CHINESE LEADERSHIP WISDOM FROM THE
BOOK OF CHANGE

Chinese Leadership Wisdom
from the
Book of Change

Mun Kin Chok

The Chinese University Press

Chinese Leadership Wisdom from the Book of Change
  Mun Kin Chok

ISBN 962–996–293–4

THE CHINESE UNIVERSITY PRESS
The Chinese University of Hong Kong
SHA TIN, N.T., HONG KONG
Fax: +852 2603 6692
     +852 2603 7355
E-mail: cup@cuhk.edu.hk
Web-site: www.chineseupress.com

Printed in Hong Kong

Contents

❧ ❧ ❧

Part Two: The Sixty-Four Hexagrams

Part Three: A Leadership Model from the *Book of Change*

Part Four: Divination

Foreword

❦ ❦ ❦

The first time I started to read the *Book of Change* 易經, also known as the *Yijing*, I found it very difficult to understand the meaning of the texts, particularly those ancient Chinese words which I don't even know how to pronounce. Although the text has been translated into modern Chinese, its meaning is still not clear since it is interpreted differently by different people. However, I have tried to interpret the text according to my own understanding and have used other works as references. Gradually I have come to realize that the *Yijing* is a book for guiding people in how to behave in their daily life in order to become good and to get rid of evils. In different times and places, people are advised to act in the proper way in order to receive "fortune" and to avoid "misfortune." Since the advice provided in the *Yijing* is not expressed directly or explicitly, but rather implicitly, the ordinary reader will have difficulty in understanding it if they lack patience.

As a university professor in the business school, with many years' experience in teaching and consulting, I have realized that the guidelines in the *Yijing* for daily life can also be usefully applied to any organization, whether these are public or private. Indeed the *Yijing* has for the past two thousand years been considered in China as a classic book for government leaders. The qualities of a "superior man" or an enlightened person as indicated and emphasized in the *Yijing* should remain the same for the leaders of any organization today. However, I must admit that a "perfect leader" who can meet the standards set by the *Yijing* is difficult to find in the real world. But the expected qualities of leadership can still lead people to move in that direction.

In this book, the wisdom of leadership within the framework of the *Yijing* will be used to indicate how a leader should act in different situations, including both good and bad. I have found that there are a number of leadership principles that can be derived from the philosophy of the *Yijing* which should not be handled and discussed exclusively in the academic field but also used in practice. Wisdom and practice should go hand in hand. Wisdom that can be practiced is real wisdom.

The *Yijing* has been used as a book of divination for three thousand years in China and still is by some people today, including in the Western world. However, there are different views on divination. Some believe in it, some don't, and others keep an open mind. I would consider divination as a method of broadening a person's thinking or intuition power when he or she is facing a situation in which there is no information and data available. By using divination, one is able to get new insights and "advice" from the *Yijing* and can use them as guidelines in deciding the right action to take. One of the spirits of the *Yijing* is to allow different views among people. I highly respect this principle. Therefore, the main objective of this book is to introduce the leadership principles derived from the wisdom of the *Yijing*. Concurrently, readers can also learn what the *Yijing* really is.

Mun Kin Chok
April 2006

PART ONE

■ ■ ■ ■ ■ ■ ■ ■ ■ ■ ■ ■

The Fundamentals

Understanding the *Book of Change*

❦ ❦ ❦

The *Book of Change*, that is, the *Yijing* 易經, is an ancient Chinese book of divination. *Yi* 易 means change and *jing* 經 a canon. The *Yijing* is considered the oldest of the Chinese classics. It is the only book that has been subject to so many interpretations by so many people in both the past and the present according to their own perceptions, understanding, values, and background; for example, fortune-tellers, philosophers, politicians, Chinese herbal doctors, ancient astronomers in China, architects, mathematicians, litterateurs, scientists, historians, feng shui masters, and boxing masters. Thus, the *Yijing* has been used as a kind of "basic material" which can be further processed by different people according to their interests and objectives.

People use the materials provided by the *Yijing* as a basis. The materials in the *Yijing* are like the food ingredients for a cook, who can use them to make his own style of dishes. Different cooks have different styles of cooking. They will use their imagination to develop new dishes for the diners. Whether their dishes are tasty or not is determined by the diners. Different diners have different tastes, so a cook will determine who his target diners are before he cooks. The ingredients provided by the *Yijing* are so "round" or highly adaptable that people with different backgrounds can always find it useful in meeting their needs and applying it to their own purposes. This is probably the reason why the *Yijing* has maintained its attraction for the past three thousand years and has never been discarded.

NATURE OF THE *YIJING*

The *Yijing* was originally a divination manual named **Zhouyi** 周易 [*The Zhou Book of Changes*]. It is said that the contents of the *Zhouyi* were contributed by three people: the legendary sage **Fuxishi** 伏羲氏 (sometime 3000 B.C.), **King Wen** 周文王 of the Zhou Dynasty

(1171–1122 B.C.), and his son, the **Duke of Zhou**. Fuxishi created the eight trigrams called *bagua* 八卦 in Chinese. Each of these is formed by three lines in a combination of solid (yang) and broken (yin) lines. Each trigram represents an aspect of nature: heaven, lake, fire, thunder, wind, water, mountain, and earth. King Wen further developed these eight trigrams into sixty-four hexagrams, each comprised of two trigrams. He also wrote the hexagram statements which are the commentaries on the sixty-four situations indicated in the hexagrams. The Duke of Zhou wrote the line statements to explain the situations as presented by the six lines of a hexagram. A comprehensive explanation of these will be found in the later chapters.

In divination the hexagrams and the statements are used as the basis for prediction, so they are considered as a canon in English or *jing* 易 in *Hanyu Pinyin* and *ching* 經 in the Wade-Giles system. As *yi* or *I* means change, the two words *yi* and *jing* together become *Yijing* or *I Ching*, which means a canon for the exposition of change. Hence the meaning of the *Yijing* in English is the *Book of Change*. After the *Zhouyi* acquired a high status in the Han Dynasty (206 B.C.–A.D. 219) as a book of wisdom and philosophy rather than a book of divination, it was then named the *Yijing* and has become one of the important Chinese classics for intellectuals.

There are a lot of commentaries on the *Zhouyi* including the most important ten essays called the Ten Wings [*Shiyi* 十翼], which elaborate on different aspects of the text of the *Zhouyi* as auxiliary "wings" to the explanations of the text. They are also called Great Commentary [*Dazhuan* 大傳], as appendices to the *Zhouyi*. It is said that Confucius also added his commentaries in some parts of the Ten Wings. These two names—*Zhouyi* and *Yijing*—are used interchangeably today, but the contents of the respective books can be different. Some will include the texts of hexagram and the lines as well as relevant parts of the Great Commentary. Some however include only the text of the hexagrams and lines without the latter. In this book, the author has adopted the second approach based on the reason that the original text of the hexagram and lines together with the structure of the hexagrams should be understood first by readers who are beginning to learn the *Yijing*. Once they become more familiar with the hexagrams and understand better the meanings of the original text, they will be able to develop their own thinking about the text independently from those commentaries made by others. This is one of the main objectives of this book.

What can a person learn from the *Yijing*? He may think the *Yijing* is used to make predictions of future events. It is true that the *Yijing* was originally a book of divination and some people today still hold the same view, but the value of the *Yijing* is more than that. It is a book which provides the guidelines or principles for a person to behave as a cultivated man in his daily life. If he can earnestly follow these guidelines, he is on the path to enlightenment which is the path of a "superior man." A superior man is a person who knows how to handle relationships with others in the right way. According to the philosophy of the *Yijing*, by acting in this way he will be fortunate; otherwise he will be unfortunate.

The main purpose of a divination is to predict whether or not an event or an action will be fortunate. The advice given in the *Yijing* acts as practical guidelines or principles to be used to direct a person as to how to behave as an enlightened or a superior man. From this aspect, a divination can be seen as a medium between the actual world of an ordinary man (inferior man) and the ideal world of a superior man, directing the former how to move onto the right path to the latter. Thus, the *Yijing* explicitly appears to be a divination book, yet implicitly it is rather a book that instructs people how to behave as a well-cultivated man or a superior man.

QUALITIES OF A SUPERIOR MAN

A model of superior man is introduced in the *Yijing*. If a person acts as a superior man he will be fortunate and able to avert misfortune. In fact most of the texts of the hexagrams in the *Yijing* give advice to people on how to follow the behavioral pattern of a superior man; this advice is particularly found in the Great Images [*Daxiang* 大象] which is part of the Great Commentary. In the Great Images there are twenty-nine guidelines suggesting how to cultivate the superior man, and concepts which are identified with Confucianism. The opposite meaning of superior man is a "inferior man." These two terms are frequently used in the texts when the behavioral patterns between the two types of people is compared. The guidelines for superior man in the *Yijing* can well be applied to the organizational field as the qualities of a well-cultivated leader. These qualities are stated as follows:

- He is outwardly gentle and graceful but inwardly strong and vital.
- He has a moderate manner without superficial refinement, nor is he simple and uncouth.
- He is balanced, just, and correct.
- He is tolerant but not indulgent.
- He is active but not reckless.
- He is decisive but not obstinate.
- He is modest but not servile.
- He is not self-complacent and self-conceited but is self-energizing.
- He thinks ahead but reviews the past.
- He knows when he should advance and when he should stop or retreat.
- He knows when he should insist and when he should adapt.
- He knows when he should concentrate his power and when he should delegate it to others.
- He knows when he should prepare resources for future needs.
- He knows when he should show his brilliance and when he should hide it.
- He knows when and when not to restrain his desire.
- He knows how to develop relationships with others based on the principle of mutual trust and respect.
- He knows how to bind people together based on the principle of "seeking identical points by allowing different views."
- He knows how to lead people without by force.
- He knows what is enough and what is not enough.
- He knows what his right position is and will not go beyond it.
- He knows how to restore harmony when there is divergence among people.
- He knows how to use his power appropriately.
- He knows what the right move should be.
- He understands the cyclical change between gains and losses or success and failure.
- He knows the law of nature—the cycle of harmony and obstruction.
- He knows how to adapt to the changing conditions of the environment.
- He pays respect to others and therefore receives respect.
- He is willing to give benefit to others without expecting returns.
- He is willing to take blame without shirking his duties.

- He is willing to enlighten inexperienced juniors.
- He is stable and unemotional.
- He is calm and cautious when facing danger.
- He is aware of danger in good times and maintains optimism in bad times.
- He has the determination to remove evil things or thoughts.
- He has the courage to change old practices to new ones.
- He is patient and persevering when facing obstruction, but does not lose his drive to seek opportunity.
- He insists on his principles without having his own prejudices.
- He is true to himself and others.
- He is self-aware and corrects the corresponding errors.
- He emphasizes the strengths of others rather than their weaknesses.
- He has the flexibility to meet another party halfway when there is a conflict between them.
- He keeps his inner strength and self-confidence in a time of adversity.
- He sets a good example to others instead of a show.

It may not be realistic to expect a leader to possess all the qualities of a superior man, but the guidelines can still serve as the basis for anyone who wishes to be a good leader.

HOW TO READ THIS BOOK

Part One

Basic Concepts

In Part One of this book the fundamentals of the *Yijing* will be elaborated. The meaning of *taiji* 太極, **yin–yang** and the **five elements** will be explained in detail as they are the basis of the philosophy behind the *Yijing*. Without a good understanding of these concepts one will not have a comprehensive framework for the *Yijing* and will not be able to apply its useful concepts effectively to the real world.

Hypothetical examples will be given to elaborate how to apply these concepts to an organization, particularly in human relations. The author will intentionally not use actual examples because they may be twisted in making an explanation. Another concern is the time/space element as the responses of people to an action can be different in a different time/ space. A case that may be able to explain a situation in time/space I may not hold true in time/space II because of changing conditions. This is not a case book, but a book indicating how the traditional thinking methods of the *Yijing* can be applied to the today's world. Once readers are familiar with these methods they will be in a good position to use them to analyze their own specific situations and to understand the situations being faced. Examples can always be derived from new situations. As long as readers can master the basic concepts and principles, they will behave in a right way.

In Part One of this book, the nature of a hexagram and the structure of its six lines will be elaborated in detail. Readers are advised to familiarize themselves with these technical relationships since the statements of the lines are closely related to the lines themselves.

Part Two

Hexagrams and Hexagram Statement

Part Two of this book gives a comprehensive explanation of the sixty-four hexagrams including the hexagram and line statements. A **hexagram** is a six-lined graphic configuration composed of a combination of solid and broken lines used to picture the image of a situation. It is a situation stated in a macro aspect. A **hexagram statement** is an explanation of such a situation in words. As indicated earlier, the hexagram statements of the *Yijing* were written by King Wen and the interpretations were based on his own understanding and judgment. So these hexagram statements could be personally biased and therefore should not be considered as the sole explanation of a situation as presented by a hexagram, but one of the possible explanations. As opposed to a subjective or more personal interpretation which is based on words, the hexagram itself can be used as the basis for interpretation in a more objective way. Readers are encouraged to interpret the hexagrams according to their personal understanding and judgement. It is not necessary to follow the original hexagram or line statements. **This is one of the main purposes of this book—to encourage people to use these hexagrams as a tool for thinking and for developing their own creativity or imagination.**

Line Structure and Line Statements

A hexagram is constructed in six lines and each line represents a particular stage of a development or a situation and people's behavior in that particular stage. So the line structure of a hexagram indicates relationships between the people. An understanding of the **line structure** is therefore helpful in understanding human relations. A **line statement** is a description of a situation in words about how people behave in a particular stage and makes a judgment as to whether the situation is favorable or not, either in an explicit or an implicit way.

The line statements play an important role in the explanation of the *Yijing* principles as they have been interpreted by different people, including Confucius and many intellectuals in the past and today. Beginners in the study of the *Yijing* are advised to know the meaning of these line statements. The line statements, which are written in ancient Chinese, are rather difficult to understand even for people in China today because they may not know how to pronounce the words and what their meanings are. However, this problem can be solved by reading the texts which are translated into modern Chinese. This difficulty with ancient Chinese is avoided in this book. So for English readers it is a problem whether or not the text is correctly translated. Even in Chinese versions, interpretations of the line statements differ from person to person. In some English versions, the original line statements are not presented at all, but rather the applications are based on the author's own interpretations. In English versions, which have the original line statements their interpretations, as in the Chinese versions, are different. Since the target readers of this book are executives of different types of organizations, the author has tried to translate the original text into English as simply as possible so that readers can grasp the essence of the meaning of the hexagram and line statements, even though the translations will not meet the standard of professionals.

In analyzing the line structure or the relationships between the positions of the six lines in a hexagram, a particular symbolic name will be used for each line to simplify the description in the analysis. This is the old practice used in the *Yijing* in the Chinese versions and also in some of the English versions. At first the reader may feel a little bit confused, but will gradually get use to these symbols. As the *Yijing* is seen as a kind of symbology, it is natural to use the relevant symbols in the explanation of the text. Another example of this is the hexagrams.

Each of them, as indicated earlier, symbolizes a particular situation. Readers are advised to familiarize themselves with these symbols so that reading the text will be easier.

The reason why the author includes the original text in this book instead of merely indicating the applications of the *Yijing*'s principles to practise is that he wishes readers to achieve both the benefit of understanding the original spirit of the *Yijing* and of how to use it in the real world. The original text will help to generate new insights in the readers themselves.

In the ancient Chinese text, the third person in masculine form was used, so in this book "he," "his," and "him" will be used throughout instead of "he/she," "his/hers," and "him/her" so as not to make the text cumbersome for readers. This is not meant to display any prejudice against the female reader.

Knowledge and Wisdom

In a knowledge-based economy, modern executives are generally advised to acquire the most up-to-date knowledge as far as possible in order to survive in a competitive world. It is true that knowledge is indeed important to the executives of any organization today. But with knowledge alone the executives may still not be qualified to be a good leader. There is a major difference between an executive and a leader. An executive needs professional knowledge in his specialized field because most of his responsibilities lie in increasing efficiency in his specialized functions. But to improve in his functional abilities, he also needs to know how to deal with people. No one can be without contact with other people or without any support from others.

An executive who only has professional knowledge and skills may not be good in handling human relations. Here he needs the wisdom of leadership. As indicated above, the *Yijing* provides useful guidelines for leaders as to how to behave in the right way with people. In the Western world the word "wisdom" generally means knowledge. Whoever has knowledge will have power. But in the classic Chinese perspective, as indicated by the *Yijing*, the word "wisdom" has more to do with the ability to handle human relations and to lead people. A man who lacks knowledge in this field is considered a man with no wisdom. He only knows how to use his professional knowledge to increase or improve the efficiency of his specialized functions, but ignores how other people's knowledge and talent can be used for the benefit of the whole organization. He lacks an **interdependence** perspective or a **mutually supportive** outlook. The word "knowledge" probably needs a new definition in the context of an organization.

In an organization today, people can acquire their knowledge from different channels, such as self-study through reading books and participating in formal and special programs as well as short-term seminars or training courses offered by various academic or professional institutions in the community. Also, their experience gained from their actual activities. So in the context of an organization the word "knowledge" should not only include new knowledge but also personal experience from past activities. Actual experience is a kind of knowledge and considered sometimes even more valuable and useful in practice than theoretical knowledge, particularly when handling human relations. A man with good theoretical knowledge may not be competent to handle actual problems in the sophisticated human world. Under such circumstances, a person's practical experience can become "wisdom" to help him. On the other hand, new knowledge is also important for it can stimulate insight and vision. In the context of an organization the relationship between knowledge and wisdom is mutually supportive as reflected by the following: **knowledge makes wisdom grow and wisdom makes knowledge flourish**. It seems that an ideal leader should have both qualities—knowledge and wisdom. But it is rather difficult to find a person who is well balanced in both. If one of these two qualities has to be chosen as the most important one for a good leader, wisdom appears to have more weight. The *Yijing* will not give knowledge to the leader of an organization, but will provide wisdom for proper conduct in the human world.

Self-cultivation, Ethics, and Leadership

In the framework of Confucianism, the *Yijing* can be seen as a book of self-cultivation for those who would like to be a person who conducts themselves in the right way. All words of advice provided by the *Yijing* or divination are in fact the rules or guidelines for people to behave rightly in the human world in order to be a superior man. Some these have already been stated above. The basic criterion for a superior man is **to turn to good and stay away from evil**. To behave in this way, one is most likely to be "fortunate" instead of "unfortunate."

Only a virtuous person will be concerned about the influence or consequences of his conduct to others, and whether these are favorable or harmful. So an individual's standard of morality can influence the ethics of the people in the community. The higher an individual's moral sense, the higher the ethics of a community is to be expected, vice versa. This is why an individual's moral sense is so much emphasized by the *Yijing*. As a matter of fact, the predictions of divination also follow this philosophy or principle. This issue will be further elaborated later.

Business ethics are emphasized by companies to benefit their stakeholders (customer, shareholders, and employees). However, an emphasis on business ethics without improvement of an individual's morality is pointless because the standard of an individual's morality is the basis for a community-wide ethics. And self-cultivation as emphasized by the *Yijing* is the foundation of building up an individual's moral sense.

Part Three

The Natural Law and the Principles of Leadership

The meanings of the text in the *Yijing* are not only related to the thought or ethics of Confucianism, but also the law of nature as emphasized by **Laozi** 老子, who is seen as the founder of the **Daoism**. Both the *Yijing* and Laozi considered that yin and yang are the two forces of the universe which create myriad things. Both believed that human conduct should follow the law of nature. The difference between the *Yijing* and Laozi is that the yang element plays the main role in the framework of the former, whereas the yin element is considered more superior to yang by the latter.

From the sixty-four hexagrams of the *Yijing* there are several principles which are derived from the natural laws, for example:

- **The law of change**: Everything will change as time flows.
- **The law of cyclic change**: Everything changes in a cyclic pattern.
- **The law of continued self-renewal**: The superior man should make himself as strong and untiring as the heavens.
- **The law of tolerance**: The superior man should be as tolerant as the earth, which nourishes myriad things including humankind without receiving returns.
- **The law of modesty**: The hexagram QIAN 謙 [Modesty] (15) is considered the most fortunate situation among all sixty-four hexagrams (situations).

- **The law of opposites and complement**: The relationships between things in the world are both contradictory and complementary. Human relationships follow the same pattern.
- **The law of harmony**: The basic relationship among the myriad things in nature is harmony; any deviation from this will result in backward movement. Disharmony is a phenomenon in the adjustment process from an unbalanced situation to a balanced one—harmony, which is the ideal state that can be achieved in human relations.

The different laws of nature stated above can be named principles when they are applied to human relations or leadership in an organization. In Part Three of this book, **a conceptual model of leadership** will be used to illustrate application in the real world. This leadership model includes two parts: **nine yin–yang principles** and **the qualities of a leader**. The nine yin–yang principles, which are derived from the laws of nature in their different aspects, can be used as a basis for understanding what types of changes there can be in the human world. If a leader can master these nine yin–yang principles, he will be in a good position to predict future event without divination. He can prepare in a timely fashion the necessary plans or measures to adapt to the coming changes. Consequently he will most likely be "fortunate" rather than "unfortunate."

However, with these nine yin–yang principles alone, a person, according to the philosophy of the *Yijing*, can still not become a good leader unless he also possesses the qualities of a superior man as stated above. In the leadership model of this book, these qualities will be presented in a summarized form. So a good leader within the framework of the *Yijing* should have both qualifications. One must have the inner qualities from self-cultivation as well as being able to grasp the nine yin–yang principles.

Part Four

The Meaning of Divination

Since the *Yijing* is traditionally treated as a book of divination, it is necessary to present the relevant methods in the Part Four of this book including the widely used **Three Coins Method** and **Yarrow Stalks Method** as well as various simplified methods. In addition, an old method called the **Five Elements Method** will be introduced in this book. The five elements method was originally named **Plum Blossom Numerology** in Song Dynasty (A.D. 960–1279) in China and is almost unknown in the Western world. The special feature of this method is not to use the text for the interpretation of divination but to use the relationships between the five elements.

No matter what a method is used for divination, it is important to know what the value of a divination is. To some people, a divination based on the *Yijing* can provide them with advice as to whether their future moves are considered fortunate or unfortunate. If the *Yiijing* is used in this way it is a book of fortune-telling. Some people may not entirely believe in fortune-telling but still like to have some advice from a divination as this can provide interesting information or references for them. Others will not make a divination at all as they believe whether a person is fortunate or not is primarily determined by his own conduct. If a person behaves in the right way, he will most likely be fortunate. Confucius and Xunzi 荀子 emphasized the text of the *Yijing* rather than divination.

Carl Jung, the twentieth-century psychologist, in his foreword to the English translation of the *Yijing* (*I Ching*) by Richard Wilhelm (translated by Cary F. Baynes), claimed that there is an interdependence between objective events and the subjective state of the diviner (and also among the objective events themselves). He called this phenomenon as "synchronicity," *syn* means "together" and *chron* "time." Synchronicity means therefore "together in time." As things in the world share in time and space, they are "in synch" and changing together. The hexagram obtained from throwing coins is not meaningless, but a meaningful coincidence. The advice or wisdom given by the resulting hexagram to the question asked by the diviner may already exist in his unconscious mind but is largely hidden. Through divination one can interpret the situation from the divined hexagram by using one's knowledge of the subjective and objective conditions as well as the character of the subsequent events. By doing this, one is able to understand the problem asked and the advice of the *Yijing* in deeper levels.

The author, however, will consider divination as a tool for broadening one's thinking power. When the leader of an organization finds himself in a situation in which he has no information or data about the problem he is facing, he can use divination to see what kind of situation he will meet and what the *Yijing* advises. If the commentaries on the divined situation are on the good side, he should not be too easily pleased as there may be some hidden problems or trouble. He can use the various methods as suggested by the *Yijing* to "predict" what they are, so that he will be quickly in a position to know whether or not he will be able to solve them. This additional "information" obtained from the changes in hexagrams can be useful to the leader, because he has not yet thought of this in his original plan. If he thinks this information is not meaningful to him, he just ignores it. If the situation "predicted" by a divination is not favorable, the leader will think what difficulties might happen in the future and what the corresponding measures can be prepared to overcome them. In either situation, whether it is favorable or not, the leader can benefit from a divination because it will broaden his mind in a specific situation. In this aspect, the divination using the *Yijing* has an educational value rather than merely a predictive one as people used to believe.

In the commentaries on the hexagrams (the macro aspect of situation) and the lines (the micro aspect of each individual situation), their judgment on a respective situation can be "fortunate" or "unfortunate," "regret" or "no blame." How should the diviners respond to them? As these statements were written in ancient China based on the writers' own understanding, values, and interpretation, their judgments were inevitably of a subjective nature. Therefore, a diviner today should not blindly follow or accept the commentary made in a statement; instead he should make a judgment of his own based on the following guidelines:

1. He should check whether the situation indicated by the divined statement is relevant to the question which he has asked. If yes, he can make a further analysis by using the changing lines or changing hexagrams to generate new insights.
2. The situation is not relevant to his question at all even though he has unsuccessfully tried to derive meaning from it. In this case he needs to forget about this divination. It is advisable to make another divination immediately after the preceding one.
3. If the situation stated by the respective statement is relevant to the question asked but the commentary of the statement is, however "not favorable," the diviner need not be sad; instead he should consider this commentary useful to his future action. What he should do is to avoid the conduct indicated in the statement as it would lead to a situation of "misfortune." Instead he can act in the opposite

direction to the situation indicated by the statement. As a consequence his action will become "fortunate." Alternatively, he may ignore the judgment of the commentary if he strongly believes that he will be able to overcome the difficulties and solve the problems as mentioned in the statement.

4. Whether the future situation is "fortunate" or "unfortunate" depends much on a person's own act. If he acts in the right way, an "unfortunate" situation can possibly turn into a "fortunate" one. From this perspective, the action of a person is considered the independent variable and the result of his action the dependent variable. **A person's act will determine his own fate**, but not the other way round. This is the philosophy of the *Yijing* and it should be used as the main guideline when making a divination.

Taiji, Yin–Yang, and the Five Elements

✍ ✍ ✍

CONCEPT OF *TAIJI*

In Chinese thought *taiji* 太極, also known as *taichi*, means the great ultimate or the primal beginning of the process of universal evolution, which is based on the interplay between the two forces: yin and yang. Yin and yang are separate and united like the relationship between the head and tail of a coin. If a coin is seen as a *taiji*, its two sides are yin and yang. One can be divided into two and two can be united into one. *Taiji* means the whole of the coin and yin–yang refers to the two forces generated from *taiji*.

When yin and yang are separated, the relationship between the two is opposite. But it will become complementary in nature when they are united. This is the principle that can be called **the unity of complementary opposites** or the unity of yin and yang. *Taiji* is the origin of the interplay between yin and yang, and these two forces produce myriad things in the world including the manifestations of the eight trigrams. *Taiji* is, therefore, the primal beginning of the dynamic process of evolution. In this respect everything in the world has a *taiji* of its own, for example, human beings, animals, plants, countries, governments, organizations, companies, cultures, thinking, values, and so forth. Everything in the world is forever changing and the origin of a change is *taiji*. So *Taiji* is the concept of a whole whereas its evolutionary process is the subsystem of the whole. This is **the principle of totality**.

EVOLUTIONARY PROCESS OF *TAIJI*

The evolutionary process as generated from *taiji* can be illustrated by using a tree diagram as follows:

Taiji generates the two primary forces yin − − and yang ——. The two forces yin and yang generate the four states: old yin ≡ ≡, young

The Evolutionary Process of *Taiji*

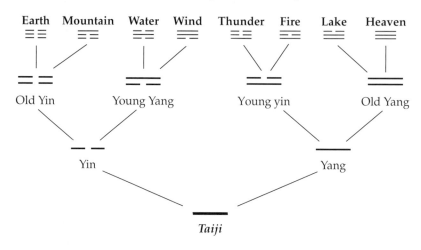

yang ══, young yin ══, and old yang ══. The four states generate the eight trigrams. The eight trigrams together are considered as *taiji*, as are yin and yang and the four states. Therefore, *taiji* can be seen as a whole system and other systems generated by it are its subsystems. In this respect *taiji* is considered as oneness in nature as are yin and yang, the four states and the eight trigrams. This is the principle of oneness or the principle of unity or the principle of totality. This is the fundamental concept in the philosophy of the *Yijing*. The two trigrams of a hexagram are considered as one system, as are the six lines of a hexagram.

The concept of *taiji* was initially introduced in the *Xici* 繫辭 [The Great Commentary], one of the Ten Wings. It is regarded as an early foundation of the philosophy of the *Yijing*. It stated:

> **There is *taiji* in *Yi*, which produces two forces (yin and yang); the two forces produce the four states, the four states produce eight trigrams; the eight trigrams determine fortune and misfortune.**

Hence, it said:

> **The successive movement of yin and yang constitutes *dao*.**

Since yin and yang are generated from *taiji*, so *taiji* is also defined as *Dao*. Every organization can be seen as a *taiji*. All departments within it are its subsystems, but they are considered as one unity or as a whole in respect to their objective and value. The plans and actions of each unit of the organization appear outwardly separate but they are inwardly coordinated in pursuit of the common objective. From the perspective of the whole organization, the different activities of its subunits are in fact interlinked and coordinated with each other, moving towards the common objective, as every unit of the organization aims towards the interests of the whole rather than towards its own interests. If this is not the case then the entire system lacks the *taiji* spirit.

Taiji Diagram

The concept of *taiji* or yin–yang can be best illustrated by using the *taiji* diagram below:

Taiji Diagram

Unity of Opposites and Complementarity

There are two fishes in the *taiji* diagram. The white fish represents yang and the black represents yin. The white fish's head adjoins the black fish's tail and vice versa. These two fishes are interlocked with each other and are inseparable; each of the two is a part of a whole like one coin with two sides. The whole is represented by *taiji* and the two forces by the two fishes. The relationship between the two is both opposite and complementary in nature.

An opposite relationship between two forces indicates a situation in which the two parties have different views or positions because of their different interests. However, these two relationships are not absolute but relative. Under different conditions or at different times and in different places, the relationship between yin and yang can change from an opposite relationship to a complementary one. For example, people who were originally "enemies" can change into "friends" because of the changes in their interests.

The relationship of opposites and complementarity can also be found in the same time and place. If this is the case, it should be considered beneficial to the whole of an organization. If people under a leader hold differing views, this is not necessarily "bad" but can also be seen as "good." A leader should be able to tolerate different views and select the most useful among them. Acting in this way a leader who is open-minded will be able to get new ideas about the direction, structure, and policy of his organization. As a result, the organization will be able to benefit from both opposite and complementary relationships.

TAIJI AND HARMONY

One of the important concepts of *taiji* is harmony, which is implicitly illustrated in the *taiji* diagram. The relationship between the black and white fish or yin and yang images a harmony which is desirable in different situations:

- A balance between the two forces of yin and yang
- A balance between toughness and gentleness
- A balance between activeness and cautiousness
- A harmony between the units of an organization
- A harmony between an organization and its stakeholders
- A harmony between an organization and the public
- A harmony within the objectives of an organization

The state of harmony is a dynamic concept. Any development is a continuous movement between balance and imbalance. A balance provides the conditions for an imbalance and vice versa. The complementary relationship between yin and yang establishes a balance and the opposite relationship between the two forces breaks the balance and moves into imbalance. Following the yin–yang cycle the imbalance between the two will be reunited to one in a complementary relationship, a new balance between the two. However, the changes in the state of balance and imbalance are still within a whole or oneness—*taiji*.

YIN–YANG CYCLE

The tail of the white fish represents the initial stage of the yang force moving upwards: the body of the fish is the midlevel of the yang movement and the head the high level of the yang. The tail, body, and head of the white fish symbolize the stages of the development of the yang force. Similarly, the black fish represents the development stages of the yin force. The head of the white fish connected with the tail of the black fish indicates a situation in which the upward movement of the yang force has reached its extreme and the next stage beyond it is the beginning of the upward movement of the yin force. When the growth of the yin force has reached its peak or the head of the black fish, it is the signal for the return of the yang force in the next stage. The interlocked relationship between the white and black fish symbolizes the cyclic change in nature, or the cycle of yin and yang.

The concept of the yin–yang circle can be applied to many situations to explain the changes between two opposites. For example:

- Gain and loss
- Hardness and softness
- Strength and weakness
- Advance and retreat
- Attack and defence
- Expansion and contraction
- Peak and depth
- Like and dislike
- Friend and enemy
- Outward and inward
- Good and evil
- Fortune and misfortune

A cyclical movement between the situations of two opposites as stated above can be found in a natural change as indicated by both the *Yijing* and **Laozi**. In the *Yijing* a yang-dominated situation can change into a yin-dominated one, a favorable situation can change into an unfavorable situation, an advanced situation can change into a retreat, a dispersed situation can change into a united one, and so forth. In Laozi's doctrine the cyclical movement of yin and yang plays an important role: **"Disaster is the avenue of fortune and fortune is the concealment for disaster."** However, he advised people to stand on the side of the yin which he considered as the Dao for human activities: **nonbeing** or *wu* 無 in his cosmological outlook.

The yin–yang cycle can also be used by the leader of an organization as the basis for his future planning. For example, a company suffers losses from its direct investment in a new sector but the leader decides to continue to inject resources into this sector as he believes that the loss resulting from the action at present will eventually become a gain tomorrow. Compared with the **natural yin–yang cycle** as described above, this is a **planned yin–yang cycle**.

INTERDEPENDENCE BETWEEN YIN AND YANG

Neither yin nor yang can exist alone without the other. The existence of yin is the condition for the existence of yang and vice versa. Thus, yin and yang are considered as oneness or a unity. For example, two persons or two companies having an intimate relationship and acting for the benefit of their common objective as an integrated group, yet neither of the two alone can reach the objectives of their side. The union of yin and yang produces energy for development. Neither of the two alone has the force to do so. The union of yin and yang therefore gives strength.

YIN WITHIN YANG AND YANG WITHIN YIN

In the *taiji* diagram the black fish (yin) has a white eye (yang) and vice versa, indicating the fact that neither yin nor yang is pure in nature as each of the two has also an ingredient of other. This is the principle of mutual containment: yin within yang and yang within yin. In good times there are still bad times and vice versa. Within opportunity there is danger and within danger there is opportunity. In a state of economic prosperity, there is always danger hidden somewhere and it is equally true that in a recession an opportunity can be identified. A good man or a superior man may sometimes still have an evil idea, and a bad man or an inferior man may also have good intentions too.

INTERCHANGE BETWEEN YIN AND YANG

The positions of yin and yang are not fixed but are interchangeable. In time I an object is seen as yang but in time II it can change to yin and vice versa. The sky in the day is bright (yang) but in the night is dark (yin) even though the sky itself remains the same sky.

The top management of an organization can be seen as a yang unit whereas others are yin units, including the staff or labor union. If the staff or labor union requests a wage rise in times of economic prosperity, then it becomes a yang unit in nature. If the top management is willing to accept their view with some modifications, it becomes a yin unit as it reacts more or less in a passive way. In a contrary case, the top management wants to cut wages in times of recession and the staff or labor union accepts it because its bargaining power is becoming weaker. In such a situation, the top management retains its status as a yang unit whereas the labor union remains the yin unit. If both sides insist on their own position without compromise, both of them become yang unit in nature and the organization suffers from an imbalanced situation or disharmony even though this may be temporary.

Equally, today's allies (yang) may become tomorrow's enemies (yin); today's gains may become tomorrow's losses and vice versa. The main reason for the change in yin and yang is due to changes in time and place. Yin and yang can interchange their positions as time and place changes.

In the *taiji* diagram, the two black and white fishes appear to be moving and hence create a dynamic image. The positions of these two fishes, or yin and yang, are not fixed but changeable. The leader of an organization should understand the impact of changes in time and place on the yin–yang relationships as explained above and make the appropriate plans or take the appropriate actions to adapt to them.

INTERDEPENDENCE BETWEEN THE WHOLE AND INDIVIDUALS

Taiji explains the relationship between the whole and its individual units. The leader of an organization should formulate his plans based on the benefit of the whole organization rather than on that of an individual unit. However, the relationship between the whole organization and its individual units is not independent but interdependent. What is good for the whole organization can also be good for its individual units and vice versa. Based on the above, *taiji* is considered as a total system comprised of a number of subsystems within it.

DYNAMIC NATURE OF *TAIJI*

Taiji is not static but dynamic in nature. The size of the *taiji* as indicated in the diagram is also changeable, depending on the strength of the interactive effect between the two forces yin and yang in a development. The greater an interactive effect of yin and yang, the larger will be the size of the *taiji*. Vice versa, the smaller the interactive effect of yin and yang, the smaller will be the size of the *taiji*. If there is no interaction between yin and yang, the size of the *taiji* will remain unchanged or its growth will be zero.

Since the size of the *taiji* is influenced by the interactive effect of yin and yang, the leader of an organization should properly understand and master this principle. For example, good coordination between the departments of an organization will positively contribute to its expansion and hence the size of the *taiji* will be enlarged. An enlarged *taiji* is identical with an enlarged organization. An enlarged organization is a change with a quantitative nature and **a quantitative change will lead to a qualitative change**. For example, the organizational structure and the qualities of the people within it should also change in order to meet the new conditions.

A DIALECTIC METHOD OF THINKING

Taiji thinking provides the leader of an organization with a dialectical method to analyze the situations or problems he faces. The leader should be able to identify both positive and negative factors in an event as stated as follows:

- A favorable situation (yang) has also unfavorable factors (yin) within it.
- A difficulty (yin) also provides an opportunity (yang).
- A wise decision (yang) has also unwise ingredients (yin).
- A success (yang) contains also the elements of a failure (yin).
- A sharp rise (yang) leads to a sharp fall (yin).

By using the dialectical method, a leader can be in a better position to identify both the positive and negative factors related to the situation he faces. The dialectical method will provide a leader with analytical power when making his decisions.

A LEADER AS A *TAIJI*

The universe is a *taiji*, so is the world, a country, a government, a community, a company, and a man. Following this concept, a leader is also seen as a *taiji* as his attributes can be divided into two major categories—yin and yang:

Yang	Yin
Masculine	Feminine
Strong	Soft
Straight	Pliable
Creative	Receptive
Decisive	Flexible
Projecting	Open
Confident	Anxious
Excited	Relaxed

It is difficult to say whether a leader should have a yang character or a yin one since it depends much on the situation or in what time and place he is facing it. The influences of these two types of leadership characteristics differ in different times and places. Neither a pure yang nor a pure yin character would be a strength in a leader. They would be a weakness. **Monocharacter in a leader will reduce his adaptability to the changing environment or time and place.** Conversely, **a leader with a dual character of yin and yang will be more flexible and adaptable**.

Based on the *taiji* concept or the yin–yang mix, the types of leadership can be grouped into two categories: the type of inward-yang–outward-yin and the type of inward-yin–outward-yang, or the type of inward-strong–outward-soft and the type of inward soft–outward strong. In the traditional perspective of the *Yijing*, the first type (inward-strong–outward-soft) is more preferable to the second type (inward-soft–outward-strong) and is considered to be the general character of a superior man or an enlightened man. A superior man is a person who is inwardly strong, creative, upright, and fair (yang) while outwardly broad minded, considerable, flexible, and adaptable (yin). In the traditional perspective, the second type is seen as the character of an inferior man or not an enlightened man, for he is insidious inwardly (yin) and supercilious outwardly (yang). The attributes of yin and yang can be interpreted differently in their positive and negative sides in different times and places. This is a special feature of the *Yijing*. The first type of *taiji* leadership is seen as more civilized and cultivated than the second type.

If a leader is considered as a *taiji* then the people under him can be divided into two groups: the yang group and the yin group. The same principle can be applied to all levels of an organization and not merely restricted to the top leader. As a result, the people of a whole organization can be categorized into two groups, the yang and the yin. This grouping is particularly useful when assigning the people to a task team. The members should be allocated to create a good combination in order to obtain harmony and higher efficiency within the team.

TAIJI AND *DAO*

Taiji or yin and yang are considered as *dao* 道 in the *Yijing*. **Laozi** is the founder of Daoism, so what are the similarities and differences in the concept of *dao* between the *Yinjing* and Laozi? According to Laozi, *dao* is the great ultimate or origin of all things and the universe. He stated that:

> *Dao* **produces one; one produces two (yin and yang); two produces three; three produces all things of the world.**

From a cosmological point of view Laozi's *dao* is, therefore, similar to the *Yijing*'s *taiji* as both try to explain the origin of myriad things and their evolutionary process. In the *Yijing*, *taiji* hence can be defined as *dao*. In both concepts, dao is seen as the source of all things.

A question has, however, been raised whether the concept of dao in the *Yijing* and Laozi is the same. Laozi said:

> **All being comes from non-being.**

He believed that all things come from non-being or *wu*, so non-being or *wu* is **the origin of all things**. Nonbeing is the ultimateness or origin of the universe, it is called *wuji* 無極 by Daoists. In respect to the origin of all things, there is a difference between Laozi and the *Yijing*. In Laozi's framework non-being or *wu* or *wuji* 無極 is the origin of all things, whereas in the *Yijing* the being or oneness is illustrated in the *taiji* diagram. According to Laozi, nonbeing or *wu* or *wuji* is *dao*, which produces being. Since *taiji* **is being,** *wuji* **is therefore the prestage of** *taiji*. Both *taiji* and *wuji* are considered as *dao*, the origin of all things, **Laozi's** *dao* **starts from nonbeing or** *wuji* **whereas the** *Yijing*'s *dao* **begins with being or** *taiji*. The difference between Laozi and the *Yijing* is where *dao* comes from. Here, numbers can be used to illustrate their difference, *wuji* is represented by 0, *taiji* by 1, yin and yang by 2, the four states (old yang, young yin, young yang, old yin) by 4, and the eight trigrams by 8:

Wuji (*wu* or nonbeing)	0
Taiji	1
Yin and Yang	2
Four states	4
Eight Trigrams	8

Another difference between Laozi and the *Yijing* is their focus on the *dao*. The focus of the *Yijing* is on the side of being while that of Laozi is on nonbeing. Although both consider *dao* as the law of nature, or the law of yin–yang which is applicable to the human world, their focuses are different. The *Yijing* emphases a balance between the two forces yin and yang during their interplay, and appropriate adjustments are required to maintain or to restore their proper relations as time and space change. The *Yijing* considered yang the leading force and yin the auxiliary force in human acts or developments. In contrast, Laozi emphasized the yin force:

Gentleness overcomes strength.

In the *Yijing* both yin and yang are emphasized depending on in the time and place. Laozi believed that *dao* moves in a cyclical change:

Reversion is the action of *dao*.

This is the concept of the yin–yang cycle as indicated in the *Yijing*. However, there is a difference between the two. Laozi believed that the movement of *dao* is a cyclical change as it will return to its origin. In Laozi's concept *dao* is a static movement whereas in the *Yijing dao* is dynamic in nature. **Laozi's *dao* seems to move in a circular pattern whereas the *Yijing*'s *dao* moves in a linear pattern with cycles.** In the *Yijing* the movement of the yin and yang is directed to the future rather than the present, so the cyclic movement will not return to the origin but to a new point at a higher level of a movement. This is the difference between a static view and a dynamic view in the observation of change.

APPLICATIONS OF THE YIN–YANG CONCEPT

The yin–yang concept has not only metaphysical meaning, but is also applicable to ordinary life including the activities of the various organizations. The examples stated below illustrate the possibilities of applying *taiji* or the yin–yang concept to the real world.

Yin–Yang and Driving Force

Yin and yang represent two forces of development. Each single force is inadequate to push an organization forward and achieve success. Neither yin nor yang alone can bring their own forces into play. The development of an organization is the result of an integration of different forces or different people with different capabilities. An organization which depends on only one category of people will meet with difficulty in its development. A bank should not be considered as merely a financial institution but as an enterprise which needs different kinds of people to accomplish its tasks. An organization which has a team of people with different backgrounds will have a larger driving force or energy than one which relies on a monotype of people.

The Whole and the Individual

Since the concept of yin and yang is like one coin with two sides, the leader of an organization should pay attention to the relationship between the whole and the individual. Generally, he will make a plan in the interests of the whole organization through which the individual can achieve his or her interests. The relationship between the whole and the individual may seem to be one-sided as the latter is highly dependent on the former. However, the relationship between the whole and the individual is interdependent in nature. Without the efforts of the individual, the interests of the whole will not be achieved. The relationship between the two is therefore complementary. If the interests of the individual are not carefully considered or ignored, conflicts, or an oppositional relationship between the two, may arise and result in tension. A proper relation or balance between the interests of the whole and those of the individual is the most desirable in order to achieve harmony within the organization.

Balance between Yin and Yang

The various departments of an organization as a whole system can be divided into two subsystems or two groups: a yang system and a yin system. Line departments, like production and marketing in a manufacturing firm, can be categorized as a yang system, and staff departments handling finance and human resources as a yin system. In a university, the teaching departments are considered a yang system whereas the administrative departments are a yin system. The relationship between the two is normally a complementary one. A yang system without the support of a yin system cannot function; vice versa, a yin system without a yang system has no justification for its existence. If there is an obstruction (or an opposite relationship) between these two subsystems, the efficiency of the whole system will adversely be affected. A well-balanced relationship between these two subsystems is an important condition for achieving harmony in the whole system.

Opposites and Complementaries

A wise leader will realize that people with opposing views should not be considered as unfavorable or bad to the organization. They can be an advantage. A leader who only appreciates the people who are obedient and agree with whatever he says cannot be a successful leader because he will not get the different inputs or stimulants to broaden his mind that a brilliant and insightful leader should have. An opposite situation can be turned from unfavorable to favorable if the attitude and skills of the leader change.

A Balanced Team

The character of the team members within an organization should be balanced. If all members of a team have either yin or yang characteristics, the efficiency of the team may be unfavorably affected by the homogeneity of its members. The weakness of a homogeneous team is that the members tend to have similar values and views, whereas a heterogeneous team will be able to generate new ideas. For example, if all members of a marketing team are similar in their character this may become a hindrance to performing their function since the character of the potential clients will be diverse; two parties with similar character will be favorable in making a deal. By the same token, the composition of a leader's advisory group should have a similar arrangement. For a task force, a balanced team comprised of people with different abilities is particularly meaningful and important.

Centralization and Decentralization

Centralization can be represented by yang and decentralization by yin. In any organization, there are both centralized and decentralized functions and activities. A centralized organization or a yang-dominated organization is one in which all important decisions are in the hands of the people at the top level and which leaves only minor decisions to those at the lower echelon. In a decentralized organization, all the departments receive adequate authority to execute their tasks and the top unit reserves the authority to make the decisions related to the organization as a whole such as system, structure, direction, and coordination. An organization which operates in this way can be called a decentralized or a yin-style organization.

In a yin-dominated or -style organization, discipline is well maintained but the initiative of the employees may not be high and it may also lack flexibility and adaptability. In a yang-style organization, the initiative of employees can be high but each unit may only be interested in its own benefit at the expense of other units. It will lack good coordination. In either case the organization is not efficient due to the imbalance between yin and yang. Only when centralization and decentralization in an organization have balance, or there is a balance between yin and yang, will the organization be in harmony.

Balance in Objectives

Any organization has an objective or objectives, for example:

- Obtaining good profits through meeting the needs of the community
- Providing good returns for the shareholders
- Providing good fringe benefits and a good working environment for the staff
- Achieving a reasonable balance between corporate responsibility and social responsibility

If all these objectives are achieved the organization is in a harmony, or yin and yang are in balance. If a leader only focuses one or two of the objectives the organization is considered not to be in a balanced situation.

Responsibility and Authority

In an organization, the responsibility of a position can be seen as yang and the authority of the position as yin. If the responsibility of a position is higher than the authority that is needed, the executive cannot effectively perform his function. On the other hand, if the authority is more than the responsibility requires, the executive may abuse the excessive authority he holds. In both cases, the efficiency or the harmony of the organization is adversely affected as yin and yang are out of balance.

Rules and Practice

The rules of an organization or a position can be seen as the yang and the practices as the yin. If a practice follows the rules exactly, yin and yang are in balance; otherwise, they are out of balance. However, if conditions require there may be a need for a certain flexibility in the relationship between rules and practices. In this respect, the concept of a yin–yang balance should not be a "point" aspect but a "range" one.

Motive and Incentive

In an organization, the relationship between the incentives used and the internal motives of the members should be kept in balance. If the organization only emphasizes surface incentives to its staff (yang), regardless of their internal motives (yin), the effect can be limited. This is an unbalanced situation between yin and yang.

Appraisals and Standards

In appraising the performance of the staff in an organization, certain standards are used. If the appraisal emphasizes only the standards set by the organization (yang) but ignores other standards (yin) related to the performance of the staff, there will be conflicts within the organization. If the standards of the appraisal are set more objectively, disharmony in the organization can be avoided.

Knowledge and Wisdom

Knowledge is defined here as an understanding of the body of facts accumulated by mankind or a familiarity with these facts. In organizational activities the meaning of knowledge can specifically refer to technology, management knowledge and understanding of the external environment. Wisdom is defined here as good judgment of what is right and wrong, particularly in human acts and human relations. Both knowledge and wisdom can be obtained from learning and experience. But knowledge and wisdom are not necessarily identical. A person who is knowledgeable in his special or professional field may not have wisdom in judging his own conduct and his relations with others. The reverse is also true; a person who has wisdom in restraining his own conduct and knows how to deal with others properly may lack specialist knowledge. Generally speaking, a person possesses both knowledge and wisdom at different areas and levels. The executives within an organization may be knowledgeable or wise in their own and specific areas but may not have knowledge or wisdom in other areas, particularly in respect to knowing themselves and dealing with others in proper way.

In an organization, knowledge can be considered as yang and wisdom as yin. Knowledge and wisdom can be either explicit or implicit depending on whether it is identifiable by others. If a person's knowledge or wisdom is easily identifiable by others, his knowledge or wisdom can be categorized as explicit. In the reverse case, knowledge or wisdom can be seen as implicit. Just because a person is knowledgeable or wise in his professional field doesn't mean that he has the adequate knowledge for or is wise dealing with human relations.

Generally speaking, there is a complementary relationship between knowledge and wisdom: **Knowledge is the source of wisdom and wisdom makes knowledge flourish**. The relationship between the two is like the one between yin and yang; both of them are complementary. As with yin and yang, knowledge and wisdom form a *taiji* from which four combinations of knowledge and wisdom can be classified based on the criterion as to whether it is expressed by a man's act in an implicit or explicit way:

The Combinations of Knowledge and Wisdom in Leadership

Knowledge / Wisdom	Explicit Yang	Implicit Yin
Explicit Yang	I Leadership with explicit knowledge and wisdom	II Leadership with explicit wisdom and implicit knowledge
Implicit Yin	III Leadership with explicit knowledge and implicit wisdom	IV Leadership with implicit knowledge and implicit wisdom

Combination I:

A leader's knowledge and wisdom are both explicit and directly identifiable by others.

Combination II:

A leader's knowledge is implicit and not directly identifiable by others though his wisdom is identifiable.

Combination III:

A leader's knowledge is explicit and directly identifiable though his wisdom is not identifiable.

Combination IV:

A leader's knowledge and wisdom are both implicit and not directly identifiable.

It is hard to say which combination of knowledge and wisdom is more important to a leader since people's likes and dislikes can be different at different times and places. In a highly explicit culture, a leader of the combination I would be more appreciated and accepted by people whereas in a highly implicit culture a leader of the combination IV would have more followers. A leader of the combination II or III would have his appreciators, too.

Knowledge and Action

One of the important principles in traditional Chinese culture is that **knowledge and action should go hand in hand**. Knowledge without action cannot prove its usefulness while action without knowledge may go in a wrong direction. The relationship between knowledge and action is like that between the yin and yang of a *taiji*. Both are considered as a whole and should not be separated; pragmatism plays an important role in traditional China.

Government and the Private Sector

The relationship between government and the private sector in an economy is exactly like the one between yin and yang. A government that is active and has more influence on socioeconomic development can be considered as a yang unit, whereas a private sector that follows the policy of that government and is less active is seen as a yin unit. Vice versa if the private sector plays an active role in the overall economy and the government functions primarily as the maintainer of law and the development of the social and economic infrastructure to provide an external economy for the private sector, then the private sector becomes a yang unit and the government a yin unit.

Whether a government or the private sector is seen as a yin or yang unit in the whole economy depends on the role it plays in a direct or an indirect way. A direct role indicates the yang nature and an indirect role the yin nature. The role of a government or private sector in the whole economy can be changed as time and space changes. In a different time and space, the relationship between a government and the private sector is changeable. For example, in a time of economic recession and high unemployment, the government will become more active (yang) than the private sector (yin); in a time of economic prosperity the private sector will play a major role (yang) and the government keeps its minor role (yin).

Market Forces and Government Action

The relationship between market forces and government action is also like that between yin and yang. There is no economy that is solely dependent on market forces without any government action and the reverse case is also true. Market forces and government action together is like a *taiji* as oneness; neither can exist without the other. The relationship between the two is both opposite and complementary. When market forces function well, the government action keeps a relatively low profile which will become higher as the market forces becomes weaker. The relationship between market forces and government action change as time and space changes.

Supply, Demand, Business Cycle

From the economic aspect, either side of supply or demand can be considered as the yang or the yin. When supply and demand are in balance, it means yin and yang are in balance, indicating the most desirable situation. Supply and demand are out of balance when there are situations of over-supply or demand shortage and overdemand or supply shortage. From a macroeconomic aspect, either aggregate demand greater than the aggregate supply or aggregate supply greater than aggregate demand will result in an unstable situation. In the former case, expansion and inflation will occur. In the latter case, there will be recession and deflation.

In times of economic expansion, the yang force is more active than the yin force as people become optimistic, self-confident, determined, and are willing to take on new ventures. It is a time dominated by the yang force. In a time of economic recession, people tend to be pessimistic, frustrated, cautious, and indecisive. They prefer to stay where they are; the yin force rises above the yang force. In both cases, yin and yang are out of balance and form a cycle between the two. Once the rise of the yang force reaches its limit or the peak of the cycle, it begins to decline and the yin force starts to rise. The business cycle is like a yin–yang cycle, the movement of the two forces yin and yang follows the law of nature or *dao* as it always changes cyclically between two extremes.

Saving and Consumption

From a macroeconomic aspect, the relationship between saving and consumption is like a *taiji*. Saving plus consumption equals disposable income. A rise in savings means a decline in consumption and vice versa a decline in savings lead to a rise in consumption. There is inverse relationship between the two. In the long run, consumption can rise with increased savings and decline as savings fall. This shows a complementary relationship between the two. If savings are "too high," the economy may slide into recession or deflation. On the other hand, if consumption is "too high," the economy may suffer from inflation. The monetary policy of a central bank is to stabilize the proper relationship between the two by using interest rate policy to maintain a macro-economic balance, or a balance between yin and yang.

A Global Aspect of the World Economy

By using the *taiji* concept, the economies of the world can be categorized into two groups: the "active" group and the "less active" group. The "active" group comprises those economies which show initiative and are energetic and strong, whereas those in the "inactive" group are weak, passive, and slow. The size of an economy is not a criterion for the classification of whether it is "active" or "less active," for a large economy may be weak, passive, and slow and a small economy dynamic and innovative.

If the whole economy is considered as a *taiji*, the "active" group is the yang and the "less active" group is the yin. The relationships between these two groups are dual. On one hand, they are different in nature, yet they are also complementary to each other just like the relationship between the white fish and the black fish in the *taiji* diagram. The economies of the "active" group can only maintain their status if they continue to be active and efficient as otherwise they will be driven into the "less active" or the yin group because of their inefficiency and backwardness. Equally some of the economies of the "less active" or the yin group are able to change their status by increasing their efficiency and so to enter the "active" group. Through this transformation process those efficient economies originally in the "active" group will fall into the "less inactive" group. This is the principle of interchange between yin and yang.

Yin–Yang and Time/Space

A hexagram has six lines; the movement of the line from the bottom to the top represents the time process in a development whereas the position of each line represents the space or place in a particular time. So a change in the **yin–yang mix** reflects a change in a time–space mix. In a particular **time–space mix** there is a particular yin–yang mix. To achieve harmony, the leader of organization should be able to adjust the yin–yang mix to adapt to the changes in a time–space mix. An efficient adaptation will bring, in the terminology of the *Yijing*, "good fortune." Otherwise there will be "misfortune."

Capability and Integrity

An overemphasis on the capability of a leader but ignorance of the integrity of a leader is not balanced from the point of view of yin–yang. The capability of a leader can be objectively identified by his outward performance which is on the yang side, but it is not easy to know his integrity as it is on the yin side. A capable leader without integrity can make an organization unfair to its stakeholders and the public interests through corruption, bribery, inside trading, false financial statements, and so forth. This issue will be further elaborated later in Part Three of this book "A Leadership Model of the *Book of Change.*" Similarly, a leader who does have high integrity but low capability is equally not qualified to be a leader. A well-qualified leader is balanced in both integrity and capability.

THE FIVE ELEMENTS

The yin–yang concept provides a basis for analyzing the relationships between things in two categories: yin and yang. The concept of the five elements broadens this scope by introducing a new perspective. The five elements are: metal, wood, water, fire, and earth. These five elements do not refer to the substance but to the properties of the substance. For example, the properties of water are descending (water always flows down) and changeable. These two properties of water can be used for describing a person's character.

The relationships between these five elements can be classified in two principles:

1. The principle of mutual creation
2. The principle of mutual destruction

The Principle of Mutual Creation

Under the principle of mutual creation, metal creates water (metal can be melted into fluid), water creates wood (tree needs water), wood creates fire (fire can be obtained from wood), and fire creates earth (the dust becomes a part of earth). The relationship of mutual creation among these five elements forms a cycle of creation:

The Relationship of Creation among the Five Elements

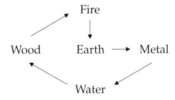

The reason for placing earth in the central position among the five elements is that all the other four elements are closely related to the earth.

The Principle of Mutual Destruction

There are also relationships of destruction among the five elements as each element can be destroyed by another element: Metal can be melted by fire, fire can be extinguished by water, water can be covered with mud, earth can be destroyed by wood or trees, and wood can be chopped down by axe. These destruction relationships among the five elements are illustrated below:

The Relationship of Destruction among the Five Elements

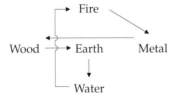

A Balance between the Two Principles

The two mutual relationships of creation and destruction among the five elements, as indicated by the first and second cycle, are an enlargement of a two-category classification of yin–yang to a five-category one. However, the two principles of the mutual relationships are still based on a yin–yang concept if the first principle is seen as yang and the second principle as yin. By combining these two principles into one, a *taiji* or a total system is obtained.

The principle of mutual creation illustrates the meaning and the importance of a mutual support system in an organization, whereas the principle of mutual destruction suggests the need for a control system in this organization. These two principles constitute a good balance or harmony among the five elements.

The Attributes of the Five Elements and Personnel Assignment

The attributes of the five elements can be used to classify people's personality into five types as follows:

Metal Type: Tough, orderly, and strict
Wood Type: Creative, imaginative, and persevering
Water Type: Flexible, sociable, and changeable
Fire Type: Optimistic, compassionate, and straightforward
Earth Type: Open, tolerant, adaptable, and supportive

These five types of personalities suggest a base for personnel assignments within business organizations according to the nature of positions, for example:

Types of Personality	Nature of Position
Metal Type	Supervision, control
Wood Type	Research
Water Type	Marketing, public relations
Fire Type	Human resources management
Earth Type	Planning and directing

A good match of personality with the nature of the position can contribute positively to the efficiency of an organization. Conversely, a mismatch of these two could result in lower efficiency.

Among the five types of personalities the earth type appears to be the most desirable for the top leader of an organization. This is because the other four elements are from the earth, and the earth plays the central position among the five elements.

Thee principle of mutual creativity can be used as a basis for personnel assignment in a work team. For example, if a work team comprises three types of person: wood, fire, and earth, the relationship amongst them tends to be cooperative, friendly, and pleasant. Conflicts between the wood-type person and the earth-type can be harmonized by placing a fire-type person in the team.

If the team members are a mix of water- and fire-type, the destructive relationship between the attributes of water and of fire can damage cooperation between them and consequently that of the whole team. This unfavorable situation can be improved by adding a wood-type person into the team because of his or her supportive relationship with the fire-type person on one hand, and his or her dependent relationship with the water-type person on the other. A harmonious relationship is obtainable through a change of the personnel mix.

A person may have a dual personality. For example, an earth-type person can also have the character of a metal-type person so he or she can be a mixed-type of person rather than a mono-type person.

A FUSION OF YIN–YANG WITH THE FIVE ELEMENTS

A fusion of the yin–yang concept with the five elements gives ten different categories as follows:

A Fusion of Yin–Yang with the Five Elements

	Yin	Yang
Metal:	Yin–Metal	Yang–Metal
Wood:	Yin–Wood	Yang–Wood
Water:	Yin–Water	Yang–Water
Fire:	Yin–Fire	Yang–Fire
Earth:	Yin–Earth	Yang–Earth

By adding the concept of yin–yang to the five elements framework, ten combinations are obtained. The yin–yang concept used here is to indicate whether a combination is explicit or implicit in nature. An explicit nature means that the attribute of a thing or the character of a person is directly identifiable whereas an implicit nature is indicated indirectly:

Metal: Toughness
  Yin–Metal: Implicit toughness
  Yang–Metal: Explicit toughness

Wood:	**Creativity**	
	Yin–Wood:	Implicit creativity
	Yang–Wood:	Explicit creativity
Water:	**Adaptability**	
	Yin–Water:	Implicit adaptability
	Yang–Water:	Explicit adaptability
Fire:	**Passion**	
	Yin–Fire:	Implicit passion
	Yang–Fire:	Explicit passion
Earth:	**Tolerance**	
	Yin–Earth:	Implicit tolerance
	Yang–Earth	Explicit tolerance

The ten combinations of the yin and yang with the five elements provide a broader basis for a better personnel assignment within an organization. A good personality match between the people working within a team creates harmony. For example, a leader who is the yin–earth type will be capable in administration but he can be an introvert. His feelings are not explicitly identifiable by his colleagues or subordinates. He does not take initiative in communication with the colleagues. As a result, a gap between the leader and others may occur. If this is the case, the yin character of the leader can weaken his capability.

On the contrary, a yang–earth type leader takes an active role in communication with his or her colleagues and provides higher transparency than a yin–earth type leader. The yang–earth type leader correspondingly creates a higher level of cohesion in the organization and displays better administrative ability and effective leadership. Nevertheless, a yin–earth type leader does have merits in comparison with a yang–earth type leader due to his quietude, calmness, and cautiousness.

If a leader is a yang–earth type and the subordinates are yin-type, such as yin–metal, yin–fire, yin–water and yin–earth, this would be good match of yin and yang and can help avoid or reduce the conflicts within the organization. If all subordinates are yang types, clashes with the superior may be inevitable.

If the members of an organization are of all same type of persons, for example yang–fire type or yin–wood type, the organization will be unable to obtain an interactive advantage between yin–yang and the five elements. A good match of different types of persons in an organization is important in order to reach a harmonious situation.

CONCLUSION

The *taiji* concept is useful to the leader of an organization as a basis on which to formulate policy. An understanding of the relationships between yin and yang will give a leader more food for thought before taking action.

- For any action a leader should consider both the positive and negative effects.
- For any development a leader should use two or more forces rather than a single force. Two or more forces will be advantageous due to the fact that they are complementary.
- Any conflicts or contradictions between two parties in human relations are not eternal but changeable as time goes by. Today's enemy can be tomorrow's friend and vice versa. A company's rival today may become its ally tomorrow. Therefore, a leader should not merely consider the present relationship between two parties in absolute terms but relative ones. Understanding the principle of opposite and complementarity is necessary for leaders of all organizations.
- The interchange between yin and yang indicates that a change in things is a general phenomenon in the world. A linear development can be found only in a particular time period, a cyclical development is closer to reality
- Any organization can be seen as a *taiji* or a total system that is comprised of a number of subsystems with the two forces yin and yang. A leader should develop a sense of interdependence in all departments or units of his organization. What is good for the whole organization is good for the individual unit and vice versa.
- Harmony is achievable when a leader is able to maintain a balance between yin and yang as well as between the five elements. Disharmony occurs when yin–yang or the five elements are out of balance. It is the responsibility of a leader to restore this balance. In a long-term development, harmony and disharmony change alternatively.

Lines, Trigrams, and Hexagrams

୧୭ ୧୭ ୧୭

THE YIN AND YANG LINES

There are two natural forces in the universe—yin and yang—which determine the development of myriad things as stated in the previous chapter. Yin is represented by a broken line and yang a solid line. Through the interplay of these two forces, yin and yang, all things are produced. Yin–yang is the key concept of the *Yijing*; without it the philosophy of the *Yijing* would not exist.

THE EIGHT TRIGRAMS

A **trigram** is a configuration of three lines in which each line is either yin or yang. A trigram is therefore a combination of yin and yang lines. The three lines of a trigram can be all yins or all yangs, or a combination of the two. There are eight trigrams are used in the *Yijing* to symbolize eight natural phenomena. Each of them has particular attributes as stated below:

1. ☰ QIAN 乾 [**Heaven**]: Strong, active, creative, dynamic, productive, and energetic
2. ☱ DUI 兌 [**Lake**]: Joyous, delighted, and pleasing
3. ☲ LI 離 [**Fire**]: Bright, clear, and understanding
4. ☳ ZHEN 震 [**Thunder**]: Powerful, authoritative, dignified, active, and moving
5. ☴ XUN 巽 [**Wind**]: Gentle, penetrating, flexible, and obedient
6. ☵ KAN 坎 [**Water**]: Dangerous, and difficult
7. ☶ GEN 艮 [**Mountain**]: Still, stable, steady, and restrained
8. ☷ KUN 坤 [**Earth**]: Soft, receptive, passive, gentle, modest, and tolerant

The attributes of these natural phenomena as represented by the eight trigrams can be used in the human world to describe a person's character and conduct.

THE SIXTY-FOUR HEXAGRAMS

Using only the eight trigrams to describe the complexity of the human world is inadequate. The solution is to expand oversight by placing the eight trigrams in pairs, one on top of the other. This results in sixty-four images, or situations formed by six lines from two trigrams. This situation, called a **hexagram**, is illustrated below:

Hexagram TONGREN 同人   **Hexagram DAYOU** 大有
[Fellowship] (13)   **[Great Possessions] (14)**

☰ Upper Trigram   ☲ Upper Trigram
☲ Lower Trigram   ☰ Lower Trigram

The sixty-four hexagrams describe sixty-four situations in the human world. Table 1 illustrates the combinations of the eight trigrams:

Before analyzing the hexagrams and their lines, it is necessary to understand the structure of a hexagram and the influences a change in a line has on the respective hexagram. Hexagrams and lines are the cornerstone of the *Yijing* since the descriptions and commentaries made by a hexagram statement are based on the image and the structure of that hexagram. Similarly, the descriptions and commentaries on the statements of the six lines of a hexagram are based on the relationships between the lines. Without an understanding of the hexagram structure or the structure of the lines, it will be difficult to understand what a hexagram and its line statements really mean.

LINE AND POSITION

A hexagram has only two different lines: the yang line and the yin line . Each represents the characteristics of the two elements yang and yin respectively. Every hexagram has six lines in six different positions:

	6th position	— —	Yin position, Yin Line
	5th position	— —	Yang position, Yin Line
Hexagram TAI 泰	4th position	— —	Yin position, Yin Line
[Harmony] (11)	3rd position	——	Yang position, Yang Line
	2nd position	——	Yin position, Yang Line
	1st position	——	Yang position, Yang Line

As a line a position can also be divided into two categories: the yang position and the yin position. In a six-line hexagram, the three positions

Eight Trigrams and the Sixty-Four Hexagrams

Upper Trigram / Lower Trigram	QIAN 乾 1 Heaven	DUI 兑 2 Lake	LI 離 3 Fire	ZHEN 震 4 Thunder	XUN 巽 5 Wind	KAN 坎 6 Water	GEN 艮 7 Mountain	KUN 坤 8 Earth
QIAN 乾 1 Heaven	QIAN 乾 1 Heaven (Force)	GUAI 夬 43 Determination	DAYOU 大有 14 Great Possessions	DAZHUANG 大壯 34 Great Strength	XIAOXU 小畜 9 Small Accumulating	XU 需 5 Waiting	DAXU 大畜 26 Great Accumulating	TAI 泰 11 Harmony
DUI 兑 2 Lake	LÜ 履 10 Treading	DUI 兑 58 Interlinking	KUI 睽 38 Diverging	GUIMEI 歸妹 54 Marrying Maid	ZHONGFU 中孚 61 Inner Truth	JIE 節 60 Regulating	SUN 損 41 Decreasing	LIN 臨 19 Approaching
LI 離 3 Fire	TONGREN 同人 13 Fellowship	GE 革 49 Reforming	LI 離 30 Brightness	FENG 豐 55 Abundance	JIAREN 家人 37 The Family	JIJI 既濟 63 Already Accomplished	BI 賁 22 Adornrning	MINGYI 明夷 36 Brightness Dimmed
ZHEN 震 4 Thunder	WUWANG 無妄 25 Without Wrongdoing	SUI 隨 17 Following	SHIHE 噬嗑 21 Biting Through	ZHEN 震 51 Shock	YI 益 42 Increasing	ZHUN 屯 3 Sprouting	YI 頤 27 Nourishing	FU 復 24 Returning
XUN 巽 5 Wind	GOU 姤 44 Meeting	DAGUO 大過 28 Great Exceeding	DING 鼎 50 Renewing	HENG 恆 32 Persevering	XUN 巽 57 Penetrating	JING 井 48 The well	GU 蠱 18 Decaying	SHENG 升 46 Rising
KAN 坎 6 Water	SONG 訟 6 Contention	KUN 困 47 Adversity	WEIJI 未濟 64 Not Yet Accomplished	XIE 解 40 Loosening	HUAN 渙 59 Dispersing	KAN 坎 29 Double Pitfall	MENG 蒙 4 Enlightenment	SHI 師 7 Leading Troops
GEN 艮 7 Mountain	DUN 遯 33 Retreating	XIAN 咸 31 Interacting	LÜ 旅 56 The Wanderer	XIAOGUO 小過 62 Small Exceeding	JIAN 漸 53 Gradual Progress	JIAN 蹇 39 Obstacles	GEN 艮 52 Stilling	QIAN 謙 15 Modesty
KUN 坤 8 Earth	PI 否 12 Obstruction	CUI 萃 45 Gathering	JIN 晉 35 Advancing	YU 豫 16 Providing-For	GUAN 觀 20 Observing	BI 比 8 Joining Together	BO 剝 23 Stripping	KUN 坤 2 Earth (Tolerance)

in odd numbers 1, 3, 5 are called yang positions, whereas the three even numbers 2, 4, 6 are yin positions. The odd numbers are seen as the yang and the even numbers as the yin. The combination of a line (yin or yang) with a position (yin or yang) can be called **line–position link**, which represents six different times and places in a hexagram.

THE SYMBOLISM OF LINE–POSITION LINKS

In a hexagram the lines or the line–position links move from the bottom to the top, indicating changes in time and place. The six line–position links of a hexagram are indicated by corresponding symbols. For example, "Initial" represents the first position and "Second" the second position, … and "Top" the sixth position. "Yang" stands for the yang line, and "Yin" the yin line. "Initial Yang" means "the yang line in the first position" and "Fourth Yin" the yin line in the fourth position. The symbols of twelve line–position links are indicated in the following two hexagrams TAI and PI:

Hexagram TAI 泰			**Hexagram PI** 否		
[Harmony] (11)			**[Obstruction]** (12)		
Top Yin	– –		Top Yang	——	
Fifth Yin	– –	Earth	Fifth Yang	——	Heaven
Fourth Yin	– –		Fourth Yang	——	
Third Yang	——		Third Yin	– –	
Second Yang	——	Heaven	Second Yin	– –	Earth
Initial Yang	——		Initial Yin	– –	

A position or place in a hexagram represents a specific time and place in an evolving process. Time moves upward and so does the place. In the framework of the *Yijing*, time and place move simultaneously as represented by the upward movement of the six lines. A line represents two characteristics, firstly its nature as either yin or yang and secondly those characteristics represented by where the line is located. Initial Yang means a yang line in the first position of a hexagram and Second Yin a yin line in the second position. The other four lines and positions are named in the same way, for example, Third Yang, Fourth Yin, Fifth Yin, and Top Yin in the hexagram TAI, and Third Yin, Fourth Yang, Fifth Yang, and Top Yang in the hexagram PI as indicated above. The name of a line–position link uses two symbols, the first symbol indicates in which position the respective line is located and the second symbol represents the type of line (yin or yang). Each hexagram has six line–position links and the sixty-four hexagrams as a whole have a total of 384 line–position links.

Proper and Improper Positions

A yang line in a yang position or a yin line in a yin position is defined as a **proper position**, for example, Initial Yang and Second Yin. A yang line in a yin position or a yin line in a yang position is called an **improper position**, for example, Third Yin and Fourth Yang. A proper position is generally considered as "favorable" and an improper position as "not favorable." A person whose character (yang or yin) matches the nature of his position (yang or yin) will be considered to be in a proper position; otherwise, he is in an improper position.

However, this classification is rather subjective as the meaning "proper" or "improper" can be interpreted differently in different situations. A person who is energetic and capable (a yang character) in a strong (yang) position will have a good chance of taking the right action to achieve his objective. This person, according to the general definition, is in a "proper" position. But if he is a man with strong self-confidence or obstinacy he may be induced by his "proper" or favorable position to take a reckless action and to move forward despite the uncertainty involved in such a movement. As a result, he will face danger ahead. In this respect, a "proper" position may not necessarily be considered favorable to him. Similarly, a weak (yin) person in a weak (yin) position may decide to stay where he is as he believes that he is in the "proper" or "right" position which rests on not moving forward, despite the fact that the conditions for such a movement appear to be favorable. In this case, a "proper" position becomes not favorable to him.

A strong (yang) person in a strong (yang) position may decide not to take any action and to stay where he is because he realizes that a forward movement is likely to be uncertain and dangerous. Under such circumstances, if he knows how to restrain his inner desire and not move forward, he will be able to maintain his "proper" or "right" position. If a weak (yin) person in a weak (yin) position does not make a forward action as indicated above, he is also acting properly.

To decide whether a position is "proper" or "improper," the criterion of **similarity** between the nature of a line and its positions is not the only one that should be used. Other factors should also be taken into consideration, such as the **personal character** of the respective executive and the **conditions** for taking an action.

Carrying Position

A carrying position is a position in which **a yin line is below or carries a yang line** ⚏. This is the position of a subordinate (yin) who carries the orders of his superior (yang), so it indicates a subordinate–superior (yin–yang) relationship from the standpoint of a subordinate. As the yin line symbolizes the obedience or docility of a subordinate to his superior, so is a carrying position generally considered favourable. In the framework of the *Yijing*, the yang generally represents a higher position than the yin, indicating the relationship between heaven and earth. In an organization the yang may represent a strong and experienced person and the yin a less experienced and capable one. The former above the latter is considered a normal situation in which the softness (yin) follows the hardness (yang), indicating the obedience of a subordinate to his superior. As a result, a harmonious relationship between the two is expected and the situation should be seen favorable.

Riding Position

A riding position is a position in which **a yin line is above or rides a yang line** ⚏. Normally the yang should be above the yin, so this "inverse" situation is considered not favorable. Hardness following softness is considered not a "normal" practice in a superior–subordinate relationship. A soft or incapable (yin) superior above a strong and capable (yang) subordinate may create conflicts between the two if the superior cannot properly manage the relationship with his subordinate.

Interconnecting Positions

The position of a yang line in one trigram of a hexagram, for example, the lower trigram, has an interconnection with a yin line in the corresponding position of the other trigram—the upper trigram. Similarly, the position of a yin line in a trigram has an interconnection with the corresponding position of a yang line in the other trigram. The reason why the **two lines with different natures interconnect with each other** is based on the principle of the yin–yang union. Between the lower and upper trigrams of a hexagram there are three possible pairs of interconnecting positions as shown below:

Interconnecting Positions

Lower Trigram		Upper Trigram	Hexagram JIJI 既濟 [Water–Fire] (63)
Third Yang	and	Top Yin	
Second Yin	and	Fifth Yang	
Initial Yang	and	Fourth Yin	

or

Lower Trigram		Upper Trigram	Hexagram WEIJI 未濟 [Fire–Water] (64)
Third Yin	and	Top Yang	
Second Yang	and	Fifth Yin	
Initial Yin	and	Fourth Yang	

In each hexagram, except the pure yang hexagram QIAN 乾 [Heaven] (1) and the pure yin hexagram KUN 坤 [Earth] (2), the number of interconnections between the two lines ranges from one to three. Except in the two "parental hexagrams"— QIAN and KUN—interconnections between a yang line and a yin line are found in all the other sixty-two hexagrams. Examples are shown below:

Complementary Advantages

Hexagram TAI 泰 [Harmony] (11)   **Hexagram XIAN 咸 [Interaction] (31)**

A union of yin and yang is always considered a favorable situation because it can provide **complementary advantages**. There is, however, no interconnection between two yang lines or two yin lines in the two trigrams since the lines are the same and hence lack the advantage of a complementarity.

Normally, there is no relationship between a yang line in the lower trigram and a yang line in the upper trigram in the equivalent position. For example, the first yang line of the lower trigram and the fourth yang line of the upper trigram, or the second yang line and fifth yang line. The reason for this is that an association of two lines of the same type, based on the yin–yang concept, will not offer any complementary advantage. This

principle is also applied to the relationship between two yin lines which
are located in the equivalent position in a lower and an upper trigram:

Similar Advantages

Hexagram Kun 困
[Adversity] (47)

Hexagram Jin 晉
[Advancing] (35)

There is no relationship between Second Yang and Fifth Yang in the
hexagram Kun 困 [Adversity] (47) and between Second Yin and Fifth
Yin in the hexagram Jin 晉 [Advancing] (35). However, under special
circumstances the relationship between two yang lines or two yin lines
in the lower and upper trigram respectively can be considered favorable
when one party needs assistance from another party with the same
characteristics, and if such cooperation between the two can benefit both
sides. Two persons of the same type can therefore establish a working
relationship in order to benefit from each other. This relationship will
not provide complementary advantages but **similar advantages**.

CENTRAL POSITION

In each of the two trigrams of a hexagram, there is a central position
which is represented by the second line of the lower trigram and the
fifth line of the upper trigram. There are four central lines in sixty-four
hexagrams as in Second Yang, Second Yin, Fifth Yang, and Fifth Yin. The
following two hexagrams indicate these four central positions:

Hexagram Jian 蹇
[Obstacles] (39)

Hexagram Xian 咸
[Interacting] (31)

There are a total number of 128 central positions in the sixty-four
hexagrams. With the exception of a few, most of the commentaries in
their line statements are favourable. They indicate that the concept of
centrality plays a major role in the framework of the *Yijing*. **Centrality**
means "a position which is just right"—which is neither too much
no too little—and includes the concept of sincerity, balance, and

uprightness. It is also called the *zhongyong* 中庸 [moderation] as emphasized in the Confucian doctrine.

A central position is more important than a proper position. A position which is "proper" or "correct" is not necessarily central, but a position which is central is considered correct. So **an improper position can still have a favorable commentary in its line statement if the position is central**, for example, Second Yang or Fifth Yin.

In the doctrine of the *Yijing* the concept of centrality is a "point" aspect, but in practice it should be a "range" concept so as to increase its adaptability.

INTIMATE POSITIONS

Intimate positions refers to the positions of **two of the same type of lines in the neighborhood of a hexagram**, for example, Initial Yang and Second Yang, Second Yang and Third Yang, Third Yang and Fourth Yang, Fourth Yang and Fifth Yang, Fifth Yang and Top Yang, Initial Yin and Second Yin, Second Yin and Third Yin, and so forth. Based on this concept, people who have similar characteristics and work in a close relationship are likely to develop an intimate relationship.

CHANGING LINE AND HEXAGRAM

Since a hexagram consists of six lines, a change in any one of them will lead to a change in the original hexagram to another hexagram within the system. For example, through a change of the yin line in the fourth position to a yang line, the primary hexagram TAI 泰 [Harmony] (11) will be transformed to the changing hexagram DAZHUANG 大壯 [Great Strength] (34):

Primary Hexagram	**Changing Hexagram**
TAI 泰 **[Harmony] (11)**	DAZHUANG 大壯 **[Great Strength] (34)**

Earth ⚏. ⟶ ⚏. Thunder
Heaven ⚌ ⚌ Heaven

The fourth line of the above two hexagrams is called the **changing line**. The situation of the primary hexagram is different from that of a changing hexagram. A changing line can be seen as an "independent variable" whereas the changing hexagram is a "dependent variable." A hexagram cannot have more than six changing lines:

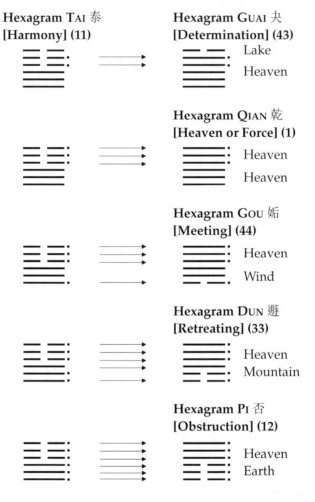

Hexagram TAI 泰
[Harmony] (11)

Hexagram GUAI 夬
[Determination] (43)
Lake
Heaven

Hexagram QIAN 乾
[Heaven or Force] (1)
Heaven
Heaven

Hexagram GOU 姤
[Meeting] (44)
Heaven
Wind

Hexagram DUN 遯
[Retreating] (33)
Heaven
Mountain

Hexagram PI 否
[Obstruction] (12)
Heaven
Earth

CHANGES IN HEXAGRAMS

Within the sixty-four hexagrams one hexagram can be changed into another using different methods:

1. The opposite method
2. The inverse method
3. The interchange method
4. The nuclear method

The Opposite Method

A primary hexagram can be transformed into an opposite hexagram by changing all its six lines into their opposite nature, for example, yin to yang or yang to yin:

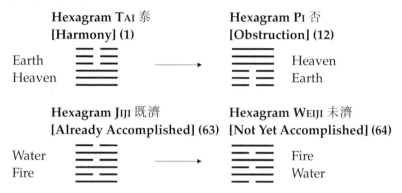

The above two examples illustrate the opposite natures of the primary hexagram and the second hexagram. The second hexagram is named the opposite hexagram. When the leader of an organization is considering whether he needs to make a significant change in structure or policy he should think of what the opposite situation will be as indicated by the opposite hexagram. If it appears to be favorable, he can start his reforms. If not he can modify his plans or simply give up.

Two more examples of opposite hexagrams are shown below:

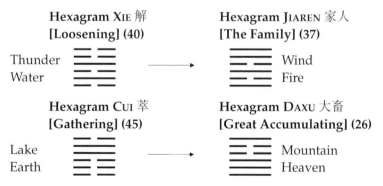

The Inverse Method

By reversing the trigrams, a primary hexagram can be turned upside down to become another hexagram as follows:

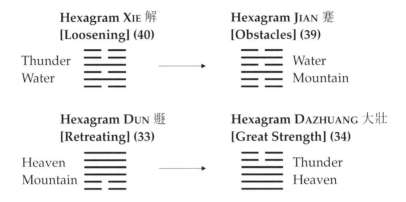

The inverse method can be applied to a situation in which the leader of an organization is, say, in negotiation with his employees over a salary increase or an improvement in fringe benefits. It would be useful for him to think about the situation faced the employees and vice versa. Use of the inverse method can help improve understanding between the two opposing parties.

The Interchange Method

Through an interchange between the upper trigram and the lower trigram of a hexagram, the primary hexagram changes to another hexagram as follows:

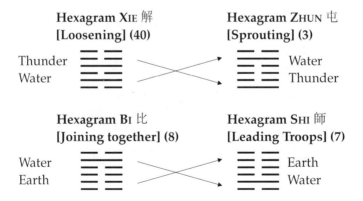

The interchange method provides another way of thinking about the situation. It can broaden a person's mind when making a decision.

The Nuclear Method

Within each hexagram there is at least one "hidden hexagram" or nuclear hexagram. The general rule is to treat the second, third, and fourth line of a primary hexagram as the lower trigram of the derived hexagram and the third, fourth, and fifth line as the upper trigram:

Hexagram BI 比   **Derived Hexagram PO 剝**
[Joining together] (8)   **[Stripping] (23)**

6	— —		5	———
5	———		4	— —
4	— —		3	— —
3	— —		4	— —
2	— —		3	— —
1	— —		2	— —

Since the derived hexagram Bo is within the primary hexagram BI, it can be called the hidden hexagram or nuclear hexagram. Another example of a nuclear hexagram is shown below:

Hexagram KUN 困   **Nuclear Hexagram JIAREN 家人**
[Adversity] (47)   **[The Family] (37)**

6	— —		5	———
5	———		4	———
4	———		3	— —
3	— —		4	———
2	———		3	— —
1	— —		2	———

A nuclear hexagram indicates a situation or a problem which is hidden within an identifiable situation or problem. The hidden situation (problem) lies within the explicit situation (problem). By using the nuclear method, the leader of an organization can think about the problem he faces in a deeper way and can identify the hidden problem that he has not yet recognized. As with the other methods illustrated above, the nuclear method can also broaden the mind of a leader.

The interrelationship between a primary hexagram and its four changing hexagrams are illustrated in the following figure:

The Interrelationship between a Primary and its Four Changing Hexagrams

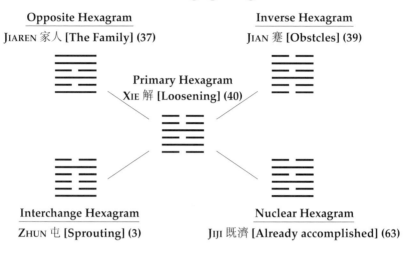

Opposite Hexagram
Jiaren 家人 **[The Family] (37)**

Inverse Hexagram
Jian 蹇 **[Obstcles] (39)**

Primary Hexagram
Xie 解 **[Loosening] (40)**

Interchange Hexagram
Zhun 屯 **[Sprouting] (3)**

Nuclear Hexagram
Jiji 既濟 **[Already accomplished] (63)**

Suppose the leader of an organization is in a situation in which the members of the organization at the middle and lower level reject the top management's proposal for a wage cut during an economic slow-down. The leader is thinking of what move he should take. He starts with the hexagram Xie 解 [Loosening] (40) in the hope of getting some **advice** from the derived hexagrams. The nuclear hexagram Jiji 既濟 [Already accomplished] (63) gives him **confidence** in his negotiations with the members, encouraged by the meaning or the name of this derived hexagram. However, he will find **difficulties in the beginning** of the negotiation and **obstacles** during the negotiation as indicated by the two respective derived hexagrams.

To solve the conflict between the two parties, the leader should convince the members of the organization that a wage cut will not necessarily be harmful to them. They would be able to keep their jobs in the organization without a lay-off, which would be imposed if a reasonable and acceptable solution cannot be obtained. If the organization members can share the values of a whole group as suggested by the opposite hexagram, Jiaren 家人 [The Family] (37) the conflict between the two parties can be resolved. The group value should probably be emphasized in the negotiations between the two parties. In addition, the leader can also examine the thirty line statements of the five hexagrams and see whether he can get any useful insights or advice for his actions.

TIME AND SPACE

Any change is to do with time and space or place. In human activities, time and place are particularly meaningful. An action in one time/place can have a different effect to that produced by the same action in a different time/place. In order to act properly one must know when and where to act, as well as when and where to stop. A leader who is able to take proper action in accordance with time/place will be able to increase his flexibility and adaptability to the changes in the environment, both internal and external. The changes in the lines and hexagrams indicate this important principle for effective leadership.

Each hexagram represents a particular situation that can be observed in six different stages by the six lines. Each line stands for a specific time/place which a person or an organization faces. Each situation can be considered favorable or unfavorable, or in the *Yijing*'s terminology "fortune" or "misfortune."

The movement of the lines from the bottom of a hexagram to the top indicates the changes in time and place. **In the framework of the *Yijing* time/space changes simultaneously. Time can be seen as the "vertical space" whereas space is the "horizontal time."** The whole system of sixty-four hexagrams can therefore be considered as a large space within which the hexagrams will change with time among themselves. Similarly, a particular hexagram stands for a smaller space or a specific situation which comprises six stages of time movement. Here, time appears to be the key variable and place a subordinate one. However, the concept of place becomes more useful in respect to the changes in a hexagram. Any change in a hexagram signifies a change of place or situation, and hence a change in time too.

HOW TO INTERPRET A HEXAGRAM

A Hexagram as an Organization

A hexagram can be seen as an organization which includes companies, governments, public and social institutions. The six positions of a hexagram represent the different levels within an organization: the positions of the lower trigram stands for executives at the lower and middle level of management whereas the positions of the upper trigram stand for the higher and top level management. A yang position means this position has the strength to take action and a yin position does not.

A leader should know whether his position meets the conditions for moving forward or not. An action which is entirely based on the leader's optimism or enthusiasm, regardless of the objective conditions, will be dangerous.

The nature of a line, whether it is yin or yang, represents the character of a leader. A yang line symbolizes a person who is active, strong, optimistic, and probably emotional. He tends to prefer an expansionary operation, moving forward regardless of the possible risks or dangers involved, particularly if he is in a yang or strong position. If the time/place is favorable he may succeed, otherwise he will fail. According to the principle of moderation or centrality as emphasized by the *Yijing*, he cannot be considered a wise leader, because a wise leader must not only have **initiative** but also be **stable** in his emotions and steady in his action. **A wise leader is one who is balanced in his character**. If a leader has a strong (yang) character but is in a weak (yin) position, he will tend to act moderately.

Conversely, a yin line represents a person who is soft, passive, and cautious. If he is in a weak (yin) position he should not move forward but should stay where he is. If the time/place is not favorable for moving forward his action can seem right even though it was not his original intention. The unfavorable time/place becomes favorable to him; his weakness is covered by favorable environmental factors. In fact, according to the *Yijing* he is not a good leader since his "success" has come about by accident. If he is in a strong (yang) position, it will be a challenge to him as to whether he should take action. If he believes the time/place will be favorable in the future, he may take action to move ahead even though he lacks the capability to do so. But he will ask the capable people in the organization to assist him in this mission, that is, those able men as represented by the yang lines in a hexagram. By acting in this way, he is a balanced person even though he is weak in capability. **A man who knows his weakness but is willing to use capable people is a wise man**.

Hexagram Statements

A hexagram statement is a judgment of a whole or "macro" situation whether it is favorable or not. In some cases, the conditions for achieving a desirable situation are suggested. Out of sixty-four hexagram statements, fifty-four situations have favorable commentaries, indicating the optimism of the *Yijing*. Only five hexagram statements have unfavorable commentaries and another five are mixed. The five hexagrams with unfavorable commentaries are SONG 訟 (6), PI 否 (12), MINGYI 明夷 (36), GOU 姤 (44), and GUIMEI 歸妹 (54). The other five statements which have mixed commentaries are LIN 臨 (19), JIAN 蹇 (39), JING 井 (48), JIJI 既濟 (63), and WEIJI 未濟 (64). However, the optimism of hexagram statements does not necessarily mean that every stage of a development within a whole situation must be favorable; the individual or "micro" situation indicated by a line statement or line–position statement may be different from the whole or "macro" situation. Another reason for the inconsistency between the commentaries on the hexagram and line statements is probably due to the different writers.

Line Statements

A line statement is a description of the "micro" situation of a line–position link with a judgment on whether it is favorable or not. Some of the line statements, however, have no direct judgment on the situation described but implicitly indicated in the text.

STRUCTURE OF LINE–POSITION LINKS AND HUMAN RELATIONS

The relationship between the six line–position links of a hexagram symbolizes the **human relations** within an organization. A carrying position == indicates a harmonious relation between a superior and a subordinate due to the obedience of the latter. A riding position == may result in a disharmonious superior–subordinate relationship because of a weak and incapable superior above a strong and capable subordinate. An interconnecting position indicates a cooperation between the executives at different levels. A leader in a central position (second position or fifth position) is most likely to have good relations with his colleagues in the organization due to his balanced character.

The fifth position and its line text are conventionally considered as the basis for learning leadership because of its central position, which stands for sincerity, balance, and correctness, and because of the favorable commentaries on its line text. The author, however, prefers to consider that all line–position statements can give valuable advice to a leader regardless of whether they are favorable or not. A leader can always learn from both. A favorable action or situation gives a leader a guideline for choosing the right direction. An unfavorable action or situation can also be useful in guiding a leader to avoid a wrong move.

THE TWELVE LINE–POSITION LINKS

A hexagram has six line–position links, indicating six particular situations. Since both position and line can have either yin or yang characteristics, there are twelve line–position links: Initial Yang, Initial Yin, Second Yang, Second Yin, Third Yang, Third Yin, Fourth Yang, Fourth Yin, Fifth Yang, Fifth Yin, Top Yang, and Top Yin. Each hexagram has six line–position links out of the above twelve. Before analyzing the sixty-four hexagrams in detail, it is useful to know the general characteristics of these twelve line–position links and their relationships.

Initial Yang

This position is at the bottom of a hexagram. It symbolizes that the position of the respective executive is low within his organization but that he is active and possesses initiative, as indicated by the properties of the yang line. When he intends to move up, say, by participating in a promising project in order to demonstrate his capability, he must not overreach himself and risk hurting his colleagues. He should act moderately. If he is ambitious or emotional he should restrain his desire at this time/place until the opportunity arises.

To decide whether he should move forward or not, he must assess what situation he is facing now and what the future situation is likely to be. If he anticipates there will be danger ahead as represented by the trigram or nuclear trigram KAN 坎 [Water] ☵, he should stay where he is. However, if he believes that he will certainly get help from his superior Second Yang or Second Yin, or particularly the senior executive Fourth Yin which is close to the top leader Fifth Yang (or Fifth Yin) as indicated by an interconnection between these two positions in respective hexagram, he can go ahead as the difficulty or danger of such a movement can be lessened through help from above. On the other hand, his strength and capability can also be of assistance to the senior executive Fourth Yin who is not "strong" as indicated by the yin line. Through the interconnection between these two, Initial Yang provides a **complementary advantage** to Fourth Yin.

If the senior executive is Fourth Yang instead of Fourth Yin, Initial Yang can still establish a connection with the senior executive Fourth Yang through their common character, shared values, and interests, as both are represented by yang lines. This can be called **similar or comrade advantages**.

Out of thirty-two line statements on Initial Yang, twenty-eight commentaries are considered favorable, "blameless," and "no regret." This is eighty-eight percent of the total, indicating the opportunities provided at this stage to prepare for a future movement.

Initial Yin

An executive in this position is seen as weak since his position is lower within an organization as indicated by its bottom position of a hexagram and his character is weak as represented by the yin line as well as having an improper position (a yin line in a yang position). An executive in this time/place is advised not to move but to remain in his position unchanged. He must acknowledge his own weakness and take precautions against any change that may affect him. His obedience to his superior Second Yang or Second Yin is helpful, but he should also seek an interconnection with those senior executives as represented by Fourth Yang who is close to top leader Fifth Yang or Fifth Yin in order to get useful assistance from the above. **Since his position is vulnerable, he must always be alert and cautious in his actions**.

Out of thirty-two line statements of Initial Yin, nineteen commentaries are considered favorable including "blameless" and "no regret." There is a need for more caution in this stage than in that of Initial Yang.

Second Yang

This is a position of an action-leader which is seen favorable due to its central position of a lower trigram, symbolizing that a person is **balanced, sincere, and correct**. He emphasizes the principle of centrality in his leadership and management. His character is **strong, active, and with initiative**. He is willing to assume the tasks assigned by the senior or top leader, as indicated by the characteristics of a yang line. On the other hand, he is strong but not obstinate, active but cautious, so he has a certain yin or soft element in his behavior too. He knows that he is in an improper position (a yang line in a yin position), or a position with constraints, so he acts in a moderate way. Consequently, the disadvantage of his improper position is compensated for by the advantage of his central position. If an improper position is also a central position, its yin–yang union is considered favorable. Centrality is one of the essential concepts of the *Yijing*.

As an action-leader, Second Yang needs to establish a good relationship with the top leader Fifth Yin to get a **complementary advantage**. If the top leader is Fifth Yang, **similar advantage** can also be obtained through an interconnection between the two.

Out of thirty-two Second Yang commentaries, twenty-seven are considered favorable. The eighty-four percent of the total indicating the importance for an action-leader to be in a central position to achieve efficient leadership.

Second Yin

Like Second Yang, Second Yin represents an executive who is also in a central position of the lower trigram with the characteristics of balance, sincerity, and correctness. Second Yin, however, is different from Second Yang in his characteristics as he is **soft, flexible, and adaptable** as symbolized by the yin line. He is in a yin position which indicates that the authority of his position may not be adequate to meet the responsibilities of his position. If this is the case, he should not move forward unless he is backed up by a top leader such as Fifth Yang.

If the top leader is Fifth Yang, Second Yin will have a chance to provide special assistance to the senior management through a **complementary advantage**. The combination of a yang-type top leader with a yin-type action-leader is beneficial to an organization. If the top leader is Fifth Yin then two yin-type persons working together, unlike two yang-type persons, may not produce the adequate energy to move forward and so a similar advantage can not be obtained as in a two Second Yang's case. For this reason, **the ideal top leader for Second Yin should be Fifth Yang instead of Fifth Yin**.

There are thirty-two line–position links for Second Yin of which twenty-one have favorable commentaries, sixty-six percent of the total. Compared with a yang type action-leader as Second Yang, a yin type one represented by Second Yin appears to be less favorable.

Third Yang

The third position is at the end of the lower trigram, in which it is difficult for an executive to make his decisions. Moving to the upper trigram from the lower trigram means leaving the present stage and entering into a new development. By moving forward there will be a chance to catch the opportunity for development, but the action may involve certain risks and uncertainties. Staying placed may avoid the risk of a move but it may also mean missing out on an opportunity. The decision to move or not to move, as well as how to move, is likely to be influenced by the character of the executive as represented by the third line of the hexagram.

If the executive is active, energetic, and capable as indicated by Third Yang, he will tend to be optimistic and will most likely prefer to take a forward action, even though present circumstances are not necessarily clear or favorable. A yang line in a yang position indicates that he is in a strong and proper position, so he may become **emotional** and **over-confident** in formulating his expansionary plans. In some cases, he may even become a **quick-tempered** or **arrogant** person. As a result, he may rush ahead impatiently without considering the consequences of his action. This kind of behavior, according to the commentaries of the *Yijing*, is considered "not favorable" or "not fortunate." A sensible executive in this situation should **stay calm** and **exercise self-control**. He must carefully assess the conditions and the possible outcomes of the planned action and seek the advice of senior and experienced people, as represented by Fourth Yang or Top Yin.

Out of thirty-two line statements of Third Yang twenty-one commentaries are unfavorable, indicating an active person in a strong position, even a proper position, needs to have control of his emotion.

Third Yin

Third Yin represents an executive who has a **soft** character and is **calm, cautious,** and **patient**. As the yin line indicates, he lacks capability. His improper position (a yin line in a yang position) reveals that his capability is below the expected standards for his position, so he may act very carefully and will not to do anything beyond his knowledge and capability. As a result, in contrast to a Third Yang, he will not take a chance to move forward. His improper position (a yin line in a yang position) has the nature of yin–yang union and hence will lead him to act cautiously in a moderate way when he is at the crossroads. But this is not to say that the way adopted by Third Yin is superior to that of Third Yang, it merely indicates that a rational decision in this situation should take other factors into consideration too. For example, anticipation of the time/place in the next stage and possible assistance from above (Fourth Yang or Top Yang).

Out of thirty-two Third Yin twenty-six commentaries are unfavorable, advising a weak person in a strong position or "improper position" needs to be particularly careful in his actions.

Fourth Yang

Like the third position, the fourth position of a hexagram is also a delicate situation for a senior executive of an organization. Fourth Yang represents a senior executive who is very close to the top leader—Fifth Yang or Fifth Yin. In either case he is one of the members of the power center within an organization. His proximity to the top leader enables him to get formal power and probably informal power too.

If the top leader is a Fifth Yang, whose leadership style tends to be strong and centralized, he needs a person whom he can trust. A senior executive Fourth Yang may be the right one as both have similar characteristics and values as indicated by the two yang lines. If this is the case, Fourth Yang will have both formal and informal authority. His formal authority comes from delegation by the top leader and his informal authority from his close relationship to the power center. The people below him will pay respect to him, not only because of his formal or informal status but also because of his capability (as indicated by the yang line). If he can get the people below him to assist him, for example, Third Yin, Third Yang, and Initial Yin, he will be able to perform his duties smoothly and efficiently. However, his strong or yang character may lead him into conflict with the top leader over some policy decisions. This would be dangerous. He must exercise **self-control**.

If the top leader is Fifth Yin, whose leadership is of the soft style, the senior executive Fourth Yang may obtain more power than in the case of a strong leadership as under Fifth Yang.

Out of thirty-two Fourth Yang twenty-one commentaries are favorable, suggesting that a capable senior executive can offer his valuable services to a top leader particularly the yin-type one such as Fifth Yin.

Fourth Yin

Like Fourth Yang, Fourth Yin represents a senior executive who is also close to the top leader and the power center. His character is soft, flexible, and cautious, but less capable than Fourth Yang as indicated by the yin line. Since he can adapt to a top leader who is either a Fifth Yang or Fifth Yin, his relationship with the power center is harmonious. To compensate for his weak capability he needs help from the people below—those who are strong, energetic, and capable such as Third Yang directly below him and Initial Yang through their interconnection. **A yin–yang union is favorable to Fourth Yin**.

However, if he is too soft and cautious, he may not be willing to initiate any new projects in order to avoid risk. He tries to safeguard his own position in the organization and not to fall into a dangerous situation. If the top leader is Fifth Yang, the impact of Fourth Yin's weakness on the efficiency of the organization may not be obvious as Fifth Yang can receive help from Second Yin through his complementary advantage, or from the action-leader Second Yang through his similar advantage.

If the top leader is Fifth Yin, **a yin–yin mix as formed by Fifth Yin and Fourth Yin may not be seen favorable to the efficiency of an organization**. A yin–yin mix in the top management would lead an organization into a situation which may lack vision and initiative. If Fourth Yin is willing to receive assistance from Third Yang or Initial Yang (see below), his situation can be improved or strengthened by a complementary advantage of a yin–yang union.

Fifth Yang

The fifth position of a hexagram symbolizes a powerful leadership position within an organization. It represents the top leader. His leadership style can be either hard or soft; a yang line represents the former and a yin line the latter. The common characteristics of these two types of leadership are balance, sincerity, and correctness, and the difference between the two lies in their personal style of doing things. Fifth Yang is **active, creative, energetic, and powerful**. He knows how to use the right people to obtain complementary advantage or a similar advantage as by using his interconnection with Second Yin or Second Yang in an organization. He also knows how to handle relations with the subordinates directly under him such as Fourth Yang or Fourth Yin. Based on this, Fifth Yang appears to be an ideal leader for any organization.

However, there is a negative aspect about this leadership "perfection." As **Laozi** said: **"The highest perfection is like imperfection."** When a leader is "too capable" in most things there will be little room for the people below him to, say, demonstrate their capabilities. As a result, the organization is led by one key man. If this is the case, "too strong a leadership" may not be good for an organization. Fifth Yang is in a proper position as represented by a yang line in a yang position; this may lead him to move to a strong leadership style.

No matter how capable a top leader is, he still needs the assistance of different capable people below him, like those represented by Second Yin. There are sixteen interconnections between Fifth Yang and Second Yin, excluding the pure yang hexagram QIAN 乾 (Heaven) and the pure yin hexagram KUN 坤 (Earth), fourteen statements of Fifth Yang have favorable commentaries, suggesting a complementary advantage between a soft action-leader and a strong top leader.

Fifth Yin

In contrast to Fifth Yang, Fifth Yin adopts **a soft style of leadership** as he is willing to delegate his authority to the people below if they are capable of assuming the responsibilities assigned to them. He has full confidence in their operating without any interference. Therefore, the subordinates have good chance to demonstrate their capabilities and specialties to the best advantage of the organization. The leadership philosophy of Fifth Yin is close to that of Laozi's "**nonaction**": "**Rule a big country as you would fry a small fish.**" Fifth Yin sees his organization as if it were a "big country," so he believes effective decentralization is the most appropriate course.

The yin line of the fifth position symbolizes the fact that the top leader Fifth Yin is not as strong, energetic, and active as Fifth Yang, but he is **tolerant, open-minded, flexible, and adaptable**. To strengthen the efficiency of his leadership, he needs to establish interactive relationships with the capable people below in order to obtain a complementary advantage. For example, he should establish an interconnection with Second Yang, who is a capable action leader.

There are sixteen interconnections between Fifth Yin and Second Yang, of which fourteen of the commentaries on Fifth Yin are considered favorable. This suggests that **a top leader with yin character needs to work with a capable action-leader**.

Top Yang

Both Top Yang and Top Yin can represent those senior people who have formal or informal influence on the top leader Fifth Yang or Fifth Yin. For example, the chairman and senior members of the board of directors or senior advisers. But they are not directly responsible for general operations. If these people are as active and energetic as a top leader Fifth Yang, they may be able to persuade the top leader to take reckless action even if the success of such an action is not certain. If the top leader follows the advice of these senior people, the organization will face danger ahead. Top Yang represents an improper position (a yang line in a yin position) where a person who is likely to make an emotional or irrational decision.

The top line at the end of a hexagram indicates also the extremity of a development. Therefore, Top Yang can also symbolize a turning point in a cycle or the final stage of a development but the best time/place for taking action has passed. A top leader in the position as represented by Top Yang must carefully assess the situation he is facing and make a prediction of potential changes in the future so that he can quickly take the necessary precautions to adapt to changing conditions or to an unexpected turn of events. If he predicts that future changes will be favorable, he should not miss this opportunity but should mobilize the resources of the organization to meet the coming challenge, for example, by organizing capable subordinates to work jointly for the future movement.

Out of thirty-two Top Yang twenty commentaries are favorable, indicating the importance of energy creativity to a senior executive who is in the turning point of the yin–yang cycle.

Top Yin

Top Yin represents the people at the top echelon of an organization, as does Top Yang. These however are **inactive, modest, flexible, and less ambitious**. As they do not influence the top leader Fifth Yang or Fifth Yin formally or informally, they function basically as "sleeping" chairman/directors/advisers. As a result the power of the organization is concentrated in the hands of the top leader Fifth Yang or Fifth Yin.

Like Top Yang, Top Yin also represents a turning point in a cyclical change. If the top leader is a yin-type person, his weak character may make him lose sensitivity to changes in conditions so that the organization will lack the ability to adapt to the new environment and hence face great danger. A yin-type leader is not energetic or strong enough to deal with the difficult situation involved in a big change if he fails actively to seek the assistance of capable people in his organization.

Out of thirty-two Top Yin twenty-three commentaries are unfavorable, indicating a soft or weak senior leader is incapable to meet the challenges facing in the turning point of a yin–yang cycle.

ELEMENTS AFFECTING THE COMMENTARY ON A LINE–POSITION LINK

The sixty-four hexagrams of the *Yijing* describe sixty-four situations in a "macro" aspect, whereas the six line statements of each hexagram indicate six individual situations in a "micro" aspect. In each of 384 line statements of the sixty-four hexagrams, there is a commentary on each situation in the respective line statement with a judgment of whether it is "fortunate," or "unfortunate," or "blameless" or "regretful." These judgments advise people to take the right actions in order to obtain "fortune" and avoid "misfortune."

Whether these judgments are "right" or "wrong" is not easy to say because they can be affected by a number of elements. For example, the time/place in which the person is in, or the character of the person. Different time/place and personal characteristics will result in different decisions and behavior, hence different outcomes or situations. An action which is considered "fortunate" for person A may not be favorable for person B because of different elements which may affect the situations faced by these two people. Based on the same reasoning, an action which is considered "unfortunate" for person A may not be unfavorable to person B. If an action is judged "unfortunate" and a person accepts this advice and does not act in that direction but in its opposite, he may have a "fortunate" situation instead of an "unfortunate" one. Similarly, if a judgment on an action is "fortunate" but the person acts in an opposite direction, they may become "unfortunate."

The elements that affect a commentary on a line–position link as to whether it is "fortunate" or "unfortunate," or other judgments, are stated in the following figure:

Elements Affecting the Commentary on a Line–Position Link

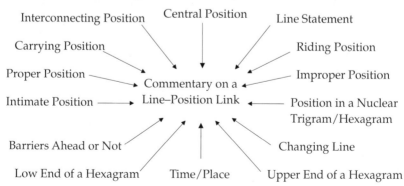

Line Statement

A hexagram has six line statements which describe the situations of six different line–position links. There are totally 384 line statements in the sixty-four hexagrams, each line statement has a commentary on the situation of the respective line–position link whether it is favorable or not.

Central Position

In the sixty-four hexagrams of the *Yijing* the commentaries on Fifth Yin and Second Yang are considered the most favorable. The commentary on a line–position link whether favorable or unfavorable is based on the meaning of the line statement and the judgment on the situation as made in the respective text.

Favorable Commentaries in Four Central Positions

Fifth Yin	28
Second Yang	27
Fifth Yang	26
Second Yin	21

(Total number of central positions in each line–position link = 32)

The importance of the four central positions in the hexagrams is illustrated as follows:

Firstly, both Fifth Yin has the highest number of favorable commentaries, that is, twenty-eight. This runs against the conventional belief that Fifth Yang, which represents a strong leadership position, should be the most favorable line–position link among all. As indicated earlier a "too strong" yang–yang mix, like Fifth Yang (a yang line in a yang position), is not necessarily favorable to a top leader as compared with one who has a balanced yin–yang mix (a yin line in a yang position) since a yang–yang mixed leader like Fifth Yang may not be as adaptable, flexible, and tolerant as a yin–yang mixed one like Fifth Yin.

Secondly, at the level of action leader Second Yang with a balanced yin–yang mix (a yang line in a yin position) appears to be more favorable than that of Second Yin with a yin–yin mix (a yin line in a yin position). This is indicated by the twenty-seven favorable commentaries on Second Yang compared with twenty-one for Second Yin. The former obviously has both advantages of yin and yang, whereas the latter only has the advantage of a single yin element.

Interconnecting Positions

There are six paired interconnecting positions in the sixty-four hexagrams: Initial Yang and Fourth Yin, Initial Yin and Fourth Yang, Second Yang and Fifth Yin, Second Yin and Fifth Yang, Third Yang and Top Yin, Third Yin and Top Yang. Except for the two "parental" hexagrams QIAN 乾 (1) and KUN 坤 (2), the sixteen interconnecting positions in the other sixty-two hexagrams range from one pair to three pairs in each hexagram. The six interconnecting positions are stated below:

Fifth Yang and Second Yin

Fifth Yang represents a strong top leader and Second Yin a soft action leader below him. A top leader in yang-type needs the complementary assistance of an action-leader in yin-type; the characteristics of a yang-type leader are different from that of a yin-type one. An interconnection between Fifth Yang and Second Yin forms a complementary relationship between a top and an action leader. There are a total of sixteen relations between Fifth Yang and Second Yin. Which of these two will get more benefits from their interconnections? The information can be obtained from the number of favorable situations at Fifth Yang and Second Yin respectively as stated in the following:

> Fifth Yang: 14 favorable situations
> Second Yin: 11 favorable situations
> (Total number of interconnections in each line–position link = 16)

The above information from the line statements suggests that the interconnections between top leader Fifth Yang and the action leader Second Yin appears to be more meaningful to the former than the latter. Since these favorable situations are also influenced by the nature of their central positions it is difficult to distinguish the **interconnection effect** from the **central position effect**. Nevertheless, a yin–yang inter-connection does suggest that **a strong top leader needs a soft action leader to assist him in order to get a complementary advantage**. Such a relationship could also be favorable to an **extroverted superior** if he has an **introverted subordinate** below him.

Fifth Yin and Second Yang

Fifth Yin represents a top leader with a soft character and Second Yang an action leader with strong character below him. The former needs the assistance of the latter in order to complement his shortages such as activity, initiative, and energy. The number of favorable situations through interconnections between Fifth Yin and Second Yang at these two levels is stated as follows:

Fifth Yin: 14 favorable situations
Second Yang: 12 favorable situations
(Total number of interconnections in each line–position link = 16)

Despite the fact that the interconnection effect of these two line–position links could be overlapped with the positive effect of their central positions, this does suggest that **a soft top leader needs a strong action leader to back him up to get a complementary advantage**. By the same token, it is probably a good idea for an introverted superior to be supported by an **extroverted subordinate** to strike a balance between their characters.

Fourth Yin and Initial Yang

The interconnections between Fourth Yin and Initial Yang indicate that the former receives more benefits than the latter as shown by the number of favorable situations at these two levels:

Fourth Yin: 13 favorable situations
Initial Yang: 8 favorable situations
(Total number of interconnections in each line–position link = 16)

Since Fourth Yin represents a soft senior executive who is close to the top leader or the power center, he needs capable people below like Initial Yang to support him, similar to the interactive relationship between Fifth Yin and Second Yang as indicated above. **The weakness of a senior executive can be complemented by the strength of the people below**.

Fourth Yang and Initial Yin

In the relationship between Fourth Yang and Initial Yin, the situation can be different from the above case as the superior is strong and capable but the subordinate is weak and cannot provide the assistance required by Fourth Yang even though there is an interconnection between the two. Out of sixteen interconnections between Fourth Yang and Initial Yin there are only six situations which are considered favorable to Fourth Yang, and five to Initial Yin:

> Fourth Yang: 6 favorable situations
> Initial Yin: 5 favorable situations
> (Total number of interconnections in each line–position link = 16)

This suggests a guideline for the superior–subordinate relationship: **a strong senior executive may not benefit from a weak executive below even if there is an interconnection between the two**.

Top Yang and Third Yin

Like the relationship between Fifth Yang and Initial Yin, the senior executive Top Yang may not benefit from a weak executive such as Third Yin below. Third Yin is in an improper position which symbolizes a person who is incapable to meet the requirements of his position. Of the sixteen interconnections between Top Yang and Third Yin there are seven favorable commentaries on the situations of Top Yang and ten unfavorable commentaries on Third Yin, suggesting that a senior executive will not benefit from a weak middle-level executive in spite of the interconnetctions between the two.

Top Yin and Third Yang

Out of sixteen interconnections between Top Yin and Third Yang, favorable commentaries on Top Yin and Third Yang are five and four respectively, both cannot benefit from the interconnections between them.

Carrying Position

In the superior–subordinate relationship within an organization two carrying positions appear to be more important than others—Fourth Yin carrying Fifth Yang and Third Yin carrying Fourth Yang. These two superior–subordinate relations are considered more meaningful than Second Yin carrying Third Yang and Fifth Yin carrying Top Yang. Since both Second Yin and Fifth Yin are also central positions, the carrying position effect can overlap with the central position effect.

Fourth Yin carrying Fifth Yang indicates a relationship between a weak subordinate and a strong superior in which Fourth Yin is obedient to his superior Fifth Yang. Out of sixteen of the carrying-relationship commentaries on Fourth Yin and Fifth Yang there are eleven favorable commentaries on both sides, suggesting that **the obedience and adaptability of a yin-type senior executive to a yang-type top leader will be able to create harmony between the two.**

Third Yin carrying Fourth Yang indicates a situation in which a weak middle-level executive shows his obedience to his superior Fourth Yang. Out of sixteen carrying relations Third Yin has thirteen unfavorable commentaries, indicating an important fact that a middle-level executive may not benefit from his carrying relations with his superior if he is incapable in an improper position.

Riding Position

A position in which a yin line is above a yang line is named a riding position, symbolizing a weak or incapable man above a strong or capable man. Since the relationship between the two is considered inappropriate, the commentary on this situation is "not favorable."

Proper Position

A person who acts in a proper position should get a favorable commentary in the relevant line statement. But if his capability is low and the time/place is also not favorable he will not be able to get "fortune" even if he is in a proper position. The situation of Third Yang (a strong line in a strong position) could be used as an example. If a capable person as represented by Third Yang wants to take a reckless action may by moving forward meet danger ahead the commentary of the respective line statement will be "unfortunate." Some cases of Third Yang support this observation. As compared with "central position" and "interconnection position," "proper position" serves an additional element or a minor role in determining whether a situation is favorable or not.

Apart from the two central positions, Second Yin and Fifth Yang, there are four proper positions in the hexagrams: Initial Yang, Third Yang, Fourth Yin, and Top Yin. The number of commentaries with judgments of "fortunate," "blameless," and "no regret" on these four line statements is stated below:

Top Yin	9
Fourth Yin	28
Third Yang	11
Initial Yang	28

(Number of line–position links in each *proper* positions = 32)

Fourth Yin appears to be the most favorable proper position among the above four, followed by Initial Yang.

Improper Position

An improper position is generally considered unfavorable due to the difference in nature between its position and line but if it overlaps with a central position, such as Second Yang, the negative effect of this improper position can be compensated for by the positive effect of its central position. Apart from the two central positions Second Yang and Fifth Yin, the other four improper positions with the number of "unfavorable" commentaries are given below:

Top Yang	12
Fourth Yang	11
Third Yin	26
Initial Yin	19

(Number of line–position links in each *improper* positions = 32)

Although Third Yin has twenty-six "unfavorable" commentaries, the highest number among the four improper positions, it is hard to say that the other improper positions are unfavorable. The relations between improper positions and commentaries are not clear.

Intimate Position

Two neighboring yang lines or two yin lines, for example Second Yang and Third Yang or Fifth Yang and Fourth Yang, indicate an intimate relationship between the two from which each of them can benefit. In some cases, this intimate relationship will have a positive effect on a situation because of their unification.

Low End of a Hexagram

The low end of a hexagram symbolizes the beginning stage of a development and hence the difficulties to be faced. There are a total of sixty-four beginning stages in the hexagrams, of which forty-one commentaries are considered favorable, "blameless," and "no regret" whereas twenty-three are judged unfavorable as shown as follows:

	Initial Yang	Initial Yin
Favorable commentaries including "Blameless" and "No Regret"	28	13
Unfavorable commentaries including "Regret"	4	19
Total	32	32

The situation of Initial Yang is considered suitable for development, whereas Initial Yin does not.

Upper End of a Hexagram

Two line–position links are located at the upper end of a hexagram, either Top Yang or Top Yin, indicating the extremity of a development. Since the best time for such a development is already over, the situation has become uncertain and bleak. Whether the situation is considered favorable or unfavorable depends much on how a person reacts to it. Different actions lead to different situations. The commentaries on Top Yang and Top Yin are given below:

	Top Yang	Top Yin
Favorable commentaries including "Blameless" and "No Regret"	20	9
Unfavorable commentaries including "Regret"	12	23
Total	32	32

Top Yin has twenty-three unfavorable commentaries as compared with twelve for Top Yang, indicating that a person who is in a weak position and has a weak character is likely to face danger at the upper end or turning point of a development. In contrast, Top Yang has twenty favorable commentaries, probably because the person's active character and strong position will lead him to overcome the difficulties encountered.

Position in a Nuclear Trigram/Hexagram

Position in a nuclear trigram/hexagram can also be an element that affects the commentary. For example, Second Yin of the hexagram Sui 隨 (17) [Following] ䷐ should be considered favorable for its central position and proper position. However, it is also the beginning position of the nuclear trigram Gen 艮 [Mountain] ☶, indicating that it is inappropriate to take action because Mountain signifies "stopping." As a result, the commentary on Second Yin advises not to move forward.

Barriers Ahead or Not

If there are barriers ahead of a line it means that a forward movement will be hindered. For example, in the hexagram DAZHUANG 大壯 [Great Strength] (34) ☳ there are three yang lines ahead of Initial Yang, indicating a forward action at this stage will encounter obstacles. The commentary on Initial Yang is "misfortune" if an action is to be taken.

Changing Lines

Any line of a hexagram can be changed to its opposite. For example, a yang line can be changed to a yin line and vice versa. Once a line is changed the trigram will correspondingly change and the changing line forms another line–position link which indicates a changed or "hidden" situation as illustrated below:

Hexagram TONGREN 同人
[Fellowship] (13)

Hexagram GE 革
[Reforming] (49)

In the original hexagram TONGREN, Top Yang has no interconnection with Third Yang. But if the yang line changes to a yin line, Top Yang will transform to Top Yin which becomes the upper trigram of the hexagram GE. Through this change Top Yin is therefore able to interconnect with Third Yang and achieve a complementary advantage through the yin–yang union. The uncertainty of the situation of Top Yang therefore can be reduced by the possible cooperation between Top Yin and Third Yang in the situation of Reforming. Changing a line means a change of behavioral style or action, which may lead to a better situation. It can also be taken into consideration in the commentary on the respective line–position link.

Time/Place

If the action described in a line statement or a line–position link is appropriate to the right time or right place, the commentary on the respective situation tends to be good. If not it will be unfavorable. The influences of the time/place element on the line commentaries under different circumstances have been elaborated above. The time/place factor appears to be the essence of the philosophy of the *Yijing*. To be an enlightened man or a superior man one must know when/where one should move and when/where one should keep still. If this principle is mastered one will receive "fortune," otherwise one will receive "misfortune."

Conclusion

In this section, the elements that influence the commentaries on line statements or line–position links are elaborated. It is not possible to know on what basis the writer made his judgment on a line–position link— whether it is favorable or not favorable. However, the **central positions** and the **interconnections** appear to be the most important criteria in determining the favorableness of a situation. Other elements could also have certain influences on writers' judgment but it is difficult to distinguish their effects from each other due to the overlapping of their positions.

SIX LINE–POSITION LINKS AS SIX STAGES OF DEVELOPMENT

The six line–position links of a hexagram symbolize also six stages of development:

- Initial Yang/Yin: The beginning stage of development
- Second Yang/Yin: The second stage of development
- Third Yang/Yin: The third stage of development
- Fourth Yang/Yin: The fourth stage of development
- Fifth Yang/Yin: The fifth stage of development
- Top Yang/Yin: The final stage of development

The development of everything in the world can be classified in different stages. The difference between them is the length of time in each stage; some are longer and some shorter.

The **first stage** of development can be represented by Initial Yang/ Yin of a hexagram with characteristics of **uncertainty and difficulty**. A person in this stage is advised to be patient, cautious, and calmly prepared.

In the **second stage** as represented by Second Yang/Yin, a person needs to be balanced, sincere, correct, active, energetic, flexible, and adaptable. There are less difficulties or obstacles for development at this stage, so it is **favorable for a person to move forward** if he can maintain the qualities indicated above.

In the **third stage**, he should control his emotion or ego, avoid being overconfident, and not go beyond his capabilities. The third stage as represented by Third Yang/Yin is like **a crossroads** which involves dangers ahead. To move or not to move can be favorable or unfavorable, depending on a person's judgment concerning the coming situation. Under such circumstances, he needs carefully to predict the changing situation, be well prepared, and obtain help from all possible sides.

The **fourth stage** represented by Fourth Yang/Yin is **the prestage of success**. A person needs to be cautious in order not to hurt established relations with those influential people whose decisions are of vital importance to the success of his operations. He should be adaptable to those people and avoid creating conflict with them. To strengthen his position, he needs the cooperation and assistance of others.

The **fifth stage** represented by Fifth Yang/Yin is **the stage of success**. This is the most favorable situation of all in which a person can accomplish his objective without difficulties. Everything runs smoothly and favorably. If he wants to prolong this successful stage, he needs to maintain his vitality: keeping high energy, creativity, and activity while holding the qualities of balance, sincerity, open-mindedness, tolerance, flexibility, and modesty.

The **final stage** of development represented by Top Yang/Yin is the **turning point**, which is unavoidable in any kind of development. Everything has a beginning and an end; this is a law of nature. There are no exceptions. When an old thing reaches the end of its development, a new thing will start to replace it and will continually move ahead. A person at the final stage of a cyclic change should not be arrogant and ambitious. Overoptimism at this stage leads to disaster. He must know when he should hold back. Good preparation for the coming changes should be auspicious.

PART TWO

The Sixty-Four Hexagrams

1

 乾
QIAN

The Heaven Hexagram
Force, Energy, Creativity, Activity

IMAGE

The Heaven Hexagram, QIAN, is the first hexagram of the *Yijing* and is considered the gate to the other sixty-three hexagrams. QIAN in Chinese means force, energy, creativity, and activity, representing the character of heaven. It is the only hexagram among the sixty-four hexagrams that has six yang lines and is thus a pure yang hexagram. The upper trigram Heaven over the lower trigram Heaven demonstrates that Heaven is everywhere and gives an image of its continuing movement as indicated in the *Yijing*:

The movement of heaven is full of power. Thus the superior man never ceases to strengthen himself.

Heaven signifies energy. It is favorable for the leader of an organization to possess the qualities of Heaven if he wants to be capable in his leadership and respected by his colleagues.

HEXAGRAM STATEMENT

The attributes of QIAN (Heaven) are creation, development, harmonization, and perseverance.

QIAN [Heaven] has the power to create myriad things, to develop them, to harmonize them, and to persevere on the right course. A leader should possess these four attributes in order to build up his abilities:

1. **The ability to create**
   He must have the creativity of vision. For example, in planning the

development of his organization in respect to new strategies, new products, new services, new methods, and so forth. It is important for him constantly to think about whether there is anything new which will make his organization more dynamic and vital.

2. **The ability to develop**

   He must know how to put his plans into practice. A vision without a practice, like a castle in the air, is just an illusion. Turning a vision into reality is the main function of an effective leadership.

3. **The ability to harmonize**

   There are always conflicts in the development of an organization. It is not realistic to expect every member to have the same values and attitudes, as differences between people's views are normal and inevitable. A capable leader must have the ability to harmonize conflicts among the people in order not to damage the benefit of the whole organization.

4. **The ability to persevere**

   A leader must be able to keep the activities of his organization constantly on the right path in order to ensure success.

STRUCTURE

Heaven over Heaven signifies that a day is followed by another day in a continuing and never-ending development. This demonstrates the dynamics and strength of heaven and the change of time in a development. In both lower and upper trigrams, three kinds of time are indicated: the time of restraining actions (Initial Yang and Top Yang), the time of taking action (Second Yang and Fifth Yang), and the time for caution (Third Yang and Fourth Yang).

The six yang lines of the Hexagram Heaven represent six different situations or six different stages of a development, which advise the leader of an organization how to adapt to changing conditions as time flows.

LINE STATEMENTS

Initial Yang ☰. Hidden Dragon: Do not act but wait for the right time

A hidden dragon does not act.

The dragon is still submerged under the water; it is not the right time to take action. The leader of an organization should be patient, calm, and keep a low profile until the time is ripe for action.

Initial Yang is at the bottom of the hexagram, indicating the beginning stage of a development. This lowest position represents a situation in which the strength for a forward movement is not yet adequate. A rash movement would bring danger. It is advisable to store energy and make all necessary preparations now in order to make the movement in the future. At this stage, the leader of an organization is advised to keep a low profile.

In business negotiations an executive should be patient when he realizes that his counterpart cannot make up his mind to close a deal, indicating that the time is not yet ripe for action. An aggressive attempt to persuade may even create an adverse effect. **In a time when it would be immature to take action, it is favorable to store energy for a future move.**

Second Yang ☰. Appearing Dragon: The right time to appear

The dragon appears in the field.
It will be advantageous to meet with the great man.

The leader believes that he is now able to take action openly as he is well prepared. It is the right time for him to come out into open. The leader should seek wisdom and advice from knowledgeable people both inside and outside his organization. His principles of centrality and sincerity will lead people to support him. Alternatively, "the great man" can be interpreted as the leader himself as he has the qualities of sincerity, balance, and uprightness symbolized by the centering position of Second Yang. **A great man is one who has integrity and a strong and firm will to control his emotions, restrain his ego, and turn inferiors into superiors.**

Third Yang ☰· Alert Dragon: Be cautious in advancement

The superior man works hard in the day and remains alert at night.
Even if there is a danger, there will be no harm.

Third Yang in a proper position (a yang line in a yang position) signifies that the leader should act correctly and cautiously since Third Yang is at the upper position of the lower trigram, which represents uncertainties in a time of transition. If the leader moves forward then he will face dangers. A proper position may not mean the right position to advance. A yang line in a yang position therefore symbolizes a leader who has a strong character with high self-confidence. A man of this type easily becomes obstinate and tempted to take action without careful consideration. This is the reason why the line statement advises people to be cautious when taking a move forward. This text gives a warning to a leader not to be carried away with his "great idea" in a stage of transition and while facing uncertainties. If he can remain hard working, alert, and cautious, he will be fortunate.

Fourth Yang ☰ **Leaping Dragon: Decision at a crossroads**

Whether the dragon leaps upward or remain in the deep,
there will be no harm.

The leader is at a crossroads and needs to make a decision on whether he should move forward or not. A miscalculation would jeopardize the whole organization. On the one hand, his position is not favorable because of his inappropriate position (a yang line in a yin position). Yet this position, on the other hand, does provides him with a yin–yang merge through which he can carefully consider his future move. As the character of yang is to advance whereas that of yin is to retreat, a decision based on the yin–yang principle should not be impulsive but calm and balanced.

If the decision is to stay where he is, it should be only temporary. An organization cannot stand still in a dynamic world. It will eventually move forward to continue its advance, as heaven moves untiringly. At this stage, a leader must make a decision whether he should go or not go. Whatever decision he makes could be a right one. His only wrong decision is to make no decision, for **indecision is the enemy of effective leadership**.

Fifth Yang ☰ **Flying Dragon: Opportunity to achieve one's objective**

A flying dragon is in the sky. It is good to see the great man.

This is the most favorable position in this hexagram. A leader who has reached his successful stage is just like a flying dragon in the sky; he has a great opportunity to accomplish many things. In a time of "flying dragon" a leader can aim high and not miss any golden opportunity. To ensure his success he needs the advice and assistance of capable people who are seen as "great men." On the other hand, the leader himself can also be seen as a "great man." Therefore, his words and deeds must be chosen carefully and well matched. Acting in this way he will be highly respected by the people around him.

Top Yang ☰ **Overbearing dragon: Pride goes before a fall**

A dragon that flies too high will have regrets.

If a leader is too ambitious and arrogant he will push matters beyond the limits and lose touch with reality, in contradiction to the balance of yin and yang. This will inevitably lead to failure. A leader should know when he should hold back since pride comes before a fall or decline comes after a peak. If a leader only knows when to advance but not when to retreat, knows only when to expand but not when to reduce, knows only when he may gain but not when he may lose, and knows only when to loosen but not when to restrain, he will have regrets. A great man with high aims may fall into the temptation of becoming an overbearing dragon if he lacks perseverance or the wisdom to know when he should act and when he should not.

USING YANG

If all six lines are divined as yang they must be changed to yin lines. This is the rule to be used in a divination:

Heaven   **Earth**

☰ ⟶ ☷

The line statement:

A group of dragons which has no head is auspicious.

This is a situation in which the yang and yin forces are perfectly balanced through the change of yang to yin. Six dragons represent the strength of the Hexagram Heaven, whereas a group of dragons with no head indicates that the members of a group are on an equal footing as there is no head of the group. The situation of this group is in harmony. Since the six yang lines will be changed to six yin lines, the mild attributes of the Hexagram Earth will be integrated with the strong attributes of the Hexagram Heaven. A merge of yin (mildness) with yang (strength) will mean that the energy is used in a more adaptable, efficient, and harmonious way.

FURTHER EXPLANATIONS

In ancient times it was believed that dragons could walk on land, swim in water, and fly in the sky. A dragon therefore has three main characters: energy, change, and concealment. This concept is well applied to any person who possesses these qualities, including the leader of an organization.

The Stage of Hidden Dragon

The hidden dragon stage is the first stage of any development. The guideline for action in this stage is to quietly prepare all necessary works for the future development so that opponents are not alerted and will not have a chance to plan corresponding countermeasures. For example, a new product development must be kept concealed like a hidden dragon. It is beneficial to an organization to keep its future plans as strictly confidential as possible in order not to let its opponents copy it.

There are three classic schools of thought in China which have a similar concept of "hidden dragon" as used in the *Yijing*: the Daoist, the Legalist, and the Military. **Laozi** 老子, **Hanfeizi** 韓非子, and **Sunzi** 孫子 are the three representatives of these three schools. The concept of hidden dragon can be found in Laozi's philosophy as "modest," "non-contention," and "fish should not be allowed to leave the deep water." Hanfeizi also emphasized the importance of "concealment" to a leader, who should know how to disguise his feelings and preferences with regard to his subordinates in order to maintain objectivity and fairness. From a military point of view, Sunzi considers "concealment" as one of the important qualities of a general. He said: "The skillful general in defense hides in the most secret recesses of the earth."

However the concept of concealment as applied by Laozi, Hanfeizi, and Sunzi is static in nature, whereas in the Hexagram Heaven it is emphasized only in the initial stage of a development and not in other five stages. In the *Yijing* concealment is associated with time and space. Whether a concept is considered favorable or unfavorable is dependent on what time and space are. A concept can be seen as favorable in time/ space I but unfavorable in time/space II.

In the *Yijing*, **Confucius** 孔子 made a commentary on this line in regard to concealment, which he considered as an important virtue of a superior man. The dragon is seen by Confucius as a superior man and the concealment is his virtue. In the *Analects* [*Lunyu* 論語] he emphasized patience or tolerance, which are indirectly related to the concept of concealment. He said: **"Lack of patience in small matters will bring destruction to overall plans."** Patience or tolerance can be the other side of concealment. Both patience and concealment are related to the ethics of human relations.

Heaven is a hexagram with six yang lines but its initial yang does have the attribute of the Hexagram Earth. This indicates that yang contains yin and vice versa: yin also contains yang.

The Stage of Appearing Dragon

When the dragon appears on the earth it means that actions no longer have to be hidden but may be revealed. A company should develop its business network. For example:

- Announce new plans for products/services to the public.
- Develop relationships with distributors, suppliers, banks, business associations, trade unions, mass media, and so forth.
- Use publicity, public relations, and advertising to provide information to the public.

The characteristic of this stage is reflected by its position in the hexagram. Second yang represents a yin–yang mix which is in the middle position of the lower trigram. This suggests that actions should be kept moderate even though they are creative, but should not be exaggerated. The most important thing is to maintain the principles of sincerity, balance, and uprightness in order to build up a favorable image of the organization in the public eye.

The Stage of Alert Dragon

In the third stage of a development, a company has successfully built up the beachhead of its business on the market but should still work hard and be cautious in making decisions, since a mistake could seriously damage the company's progress.

The third yang line is at the top position of the lower trigram; it means that a rash move to the upper trigram may face uncertainties and risks.

The Stage of Leaping Dragon

Fourth Yang is at the bottom of the upper trigram, indicating that the company needs to decide on the pace of development. Since such a movement has both pros and cons, the decision should be made cautiously. The leader needs the ability to judge the hour and to size up the situation.

The Stage of Flying Dragon

Among all six stages of the hexagram QIAN [Heaven], the stage of flying dragon is the most favorable one. Flying dragon symbolizes the ideal state, in which an organization can achieve its objectives and its members are able to apply their expertise and to work with energy.

Fifth Yang is the central position of the upper trigram. A yang line in a yang position symbolizes sincerity, strength, and balance. It is the position of the top leader of an organization.

The Stage of Overbearing Dragon

The stage of flying dragon is "high" in the whole development, but not at the "peak." Once the dragon reaches the peak or the upper limit it will begin to slide downward. This is the law of cyclical change; a fall after a peak. When yang reaches the limit, yin rises and vice versa.

A leader who has reached a high position may behave in two ways. On one hand, he will be too proud of his achievements and hence become over confident, so he tends to go to extremes. He knows how to advance, but doesn't know when and where he should stop or retreat. On the other, the leader is fully satisfied with his achievements, acts less initiative, and becomes less hard working than before. In both cases, the efficiency of the leader begins to decline. If a leader is complacent about his present successes he may lose the initiative to move forward and then the company will face obstructions.

It is important to identify what phase of a business cycle the company is in now. An expansion plan should be carefully considered and reviewed so that it will not be executed at the peak of a cycle.

Based on the concept of flying and overbearing dragon, a question can be raised about human behavior. For example, what is the objective of an individual's investment? Should he seek a maximum return or a desirable one? He may obtain a maximum return from his investment if he operates in a strictly disciplined way and has luck on his side. If this is the case, the *ex-ante* maximum return is equivalent to the *ex-post* maximum return. But in many cases, the *ex-post* return is below the *ex-ante* return, or even negative. One reason for this is because achieving the maximum return always involves uncalculated risks. To play safe one should probably not to seek a maximum return but a desirable one. The concept of flying and overbearing dragon gives this guideline. The stage of overbearing dragon can be seen as the stage of maximum return, whereas the stage of flying dragon represents the stage of desirable return. Indeed an individual's desirable return can also be seen as his own "maximum return."

No Heads among the Dragons

Since there are no heads among the dragons, each one can be considered as equal. What does this situation mean? This special situation doesn't necessary mean that the group has no leader; rather it indicates that there is a democratic relationship between the leader and the members of the group. The leader treats the people under him not as his subordinates but more as colleagues. A two-way communication system, formally or informally, is effectively developed between both parties and hence harmony within the organization can be achieved.

Authority is broadly delegated from senior to lower levels. Correspondingly the organizational structure is highly decentralized. The situation is close to the concept of **Laozi's "ruling with inaction."**

THE IMPORTANCE OF TIME AND PLACE

The stage concept the hexagram QIAN [Heaven] is closely related to time and space or place. According to the *Yijing*, every movement involves both time and place as indicated by the six lines of a hexagram. Each line indicates the specific time of a developing stage. For example, the initial line indicates the hidden dragon stage and the fifth line the specific time of the flying dragon stage. Simultaneously each line also represents a specific place for a development. The six lines of QIAN represent six different times and places in a development.

Before taking any action, time and place are the two critical factors which should be carefully considered. A successful operation is essentially dependent on whether both the time and the place are appropriate.

THE SIX DRAGON THESIS AND OTHER SIX HEXAGRAMS

In the *Yijing*, the **six dragon thesis** is traditionally indicated by the hexagram QIAN [Heaven]. Yet it can also be illustrated by another six hexagrams, namely Fu 復 [Returning] (24), Shi 師 [The Army] (7), Qian 謙 [Modesty] (15), Yu 豫 [Joy] (16), Bi 比 [Joining Together] (8), and Bo 剝 [Stripping] (23):

Fu	**Shi**	**Qian [Modesty]**	**Yu**	**Bi**	**Bo**

Let the hexagram Kun 坤 [Earth] represent the human world and the single yang line the dragon. The movement of the dragon in the world is illustrated by the above six hexagrams. The six lines of a hexagram represent the positions of three objects: first and second line for the earth, second and third line for the man, fifth and sixth line for heaven. The movement of the yang line through the above six hexagrams indicates the six stages, or time/places, that the dragon has experienced.

The dragon is under the water or ground in the hexagram Fu and appears on the ground in the hexagram Shi. Once the dragon is in the human world as indicated by the hexagram Qian [Modesty] and the hexagram Yu it must keep alert and cautious as, the human relations may be so complicated that a careless action would bring danger. Everything will be fine when the dragon enters the fifth stage, as the time and place are particularly favorable here. This stage is illustrated by the hexagram Bi. However if the dragon does not know how to restrain his ambition and flies over the reasonable limit, it will begin to slide down as indicated by the hexagram Bo.

The respective line statements of the above six hexagrams can also explain the six situations facing the dragons. The above illustration is primarily based on the structure of the six hexagrams rather than their line statements, so the situations indicated by the line statements of the above six hexagrams can differ from that of the hexagram Qian [Heaven]. However, the line statements of these six hexagrams give similar judgments on the respective situations whether they are favorable or not, despite different circumstances. Readers are advised to check the respective statements of the above six hexagrams which are given later.

The six dragon thesis in the *Yijing* can also be elaborated by using other hexagrams rather than the hexagram Qian [Heaven] alone, as is used in the traditional approach. The reason why the traditional approach uses only the hexagram Qian [Heavan] for the illustration of the six dragon thesis is because of the belief that the hexagram QIAN [Heavan] and the hexagram KUN [Earth] are the gates to the *Yijing*. The author will point out an alternative way to use the six dragon thesis.

2

 KUN

The Earth Hexagram

Tolerance, Nourishment, Docility,

Caution

IMAGE

As opposite to the hexagram QIAN 乾 [Heaven] (1), the hexagram KUN [Earth] has six yin lines, a pure yin hexagram. Both upper and lower trigrams represent Earth. It is a Double Earth Hexagram, which symbolizes the thickness and richness of the earth. Like heaven, earth also creates and develops myriad things as well as nourishes them. However, there is a main difference in their characteristics as Heaven represents power, energy, creativity, and activity whereas Earth stands for softness, tolerance, docility, and caution. Both Heaven and Earth have similar functions but perform them in different ways. Neither of these two alone can perform its functions perfectly and efficiently. This is *taiji* concept in which the ideal state is generated by a yin–yang union.

A leader who has the characteristics of heaven is still not adequate to be a good leader unless he also has the characteristics of Earth. The attributes of Earth are the complementary to that of Heaven. A good leader must have a balanced character as represented by both Heaven and Earth.

HEXAGRAM STATEMENT

KUN [Earth] has also the functions of creation and development, achieving through the docile character of a mare.
If he takes the lead of his master, he goes astray; if he follows, he finds his guide.

*It is favorable to find friends in the southwest, but to lose the friends
in the northeast.*
Perseverance in rectitude is auspicious.

While the hexagram QIAN [Heaven] uses dragon as a symbol for
representing its attributes, the hexagram KUN [Earth] adopts a mare to
represent them. A mare is considered gentle, obedient, and tolerant.
Combining the attributes of Heaven with Earth and dragon with mare
create basic leadership qualities, strength, creativity, and activity on one
hand, docility, and tolerance on the other.

A leader has a strong character is good but not good enough, he
needs to be open-minded and tolerant to different views, so that he will
not move in a wrong direction because of his strong self-confidence.
Following the right way does not mean a person is "soft" or "weak" in
his character. On the contrary, he should be considered "strong" as he
can timely and rightly restrain his desire or ego.

The "master" in the text can be interpreted as the truth. Following
the truth is outwardly docile but inwardly of a strong conduct. Docility
or obedience to the truth is considered right, but obedience to the wrong
is really wrong. This suggests that an executive must not blindly follow
his superior if he believes that the action to be undertaken is not right.
Therefore, the concept "docility" or "obedience" in the text must be
interpreted in the right way. The text "one should not take the lead of
his master" is merely an emphasis on the importance of docility to a
person who is upright, so this guideline must be used in the proper
way as indicated above.

The text "southwest" and "northeast" means "safe place" and
"dangerous place" respectively. It is said that the texts of the sixty-four
hexagrams of the *Yijing* were written by King Wen 周文王 of the Zhou
dynasty (1045–221 B.C.) when he was prisoner in the capital of the
Shang dynasty (1600–1045 B.C.). Under such circumstances, King Wen
considered his home country Zhou as a safer place than the capital of
the Shang dynasty as it was located at the southwest of the capital of
the Shang. Conversely, the capital of the Shang which was located at
the northeast of the country Zhou was naturally considered "a dangerous
place" to King Wen. This is the reason why the text says that it is
beneficial to gain companionship in the southwest instead of in the
northeast.

Another explanation of why the "southeast" is favorable and the "northeast" not favorable is because of the direction of the eight trigrams in which the trigram KUN 坤 [Earth] is located at the southwest whereas the trigram ZHEN 震 [Thunder] at the northeast. Based on this, the "southwest" hence represents the soft character of KUN, a place where people are easier to gain companionship than the place as represented by ZHEN which signifies difficulty.

STRUCTURE

Tolerance is one of the important attributes of the Double Earth Hexagram which has a broad meaning including open-mindedness, patience, understanding, and flexibility. Compared with the six solid lines of the hexagram QIAN [Heaven], the six broken lines of the hexagram KUN [Earth] gives an impression of tolerance as its broken lines, unlike solid lines, is divided into two parts which symbolize its soft or flexible character.

Since all six lines of KUN [Earth] are yin, it is called a pure yin hexagram. However, within a pure yin hexagram, there are still three yang positions as represented by the first, third, and fifth. So the influence of the yang positions cannot be ignored as that of the three yin positions in a pure yang hexagram QIAN [Heaven].

LINE STATEMENTS

Initial Yin ☷. Alertness: See small sign and think of large effect

When frost appears under his feet, it is a sign that hard ice is coming.

The leader of an organization must keep his eyes open for changes in both the internal and external environment. If a negative sign appears, he must investigate it at the earliest time and find out the causes for it, so that a remedial action can be undertaken in a timely manner before the situation becomes worse.

Negative sings in a business organization can be indicated by the following:

In **marketing**
- The growth rate of the sales begins to decline.
- Customer complaint about product quality or service rises.
- Some features of certain product are not as good as that of a major competitor.

In **general economy and finance**
- The interest rate begins to rise or fall.
- The host country of the company's overseas subsidiary suffers a huge trade deficit and consequently the exchange rate policy of the local government is likely to change.
- The bad debt rate begins to rise or fall.
- The unemployment rate begins to rise or fall.

In **human resources**
- The staff turnover rate rises.
- The morale of the people is low.
- The performances of the people in some of the departments are below the standard.

Second Yin ☷. Inner qualities as a complement to outer qualities

He is straight, square, and great; everything will work out without any effort.

In the hexagram KUN [Earth], straight signifies honesty, square stands for uprightness and greatness implies tolerance. These three characteristics of Earth, however, are also the attributes of Heaven:

	QIAN [Heaven]	KUN [Earth]
Attributes	Outer Qualities	Inner Qualities
Straight	Directness	Honesty
Square	Firmness	Uprightness
Greatness	Strength	Tolerance

The reason why Earth has the attributes of Heaven is because of Earth takes Heaven as its model due its docility. Same attributes therefore can be interpreted differently in a yin or a yang aspect. Straight in the hexagram QIAN [Heaven] can be interpreted as directness which is outward (yang) in nature whereas it represents honesty in the hexagram KUN [Earth], an inner (yin) quality in nature. Square stands for firmness in the hexagram QIAN [Heaven] while in the hexagram KUN [Earth] it means uprightness which is the principle in doing things. Greatness symbolizes strength in the hexagram QIAN [Heaven] whereas in the hexagram KUN [Earth] it means tolerance. A leader with the qualities of honesty, uprightness, and tolerance will make a complement to his qualities of directness, firmness, and strength, a balanced character for a successful leader.

Third Yin ☷· Concealment: Hide one's brilliance at a right time and a right place

He keeps his brilliance concealed but acts faithfully.
If he works for the king, he will do his best without taking any credit.

A yin line in a yang position indicates a situation in which the yin character of a man is found outwardly whereas his yang character lies inwardly. This suggests that a leader at this moment should probably be better to hide his brilliance so as not to overshadow the people under him, so that they will also be able to demonstrate their intelligence and abilities in their activities. This leadership style is based on the philosophy of decentralization. From a competitive point of view, it is also favorable for a leader not to openly reveal his new idea to prevent inspiring revivals from imitating his way. If it is not a favorable time to put a new idea into practice, the leader is advised to keep it in his mind until the right time comes.

When a company leader is invited to public services, he should not seek any credit for his efforts or achievements at this stage as his contributions will eventually be recognized and rewarded. Working quietly at present stage is beneficial.

Fourth Yin ☷· Caution: Rest and save energies for the better time

He ties up his bag, so there will be neither blame nor praise.

Fourth Yin represents a senior executive who is close to the top leader. He should be extremely cautious in his words and deeds to avoid any confrontations with his superior.

A yin line in a yin position indicates a weak situation even though it is in a proper position, so taking action at this stage would not be favorable. A postponement of his plans for expansion at a better time appears to be appropriate and desirable.

In unfavorable times, a leader is advised to keep low profile and avoid displaying his strength outwardly. A leader who is able to restrain his emotions and impulse can escape from dangers. Acting in this way he can save his energies for the better time.

Fifth Yin ☷· Balance: Use a centering approach.

He is dressed in a yellow lower garment. It will be very auspicious.

Yellow represents the color of the earth and also the middle position of Earth in the five elements (fire, water, earth, wood, and metal); therefore, yellow symbolizes the centrality too. In ancient China people's garment was categorized into two parts, the upper garment and the lower garment. The lower garment was covered by the upper garment. The lower garment indicated in the text signifies modesty. A yellow lower garment means that an enlightened person should be balanced and modest as represented by the noble position of the fifth line. In an organization, these two qualities are particularly recommended to the top leader.

There are similarities and differences between the qualities of Fifth Yang of the hexagram QIAN [Heaven] and that of Fifth Yin of the hexagram KUN [Earth]. Their similarities in their qualities are balanced, sincerity, and uprightness whereas the differences are in the characteristics whether they are outward (yang) or inward (yin) in nature as elaborated in the commentaries on the text of Second Yin stated above.

Top Yang ☷ Power Struggle: Fight for one's vision

Dragons fight in the fields, their blood is black and yellow.

When yin reaches its peak at top of a hexagram, yang will begin to rise and vice versa. The meeting or merge of yin and yang is symbolized by two dragons (yin and yang) fighting in the field. In an organization it could mean a conflict between old and new vision or approaches in policies or actions, for example, a leader facing a choice to head on in a new direction is like a situation in which two dragons are fighting.

USING YIN: TRANSFORMATION OF YIN TO YANG

When all six yin lines are divined from yin, they must be changed to six yang lines as follows:

KUN [Earth]   QIAN [Heaven]

☷   ⟶   ☰

The line statement of Top Yin:

It is always beneficial to keep to a docile way.

The attributes of Earth are docility, flexibility, caution, and tolerance. It is always right to persevere in these qualities and use them as a complement to the attributes of creativity, activity, and strength of the heaven.

The six yin lines of the hexagram KUN [Earth] signify a valley whose shape is likes a hollow, representing the great virtue or the *dao* by Laozi as he said: "The great virtue appears like a hollow (valley)."

Hollow can also be expressed as emptiness. Emptiness symbolizes tolerance and modesty and is seen as the *dao* in Laozi's doctrine. To seek fulfillment needs first emptiness. Without emptiness a thing cannot be filled. So emptiness or nonbeing is the condition for getting fulfillment or being. To a leader, emptiness signifies broadmindedness, tolerance, and modesty. In the case of using yin, the transformation of the six yin lines to six yang lines is just like the **transformation of emptiness to fulfillment**. Anything reaches its extreme shall turn to the opposite side, in this case, the hexagram KUN [Earth] will change to the hexagram QIAN [Heaven]. This is the law of nature in the framework of Laozi's *dao*.

3

 The Water–Thunder Hexagram

ZHUN

Sprouting, Difficulty in the Beginning

IMAGE

The outer trigram KAN 坎 [Water] signifies danger or difficulty and the inner trigram ZHEN 震 [Thunder] stands for movement or action. Water above Thunder indicates a situation of sprouting in which action will encounter difficulty. This is like a time of birth to many things or a time of the beginning of growth for everything. Seeds that lie in the soil struggle to rise out of the ground and sprouts grow up to break the covering earth, involving the difficulties of an upward movement. The growing process cannot be hurried as it needs effort, support, and patience. The situation is like an organization in its start-up stage, facing difficulties in getting capital, manpower, technology, and networks.

Under such circumstances the leader of an organization must stay calm, take all possible unfavorable factors into his consideration, and prepare the corresponding plans and actions in order to solve the difficulties which he anticipates. He must not move impulsively or make a reckless move forward, but conserve his energy for his future moves. **Externally a leader should be flexible and adaptable like water and internally strong and dynamic like thunder**. One of the leadership qualities is soft outwardly but strong inwardly, a desirable merge of yin and yang.

HEXAGRAM STATEMENT

The hexagram ZHUN signifies a difficult birth consisting of creation, development, harmonization, and perseverance.
It is not favorable to advance but beneficial to establish a kingdom.

The four attributes of Heaven—creation, development, harmonization, and perseverance—are well applicable to a leader who is facing difficulties just at the beginning of a development. This is the time to test whether a person can overcome difficulties to attain a success. The beginning stage of any development is crucial to an organization in determining whether it will have a future or not. Caution is one of the most important principles emphasized by the *Yijing*. A leader at this stage should not act rashly and blindly if the conditions for a movement become less favorable and the corresponding measures for dealing with the situation are not yet ready. However, a difficult time also means a good opportunity to develop a new venture, particularly to those leaders who have a challenging spirit.

STRUCTURE

This is a hexagram with two yangs and four yins. The two yangs are segregated by the four yins, indicating a situation in which the active forces (two yangs) are restrained by unfavorable factors (four yins).

The nuclear or hidden hexagram of the hexagram ZHUN is the Mountain-Earth Hexagram PO 剝 [Stripping] (23) ☶☷, which warns that unfavorable factors or difficulties could discourage people from moving forward if they lack patience or perseverance.

Another hidden hexagram is the Small YI as derived from the hexagram YI 頤 [Nourishment] (27) as formed by initial yang, second yin, third yin, fourth yin, and fifth yang:

Hexagram YI   **Small YI**

Both hexagram YI and Small YI are shaped like an open mouth with teeth, indicating that a forward development needs "nourishment" or the support of resources. This is one of the essential preparations that should be undertaken to overcome difficulties at the beginning of a development.

From Second Yin to Fifth Yang a big Mountain ☶☶ is formed. This signifies a situation for "stopping" as the unfavorable factors (represented by the yin lines) are increasing as in the situation indicated by the nuclear hexagram BO ☶☷ . Based on these hidden situations, a forward movement is considered not favorable at this stage.

LINE STATEMENTS

Initial Yang ☳. Remain steadfast when facing obstacles

He hesitates to move forward as there are obstacles ahead.
It is beneficial for him to remain steadfast and upright.
He needs assistance from capable people.

Initial Yang is at the lowest position of the hexagram, representing a leader who is right at the beginning stage of developing of his business. When he realizes that there are obstacles ahead he hesitates to move forward. Since he has a strong character (a yang line) he will not give up his development plan even though he is facing difficulties. Although he has a relationship with someone in a high position as represented by Fourth Yin, the latter is however weak (a yin line) and cannot give him the help he really needs. He should seek assistance from capable people. The text advises him to remain steadfast and upright in preparing for his future move.

Second Yin ☵. Need patience to get a better deal

In a time of difficulty, he is hesitant between going and staying as if he were mounted on a horse but stands still.
The man comes on horseback not as a robber but as a suitor.
The maiden declines to marry, she will wed in ten years.

In a time of difficulty, an executive in the position of Second Yin needs assistance from a strong partner for his advancement. He can choose a partner between Initial Yang and Fifth Yang. He is very close to Initial Yang and the two could become intimate partners. He behaves as a superior to Initial Yang as indicated by his riding position (a yin line above a yang line) but Initial Yang is not convinced by his act, and clashes between the two may arise. Since the assistance from Initial Yang is not as much as he really needs (Initial Yang is at a lowly position of the hexagram), he will give up the relationship with Initial Yang.

He wishes to get assistance from a powerful person Fifth Yang who is capable and has also indicated an interest in establishing a relationship with him. The potential for a development of a relationship between the two is shown by the interconnection between the second yin line and the fifth yang line. However, there are hindrances in establishing such a partnership as represented by the two yin lines—Third Yin and

Fourth Yin. For this reason, Second Yin is hesitant to make a deal with Fifth Yang as if he were "mounted on a horse, not going forward." In order to get better terms, Second Yin needs **patience** or **perseverance** while negotiating with Fifth Yang: as the text says, "a maiden will wed in ten years."

Third Yin ☷ Going forward needs necessary support

If he chases the deer into the forest without a guide, he will get lost in the forest.
A superior man can see the difficulty ahead and therefore will give up his chase as such an act will earn nothing.

Third Yin is in an improper position (a yin line in a yang position). A move forward without assistance and back-up will face difficulties. A wise leader should not take action if the resources required are not available. If a weak and incapable leader, as represented by a yin line in a strong (yang) position, undertakes a venture which involves uncertainties he will get lost and suffer from serious defeat.

Fourth Yin ☵ Seek the right partner for progress

He doesn't know in which direction he should go.
He should take action to seek a right partner as if to propose marriage.
Acting in this way is auspicious in going forward and there will be no disadvantage.

A leader plans to move forward but doesn't have the adequate knowledge and abilities, so he should use the capable people (Initial Yang) to resolve difficulties. With the assistance of Initial Yang, he can progress.

Fifth Yang ☵ Choose a moderate way

It is beneficial to grant favors to those who are at the beginning of difficulty.
Small measures lead to good fortune whereas drastic measures bring misfortune.

Although Fifth Yang is in a noble position, it is located between two yin lines which symbolize difficulties. Under such circumstances a leader will find difficulty in his movement. He can obtain the assistance from the person below him as indicated by Second Yin, but the support is weak as reflected by the yin line. Therefore, the leader is advised to take small steps rather than giant leaps when the conditions are not right. Being too eager for success will lead to failure.

Top Yang ☵ **Need a positive attitude**

He is astride a horse and does not go forward or go back.
He weeps tears of blood.

Top Yang is at the end of the hexagram, symbolizing extreme difficulty. A leader hesitates to move forward because he lacks the ability to overcome difficulty and assistance from others (no interconnection between Top Yang and Third Yin). He should not let the wary impede his progress but should patiently carry on until he makes a breakthrough.

4

The Mountain–Water Hexagram

Enlightenment, Education

IMAGE

Mountain symbolizes stillness or stopping and Water means difficulty or danger. If a person goes forward, he will find the mountain as an obstruction blocking his way. But if he goes backward, he will be in danger as represented by the water. This is a situation in which someone does not know where he should go. In a confused and chaotic state, one needs guidance or advice from a wise man. Fifth Yin represents the leader of an organization who is humble and seeks guidance from a capable man Second Yang, as a pupil learns from his teacher. **Life is a continuous learning process**. A person can be a teacher in some areas but he can also be a student in others; likewise a leader of an organization.

One of the important functions of an organization is to make its members efficient and productive. People's minds can become clearer through effective enlightenment or education. The process of education cannot be short or fast like water that flows underneath the mountain to cross many rocks before it reaches the streams and becomes a river. Once the water penetrates through the mountain and flows out, the obstacles to a development are overcome. This is like the process of enlightenment, through which people's minds will become clearer and more judgmental.

HEXAGRAM STATEMENT

Enlightenment brings benefit. It is not I who want to teach the pupil but the pupil comes to me for enlightenment.

*Like in divination, I will answer his question seriously if he asks me
sincerely the first time.*
*But if he continues to ask me irrelevant questions, he is disrespectful,
I will not advise him. It is advantageous to be firm in enlightenment.*

In education both teacher and student should have a right attitude. The
teacher should know how to use the proper methods to stimulate the
interest, curiosity, and creativity of the student. On the other hand, the
student should have a sincere attitude and pay high respect to the teacher
as a diviner to the *Yijing* for consultation. **Teaching and learning is a
two-way interactive process like a merging of yin and yang, one
without another in complement is pointless**. The relationship between
a leader and his subordinates is like the one between the teacher and the
student. His instructions should be clear and encouraging while keeping
his punishment and reward system in a strict but right way.

STRUCTURE

The upper trigram GEN 艮 [Mountain] means difficulty and stopping. If
a person meets difficulty and stops there, he will never get chance to get
through. In education it means that he will remain ignorant and
immature. As a result the situation is not favorable and is dangerous to
him, as illustrated by the lower trigram KAN 坎 [Water] (danger).

If a leader wants to be a good educator, he must hold to two
principles:

1. He must be open-minded as the shape of the Small YI 頤 [Small
   Nourishment] ☶☷ formed by Second Yang, Third Yin, Fourth Yin,
   Fifth Yin, and Top Yang. The small YI is derived from the Big YI ☶☷.

2. He must take significant action to enlighten the people in his
   organization other than merely by words, for example, encouraging subordinates to participate in refresher courses and training
   programs. As the trigram ZHEN 震 [Thunder] symbolizes action, the
   nuclear hexagram FU 復 [Returning] (24) ☳☷ (formed by Second
   Yang, Third Yin, Fourth Yin, and Fifth Yin) of the hexagram MENG
   is like a "big action," indicating that significant action for
   enlightenment is required to improve the quality of the people.

LINE STATEMENTS

Initial Yin ☶. Need discipline in education

To enlighten the ignorant people, it is necessary to restrict their conduct with discipline at the very beginning of an educational process.
If not, they could act in a wrong way.

To educate the members of an organization, it is appropriate to indicate the rules that they have to follow right at the beginning of an action. Self-discipline is called for. Once restrictions are imposed, people are conscientious in self-correction and will not rush into something they will regret. Initial Yin symbolizes the ignorant people who need enlightenment from Second Yang—the educator.

Second Yang ☵. The educator needs tolerance and patience

It is auspicious to show tolerance and patience with the immature just like marrying a woman or letting the son run the family.

As the leader of an organization he should be patient and tolerant with the people under his instruction and training, particularly those taking on new responsibilities for the first time. Second Yang is encircled by the yin lines indicating his role in the organization is not only an administrator but also as an educator of his subordinates, particularly the inexperienced ones represented by the yin lines.

Third Yin ☵. Do not use a person who lacks dignity and self-respect

He should not take a woman who seeks a rich and handsome man.
She loses herself. Nothing good will come out of the marriage.

If a woman represented by Third Yin cannot keep her long established relationship with Top Yang but turns to a rich and handsome man represented by Second Yang, she is apparently not reliable and trustful. A leader should not use a person who lacks dignity and self-respect.

Fourth Yin ☶. Stuck in ignorance and isolation

It is regrettable to be stuck in ignorance and isolation.

Fourth Yin represents a senior executive who is weak, unbalanced, and ignorant. He needs help from others but there is no relationship between Fourth Yin and Initial Yin. Fourth Yin is located away from Top Yang and Second Yang; both of them represent capable people. Thus the senior executive Fourth Yin in this position is most likely to get stuck in ignorance and isolation. If a person is ignorant and not open-minded, he tends to be stubborn about listening to others. As a consequence, he lacks friends to help him. An ignorant person gets stuck in his own mental cage.

Fifth Yin ☷ Innocence as a drive to learn and a power to lead

Innocence is auspicious.

The leader of an organization should be modest and open-minded like an innocent child. With this attitude he is willing to seek advice from those below and to delegate authority to the able person as represented by Second Yang. This concept is close to the philosophy of Laozi's "rule by inaction." A leader cannot be an all-around man; therefore, the delegation of authority to able subordinates is necessary. **A wise leader is a man who has an innocent attitude.**

Top Yang ☷ Need discipline in education

A punishment of the ignorant should be proper in order to prevent hostilities.

When people being in educated become undisciplined and disorderly, punishment of them is necessary. However, appropriate measures should be used since a measure that is too tough can make the people hostile to the educator.

5

円
XU

The Water–Heaven Hexagram

Waiting, Patience

IMAGE

Water above heaven or sky indicates that the rain has not yet come and waiting is necessary. The upper trigram KAN 坎 [Water] signifies danger, whereas the lower trigram QIAN 乾 [Heaven] represents strength. It means that a forward movement based on strength will face danger, so waiting is the right action. Water symbolizes the outer difficulties facing a man or an organization. Heaven represents the inner strength and firmness of a man or an organization.

To resolve difficulties an organization needs time to prepare the appropriate actions. Therefore, waiting does not mean doing nothing but means preparing for the future. Waiting is associated with patience. If the time is not appropriate for action, the leader of an organization should be able to control his emotions and remain calm and patient. A rash action would bring danger.

HEXAGRAM STATEMENT

Sincerity leads to a bright future. Uprightness brings a good fortune. It is favorable to cross great rivers.

In a time of waiting, a leader needs sincerity and uprightness to cultivate a positive attitude toward the stress. With these two qualities he will be able to overcome difficulties and achieve success.

STRUCTURE

This is a hexagram with two yins and four yangs; the yangs appear to be more important than the yins with respect to the strength of QIAN

[Heaven]. Fifth Yang is encircled by two yins (Fourth Yin and Top Yin), indicating the importance of uprightness and strength during the time of waiting.

LINE STATEMENTS

Initial Yang ☷. Wait with patience

He waits in the outskirts and keeps his way unchanged.

When a leader anticipates danger ahead, he will not move forward but will wait for the right time. Since Initial Yang is located farthest from danger or difficulty as represented by the upper trigram Water ☵, waiting represented at the first line of a hexagram is like waiting at the outskirts of a city and avoiding a dangerous situation. A leader who is found in this situation should wait patiently without anxiety.

Second Yang ☷· Wait with steadfastness

He waits on the sand and there are some criticisms, but he is fortunate in the end.

Second Yang is closer to the upper trigram Water than Initial Yang. It is like sand near water, that signifies danger. "Waiting on the sand" means that danger is approaching. A leader in this position should maintain balance, uprightness, flexibility, and steadfastness (the characteristics of Second Yang) in waiting even though others may hold a different view.

Third Yang ☰· Wait in troubles

He waits in the mud, this could lead to disaster.

Like sand, mud is also near water but more dangerous because people can be trapped in it. Third Yang is in a strong position (a yang line in a yang position), which is seen as "unbalanced" at the top of the lower trigram. A leader in this position may be tempted to move forward through emotion or ambition. If he does so his obstinacy could bring disaster. A leader needs to be particularly cautious in his actions when he is in a strong position.

Fourth Yin ☵˙ Wait in danger

He waits in blood and escapes from the danger.

Fourth Yin is at the beginning of the upper trigram Water, symbolizing a dangerous situation. A leader in this position is like in a state of "waiting in blood." Since he is weak (a yin line in a yin position), he is not able to get out on his own. He should stay calm and upright, and wait for any chance to escape from the difficult situation.

Fifth Yang ☵˙ Wait leisurely with confidence

He waits with food and drink, uprightness brings good fortune.

Fifth Yang represents a leader who has the qualities of sincerity, balance, and uprightness. He has strong confidence (a yang line in a yang position) in believing that his chance is on its way, so he is waiting in a leisurely manner as if he was waiting with food and drink. But he must not be self-indulgent, for **there is a boundary between self-confidence and self-indulgence**.

Top Yin ☵˙ Prepare for unexpected change

He goes into a cave. Three uninvited guests arrive.
If he honors them, all will be well.

Top Yin is at the extreme of the upper trigram Water, indicating a time of great danger. The three yang lines of the lower trigram Heaven move upwards like three "uninvited guests" arriving. The relationship between Top Yin and Third Yang and its associates, as represented by other two yang lines, is helpful for Top Yin to get out of the difficult situation. If a leader in the position of Top Yin can treat those capable people under him with sincerity, this brings about a merger of yin with yang through which the situation will turn out well.

6

訟
SONG
The Heaven–Water Hexagram

Contention, Conflict, Litigation

IMAGE

The sun rises in the east and sets in the west whereas the water in the two main rivers in China, the Yellow River and the Yangtze River, flows from the west to the east. The opposing direction of the rising sun and the flow of the two rivers give an image of confrontation.

The heaven symbolizes the external actions of an organization and the water the internal danger. If action is not taken at the right time and the right place, the internal stability of the organization will be damaged. External actions and internal instability sometimes cause a state of disharmony. Another interpretation of the relationship between the upper and lower trigrams is that the leader should be as strong as heaven when facing difficulty.

If there is a disagreement between two parties, confrontation between the two can arise. This could lead to **a lose–lose situation** even though one party would finally "win" the "battle." The leaders of the two parties should stay calm and keep cool. Before taking any confrontational action, it is sensible to ask what they really want to achieve and whether they would have a net gain from such a confrontation.

Both upper and lower trigrams QIAN 乾 [Heaven] and KAN 坎 [Water] are yang in nature. Since the two are of the same nature and thus do not complement each other, a contention or confrontation between them will arise soon or later. The upper trigram Heaven represents a man who has a strong and stable character and the lower trigram Water stands for another man whose character is also strong but venturous. If there is any disagreement between these two persons, a conflict between them is unavoidable.

HEXAGRAM STATEMENT

In contention he should always keep sincerity.
When he anticipates he will not be able to win the case, he must
remain cautious and balanced. Acting in this way is auspicious.
If he persists in the contention to the end, there will be misfortune.
It is the time for the great man to come out, but not favorable to cross
great rivers.

When a leader realizes that a contention is likely to happen he must first think whether or not it is worth it. Is it a zero-sum game or a lose–lose game? If the cost of winning from such a contention is larger than the benefit, why should he proceed? A careful comparison of the pros and cons of a contention before taking any action is advantageous. To solve the conflict between two parties, a respectable person who is balanced, upright, and trustworthy is needed to moderate the situation such as represented by Fifth Yang in this hexagram.

STRUCTURE

This hexagram with two yins and four yangs indicates an organization which is dominated by a strong senior management as symbolized by the three yangs at the upper trigram. There is no interaction between Fifth Yang and Second Yang, revealing a poor relationship between the leader and the people at the execution level. Misunderstandings and conflicts are therefore found between the people at these two levels.

Second Yang is encircled by two yins, symbolizing that the leader is in a dispute or a confrontation. But if he can control himself and remain calm, he will realize the harm which may be caused by a confrontation. If he is prepared to meet the other party halfway, a confrontation can be avoided. If an organization looks strong outside (upper trigram) but is weak inside (lower trigram), it should not be confrontational with others.

LINE STATEMENTS

Initial Yin ☵. Avoid a protracted dispute

If he does not pursue the case, there may be some talks, but all will be well in the end.

A leader should avoid a dispute that cannot be settled in a short time, particularly if he is in a weak position (a yin line). Contention is like war: it exhausts time and resources. If a contention is prolonged it can be harmful to both sides. Before a dispute the leader should carefully examine the situation and estimate the possible outcome and decide whether or not it is worth it. Initial Yang is at the low end of the hexagram, symbolizing the weak position of the leader in a contention and that the chance of winning is low. To complement his weak position, Initial Yin needs help from a strong person like Fourth Yang at the higher echelon of an organization as indicated by the interconnection between the two.

Second Yang ☵. Retreat from an unfavorable situation

He loses the case, then he runs back home and hides in the small town of three hundred households. There will be no misfortune.

A leader must know when he can advance and when he should retreat. If he anticipates a dispute that he cannot win, he should admit his "failure" and retreat from it at the earliest time in order to avoid more losses which might occur in the future. The position of Second Yang appears to be unfavorable as compared with that of Fifth Yang because it is in an improper position (a yang line in a yin position), whereas the latter is in a proper position (a yang line in a yang position).

Third Yin ☵. Keep a low profile

He lives on his inheritance. If he is steadfast, he will receive good fortune in the end.
He devotes himself to the service of the king, but he does not claim the merit of his achievement.

Third Yin is in an improper position and encircled by Second Yang and Fourth Yang, indicating that a confrontation will lead to an insecure situation. An executive in this position is advised to follow the ancient Chinese virtue of not contending with others as far as possible. This is why the text says "he lives on his inheritance." "Inheritance" here refers to the "old virtue." Perseverance in noncontention is considered one of the old virtues.

A weak executive Third Yin must not contend with a strong superior like Top Yang, but should keep a harmonious relationship between the two as indicated by their interconnecting relationship.

Fourth Yang ☰ Return to rationality

He should not engage in conflict but stay calm. He can have good fortune in the end.

If a person can avoid any unnecessary contention and go back to rationality, he will avoid insecurity and obtain security. An executive who is in the position of Fourth Yang should not confront his superior Fifth Yang and his subordinate Third Yin. He should control his temper and cultivate a calm nature since impulsive action in contention could lead him to the wrong way. However, he should be able to secure his cooperative relationship with Initial Yin as indicated by the interconnection between the two.

Fifth Yang ☰ Need a just and fair judgment on dispute

Contention can be auspicious if it is balanced and correct.

Fifth Yang is in a position of balance and correctness, suggesting that a leader should solve a conflict in a just and fair way if a contention is unavoidable.

Top Yang ☰ Not worth winning a short-run victory with high cost

He is awarded a belt of honor, but it will be taken away from him three times in one day.

Even if an aggressive leader can win in a contention with others, his victory may not be secured as others could fight back later. His victory is not worth having because it costs too much. The gains of taking action may not be sufficient to offset the losses.

7

師
SHI

The Earth–Water Hexagram

Leading Troops, Generalship

IMAGE

The earth bears all things including human beings, animals, plants, crops, and natural resources, and water nourishes all things. However, things cannot produce a marked effect unless they are organized by a person or a group of people. The Earth–Water Hexagram is therefore concerned with leading and organizing a military action. When this concept is applied to an organization, it refers to the leader of a group. If the people are represented by the trigram KUN 坤 [Earth], Second Yang in the hexagram SHI ☵☵ stands for the commander of the troops or the active leader of an organization. The outer trigram Earth represents the troops with the characteristic of obedience and the inner trigram KAN 坎 [Water] stands for danger. This means the troops of a legion or the people of an organization follow their leader obediently in an action that can be dangerous.

The five yin lines surrounding the only yang line in the hexagram indicate that the people are united under one leader. The hexagram suggests that these people will support their leader if he is sincere and upright (a yang line in a central position of the lower trigram). If not, people will take action against him as indicated by the characteristic of water—**Water (here it also stands for people) can carry a boat and can also sink it.**

HEXAGRAM STATEMENT

If an army has an upright and experienced leader, there will be fortune and no blame.

Like an army, an organization needs its leader to be an upright and experienced person as his integrity, capability, and vision can inspire people to follow him; a high team spirit will be built up.

STRUCTURE

The hexagram represents an organization in which Fifth Yin is the **top leader** who adopts a soft management style as shown by its nature of yin. Second Yang is an **action leader** who derives authority from the top leader—Fifth Yin. Mutual trust between the top leader and the action leader should be established in order to get a two-way communication between both sides. The interconnection between Fifth Yin and Second Yang reveals this important relationship in an organization. The qualities of an action leader as suggested by the commentary of the hexagram are experience, capability, integrity, and initiative.

A military action is a big mobilization of resources, and this requirement is indicated by the hidden Big ZHEN or Big Action from Second Yang to Top Yin. To be successful, **a military action needs discipline and common belief**. The opposite hexagram of SHI ☷☵ is TONGREN 同人 [Fellowship] ☰☲ (13), which pinpoints the importance of shared values to the success of a group action.

LINE STATEMENTS

Initial Yin ☷☵. Need for proper order and discipline

The army must set out in strict order. If not, good turns out bad. There will be misfortune.

Initial Yin symbolizes the beginning of an operation: it is wise to make the rules of conduct clear to all members who are involved in it so that they will not be confused in their actions and will know the boundaries between what they can and cannot do. Setting the rules right at the beginning of an action is advantageous to the whole operation.

An organization must keep proper order and discipline in its operations as both effective system and structure are needed to achieve an organizational objective. Unless an organization can maintain good order and discipline there will be chaos and inefficiency. In entering a "battle" with an opponent, an organization must first examine its resources and make sure they are adequate for such an action. If not, the action should not be undertaken at the present stage. An action leader should not only be responsible for setting the rules for those below him, but for should also be responsible for setting the rules for himself. He must set an example through his own actions and act as a role model for the people under him.

Second Yang ☵ · Need for a balanced course

He steers a balanced and middle course in the army. He is fortunate and blameless. The king will honor him three times.

If an action leader is weak in character when undertaking an operation he may not be able to achieve the planned objective. But if he is too strict, he may not be able to attain it either. If he can just follow the principle of centrality in leading his group, he will find few difficulties. The top leader will reward the action leader according to his contributions in due course.

Second Yang is at the central position of the lower trigram and the only yang line in the hexagram. This symbolizes an action leader who is respected and trusted by his colleagues and subordinates as well as by the top leader because of his balance and sincerity. A yang line in a yin position is not necessarily disadvantageous if it is in a central position of a trigram, which represents the principle of centrality.

Third Yin ☷ · Conflict in multiple chain of command

The army carries corpses in the wagons. It is inauspicious.

There are two explanations for this text. First, the army is defeated and carries the corpses of the generals in wagons back home (the corpses of the soldiers are simply buried in the battle field). The reason for the defeat is due to the incompetence of the commander. The weak line in an inappropriate position (a yin line in a yang position) indicates the unfavorable situation which the army faces.

The second explanation involves conflicting leadership in an army or an organization. In ancient China, a "corpse" was a wooden statue of the past or the present king carried by a wagon in an army. The purpose of carrying this wooden statue of the king was that the chief general (Second Yang) could use it to show the army that he had received authority from the king. The wooden statue therefore served the purpose of leading and supervising an army.

If a general who is in the position of Third Yin shares the authority of the commander Second Yang in leading and directing the army, there is likely to be conflicts between the two and the command of the military expedition is hence not unified. When an organization allows two or more bosses in its administrative structure, disorder and failure are likely to happen.

If a weak or incapable (a yin line) leader like Third Yin is in a strong (yang) position, he may make a rash advance; his action can be harmful to the organization.

Fourth Yin ☷˙ Timely retreat

The army retreats. There are no mistakes.

If a leader realizes his weak (yin) position and retreats in a timely fashion he will not be to blame. A wise leader is the one who can make the right judgment as to whether conditions are favorable or not for advancement or retreat. If the time is not favorable for advance then a strategic retreat is needed in order to stay away from danger.

A yin line in a yin position is considered proper and makes a leader more cautious in taking action. If he realizes that the chance of achieving his objective is low, he retreats.

Fifth Yin ☷˙ Avoid multiple "bosses"

If there are beasts in the field, it is advantageous to capture them; there will be no mistakes.
A mature person is trusted with authority to lead the army. If the army is also under the direction of another person who is immature, there will be misfortune.

Fifth Yin symbolizes a top leader who is moderate, balanced, and tolerant. He will not attack others unless he is first attacked by others.

An effective organization can only have one leader who has the power for making the final decision, for which he is fully accountable. If there are more "bosses" in the organization who share the authority, this will affect the principle of a unified chain of command. As a result, the organization will be in a situation of disorder and inefficiency. Multiple leadership may have the advantage of avoiding abuse of power, which may happen with a single leader, but it can also make the organization less adaptable and hence inefficient.

Top Yin ☷ **Fairness is the basis for reward**

The great lord rewards the people who have made contributions to the victory of a war. He chooses people to be the ruler of the states and installs feudal families.
However, he does not employ the inferior people.

The leader of an organization should employ the principle of fairness in rewarding those who merit promotion. But he should not use people who lack integrity even if they have made contributions to the organization.

8

比
BI

The Water–Earth Hexagram

Joining Together, Association

IMAGE

The hexagram Bi is an inversion of the hexagram Shi 師 [Leading Troops] (7). After an inversion of the upper and the lower trigrams, the Earth–Water Hexagram transforms into the Water–Earth Hexagram. Water flows on Earth, indicating an intimate relationship between the two trigrams. On the other hand, Water also stands for danger and Earth represents a group of people (friends or alliances). Water over Earth symbolizes that a group of friends is getting together to face danger. A leader who belongs to a group of friend will receive strong support and will be well protected when he is in trouble. If a leader can develop a cooperative relationship with the members of his organization, harmony is obtained.

The inner trigram Kun 坤 [Earth] ☷ represents the resources or the members of an organization, and Fifth Yang in the upper trigram Kan 坎 [Water] stands for the leadership position. The hexagram Bi indicates a situation in an organization in which the members are obedient under the top leader Fifth Yang. Though an organization has troubles outwardly as indicated by the upper trigram Water ☵, it does have adequate resources (people, technology, and capital) within it to support its operations, as symbolized by the lower trigram Earth ☷. Therefore, the organization should be in a good position to move forward.

HEXAGRAM STATEMENT

Joining together is auspicious if it is based on uprightness and steadfastness.

Those who did not follow in the past will gather together now.
Those who come late will meet with misfortune.

People are willing to join a leader for fellowship or companionship if he is sincere, balanced, and upright as represented by Fifth Yang in the central position of the hexagram. The relationship between the members of the organization and the leader is entirely spontaneous and voluntary on both sides. But there are still people who are hesitant to join the leader as they are not quite sure about his vision or policy, so they prefer to wait until the situation becomes clearer. However, they will regret their late action as they may not be able to fit into this group if they decide to join together later.

STRUCTURE

Like the hexagram SHI, BI is also a hexagram with one yang and five yins. The main difference between the two is the position of the yang line in the two hexagrams. One is in the lower trigram of SHI and the other in the upper trigram of BI.

From the structural point view, the two hexagrams are interchangeable:

SHI   **BI**
☰☰ ⟶ ☰☰

The hexagram BI can also be named the hexagram SHI, because here Fifth Yang plays a dual role as a top leader and also an action-leader. In this case, the leadership style in the hexagram BI is centralized as compared with the decentralized one in the hexagram SHI, where Fifth Yin represents the position of a top leader whereas Second Yang stands for an action leader. The top leader delegates his authority to the action leader but holds the ultimate authority. In the hexagram BI, the top leader and the action leader are same person.

LINE STATEMENTS

Initial Yin ☷. Associate sincerely with others

If he associates sincerely with others, he is free from making mistakes.
Sincerity is like a plain vessel that bears fruits without flower.
Eventually it brings good fortune.

A leader should be sincere and truthful with the members of his organization like a plain vessel that is filled within and unadorned without. When he seeks closeness with his colleagues he doesn't need to adorn himself outwardly but he must be true inwardly. If he acts in this way, people are willing to follow him.

Initial Yin is not interconnected with Fifth Yang and is located farthest from it, but with sincerity and truthfulness Initial Yin will be able to win intimacy with Fifth Yang in the end.

Second Yin ☷. Associate with others from one's inner truth

Association that comes from within is correct and auspicious.

Association with others must come from one's inner truth in respect to sincerity, honesty, dignity, and self-respect. A relationship that is formed based on the inner truth of both sides will last long. The interconnection of Second Yin of the inner trigram with Fifth Yang of the outer trigram indicates the principle of association.

Third Yin ☷. Do not associate with a wrong person.

He joins in closeness with a wrong person.

It is a mistake to associate closely with a wrong person. The executive Third Yin will not have an association with his colleague Second Yang, even though the latter is sincere and balanced, because Second Yang already has a close relationship with Initial Yin. But Third Yin cannot associate with the senior executive Fourth Yin, for he is weak and unbalanced. Moreover, Fourth Yin prefers to associate with his superior Fifth Yang—the top leader. So Third Yin can only associate with Top Yin, but Top Yin is too weak and changeable as reflected by the yin line located at the turning point of the hexagram and the extreme of the upper trigram. If Third Yin wants to associate with Top Yin he will face a situation of insecurity and uncertainty.

Fourth Yin ☷. Associate with people who are capable, sincere, and upright

Outward association is auspicious.

A top leader Fifth Yang should target as a senior executive a Fourth Yin as his associate as through this a yin–yang relationship is achievable. In looking for association with the members within the organization, it is sensible for Fourth Yin to associate with the top leader Fifth Yang who is capable, sincere, and upright. Since Fifth Yang is above Fourth Yin, so it is correct for Fourth Yin to have an outward association.

Fifth Yang ☵ Do not press others to follow

He openly associates with others just like a king hunts game in the surrounding three sides and allows the animals to escape from the open side.
He treats his faithful followers in the same way. There will be good fortune.

The best way for a top leader to attract followers is for him to allow them to be with him at their own will. He should be impartial to everyone as reflected by the leadership position of Fifth Yang which is centered, balanced, and upright. The association of others with him will be inspired by his personal style and charisma.

Top Yin ☵ A good beginning leads to a good end

He does not get close to others in the beginning, he will be inauspicious.

Whether an association with others at the end is good or not is also influenced by how it begins. If an association between the two parties in the beginning is good, it is likely to lead to a good association at the end. It is possible to have a beginning that doesn't have an end. However, it is certain that if there is an end, there must have been a beginning. A good beginning leads to a good end.

Since Top Yin has no interconnection with Third Yin, the leader in this position lacks support from those in the lower echelons. Top Yin is at the end of the hexagram, representing the end of association. It is therefore an unfavorable position since it is located at the top of the upper trigram Water, symbolizing danger or difficulty. The reason for this is due to a lack of good beginning when making associations with others.

9

小畜
XIAOXU

The Wind–Heaven Hexagram

Small Accumulating

IMAGE

The Wind–Heaven Hexagram XIAOXU gives an image of the wind blowing across the sky. The wind restrains the clouds so that they can become denser to produce rain, but rain has not yet come. One must have patience and wait for it.

Fourth Yin as the single yin line of the hexagram is encircled by five yang lines as if the small yin domesticates the big five, so the hexagram can be named Small Domesticating. Since there is only one yin in the hexagram its strength is apparently not adequate to support the five yangs, but it needs more power to do so. Therefore, this situation can also be called Small Accumulating: the power of the small yin needs to be further accumulated. At present, the small yin is accumulating its strength, so the time for it to domesticate the five yangs has not yet come. Accumulating with patience is necessary.

When a new subsidiary of a business group, like Fourth Yin, is still in an early stage of its development, it is unrealistic to expect it to make immediate contributions to the whole group despite of its good growth potential. This means the time is not yet ripe.

The outer trigram XUN 巽 is also considered as Wood. Wood can represent the outer part of a tree on the ground; the inner trigram QIAN 乾 [Heaven] correspondingly stands for the roots of a tree under the ground. The stronger the roots of a tree, the faster the tree will grow and the longer life it will have. Compared with the traditional explanation of this hexagram as Small Accumulating, this **new observation** suggests an important principle for the growth of an organization: **formation of**

a strong base (represented by the trigram Heaven) is essential for the healthy or sound development of an organization. Under this new image, the name of this hexagram can be called Cornerstone instead of Small Accumulating.

HEXAGRAM STATEMENT

Dense clouds do not produce rain; they start from the west.

Clouds can produce rain. But if they are from the west (in China) the chances are low because the air from the west is too dry to transform the clouds into rain, whereas the wind from southeast with wet air is more likely to do so. The reason for this is that a merging of yin and yang can produce something new; the rising vapor from the wet air will turn into rain. When the time is not ripe to take an action, a leader should be patient and it would be unwise for him to make a show of his abilities and strength. **Self-restraint is necessary and beneficial.**

STRUCTURE

The one-yin–five-yang hexagram is traditionally interpreted as Small Domesticating or Small Accumulating. However, this hexagram can also be in interpreted in a reversed way as the hexagram indicates a situation in which the five yangs domesticate the only yin. Using this definition, this hexagram should be named Large Domesticating instead of Small Domesticating. Obviously there is a contradiction between the hexagram name and the hexagram structure.

The organization in this hexagram is dominated by the yang forces; both top leader Fifth Yang and the division leader Second Yang have the same yang character. Conflict rather than cooperation between the two is likely to happen.

LINE STATEMENTS

Initial Yang ☰. Return to the right path

He returns to the right path, what blame could there be? There will be good fortune.

When a leader finds difficulties in a new direction, he should return to the old or the right way. Initial Yang moves forward to seek an interconnection with Fourth Yin, but the way is blocked by Second Yang and Third Yang, so an executive in this position would be more sensible to stay where he is.

Second Yang ☰. Cooperate with those who have the same interest

He is dragged back to his proper way. There will be good fortune.

Since there are obstructions to moving forward as symbolized by Third Yang and also no interconnection with Fifth Yang, the executive Second Yang is advised to cooperate with the two capable persons Initial Yang and Third Yang in order to overcome the mutual obstruction ahead. Solidarity is power.

Third Yang ☰. Obstinacy leads to dissociation

The axle falls off the wheel of a cart just as husband and wife turn away from each other.

Third Yang indicates a situation of a yang line in a yang position, symbolizing obstinacy. If a leader is obstinate or overconfident in his judgment or decision, he may have conflicts with his colleagues and this would lead to disharmony in the organization. He cannot progress efficiently unless his colleagues' views are also considered.

Fourth Yin ☴. Sincerity and truthfulness wins trust

When there is sincerity, blood goes and fears give way.

A senior executive Fourth Yang who is close to the top leader Fifth Yang may face danger if the top leader looses faith in him. To avoid this, he must get the trust of the top leader by remaining sincere and truthful.

Fifth Yang ☴. Cooperation through mutual trust

His sincerity enables him to form a good bond with his neighbors.

If a leader Fifth Yang is sincere to the executive Fourth Yin, Fourth Yin will be sincere also. Mutual trust between the two parties forms the basis of their cooperation which will benefit both sides.

Top Yang ☶ **Restraint after success**

The rain falls and stops, yin and yang reach a harmony.
The yin rises to its limit like a moon that is almost full. There will be
danger if the yin continues to rise. It is inauspicious for a superior
man to go on an expedition.

In its early stage of development the new subsidiary of a business group
is the hope of the whole organization as its promising future may bring
essential gains to support the organization. At this stage, all other large
units support the growth of this small new subsidiary, so it is a form of
Large Domesticating. When the new subsidiary has reached success, its
relationship with the other large units of the organization may transfer
to a Small Domesticating form. The small and new subsidiary begins to
support other large units of the organization. However, as the influence
of this small (yin) unit grow within the organization, conflicts between
the small and large (yang) units are most likely to occur and a fight
between the two forces (yin and yang) becomes hard to avoid. In such
an unstable situation, any expansion is definitely not suitable.

10

 履
LÜ

The Heaven–Lake Hexagram

Treading

IMAGE

Heaven over Lake symbolizes the strong above the soft or that the strong is ahead of the weak. The hexagram gives the image that the weak follows the strong just like a man treads on the tail of a tiger. Whether he will be bitten by the tiger depends on his own actions. If he is cautious, he will be able to avoid the danger ahead. **Working under a powerful leader is like following a tiger.** As long as the subordinate works properly and does not provoke the superior to anger, he will be safe. The upper trigram QIAN 乾 [Heaven] represents hardness whereas the lower trigram DUI 兑 [Lake] stands for docility. This hexagram gives an image of **the weaker following the stronger in an obedient manner**.

The hexagram LÜ can also mean that one follows the standards required by an organization or a community. Heaven represents the standards associated with regulation, discipline, and transparency. The attributes of Lake are those of joyfulness and receptiveness. The Heaven-over-Lake Hexagram indicates that one is pleased to follow the standards set by an organization or a community. If Heaven symbolizes the system, Lake then represents obedience to it in a pleasant manner. **In a state which is ruled by law, people tend to see the law as a tiger;** they become therefore more cautious in order not to violate it.

HEXAGRAM STATEMENT

He treads on the tiger's tail cautiously, but the tiger does not bite him. It is fortunate.

If a leader undertakes a risky project cautiously and achieves success, it does not mean the project itself is risk free but indicates that his cautiousness has enabled him to avoid the dangers in a particular time and space. It is, however, difficult to say whether his experience can be successfully repeated in a different time and space.

When a small company follows the direction of a market leader, it can save a lot of expense and work in discovering the new trends in the market. But the small company must be very careful in its operations so as not to step into the market leader's territory, otherwise the market leader will attack it.

In working under a powerful boss one could be fortunate because of the access gained from him. But there could equally be the danger of confrontation. Unless a person is well prepared to protect himself, for example, by being able to move to another organization, he should not offend the boss but should respond to him carefully. He should be sensitive to the superior's feelings. If the superior is a bad-tempered or impatient person it would not be wise to injure his pride or wound his vanity. One needs to be tactful and considerate.

STRUCTURE

As illustrated above, a one-yin–five-yang hexagram can also be called Small Domesticating based on its structure. The meaning of the hexagram structure can be different from that of the hexagram name. The meaning of a hexagram is therefore dependent on what concepts and methods are adopted, since different concepts or methods give different meanings. This indicates that the explanations given in the *Yijing* are changeable, depending on how the statements, wording, and structure are interpreted.

LINE STATEMENTS

Initial Yang ☰. Keep simplicity in a lower position

He conducts himself with simplicity, so there will be no blame.

An active leader should be able to restrain his eagerness for moving forward when his organization is still in the early stage of development as Initial Yang is at the lowest position in the hexagram. If he acts according to the capacity and resources of his organization, he will make no mistakes. An action based on plainness and naturalness is an example of simplicity, through which one will not act greedily and impetuously.

Second Yang ☱. Be calm and quiet

He walks on the smooth and easy path. If he is quiet and steadfast, he will be auspicious.

The second line is yang in character. A leader in this position could be obstinate in making decisions regardless of other people's views. If he acts this way, he will be inviting trouble. But if he is calm and quiet (a yin position), honest and balanced (a central position), things will go his way.

Third Yin ☷ Do not act beyond one's capability

A one-eyed man thinks he can see, a lame man thinks he can walk properly.
The man who treads on the tail of the tiger gets bitten, to his misfortune.
It is similar to a general who believes that he is able to take the position of the king.

The leader of a growing company must not be overconfident in taking action that would have an influence on the market leader, for the market leader could strike back to defend his current position. **An impulsive action would lead to disaster.**

A yin line in a yang position indicates a person who is weak but wants to be strong. He may try to do something beyond his capability and he will have trouble if he thinks that he can do more than he is actually capable of.

Fourth Yang ☳ Be careful under a strong leader

He treads on the tail of a tiger. He will be auspicious in the end if he is very cautious.

Similarly when the conditions of the environment are poor, any movement in an organization must be undertaken with care. Fourth Yang is close to the top leader Fifth Yang. A person in this position is in danger because he is near the leader. His relationship with the leader can be favorable if he follows the values and style of the leader. But once a conflict arises between his boss and him, the relationship between these two may be damaged and he becomes vulnerable. Therefore, the situation Fourth Yang faces is just like an old saying in China: **"To accompany a king is like accompanying a tiger."**

Fifth Yang ☰ A strong determination leads to obstinacy

A strong determination could be dangerous.

Determination is one of the important qualities of a leader. But if he always acts in this way, he may become overconfident and tend to believe that whatever decision he makes must be right. With this attitude, he will gradually become a person who is obstinate. As a consequence, he will certainly face danger.

Fifth Yang is a leadership position, representing authority and resolution (a yang line in a yang position). On one hand, a decisive leader is considered efficient. On the other, he could be seen as an authoritative person who fails to take account of the views of others. If a leader always makes decisions by himself, he walks on a dangerous path. He needs to restore his inner balance.

Fifth Yang is in a central position in the upper trigram and surrounded by both Fourth Yang and Top Yang with their firm support, so the three yangs form a power group which is as strong as a tiger.

Top Yang ☰ Examine past acts

He examines his conduct as to whether it is good or bad and how much good or bad he has done. It is auspicious to do so.

Top Yang is at the end of treading or the final stage of an operation. It is therefore necessary to review the outcome in the past. A leader who acts in this way will be in a good position to identify the reasons for the success achieved and the failure experienced. A good review at the end of an operation will provide the organization with useful information and insights for future development.

11

The Earth–Heaven Hexagram

Harmony, Tranquility

IMAGE

In reality, Heaven is above Earth, but for the purpose of harmony an inverse relationship between the two appears to be desirable. The reason for this is that the yang element by nature moves upwards whereas the yin element moves downward. Heaven (yang) and Earth (yin) cannot interact unless their positions are interchanged as the hexagram TAI suggests. So the relationship between Heaven and Earth in this hexagram is a desirable state rather than a real one. The hexagram statement says:

The small goes, the great comes.

It means that the three yin lines are going outside (outer trigram) and three yang lines are coming inside (inner trigram). Yang energy is strong inside and yin energy is submissive outside. Yang energy rises and yin energy descends. The two energies commingle and create a mixing of yin and yang. When yin and yang are harmoniously combined, myriad things can grow.

To achieve an overall harmony in an organization, a leader is advised not to emphasize his formal authority but to act more informally as in the inverse relationship indicated above. If he puts too much emphasis on the formal relationship, the harmony of his organization could be adversely affected. Conversely if a leader is willing to place himself mentally under his colleagues or subordinates despite his formal position, an internal harmony in his organization can be achieved.

Similarly if a government sees itself as an organization serving the people or the community, the government officials will think that their position is not higher but lower than that of the people served by them, as suggested by this hexagram. If they act in this way, a harmonious relationship between the government and the people can also be achieved. The inner trigram QIAN 乾 [Heaven] represents strength, initiative, and activity. The outer trigram KUN 坤 [Earth] stands for softness, tolerance, and obedience. A desirable leadership should be a mixture of the characteristics of both heaven and earth, soft outside and firm inside, so that a good balance can be obtained through the leader's thoughts and actions.

To achieve harmony between an organization and the public, it is necessary to have an interconnection between the organization as represented by the inner trigram and the public in the external environment as represented by the outer trigram. The inner trigram Heaven stands for the achievements and future action plans of an organization; the outer trigram Earth is seen as people or the public. Through an interconnection between an organization (inner trigram) and the public (outer trigram) the message of achievement or future movement of an organization will be transmitted to the people in the external environment, creating a favorable relationship between the two parties—the organization and the public.

HEXAGRAM STATEMENT

The small goes and the great comes, with auspicious success.

The small stands for yin and the great for yang. "Going outside" means the three yin lines in the outer trigram and "coming inside" refers to the three yang lines in the inner trigram. The small can also represent a man's character that is soft, flexible, and adaptable, whereas the great stands for a character that is firm, active, and creative. To be a leader with charisma, a leader should keep "the small" outside and "the great" inside.

STRUCTURE

This is a hexagram with three yin and three yang lines. The three yang lines of the lower trigram Heaven represent the first half of a development. The hexagram gives a warning that the harmony achieved in the first half of a development could change into disharmony in the second half of a development (three yang lines change to three yin lines in the upper trigram). The situation indicated by the line structure is, however, different from the situations as indicated by the line statements of the outer trigram as they tend to be more favorable. The reason for this is due to the difference in a macro (structural) and a micro (line statement) aspect. The changes in a development from harmony to disharmony in a structural aspect reflect a cyclical movement between expansion and contraction, or between favorable and unfavorable situations in a development.

LINE STATEMENTS

Initial Yang ☷. **Advancement needs solidarity**

When grass is pulled out, it pulls up others of its kind with it. It is auspicious to take on a venture.

A leader should be able to make people who share the same values and aims to join him. The three yang lines of the lower trigram symbolize solidarity among the members of an organization like grass roots clinging together. When Initial Yang moves, the other two yangs will join the action as the three have common values and the same objective.

Second Yang ☵. **Tolerance, courage, and balance are the leadership qualities**

His tolerance and resolution enable him to cross the river. He does not neglect those who are far away and does not form cliques. He acts in a middle way.

A leader should tolerate the people with different views in his organization; his broad-minded attitude is advantageous in attracting capable people to follow him. He should unite with everyone regardless of distance. The central position of Second Yang suggests that the principle of balance should be used in employing people with different abilities. A leader should be firm and decisive in order to overcome difficulties and be courageous in leading changes in his organization.

Third Yang ☳. **Everything has an opposite**

There is no plain without a slope, no going without a return.

If he keeps steadfast in difficult times, he will make no mistakes. He should not worry as his sincerity will bring him fortune.

Nothing can last forever. An economic expansion will have a limit as does an economic contraction. If there is an expansion, there must be a contraction. **Everything has an opposite and moves in a cyclical pattern.** If a leader understands the yin–yang polarity well, he will be able to predict future changes.

Third Yang is at the top of the lower trigram and below the three yin lines of the upper trigram. It paces a change in the situation moving from the lower trigram to the upper trigram. While the first half of the hexagram is yang in nature, its second half is however dominated by yin. This indicates a change from a favorable state to a less favorable one. Therefore **during a time of peace a leader should think of perilous times ahead.**

Fourth Yin ☷ Modesty and sincerity as forces for building up team spirit

He flutters down amicably together with his neighbors. They trust him without any precaution.

A person in the position of Fourth Yin tends to be modest and sincere, for a yin line in a yin position means docility and uprightness. With these two qualities he will be trusted by those in higher positions such as the top leader Fifth Yin and Top Yin. Fourth Yin and his two colleagues with the same character (yin line) and shared values will build up a team spirit to strive for their common goal.

Fifth Yin ☷ A union brings a relationship of mutual trust

King Diyi gave his younger sister in marriage. There were blessings and good fortune.

Diyi 帝乙 was a king of the Shang dynasty and the father of the last king Zhou of Shang. He gave his younger sister to King Wen of Zhou for the purpose of setting up a political union between the two states. In today's business activity, this is just like the formation of a strategic alliance between two companies. In an alliance, Fifth Yin represents a large company whereas Second Yang a small and growing one.

Top Yin ䷁ **Do not resist a natural change**

The walls of the city collapse into the moats. Military action should not be mobilized. The orders can only be carried out in one's own domain. Even if he keeps to the right way, there will be regret.

When a favorable phase of a cycle reaches its extreme, there is no point in resisting this natural change. Any attempt to resist it will be in vain. A leader must realize that it is the end of the era of harmony and he can do nothing to stop it. He should withdraw his current actions and make the necessary preparations for the coming bad time.

12

The Heaven–Earth Hexagram

Obstruction, Disharmony, Stagnation

IMAGE

The Heaven–Earth Hexagram PI is the reversed pattern of the Earth–Heaven Hexagram TAI 泰 [Harmony] (11), indicating that both heaven and earth are in their true positions—Heaven above Earth. But a true position may not be a right or desirable one. By their characteristics the yang element moves upward and the yin element downward. As a consequence, Heaven with yang characteristics cannot interconnect with Earth, which has the yin nature. Heaven and Earth are isolated from each other due to the absence of communication or interconnection. Under such circumstances, obstruction will occur between the two. An inverse position between the two appears to be more desirable as indicated by the Earth–Heaven Hexagram. In the hexagram PI, the outer trigram as yang and inner trigram as yin represent the character of an "inferior man" who acts as a "superior man" outwardly but is egocentric and dishonest inwardly. The leader of an organization can be a person with double character: outwardly he appears to be a person with high integrity but inwardly he is just the opposite. The three yin lines in this hexagram symbolize egocentrism, dishonesty, unrighteousness, and unreliability.

The three yang lines can also symbolize the power or authority of the senior management of an organization and the three yin lines stand for the middle and lower management. The structure of an organization in this hexagram tends to be centralized. Communication or interconnection between the senior management (upper trigram) and the middle/lower management (lower trigram) is from the top down, or one way. If the people at the lower level are obedient, harmony can be found within the superior–subordinate relationship. But if the people at the lower level do not act in this way conflicts between the two groups will arise and adversely affect the harmony of the organization. An organization with the Heaven–Earth structure will sooner or later be found in a disharmonious or unstable situation.

In contrast to the traditional interpretation of this hexagram as stated above, the hexagram can also be interpreted in a positive way. The upper trigram Heaven represents the outward characteristics of a superior man as indicated by his activity, firmness, and straightness, and the lower trigram stands for the inward characteristics of a superior man as tolerant, open-minded, and adaptable. By using this approach this hexagram, unlike the traditional interpretation, can also represent a superior man as judged by both his outward and inward characteristics. The argument here points out that the hexagram name as given by the traditional way in the *Yijing* is one approach, but not the only one. In fact, the hexagram name is determined by how the hexagram is interpreted. Different perceptions have different names.

Hexagram Statement

At the time of obstruction as the great goes and the small comes, humanity and rationality are not practiced, so it is not advantageous for the superior man to adhere to uprightness.

The three yang lines in the outer trigram and the three yin lines in the inner trigram represent the great and the small respectively. Since yang goes upward and yin downward, there is no interaction between yin and yang. The right way for development is blocked. It is a time of obstruction or disharmony. It will be disadvantageous for an upright man to persist in his principles of honesty and integrity as the inferior man will not let him preserve justice and truth. He should adapt to the conditions of the time while maintaining his inner truth.

Structure

In the Heaven–Earth Hexagram Pi, the three stages of the first half of a development signifies unfavorable situations as indicated by the three yin lines, but the situation becomes more favorable in the second part of the development as indicated by the three yang lines. So **the hexagram**

PI does not mean that every situation in a development must be unfavorable, it merely indicates that unfavorable situations can be found at a specific time in a development. The word "misfortune" is not used in the commentaries on the six line statements in this hexagram. Obviously there is a difference in perception between a structural aspect and that of the line statements. The former is concerned with the relationships of a whole whereas the latter suggests the guidelines for dealing with the individual situations of an obstruction; not all six stages of a development are "unfavorable." In the upper trigram Heaven, the three yang lines indicate that the situation is gradually improving from unfavorable to favorable.

LINE STATEMENTS

Initial Yin ☰☰. Need a union in the time of obstruction

When grass is pulled up, it pulls up others of its kind with it.
Uprightness brings good fortune and success.

At the beginning, when faced by an obstruction, the leader should be able to strengthen the spirit of teamwork in his organization so that people are willing to work cooperatively like the close relationship between the grasses.

This statement is almost the same as that of Initial Yang of the hexagram TAI 泰 [Harmony] (11) but with different implications. The spirit of union is emphasized a time of advancement in the hexagram TAI whereas it is emphasized in a time of retreat in the hexagram PI.

Second Yin ☰☰. Keep away from flattery and maintain inner firmness

Flattery is good fortune for the inferior man, but it is not for the superior man.

In a time of obstruction an upright leader will not flatter someone to tide over a difficulty as an inferior man does. He will maintain his inner firmness and avoid acting in an unrighteous way. The central line of the inner trigram suggests this principle.

Third Yin ☰☰. Need a right choice between proper and improper acts

He bears with his shame.

A yin line in a yang position signifies an improper act. This suggests that an inferior man is not ashamed of his incorrect practices. He is impudent. An ordinary leader may achieve his objective by using ill means without shame whereas a good leader is ashamed of improper conduct.

Fourth Yang ☳ Adapt to the law of nature

If he follows the will of heaven, he will be free from any blame.
People gathered around him will share his blessing.

In a time of obstruction the second half of a development begins to move toward a more favorable direction in cyclical change. It is the law of nature, or "the will of heaven" as is termed in the text. If a leader can make adaptations to change in a timely manner, he and his followers will share the benefit.

Fifth Yang ☴ Secure a firm position in time of transition

The obstruction is about removal. The great man is fortunate.
He should keep destruction in mind and stand firm as mulberry trees.

When good times are coming, a leader should not forget the obstruction that may arise again in the transition and hence he should make all necessary arrangements to strengthen his position. He should not forget danger when he is safe.

Top Yang ☴ Prepare for the coming good time

The time of obstruction comes to the end. Distress is followed by
happiness.

The time of obstruction is ending. Adversity followed by felicity and vice versa is the law of nature. A leader who can master this principle will be able to reduce risk in his strategic moves.

THE RELATIONSHIP BETWEEN HARMONY AND OBSTRUCTION

In the above two hexagrams TAI [Harmony] and PI [Obstruction] are treated as two "independent" situations in a development. However, each of them can be considered as part of a cyclical change as shown below:

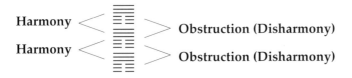

From a long-term point of view, the relationship between the two situations—Harmony and Obstruction—are cyclical in nature, indicating the alternative changes between "good" and "bad" in a development. However, harmony and obstruction are not absolutely independent from each other as shown above; the second part of the hexagram Tai can be seen as the first part of the hexagram Pi. Obviously some stages of the situation Harmony can overlap with some stages of the situation Obstruction in a development. This illustrates **the principle of mutual inclusion** between yin and yang—the character of one thing includes the character of another. The relationship between Harmony and Obstruction illustrates also **the principle of vicissitude** (rise and fall between yin and yang) and **the principle of opposites**. These three principles will be further elaborated in Part Three of this book.

USING HEXAGRAMS HARMONY AND OBSTRUCTION TO ILLUSTRATE SUNZI'S CONCEPT OF ILLUSION AND REALITY

One of the essential concepts of Sunzi 孫子 is his concept of **illusion and reality**, or **weakness and strength**. According to him a wise leader is a person who knows how to use these two concepts to confuse or mislead his opponent into making a wrong decision. The concept of illusion or weakness can be represented by the trigram Earth ☷ due to its nature of **emptiness**, and the concept of reality or strength by the trigram Heaven ☰ due to its nature of **firmness**:

Illusion or Weakness   **Reality or Strength**

☷   ☰

If a leader wants to mislead his opponent that he is "weak" outwardly by hiding his strength inwardly, his action can be illustrated by the hexagram Tai:

Hexagram Tai

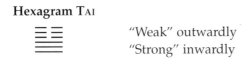

"Weak" outwardly
"Strong" inwardly

The opponent who is misled by his tactics will fall into a trap. Conversely a leader can confuse his opponent by pretending he is "strong" outwardly while in fact he is "weak" inwardly. This situation can be illustrated by the hexagram Pɪ:

Hexagram Pɪ

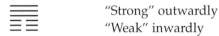

"Strong" outwardly
"Weak" inwardly

The above examples show that the hexagrams of the *Yijing* can be used as a tool to plan corresponding strategies or tactics in a business war.

13

同人 **The Heaven–Fire**
TONGREN **Hexagram**

Fellowship, Concord between People

IMAGE

Fire under Heaven symbolizes a situation where like-minded people gather around a fire under the sky. Both sky and fire have the nature of upward movement. This provides the basis for people who would like work together toward a common goal.

Within a group it is normal for there to be differences between the members' values and expectations, so the leader of an organization should allow such differences as long as these will not adversely affect the common goal and the benefit of the whole. The leader should allow individual diversity within a group. **Confucius** said: **"A superior man unites with people of principle and never follows others blindly."**

A leader should be broad-minded and open in respect to the recruitment of people for his organization, which should be primarily according to their ability and integrity. He should not be prejudiced against a certain type of person.

The lower trigram Fire means clarity. Clarity in an organization may refer to its objectives, policies, and rules. The greater the clarity, the higher the morale of the members of an organization.

The trigram QIAN 乾 [Heaven] symbolizes the strength and activeness of the senior management. However, a strong leadership like Fifth Yang does not necessarily mean centralization. Decentralization at middle and lower levels can also be efficient. It is important for a leader to know in which managerial functions centralization is more appropriate than decentralization and vice versa. The principle here is that benefit to the organization should not be damaged by either of these approaches.

A well-developed fellowship within an organization brings union and coherency, and harmony will overcome its difficulties. As Confucius said: **"When two men are one in heart, they cut iron into two."**

HEXAGRAM STATEMENT

Making fellowship with others in the wilderness is auspicious. It is beneficial to cross great rivers. It is advantageous for the superior man to keep to the right way.

The term "wilderness" means remote places. Gathering people together is not based on feelings of closeness but on broadness, openness, and impartiality. Using these principles a leader is able to form a strong group that can face challenges.

STRUCTURE

The Heaven–Fire Hexagram has one yin and five yangs. Here the only yin line in the second place plays a major role in the line structure, indicating that **the yin character is an important factor in developing fellowship in an organization** using such factors as mutual respect, modesty, softness, flexibility, and adaptability.

The superior–subordinate relationship tends to be favorable as the subordinate has the character of fire—soft and clingy—whereas the superior is as strong and active as heaven. **An adaptation of softness to hardness and vice versa results in peace and harmony**. An organization in which members have shared values will be able to create a warm atmosphere internally as symbolized by the lower trigram Lɪ 離 [Fire], through which the organization will become much stronger externally as represented by the upper trigram Heaven.

LINE STATEMENTS

Initial Yang ☰. Openness as the basis for making fellowship

He makes fellowship with people out of his house, there will be no blame.

If a leader can make fellowship with people based on his openness and impartiality, he will attract them to follow him. It is important to make personal associations without prejudice. Since Initial Yang has no interconnection with Fourth Yang, this implies that a leader should not have personal bias when making fellowship with others, as if he were associating with people "out of his house."

Second Yin ☷. Do not make fellowship in a narrow circle

He makes friendship only with people in the clan; it is regrettable.

If a leader builds up fellowship with people in an exclusive clique, he is narrow-minded. As Confucius warned: **"A superior man unites instead of forming cliques, an inferior man forms cliques instead of uniting."** The reason why a leader associates with people in a clan is primarily due to insecurity or ego. Making fellowship without the principle of impartiality brings conflict between people in an organization and hence damages harmony.

Third Yang ☶. Patience in making fellowship

While the troops hide in the bush, he climbs up the high hills to watch the enemy closely. For three years, he dare not attack the enemy.

Mistrust may arise among the members of an organization even though they have a common goal or shared values. If a leader is not able to solve the conflicts in a timely manner, confrontations can spread within his organization.

The third line, which is in the rightful position (a yang line in a yang position), attempts to take action against the top line, for both are yang in nature. But the top line gets support from Fifth Yang and Fourth Yang. The solidarity of these three yang lines in the upper trigram makes the third line of the lower trigram give up its intention to attack the top line. It is advantageous for a leader who is in a strong position like Third Yang to avoid acting impulsively. Fellowship cannot be made in a short time; it will take a longer time to build mutual trust. **Patience plays an important role in making a reliable and strong fellowship.**

Fourth Yang ☴. Correct the wrong actions

The troops climb the wall but give up the attack, it is auspicious.

If a leader is able to restrain himself from taking an unjust action against others, this will be auspicious. Unlike in the case of Third Yang, a person in Fourth Yang's position knows his own limits (in an improper position); he is flexible and willing to turn back if he realizes that his forward movement is not on the right path.

Fifth Yang ☰☰ Seek a common goal but allow differences

He makes fellowship with the allies. He weeps first but laughs later as they meet each other after they beat the enemy.

Fifth Yang seeks association with Second Yin but the way is blocked by Fourth Yang and Third Yang. However, the obstructions will eventually be overcome by the combined complementary force of Fifth Yang and Second Yin. If a leader makes fellowship only with like-minded people, this narrow-mindedness will prevent him from making a broader association with people who can give him complementary assistance.

Top Yang ☰☰ Make fellowship on a broader basis

Making fellowship on the outskirts is free from regret.

In this hexagram the geographic distance between the home and the place of making association with others is the major criterion for judging whether a fellowship is made on a broad or a narrow basis. The broader the fellowship, the better is its influence. The line statement suggests the "outskirts" as the second broadest basis for making fellowship compared to the "remote places" of the hexagram statement given above. If a fellowship is made "out of his house," its basis is moderate. But if the fellowship is made on a "clan" basis, as the line statement of Second Yang points out this is the narrowest basis for making fellowship.

COMPARING THE HEXAGRAM TONGREN WITH THE HEXAGRAM SHI

The structure of the hexagram TONGREN ☰☰ is the opposite of that of the hexagram SHI 師 [Leading Troops] (7) ☷☷ . While Second Yang plays the major role in the The Army, Second Yin in Fellowship has the same important position. Both represent action leaders. In Hexagram The Army the action leader with yang character as indicated by his energy and strength is particularly suitable in a situation in which an organization is in expansion. In the hexagram TONGREN, the action leader with the yin characteristics of tolerance and softness is in a good position to deal with human matters. An efficient action leader should possess the qualities indicated by these two hexagrams.

14

大有 DAYOU The Fire–Heaven Hexagram

Great Possessions, Great Holdings

IMAGE

Fire over Heaven symbolizes the sun at noon, illuminating all things on the earth. This hexagram gives a picture of the peak of richness, or a situation of great possessions. The lower trigram QIAN 乾 [Heaven] represents resources or richness and the upper trigram Fire a rational senior management. The whole hexagram therefore signifies an organization under a soft management as indicated by the yin line in the fifth position.

If a leader is modest and open-minded, he will be able to gain the respect and support of his colleagues and this would become his "great possessions." However if a leader believes that he has reached a position with abundant possessions, he may become arrogant and will get hurt eventually.

Heaven also symbolizes power and Fire represents lucidity. A man should use his power in a righteous way like the sun shining in the sky, unhidden and clear to others. If he acts in this way he will benefit greatly from it.

HEXAGRAM STATEMENT

Great Possessions means the time of great achievement and prosperity.

This is a time of great achievement. A leader in this situation should remain humble or modest as indicated by the yin line in the fifth position.

STRUCTURE

This is a one-yin–five-yang hexagram. The leader of an organization as Fifth Yin in the hexagram adopts a soft style of management and effectively delegates authority to the strong and active person—Second Yang—under him. Through this yin–yang union, the organization will be able to achieve harmony.

LINE STATEMENTS

Initial Yang ☰. Be humble when there are no connections

If he does not involve himself with what is harmful, he will be free from blame.
If he is aware of difficulty, there will be no mistakes.

A person as Initial Yang in the beginning stages of a development (the lowest position of the hexagram) without connections (no interconnection between Initial Yang and Fourth Yang) should be humble and constantly aware of difficulties. He should not be arrogant.

Second Yang ☰. Sincerity and centrality as the basis for assuming responsibility

A big wagon is able to transport heavy things. It is beneficial to move forward. There will be no blame.

Second Yang represents an executive who is assigned a task by his superior Fifth Yin. If he acts on the principle of sincerity and centrality he will have less difficulty in performing his duties. A person who has inner balance is capable of mastering his responsibility, just as "a big wagon is able to transport heavy things."

Third Yang ☰. Be devoted in work for the benefit of the group

A duke can present offerings to the Son of Heaven (the king) whereas an inferior man cannot.

A good leader will be devoted to his work for the benefit of his organization whereas a mediocre leader will not do this. The former always thinks his personal benefit is tied to that of his organization; the latter is only concerned with his personal benefit. The former is welcomed and trusted by his colleagues; the latter is not.

Fourth Yang ☲ · Restrain one's complacency

By avoiding complacency, he averts harm.

A yang line in a yin position suggests that a restraint of one's complacency is beneficial when an expansion is taking place. If a leader does not boast of his great possessions, he will be able to avoid the resentment of others and can be free from blame.

Fifth Yang ☲ · A union of mutual trust and dignity strengthens leadership

When mutual trust is developed between his colleagues and himself, he is able to maintain his dignity. This will be good fortune.

If a leader adopts a soft style of management (a yin line in a yang position), which is based on mutual trust between the members of the organization and himself, he should act with dignity in front of them so that they will respect him. Through a union of yin (mutual trust) and yang (dignity) effective leadership can be obtained.

Top Yang ☲ · Knowing the natural law is auspicious

He receives the blessings from heaven. This is good fortune and nothing will be unfavorable.

Heaven here refers to the natural law. Top Yang is at the end of the hexagram, symbolizing a person at the peak of possessions. In this a person should be modest and avoid being self-satisfied and arrogant. Acting in this manner is in conformity with the law of nature or *dao*, hence he will "receive blessings from heaven."

A COMPARISON OF THE HEXAGRAM DAYOU WITH THE HEXAGRAM BI

The relationship between the line structure of the hexagram DAYOU 大有 [Great Possessions] (14) and that of the hexagram BI 比 [Joining Together] (8) is one of opposites:

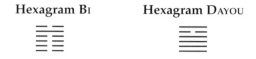

Hexagram Bɪ   **Hexagram D**ᴀʏᴏᴜ

The leader of the hexagram Bɪ (Fifth Yang) is capable of uniting the members of his organization under his direction, whereas the leader of the hexagram Dᴀʏᴏᴜ (Fifth Yin) relies on a well-established mutual trust between his colleagues and himself by effective delegation. The leader of the hexagram Bɪ tends to be a hard-style person, in contrast to the leader of the hexagram Dᴀʏᴏᴜ who acts in a softer way.

Despite the differences in their leadership style, both are able to inspire the members of their organization to follow them. Whether the leadership style should be hard, soft, or a mixture of these is dependent on the time and place. Different times and places need different leadership styles. As long as a leader has integrity, sincerity, fairness, and balance, he will be able to lead an organization regardless of what management style he chooses.

If the above view is accepted then the names of these two hexagrams are interchangeable without a loss of the original meaning. If the hexagram Bɪ ☷☵ uses the name Dᴀʏᴏᴜ, the new Dᴀʏᴏᴜ hexagram can be explained as follows: "The leader with yang character is surrounded by the members of his organization, who are soft, docile, and obedient." This new Dᴀʏᴏᴜ hexagram (the original hexagram Bɪ) indicates therefore a situation in which the resources of the organization are under the direction of a hard style leader as contrasted with a soft style leader as in the situation of the original hexagram Dᴀʏᴏᴜ ☲☰ .

GOVERNING BY INACTION

The hexagram Dᴀʏᴏᴜ also indicates the concept of **Laozi—Governing by Inaction** [*wuwei* 無為]. A leader can govern a country efficiently by non-interference, since people know what their interests are and what they should do. From an organizational point of view this suggests high decentralization. In this hexagram the only yin line—Fifth Yin—represents soft leadership which is supported by the capable people represented by the five yang lines. Since Fifth Yin is open-minded, flexible, balanced, and sincere, people are warm and respectful towards him. He becomes, as Confucius said, "a Polar Star encircled by all other stars."

15

謙
QIAN

The Earth–Mountain Hexagram

Modesty, Humility, Humbleness

IMAGE

Mountain under Earth indicates that the high mountain dwells under the lowly earth, symbolizing modesty or humility. This hexagram therefore suggests that a person in a high position should be modest and keep his true nature. A person who has true nature respects the power of objectivity or nature; he follows the truth and acts in a righteous way while retaining an open and unstructured attitude without fixed ideas. A modest person does not think of himself as being superior to others. However, modesty does not mean servility. A modest person does not undervalue himself as he knows when he should reveal his intelligence and ability appropriately. A modest person will find the right course between arrogance and servility.

Of the sixty-four hexagrams, QIAN [Modesty] is the only hexagram in which all six line statements receive a favorable commentary. A Chinese proverb says:

Haughtiness invites losses while modesty brings profits.

Lao Zi also said:

Superior character appears like a hollow.

The concept of modesty is deeply rooted in classic Chinese culture and it has been the most important quality of a chief government official for the past thousand years, as reflected by a Chinese proverb:

The belly of a chief government officer should be large enough to pole a boat.

Modesty as emphasized by the *Yijing* is also considered as one of the essential qualities of effective leadership. The concept of modesty includes **tolerance and open-mindedness**. A leader with a modest attitude will be the most willing to accept different opinions and suggestions raised by his colleagues or subordinates regarding the organizational structure and policy. **Modesty strengthens one's leadership.**

Hexagram Statement

If the superior man can remain modest all his life, he will have bright prospects.

An enlightened leader should not flaunt his achievements or his abilities. **Complacency is the beginning of failure**, in the same way as the sun begins to set after noon and the moon begins to wane after it is full. Complacency is the enemy of success. But **modesty must be from the inner heart and not hypocritical**. People respect a leader and are willing to follow him if his modesty is sincere.

Structure

This is a one-yang–five-yin hexagram in which Third Yang represents a person who has a strong (a yang line in a yang position) but modest character (a position in the lower trigram). Five yin lines are around a yang line, symbolizing a situation in which the members of an organization are inspired by this person's modesty and follow him. A yang line under three yin lines indicates that Third Yang is humble towards the three yin lines although it is stronger and more capable than them.

A yin line in the fifth position suggests that the leadership style of the organization tends to be soft and decentralized. The upper trigram Kun 坤 [Earth] indicates that the senior management of an organization should have a tolerance as broad as that of Earth. The decentralized management is inspired by the modest character of the senior executives as symbolized by the three yin lines of the upper trigram. In turn, this will have a positive effect on the attitude and behavior of the members of the organization. The relationship between upper and lower management will therefore become harmonious and steady as a mountain—the image of the lower trigram.

LINE STATEMENTS

Initial Yin ☷. Modesty gains help and support

A person who is extremely modest can successfully cross big rivers.

A modest leader should easily overcome barriers as he will find it easy to get help and support from the members of his organization. His modesty draws others' modesty to him and thereby will protect him from harm. Initial Yin at the lowest position of the hexagram symbolizes modesty.

Second Yin ☷. Outward modesty is acceptable

Outward modesty is auspicious.

If a leader shows his modesty outwardly in talk and deed, he will be auspicious. However, true modesty should come from a man's inner heart rather than his outward actions, for outward modesty could be an artificial one. But if a leader acts sincerely and in balance as indicated by the centrality of Second Yang, outward modesty can still be acceptable.

Third Yang ☶. Diligence yet modest wins respect

He is diligent yet modest. By keeping this way he will enjoy good fortune.

Third yang is the only yang line in the hexagram and plays the role of a master for all the yin lines including Fifth Yin. Third Yang represents a capable leader who gains the respect of his colleagues due to his diligence and modesty. He is a man of action and of words, his efforts will be recognized by the members of his organization in the end. The position of Third Yang can be seen as the "mental position" of a modest leader rather than his actual position in the organization.

Fourth Yin ☶. Keep modesty in full

Keeping modesty in full is beneficial in all cases.

Fourth Yin represents a senior executive in a position between the top leader (Fifth Yin) and a capable leader at middle level (Third Yang). Both of them are strong either in formal power (Fifth Yin) or informal influence (Third Yang). The executive in this position should be particularly cautious in handling delicate relationships with his superior and subordinate.

Fifth Yin ☷ **Gentleness followed by toughness**

He deals with the neighbors not on the basis of his wealth and power. However, if someone is disobedient and unmanageable, it is appropriate to defeat him with force.

A yin line in a yang position indicates a situation in which a leader in a yang position can obtain the trust and support of his colleagues by using yin measures or nonauthoritative influences and devices. If soft measures are not effective and workable, "hard" measures can be applied to achieve his objective as suggested by the use of "force" in the text.

Top Yin ☷ **Be not too modest**

When his outward modesty becomes a fault, it is beneficial to mobilize the army to overrun his own state.

A yin line in a yin position at the end of the hexagram indicates extreme modesty. If a leader is too modest, people may be skeptical as to his truthfulness. He should overcome himself by showing less humility. Moderate modesty is advisable. The text "it is beneficial to mobilize the army to overrun his own state" means using unyielding strength to overcome oneself. A truly modest person has the courage to get rid of his own inferiorities—falseness and artificialness.

SIMILARITIES AND DIFFERENCES BETWEEN LAOZI AND THE *YIJING*

Modesty is one of the important concepts in the philosophy of Laozi. According to Laozi, *dao* has the following meanings:

- Nonpossession
- Noncontention
- Contentment
- Standing at a low position
- Gentleness over strength

The above concepts are all related to modesty. Both Laozi and the *Yijing* believe that modesty is advantageous to individuals. Modesty is considered the highest virtue in Laozi's philosophy whereas in the *Yijing* it is seen as a tool for achieving a win–win or a harmonious situation. In Laozi's doctrine, modesty is yin in nature and is soft and passive. In the *Yijing* modesty is, however, not an independent element but one that contains also a yang element, as modesty can be used as a tool of achieving good relationships. According to Laozi, yin is superior to yang, but in the *Yijing* yin and yang are treated as a whole like a *taiji* that has both elements. This is the one coin with two sides' concept. The relationship between yin and yang are interdependent as they are mutually supportive. Neither yin or yang can exist alone.

THE IMAGE OF QIAN [MODESTY] IN OTHER HEXAGRAMS

The traditional approach for expressing the image of QIAN [Modesty] is based on the position of Mountain which is below that of Earth as shown in this hexagram. However, this concept is also implicitly revealed in other hexagrams, for example, LIN 臨 [Approaching] (19), TAI 泰 [Harmony] (11) and DAXU 大畜 [Great Accumulating] (26). In the hexagram LIN ☷☱ , the position of Lake is below that of Earth, in TAI ☷☰ Heaven is below Earth and in DAXU ☶☰ Heaven is below Mountain. Should the concept of modesty be focused on in these three hexagrams they can also be named Modesty as is this hexagram. Therefore, the traditional names of the hexagrams in the *Yijing* were given for one specific aspect, but not the only one. Different perspectives may give different names.

16

豫
YU

The Thunder–Earth Hexagram

Joy, Delight, Preparation, Contentment

IMAGE

The Thunder–Earth Hexagram has two different meanings: preparation and joy. These two names can be used interchangeably. From the point of view of the hexagram structure, the name preparation is more appropriate. But according to the commentaries on the lines the concept of joy is more emphasized. This indicates the special feature of the *Yijing* as the name of a hexagram can be interpreted differently in different aspects.

The upper trigram is ZHEN 震 [Thunder] which means action or movement. The lower trigram KUN 坤 [Earth] means providing the resources for an action. The Thunder–Earth Hexagram as a whole indicates a situation in which necessary preparation is needed for a future action. So an effective action as represented by the image of Thunder is much dependent on its preparations, as symbolized by the resources provided by Earth. The better the preparation, the better is the action, and vice versa. A leader must think ahead and prepare for all the needs of the planned action. The members of an organization will follow the planned action with enthusiasm. People are joyful when the action ends in success.

Earth also symbolizes obedience. When the members of an organization are obedient to their leader, it is advantageous to undertake the planned action. Earth can also be seen as the troops and Thunder as the orders of the general. The whole hexagram signifies obedience in following orders.

HEXAGRAM STATEMENT

In a time of pleasure and contentment, it is favorable for the king to establish feudal states and prepare to take action.

When the members of an organization are contented with their life they enthusiastically follow the leader's policy in preparing for actions to be taken. In a bad time it is difficult to do so. Peoples' obedience is closely related to their pleasure. They will follow what and who can please them. It is beneficial for a leader to mobilize his people at a time when they are contented.

STRUCTURE

Again this is a one-yang–five-yin hexagram. Fourth Yang is the key line of the hexagram for it is the source of energy of a movement. Three yin lines below the yang line symbolize their obedience to the person above. Fourth Yang is below Fifth Yang, indicating his close relationship with the top leader of the organization. However, it is difficult to judge whether such a close relationship with the top leader can really bring him an advantage, for a close relationship can also be unfavorable to him. **Everything can be looked from two sides**. If there is mutual respect and trust between the top leader and this senior executive then a harmonious relationship between the two is achievable. If there is not, an unfavorable relationship or tension could arise between the two.

LINE STATEMENTS

Initial Yin ☷. Boasting is harmful to teamwork

It is unfavorable to flaunt pleasure.

The interconnection of Initial Yin with Fourth Yang brings a union of yin and yang which is favorable to both. But the person in this low position (Initial Yang) should not flaunt his relationship with the superior Fourth Yang in a high position as indicated by the interconnection between the two. If he boasts about the superior he is connected with, he will alienate his colleagues. The gains from the relationship with his superior may not be fully compensated for by the loss of a harmonious relationship with his colleagues. His act is shallow, as boasting in public is harmful to teamwork. It turns joy into sorrow.

Second Yin ☷. Persevere in one's belief and vision

He is firm as a rock and will take action in a timely manner. He can receive good fortune through his persistence.

Perseverance is one of the important qualities of a leader and it should be strong like rock. He should maintain principles that are widely recognized and accepted by the community. He should not give up his principles easily even under pressure from different groups which are protecting their own interests. Also, he must not be carried away by other people's enthusiasm. He should rely on his own judgment as to whether the time is good or bad. However, persistence may make a leader stubborn; he needs to be flexible if required.

Third Yin ☷. Be self-reliant

He carries favor with one above for pleasure. This only brings regret. Late regret will have more regrets.

A yin line in a yin position symbolizes a weak executive who lacks independence and self-confidence. He is anxious to please his superior in the hope that he will get a cue for his actions. He also tries to please the people below him by adopting a rather loose leadership or management style. He will regret his cowardice for it will eventually damage the efficiency of his organization. If he cannot change his attitude and style early on he will also regret it. He should be self-reliant in the things he wants to do if he believes they are right.

Fourth Yang ☳. Inspire people to gather around by sincerity and capability

He is the source of joy and able to achieve great gains. His sincerity and capability attracts friends to gather around him.

Fourth Yang signifies a senior executive of an organization whose sincerity, capability, and strength (the characters of a yang line) can inspire trust in people. The three yin lines of the lower trigram Earth symbolize a crowd of followers who will join him when he takes an action (as indicated by the upper trigram Thunder). He will win the support and cooperation of the colleagues he needs to fulfill his aim.

Fifth Yin represents the top leader of an organization, who trusts the senior executive Fourth Yang and delegates him the adequate authority to fulfill his responsibilities. If Fourth Yang treats everyone equally with sincerity, he will win the respect of the colleagues and subordinates. While Fifth Yin is the formal leader of this organization, Fourth Yang can play the role of an informal leader.

Fifth Yin ☷ Decentralization doesn't necessarily mean a weak leadership

Although he is ailing, he is steadfast and does not die.

Fifth Yin represents a soft style leader as compared with the strong leadership of his assistant Fourth Yang. From the point of view of the power structure, Fifth Yin could lose his formal power to Fourth Yang and become a "weak leader." However, as long as Fourth Yang is capable and has no ambition to undermine the formal authority of Fifth Yin, a "weak leadership" can be considered an effective leadership under a decentralized policy. Fourth Yang offers his advice and services to Fifth Yin. What Fifth Yin should know is how to delegate his authority effectively to colleagues or subordinates.

Top Yin ☷ Do not indulge in pleasure

He indulges in pleasure. If he can change his ways, he will be free from blame.

If a leader indulges in pleasure over his success he is in danger, since too much pleasure will eventually ruin him. If he can change his direction in a timely way then there will be no fault. Top Yin in an improper position (a yang line in a yin position), which indicates misconduct in a successful leader. He should not be intoxicated with success.

17

SUI

The Lake–Thunder Hexagram

Following, Adaptation

IMAGE

Thunder within Lake symbolizes that the water in the lake is shaken by thunder to make big waves; waves hence follow the thunder. A leader should understand the principle of following. A leader should not blindly follow his subordinates for the sake of pleasing them in order to get their support and hence a harmonious relationship. This is a false definition of following. According to the *Yijing*, following should be based on the principle of whether to do so is right or not.

Since Thunder has the characteristic of dignity a leader should use this concept as the guiding principle for his act of following. A leader should know when and how to follow the people and not follow blindly. If a leader wants people to follow him, he must learn how to adapt to them first. A leader who can serve his people will gain returns from them.

HEXAGRAM STATEMENT

If a following is in the right way, it is favorable and there will be no blame.

People can follow a leader or a leader can follow the people. Everyone can be a leader in some ways and a follower in others. The main concern in following is whether the direction is right or not. Generally, people tend to follow a direction which they believe is the right one, but under special circumstances they could also blindly follow a wrong direction by impulse. The difference between the two directions is that the first will have a good prospect whereas the second will not.

STRUCTURE

This is a hexagram with an equal number of yin and yang lines. Between the upper and lower trigram there is a yin–yang union as indicated by the interconnection between Fifth Yang and Second Yin. Both lines are in a proper position. A yin–yang union creates harmony between the upper and lower trigrams. A relationship of mutual trust between the leader and those below him can be developed and mutual support is achievable.

A leader in the fifth position has the yang characteristics of activity, creativity, and strength, as does his major assistant Fourth Yang. If both superior and subordinate are the same type of person there will be both pros and cons. On the pro side they may have similar motivation, attitudes, and objectives. This provides a good basis for their cooperation because an active leader needs an active subordinate to match his style. But on the con side they may have confrontations when their views are divergent.

The leader can also get good support from subordinates as represented by Second Yin. Their expertise and skills can complement his. This will produce a yin–yang interaction which is advantageous to improvement of the relationship between the leader and the members of his organization.

LINE STATEMENTS

Initial Yang ☷. Adapt to a right direction

Following the change of time is auspicious. Obtaining relationships outside the gate is advantageous.

An executive must know when he should adapt to the change of time. A right adaptation to such a change is advantageous to the steady growth of an organization. He is advised to have a broader view when adapting to a change.

In a normal relationship between yin and yang, the former should follow the latter. But under special circumstances, yang following yin can be considered appropriate and favorable like the case between Initial Yang and Second Yin. Initial Yang represents a capable man who is under a weak leader Second Yin (a yin line) and he may feel unhappy in following his superior although he has to do so. When there is such a need for cooperation between the members of an organization for the benefit of the whole, the capable subordinate will follow the weak and incapable superior.

The second interpretation of this line statement is positive. Initial Yang represents a capable executive who is willing to listen to other people's opinions and will change his own position if he realizes he is wrong. Following Second Yin indicates his openness and willingness to associate with others. This is why the text says "relationships obtained outside the gate are advantageous." The "gate" here means one's own position.

Second Yin ☷. Do not lose a large gain because of trifling considerations

If he clings to the young man, he will lose the able man.

The "young man" in the text refers to Third Yin and the "able man" means Initial Yang, as yang represents "senior" or "strong" and yin stands for "young" and "weak." A leader should be careful in choosing his business partners. If he is closer to the new client (Third Yin) he may lose the connection with his old client (Initial Yang) and vice versa—he will not get the new client if he keeps the relationship only with his old client.

Second Yin is in the middle position of the lower trigram. It implies that the leader should apply the principle of centrality to achieve a balance in the relationship between the two business partners. An over-emphasis on one relationship may result in losing the other, although this may not matter if the gains from the former are obvious more than that of the latter.

Third Yin ☷. Choose the right partner

He clings to the able man and loses the young man. Following this way, he obtains what he seeks. It is beneficial to remain correct.

Like the text of the second line, the "able man" here refers to Fourth Yang and the "young man" the Second Yin. If a leader purposely develops a relationship with a business partner who has good prospects (Fourth Yang) and gives up the less promising one (Second Yin), he will get what he wants. However, he should act in a right way. Otherwise, he is advised to stay where he is.

Fourth Yang ☳ Follow the superior with faithfulness and respect

He is followed by others and may have misfortunes. But if he keeps his sincerity, he will not be blamed.

Fourth Yang represents a senior executive who is close to the top leader Fifth Yang. If other people as represented by Third Yin and Second Yin are willing to follow him more than his superior Fifth Yang—the top leader of the organization, Fourth Yang will be in a dangerous position if his superior is not an open-minded person. However, if he sincerely follows his superior Fifth Yang with high respect, he will be free of blame.

Fifth Yang ☳ Follow what is good

Follow what is good, there will be good fortune.

If the leader of an organization follows what is good, the good people will follow him too. For example, he will delegate authority only to those subordinates who are very capable and he will also accept good advice from other members of the organization. His qualities are indicated by the nature of Fifth Yang as sincerity, balance, and uprightness.

Top Yin ☳ Mutual trust based on sincerity and faithfulness

He sincerely follows the king as if he is bound up with him. The king asks him to make sacrifices on Western Mountain.

Top Yin represents a capable man who is, for example, the adviser to the leader Fifth Yang. As he is loyal and sincere to the leader, the leader in return also trusts him by giving him an honor. The hexagram statement indicates the importance of mutual trust between superior and subordinate in a time of following.

18

GU

The Mountain–Wind Hexagram

Decay, Degeneration, Renovation

IMAGE

Mountain above Wind or Wind below Mountain symbolizes wind blowing on the lower side of the mountain, resulting in two possible situations:

Situation I:
The wind blows on the lower side of the mountain and spoils the vegetation there.

Situation II:
Since the wind does not blow on the upper side of the mountain, the vegetation there degenerates.

In both situations vegetation is devastated or degenerated. In the first situation, the root of decay is at the lower level of the mountain whereas in the second situation it is at the upper level of the mountain. Both situations can be found in the human organizations. Decay in an organization can start either from a lower level or a higher level. In both cases, the organization suffers from rottenness, inefficiency, and disorder.

The Chinese character *gu* 蠱 means that food rots in an urn and is infested with worms. Similarly, an organization that has not changed its degenerating structure and system for some time will gradually be eroded by its own rigidity, just as worms breed in a plate.

The upper trigram GEN 艮 [Mountain] symbolizes stillness and the lower trigram XUN 巽 [Wind] represents softness. The Mountain–Wind Hexagram as a whole can therefore be interpreted as a situation in which an organization fails to change like a mountain remains still, and its members just accept the fact without any resistance. **The degeneration of an organization is caused by its own stagnation.**

Wind can also be seen as wood or tree in this hexagram. If degeneration is at either the lower or higher part of the mountain, the trees will not grow on either side. Action is needed to cure the decay.

HEXAGRAM STATEMENT

Like crossing a great river, to cure decay is difficult but favorable. Well-prepared plans are required before and after the reform.

To reform and to remedy decay in an organization, it is of vital importance for the leader to choose the right time to do so. An early action may not be effective if the necessary preparations have not been made. A late action may not be effective either since the problem may have become deeper and resulted in more difficulties, whereby it becomes harder to resolve.

A situation of decay in an organization should not only be considered "bad." It can also be seen as "good" for the organization. According to the law of reversion or cyclical change, a bad time will be followed by a good time. In decay, people will take corresponding action to remove the roots of corruption in the organization. Once the worst situation is overcome, the way to prosperity is then opened. Decay and prosperity are opposite. **Without decay there is no prosperity and vice versa.** So in the reverse perspective, decay should not necessarily be seen as unfavorable.

STRUCTURE

The structure of the Mountain–Wind Hexagram symbolizes a soft style of management or leadership in an organization, as indicated by the interconnection of Fifth Yin and Second Yang. A soft style of leadership can be seen as positive or negative depending on whether it is used in a proper time and place. As a practice, a hard style of management seems to be more effective for a situation of decay or degeneration.

If the leader adopts a hard style of management as indicated by a yang line in the fifth position—Fifth Yang—the original Mountain–Wind Hexagram is changed to the hexagram XUN 巽 [Double Wind] (57) ☴. In this Double Wind Hexagram, there are four yang lines and two yin lines. In both the outer and inner trigram the yin line is below the yang line, indicating a hard leadership after reorganization. This will be elaborated in more detail in the hexagram Xᴜɴ.

LINE STATEMENTS

Initial Yin ☷. Correct the mistakes made by the predecessor or superior

The son corrects what has been mishandled by his father without difficulties.
Although there are problems, things will work out well in the end.

If an executive can carefully clear up the mistakes made by his predecessor or his superior without putting blame on either of them, things will turn out well in the end. However, he should be alert when he is making changes for there may be some danger or resistance involved in these changes. Initial Yin at the low position of the hexagram symbolizes that the decay is still in an early stage and should be addressed now before it spreads.

Second Yang ☵. Correct the mistakes in moderation

The son corrects what has been mishandled by his mother. He should not use rigid and direct measures.

The interconnection between Fifth Yin and Second Yang is like the relationship between mother and son. When an executive (Second Yang) deals with the problems caused by his superior (Fifth Yin) he should use a moderate approach (the second line is in a central and yin position) instead of a rash and hard one. He should deal with the situation in a gentle manner in order to avoid any adverse effect on morale and the stability of the organization.

Third Yang ☶. Use hard measures in limit

The son corrects the wrong things caused by his father. There is a little regret but no mistakes.

If the executive use a hard approach (a yang line in a yang position) to correct the mistakes made by his predecessor, he may face resistance and frustration. But if he does not lose his courage and does not push things too far, he will do it well and the problems will be smoothed out. A leader in a strong position like Third Yang is advised to use the tough measures in a time of decay even though there is a little regret.

Fourth Yin ☷ Do not tolerate the mistakes

If the son tolerates the mistakes made by his father without making corrections, he will regret it.

If the executive is weak (a yin line in a yin position) and indecisive he may not take the appropriate actions to correct the mistakes made by his predecessor. Over a period of time, his weakness and indecision will cause the situation to deteriorate.

Fifth Yin ☷ Use a balanced approach

The son who uses the appropriate measures to remedy his father's mistakes will get praise.

The new leader Fifth Yin will use a balanced approach (a yin line in a yang and central position) to remedy the mistakes of his predecessor. Unlike the hard approach used by Third Yang and the soft approach by Fourth Yin, Fifth Yin uses the right approach to tackle the problems. The interconnection between Fifth Yin and Second Yang symbolizes the delegation of authority by the former to the latter so that the strong and capable people can help the leader to make the necessary reforms in the organization. The new leader is therefore considered as a good successor and wins a good reputation.

Top Yang ☷ Have a high purpose

He doesn't work for the king or his lords, for he sets himself a higher purpose.

A leader deals with the problem of decay in his organization not because of ambition, status, or money. He is primarily concerned with a higher purpose of his own, namely "serving the organization." Top Yang at the end of the hexagram symbolizes the stage in which the problem of decay is solved. There are some people who have made their contributions to the reorganization or reengineering but they do not seek the corresponding rewards.

19

LIN

The Earth–Lake Hexagram

Approaching, Overseeing

IMAGE

Earth over Lake symbolizes the relationship between a leader in a high position and the people below. Earth borders upon Lake from above, indicating the situation in which a leader approaches the members of his organization. Earth is the land with the characteristics of tolerance and generosity, which signify leadership qualities. Lake has water that represents the people. The relationship between Land and Water is as intimate as that between the leader and his people. The land provides the lake a place to accommodate water. A leader should know how to approach the members of his organization in a right way.

The Earth–Lake Hexagram is named Approaching since it indicates a situation in which the superior superintends the subordinates by using a proper approach. In this hexagram a soft approach is suggested by the three yin lines of the upper trigram.

HEXAGRAM STATEMENT

Approaching is the right way to be auspicious. There will be misfortune in the eighth month.

If a leader is willing to approach those under him, this will narrow the gap between those above and those below and will therefore increase communication and interconnection in an organization. Through approaching, a leader is in a better position to know what people think about the operations and problems of the organization and so can make timely and appropriate corrections. As a result, the team spirit and the efficiency of the organization can be increased by a large extent.

The text "there will be misfortune in the eighth month" means yin will be on the rise and yang on the fall; here yin refers to the negative factors and yang the positive factors. The text gives a warning that one should not only look at the positive side of an action and ignore its negative impact, which may occur as time goes on.

STRUCTURE

This is a hexagram with four yin and two yang lines. The two yang lines are at the lower position of the hexagram, representing the leader's humility towards the members of his organization. Yang symbolizes "big" and "high" whereas yin stands for "small" and "low." In this hexagram, **the two yang lines at the lower position represent the open-minded mentality of the leader towards those below him** as the situation indicated by the hexamgram TAI 泰 [Harmony] (11) ䷊ illustrated earlier. Yang lines below the yin lines can be interpreted as the modest mentality of a leader rather than his formal and authoritative position in the organization (or in the hexagram).

The two yang lines indicate that the yang energy is moving upward, providing favorable conditions for the leader to take action to benefit his people. However, this action could face resistance from people who are in disagreement with it. To overcome this resistance there is a need for understanding and cooperation between the leader and those below, as suggested by the interconnection between Second Yang and Fifth Yin. To do this the leader needs to be skilled in persuasion.

LINE STATEMENTS

Initial Yang ䷒. Approach through integrity

He approaches with integrity and will have good fortune.

If a leader can maintain his relationship with the members of the organization based on his integrity (sincerity, honesty, and fairness) rather than his formal authority, he will be able to gain high respect from them. The interconnection between Initial Yang and Fourth Yin indicates that yang can influence yin by its virtue.

Second Yang ☷. Approach with integrity

He approaches with integrity. Nothing will be unfavorable.

A leader approaches people with integrity by emphasizing particularly the principle of centrality as indicated by the central position of the yang line in the lower trigram. His act is advantageous. Second Yang in a central position with balance and uprightness interconnects with Fifth Yin, which has similar characteristics. This interaction is auspicious.

Third Yin ☷. Do not use sweet words for the purpose of approach

He approaches with sweet-sounding words but will have no benefit. If he is concerned about this, he will be free from blame.

A leader who uses an improper approach in order to interact with the members of his organization will not benefit. The yin line in a yang position indicates that the approach used is not a proper one.

Fourth Yin ☷. Approach with intimacy

He approaches people with intimacy. There will be no mistakes.

A leader approaches the people below him through interaction, as indicated by Fourth Yin with Initial Yang. A yin–yang union produces harmony in which the leader knows how to employ capable people to the best advantage.

Fifth Yin ☷. Rule with wisdom

He rules with wisdom like a great leader. He will have good fortune.

If a leader can use his wisdom to attract capable people to his organization and gives them freedom to do their best, this will be auspicious. Fifth Yin is a position which is characterized by balance, uprightness, and a soft leadership style.

Top Yin ☷. Rule by tolerance and generosity

He rules with tolerance, generosity, and honesty. He will have good fortune.

As the upper trigram Earth of this hexagram symbolizes tolerance, generosity, and honesty, Top Yin at the extreme of the upper trigram indicates that a leader should possess such qualities in his relationships with people. A generous and open-hearted approach will lead to good fortune.

20

GUAN

The Wind–Earth Hexagram

Observing, Viewing

IMAGE

Wind moves above Earth, symbolizing a situation of observing. When a leader of an organization reviews or examines the operations of the departments under him, his action is one of observation. The purpose of observation is to find out what has been done right or wrong in the past so that he can make timely corrections as needed.

Wind signifies the policy of the leader and the earth the people under him. These people follow the leader's policy. **Confucius** said: **"The ruler is like the wind, the common people are like the grass. Whichever way the wind blows, the grass cannot help but bend."**

The leader's policy is like the wind which can make people follow his direction. It is therefore necessary for the leader to constantly review the impact of his policy on the whole organization to see whether it is effective or not.

The hexagram can be seen as a picture of a tower with the yin lines representing the supports and the two yang lines the platform. At the top of the tower one can have a wide view of the surrounding area, indicating that a leader should constantly oversee the changes in both the external environment and the internal situation in his organization. This will give him an understanding of what has happened and he can make timely and appropriate adaptations.

HEXAGRAM STATEMENT

The king washes his hands before making an offer, his dignified appearance and manner inspire confidence in those below.

Since a leader's conduct can inspire or influence the people below him, he should set a good example by acting in a proper way. People will respect him for his dignity. The text "washing hands" here symbolizes that one's act is a clean one.

STRUCTURE

Like the hexagram LIN 臨 [Approaching] (19), GUAN also has a structure with four yin and two yang lines. The difference between the two hexagrams is the position of the two yang lines. In the hexagram LIN, the two yang lines are in the lower trigram and the four yin lines in the upper trigram, indicating a decentralized management style in the organization as the leaders (Fifth Yin and Top Yang) are willing to delegate their authority to the people below them (the four yin lines). The hexagram GUAN indicates a centralized management under which the leader Fifth Yang and his senior assistant Fourth Yang are active and capable; the people under them just follow their orders or policies.

LINE STATEMENTS

Initial Yin ☷. Do not observe things like a child

An ordinary man who observes things like a child is not blamable, but it is regrettable for a superior man.

A leader should not look at things like an ordinary man who has a shallow view; instead he must look deeper and wider within himself. A leader with a deeper and wider perspective will have a better understanding of the strengths and weaknesses of his organization as well as a long-term vision. Initial Yin is weak and far from Fifth Yang, symbolizing a man who is incapable and lacks vision.

Second Yin ☷. Do not observe things with a narrow view

Peeping out from a door is advantageous only to a woman.

In the traditional Chinese perspective, a woman has a soft and passive character (as represented by the yin line here) whereas a man is considered strong and active. A leader's outlook should be deeper and wider like that of a man instead of "narrow" and "shallow" like that of a woman. However, here the term "woman" refers to the characteristics of a person rather than their physical sex, as the word "woman" is identical with "yin." The line text suggests that a leader should have a yang character instead of a yin one when observing the things. An interconnection between Second Yin and Fifth Yang suggests that through interaction people of different backgrounds can broaden their minds.

Third Yin ☷· Observe the situation before taking an action

He examines his life in order to decide whether to advance or retreat.

Third Yin is in a position that is at the top of the lower trigram. A leader in this position must decide whether he should move forward or stay where he is. Observing the current situation before making a future move is necessary. He needs to be objective and careful in evaluating his situation in order to make the best choice.

Fourth Yin ☴· Know more about the leader

He observes the glory of the state; it is favorable for him to become a guest of the king.

A senior executive like Fourth Yin is in a good position to learn about the top leader: his vision, values, attitude, and behavior. If he has a good knowledge of the top leader he can better serve the organization. In the text "the state" means "the king."

Fifth Yang ☴· Need a self-audit

A superior man who will examine his own conduct is blameless.

A leader must constantly review his own conduct and see whether he has ever violated the regulations of the organization or the ethical principles and the rules he has set. **A self-audit is necessary for effective leadership**. The qualities of the noble position Fifth Yang, for example, sincerity, balance, and uprightness, can serve as the basis for such a self-audit.

Top Yang ☴· Need advice from an enlightened person

An enlightened person watches what the noble man does, the noble man is auspicious.

Top Yang represents an enlightened person who has an honorary or a high position in the organization such as an adviser, a nonexecutive director, or a retired senior executive. This person is much concerned with the actions of the leader Fifth Yang and is willing to offer his services to assist the top leader.

21

噬 嗑
SHIHE

The Fire–Thunder Hexagram

Biting Through

IMAGE

Fire over Thunder is the image of the hexagram SHIHE. Since fire produces lightning, the image of this hexagram is like thunder and lightning in a storm. Thunder symbolizes sternness or law (enforcement) and lightning means understanding. The hexagram indicates that when one understands the consequences (punishments) he will incur if he violates the law, he will act properly. The hexagram emphasizes **the importance of law as guidance for one's conduct**. One has to think twice before doing something that might violate the law or the regulations of an organization.

The Fire–Thunder Hexagram also portrays a man who is biting food. The two yang lines at the top and the bottom of the hexagram represent the upper and lower jaws of a man, with the three yin lines as teeth. The yang line in the fourth place stands for an obstruction in the mouth. To remove or to bite through the food (obstruction) in the mouth, it is necessary to close the jaws. By the same token, **the leader of an organization should have strong determination and take decisive action to break through obstacles in order to achieve cohesive union or harmony**.

From a macro point of view, the lightning of the upper trigram symbolizes **understanding**. Before a person acts on something he should first understand whether it is within the law. The **law** as symbolized by Thunder of the lower trigram provides **the basis of the order of a harmonious society** as represented by the lightning of the upper trigram. Rule by law will be favorable to the order of a society.

Since the lower trigram Thunder also symbolizes an action, the hexagram advises that an action should be based on understanding as understanding gives clarity to an action. Therefore, understanding should always come first. **A rational action is based on understanding whereas an irrational action is not.**

HEXAGRAM STATEMENT

Biting through is like the use of force in criminal punishment. It is auspicious.

Biting through a thing in the mouth is like establishing law and order in an organization in order to remove the obstruction within it. The act is considered beneficial and favorable.

STRUCTURE

This is a hexagram with three yin and three yang lines. Two of the yang lines are located at the top and the bottom of the hexagram and the three yin lines are between them. The third yang line separates these three yin lines into two parts. The two yin lines of the lower trigram are surrounded by two yang lines and the one yin line of the upper trigram is also encircled by two yang lines. The structure of the hexagram therefore indicates that hardness is in a favorable position to that of softness, symbolizing the power of law over the influence of evil.

The nuclear or hidden hexagram of this hexagram is JIAN 蹇 [Obstacles] (39) ☶. This indicates that difficulties are not avoidable even in an environment of law enforcement.

LINE STATEMENTS

While the hexagram indicates the relationship between law and order, the six line statements are primarily concerned with different approaches to punishment under criminal proceedings.

Initial Yang ☳. A mild punishment for minor mistakes as an educational tool

His feet are locked in a wooden stock. There will be no mistakes.

When a person's feet are locked up, he cannot move. This is a mild punishment. A leader of an organization is advised to give a mild punishment to a subordinate who has made a mistake for the first time. In some cases, education is a positive approach and more meaningful than a negative approach—punishment. Initial Yang symbolizes a mild punishment for minor mistakes.

Second Yin ☲. Use strict and just measures to remove the obstacles

He bites off the soft meat so deep that his nose is covered.

A leader uses severe but fair measures (the principle of centrality) to remove the obstacles in his organization. In dealing with an intractable person, the use of strict punishment is justified as long as it is balanced and correct. Second Yin is in the middle position of the lower trigram, signifying that a punishment should be fair and appropriate to the respective crime.

Third Yin ☳. Resentment and resistance may arise in biting through obstructions

He bites off dried meat and is poisoned. There is a little shame, but no blame.

When a leader is biting through obstructions in his organization, he may face resentment and resistance from the members of the organization as they defend or protect their own interests if they are affected by the new policy. However, if the actions are taken in a just way, people who are adversely affected or punished will have no complaints. Third Yin is in an improper position: when advising a punishment one must be as fair as possible.

Fourth Yang ☳. Need strength and persistence

Biting on dried meat with bones, he obtains a metal arrow.
Recognizing where the difficulties are, he persists in his direction.
There will be a good future.

When a leader wants to overcome the difficulties in his organization, he needs strength like a metal arrow and to persist in his principles. The term "a metal arrow" represents a man's characteristics of strength and uprightness.

Fifth Yin ䷜ Need a combination of toughness and gentleness

He bites off dried meat and gets yellow gold. If he is steadfast in danger, there will be no fault.

A leader should solve his problems by using the principle of centrality as indicated by the "yellow gold." In the Chinese perspective, yellow is in the middle of the five basic colors (red, blue, yellow, white, and black), symbolizing justice and honesty. On the other hand, gold represents hardness and strength. "Yellow gold" therefore stands for a yin–yang combination that suggests the leader should combine toughness (yang) and gentleness (yin) in dealing with the problems in his organization. Although Fifth Yin is in a noble or leading position, it is somehow soft or weak. Therefore, the text suggests that there is a need for a combination of toughness and gentleness.

Top Yang ䷜ Listen to others

He wears a heavy cangue which covers his ears. There will be misfortune.

When a leader in a top position does not listen to the advice of his colleagues or subordinates, there will be misfortune. He is a prisoner of his own arrogance. The term "a heavy cangue" means a heavy punishment which is used for a prisoner who has committed a severe crime. "A heavy cangue covers his ears" means that a man cannot listen to others as if he were a deaf.

22

The Mountain–Fire Hexagram

Adorning

IMAGE

Mountain over Fire or Fire below Mountain gives the hexagram BI. Fire below Mountain beautifies the latter; it suggests a function of adornment. Any organization needs a certain adornment for the purpose of establishing or improving its public image. In business firms, public relations is generally used for this purpose and advertising for the image of the product. Through adornment a simple thing can be changed into a "new" thing with a special image. A person can also be adorned in his appearance, manner, and speaking methods. However, overadornment may have an adverse effect.

The second interpretation of this hexagram is based on the nature of Mountain and Fire. As Mountain symbolizes steadiness or stability and Fire stands for understanding, Fire below Mountain indicates a situation where an understanding of people is the foundation of a stable organization.

HEXAGRAM STATEMENT

Adorning is beneficial for development if it is on an appropriate scale.

Like a person, an organization also needs adornment to create a favorable image but it should not exceed the appropriate scale. As stated above, overadornment would result in an adverse effect. This concept is another expression of the principle of centrality or moderation. Substance and adornment (appearance) are complementary in nature. Substance without adornment makes a thing simple but unattractive. Adornment without substance is like flower which does not bear fruit. Being merely impressive in appearance is considered exaggerated and unreliable. A balance between substance and adornment is achievable through adornment on the appropriate scale—neither excessive nor inadequate.

STRUCTURE

A Comparison of Two Similar Hexagrams

Like the previous hexagrams SHIHE 噬嗑 [Biting Through] (21) ☲☳, BI is another hexagram of three yin and three yang lines. Thus the line structures of these two hexagrams are quite similar. The only difference in their structure is the position of the yang line ☰ between the upper and lower trigrams. Third Yang is located at the fourth position of SHIHE whereas it is at the third place of BI.

Hexagram Name and Structure

In fact the name of these two hexagrams can be interchanged. If the hexagram Adorning [BI] is renamed Gnawing or Biting Through [SHIHE], its image can still be remain a man who is biting food. Similarly, if the name of the hexagram Biting Through is changed to Adorning, Fire above thunder can also be interpreted as "an action (Thunder) for adornment must be clearly defined and understood (Fire) by the people who assume responsibility."

Among the sixty-four hexagrams, only the two hexagrams Biting Through and Adorning have a situation in which three yin lines are separated by three yang lines into two parts and the yang forces are able to control the yin forces completely. If this argument is accepted, the hexagram Adorning can be renamed as Control in order to reflect the situation indicated above.

This argument indicates that the name of a hexagram in the *Yijing* can be changed if the interpretation of the hexagram structure is different. The name of a hexagram in the *Yijing* is therefore not immutable; it is changeable depending on what basis of interpretation is used.

LINE STATEMENTS

Initial Yang ☲. Adorn simply

He adorns his toes. He abandons the carriage and walks.

If adornment is necessary for a leader, he is advised to adorn himself in a simple or plain way instead of a beautiful or exaggerated one. The text "he abandons the carriage and walks" is a way of indicating his simplicity. The low position of Initial Yang suggests a low profile in adornment.

Second Yin ☷. Adorn properly

He adorns his beard.

If a leader needs adornment he can follow the proper ways taken by others. A person in the position of Second Yang has the characteristics of docility and will follow Third Yang, which represents hardness and real substance. A beard is an adornment but it cannot exist without substance. Adornment emphasizes the outward appearance whereas substance focuses on inward qualities. Whether an adornment is considered good or not is much dependent on the real substance.

Third Yang ☶. Do not cover up the essence with adornment

An adornment is fortunate only if the right way can be kept constantly.

Overadornment can damage the real substance. A wise leader should not cover up the essence with adornment. An adornment with elegance is advantageous. Third Yang stands in the middle of two yin lines (Second Yin and Fourth Yin), symbolizing a dangerous position. A leader is advised to keep adornment on a proper scale, neither excessive nor inadequate. Sacrificing substance for shadow is an unbalanced and unwise act.

Fourth Yin ☷ Return to simplicity

He adorns himself in white as a soaring white horse.

The white color symbolizes simplicity. A leader can adorn himself or his organization in simplicity. "A soaring white horse" means truth, which should be the basis for the relationship between the senior executive Fourth Yin and his subordinate Initial Yang. Superficial beauty cannot last long. Returning to the path of simplicity is one of the important principles that a leader should master. The interconnection between

Fourth Yin and Initial Yang indicates that both share the same value of simple adornment.

Fifth Yin ☷ Simplicity instead of splendor

His adornment is simple like the garden on suburban hill.
He receives a gift of small roll of silk though it looks miserly.
It seems to be regret, but there will be good fortune in the end.

"The garden on a suburban hill" represents a place of simplicity whereas a "city" stands for a splendid place. A leader is advised to pay attention to simplicity rather than splendor in his adornment. For the purpose of establishing a relationship with people, the leader needs to present a gift of small value but with immense thoughtfulness behind it.

Top Yang ☷ A plain simplicity is the best adornment

He adorns with white, there will be no mistakes.

If a leader can make a plain and simple adornment of his organization, there will be no fault. An extreme adornment can lose the basic reality of the organization. Top Yang is at the extreme of the Hexagram Adornment, indicating that it is the right time to return to simplicity or substance.

23

 剝 BO

The Mountain–Earth Hexagram

Stripping, Peeling

IMAGE

The Traditional View

Mountain above Earth indicates that the former adjoins the latter. The hexagram gives the image that the mountain is gradually stripped away by the earth. If this stripping continues, the mountain will eventually become steepened and narrow as in a "big mountain." Lacking a broad base, the mountain will topple over. This portrays the dependence of the mountain on the earth. If the mountain represents the government of a country and the earth stands for the people, the government could collapse due to the increased discontent of the people about its inefficient administration and policy.

Similarly a leader could also face pressure from colleagues or members of his organization as reflected by the five yin lines moving upward to the top position of the hexagram. These five yin lines represent forces opposing the leader or the senior management. The leader should be aware of this danger and prepare corresponding measures for dealing with this situation.

The Opposite View

The hexagram Bo can also be interpreted in an opposite way. The single yang line of the top position of the hexagram (Top Yang) symbolizes a person or a group of persons who have the ultimate authority in making the main decisions in an organization; the leader and his followers at the senior level can be named as an "**authority group**." The five yin lines represent the people below the "authority group." Normally they are obedient to this "authority group" and they can be named the **"receptive group**." The hexagram indicates an image of the dependence of the "receptive group" on the "authority group" rather than an inverse relationship between the two groups as seen in the traditional view.

Another interpretation of this hexagram is based on **Laozi's doctrine—rule by inaction**. The top line symbolizes a top leader who delegates adequate authority to the subordinates below him as represented by the five yin lines. The leadership style in this organization tends to be of a decentralized type rather than a centralized one.

In the opposite view, the hexagram Bo can be interpreted differently from the traditional way. Unlike the traditional interpretation, Mountain in the hexagram is not seen as stripped away by the yin lines. On the contrary, the top line symbolizes a leader who is able to control the whole organization and hence able to maintain his top position even though there are pressures from below. This top leader will be a person with the characteristics of balance, fairness, open-mindedness, tolerance, and uprightness. These qualities make him a man of charisma and attract people to follow him voluntarily. The situation is stable and harmonious. On the other hand, if the top leader is authoritative and backed up by the formal power, people are forced to follow him with no alternative. This situation is, however, unstable and disharmonious.

HEXAGRAM STATEMENT

Bo signifies stripping of yang. When yang is stripped away by yin, it is not favorable to take any action.

When an unfavorable trend is identified a leader must accept it, for any struggle against it would be pointless. The appropriate act for the leader in this situation is to remain calm and patient. As everything has a beginning and an end, the difficult time will pass and spring will again return.

STRUCTURE

Among the six lines there is only one interconnection between yin and yang, namely Top Yang and Third Yin, indicating that the top leader Top Yang does have support of part of the people as represented by Third Yin in the organization (indicated by their interconnection) despite the pressure imposed on him from the other part. The forces opposed to the leader are obviously divided and therefore weakened.

LINE STATEMENTS

Initial Yin ☶☷. Pay attention to the signs early

The legs of the bed are stripped away; the bed loses its foundation. Neglecting this will be misfortune.

The hexagram BI is a gradual development the position of Initial Yin is just the beginning of this process. If a leader is weak and unrighteous, people will begin to be less cooperative in responding to his policy. As a consequence his situation is dangerous, as if he were lying on a bed with destroyed legs. When the resignations of capable people in an organization increase, the senior management needs to find out the main reasons for this and adopt the right remedies as quickly as possible.

Second Yin ☷. The opposite forces are increasing

The frame of the bed is stripped away. Persistence on present position brings misfortune.

When people begin to criticize an organization with respect to its operations, structure, and policy, the leader of this organization should not simply ignore these views but should actively investigate the causes and make timely and corresponding corrections. An obstinate leader will insist that there is nothing wrong with the present management and will not abandon his position but keep the status quo. Through acting in this way the organization will further deteriorate and the opposing force will gain strength. Among the people of the opposite group as indicated by the five yin lines, some are rather moderate, as represented by Second Yin, but under the pressure of other members they have to follow the same path for solidarity.

Third Yin ☶. Do not stand on the wrong side

There will be no blame even through in a time of stripping.

A person in the position of Third Yin has to make a decision as to which group he wants to join: a "yin" group as represented by the five yin lines or a "yang" group as represented by Top Yang. If he chooses the "yang" group and keeps as far away as possible from the "yin" group, he will be auspicious. The interconnection between Third Yin and Top Yang provides this opportunity.

Fourth Yin ☶ **The opposing forces are approaching**

Stripping a man in the bed to the skin is not fortunate.

When stripping gradually has reached the skin of a man who is in the bed, the situation is becoming more serious, for it means yang has been stripped away by yin. In an organization, the opposing forces increase to a higher level and will soon affect the senior management. When danger is approaching the leader needs to be cautious and should prepare corresponding measures.

Fifth Yin ☶ **To capture a group of bandits, it is necessary to capture the ringleader first**

The court lady leads her maids-in-waiting like a string of fish to wait for the king's favor. There is no misfortune.

Fifth Yin represents the chief of the opposite forces (among five yin lines). If the leader of an organization (Top Yang) is able to get the chief of the opposite group Fifth Yin to stand on his side, he will be out of danger.

Top Yang ☶ **The evil will not triumph over the good**

The largest fruit is not eaten. The superior man gets a carriage while the inferior man is stripped of his shelter.

The yang line at the top symbolizes the seed of good. The largest fruit falls down to the ground because of stripping and the good sprouts again. The superior man will regain his influence and the support of the members of his organization as if he has received a carriage. However, the inferior man will lose his "shelter" because the actions taken by the inferior man against the superior man will eventually destroy him. He will suffer the consequences of his own actions.

Yang represents good and yin evil. Since there is an interdependent relationship between yin and yang, a destruction of yang (good) will inevitably destroy yin (evil) too. When yin rises, yang falls and vice versa, yin falls when yang rises. Cyclical change is the natural order. The negative forces in an organization can only replace the positive forces for a certain time, but the positive forces will eventually return if the leader is able to maintain the right direction.

Top Yang represents a man of virtue and the five yins the ordinary people. This is a situation as illustrated by the Chinese proverb: **"a crane stands among chickens for surpassing the others,"** or the leader stands head and shoulders over others.

24

 The Earth–Thunder Hexagram

Returning

IMAGE

Thunder inside Earth symbolizes the beginning of a movement. When yin rises to its extreme as indicated by the situation of the hexagram KUN 坤 [Earth] (2) ☷☷, the turning point comes. Yang that is banished by yin now begins its return in the yin–yang cycle. The yin–yang cycle can be illustrated by the changes in the yin and yang lines of seven hexagrams as stated below:

GOU 姤	**DUN** 遯	**PI** 否	**GUAN** 觀	**BO** 剝	**KUN** 坤	**FU** 復
[Meeting]	[Retreating]	[Obstruction]	[Observing]	[Stripping]	[Earth]	[Returning]

Moving from the hexagram GOU to the hexagram KUN [Earth] illustrates a rise of the yin lines in six hexagrams, and the yang line returns in the seventh hexagram FU. The yin lines increase (the yang lines decrease) from the hexagram GOU to the hexagram KUN [Earth] and the yang lines begin to rise (the yin lines fall) in the hexagram FU and ends at the hexagram QIAN. The yin lines rise across six different hexagrams and begin to vanish as the yang line returns. The rest five hexagrams of the yin–yang cycle are the following:

LIN 臨	**TAI** 泰	**DAZHUANG** 大壯	**KUAI** 夬	**QIAN** 乾
[Approaching]	[Harmony]	[Great Strength]	[Determination]	[Heaven]

The lower trigram Thunder of the hexagram Fu symbolizes drive and movement whereas the upper trigram Earth stands for vastness and depth. The Earth–Thunder Hexagram indicates that the yang force is so strong that it can expand. Consequently the yin (evil) force will be driven out completely by the yang force at the end of its recovery. The hexagram Fu indicates **the return of the yang force in the initial stage of recovery**.

Hexagram Statement

The hexagram Fu signifies the return of yang that is favorable.
He goes out and comes back without affliction. Friends will come, so
there is no fault. Forth and back are in the proper way.
In seven days the yang returns. It is favorable to advance.

After a period of stagnation, the period of recovery in a yin–yang cycle begins. The tide is now turning. Light comes again after the darkness. Cyclical change is a phenomenon found in the nature but also found in the lives of people. The leader of an organization must understand it and be able to anticipate the turning point of this cycle, making timely and appropriate adaptations to the upward or downward trend. In an upward movement, it is beneficial to take action to benefit from expansionary development. The term "seven days" symbolizes a complete time period or a cycle. As stated above, there are seven hexagrams from the hexagram Gou to the hexagram Fu, indicating a cyclical change in nature or human life.

Structure

In this hexagram the only yang line is located at the bottom. From a traditional point of view, the return of yang indicates that the positive forces will gradually move upward and drive out the negative forces as represented by the yin lines. This belief is based on the natural law of cyclical change. But if the negative forces try to resist the upward movement of the positive forces, the yang lines may not be able to replace the yin lines in the hexagram. The result is much dependent on how the negative forces respond to the rise of the positive forces.

The interconnection between Initial Yang and Fourth Yin is advantageous to the return of positive forces because it indicates that some members of the negative forces (Fourth Yin) will support the upward movement of the yang lines. For the purpose of overcoming resistance to its advance, the positive forces should have plans and actions in place to meet the likely responses of the negative forces. Establishing relationships with some members of the opponent group is one of these.

LINE STATEMENTS

Initial Yang ☷. Correct errors quickly

He returns before going too far. There will be no regret and be very fortunate.

If a leader realizes the mistakes he has made and corrects them as quickly as possible, he will be able to maintain balance and move in the right path. The initial line symbolizes a quick return to goodness and the leader's determination to correct the mistakes made.

Second Yin ☷. Correct by maintaining centrality

He lets things return to order which is delightful goodness.
It is auspicious.

A leader should correct his mistakes with uprightness and sincerity. He should tread the path of centrality which is the basic quality of a second line. As Second Yin is close to Initial Yang, a leader in the position of Second Yin is willing to follow the path of goodness.

Third Yin ☷. Think carefully before taking an action

His repeated return may bring danger, but there is no mistake.

Third Yin is at the extreme of the lower trigram Thunder. A leader in this improper position (a yin line in a yang position) lacks self-confidence and his emotions are unstable. Once he meets an obstruction in his actions, even a minor one, he will immediately stop the action and change to a new one. On the good side, he will admit his mistakes and makes the corrections, but on the bad side, he may lose all the effort spent on the first action without giving a thought to whether the second action is workable and appropriate. His action is based on a trial-and-error basis, which may lead to success or failure. If a leader often changes his course of direction, he may lose his direction entirely. Too many directions equals no direction. However, he is willing to correct his "mistakes" every time, so his attitude is considered positive. But such a "positive" attitude may not be good for an organization.

Fourth Yin ☷ Move in the middle way

He returns alone in a middle way.

The executive in this position will adopt a balanced action despite the different views held by most people in the organization. Fourth Yin is in a proper position (a yin line in a yin position) and is located close to the middle of the six lines of the hexagram, indicating that a balanced approach should be used. Although Fourth Yin has an interconnection with Initial Yang the latter does not have adequate strength to support the former. The executive in the fourth position therefore has to walk along in his own direction. This could mean a middle way.

Fifth Yin ☷ Choose what is good and stick to it

He returns with sincerity.

If a leader will readjust his wrong course of direction with sincerity he will be able to ride out the storm and hence have no regret. Fifth Yin represents the sincerity and balance with which a leader is able to return to the right path.

Top Yin ☷ Do not hold on to wrong beliefs obstinately

He goes astray but does not return. There will be misfortune.

If a leader stubbornly insists on going a wrong way without a readjustment, he will be inauspicious. Top Yin is an improper position (a weak line in a weak position), indicating that a leader in this situation should readjust his course of direction and return to the right path in order to avoid falling into a deep abyss.

25

無妄
WUWANG The Heaven–Thunder
Hexagram

Without Wrongdoing, No Error

IMAGE

This Heaven–Thunder Hexagram symbolizes the law of nature (or the appropriate way). Heaven stands for the law of nature and Thunder for action, indicating that one's action should follow the law of nature (or the principle of objectivity), not one's own will. The upper trigram QIAN 乾 [Heaven] is represented by three solid lines which correspond to the truth and innocence of nature. Myriad things follow the natural course of growth. When someone conducts himself properly it will help him to achieve success. Under the guidance of the law of nature as represented by Heaven, a leader should not act just as he pleases. For example, he should not throw his weight around, behave like a tyrant, display his bravery, indulge in moments of pleasure or act insincerely.

HEXAGRAM STATEMENT

To be without wrongdoing is favorable. It is beneficial to be upright. If he does not follow the right way, he will have troubles. It is not favorable for him to go anywhere.

If one acts properly on the principle of uprightness as indicated by unselfishness and sincerity, he will receive benefits from all sides. The outer trigram Heaven symbolizes the law of nature and the inner trigram ZHEN 震 [Thunder] the human action. It is auspicious if human action can follow the law of nature.

STRUCTURE

This is a hexagram with two yins and four yangs. The two yin lines are surrounded by the four yang lines, indicating that the negative or evil forces are under the restraint of the positive or virtuous forces. The hexagram has two yin–yang interconnections, Fifth Yang and Second Yin, Top Yang, and Third Yin. With these two complementary relationships, one's conduct tends to be balanced toward harmony. If the top leader of an organization has constant interaction with the people under him and is also willing to listen and accept useful suggestions, his decisions will be made properly. The subordinates' views can serve as a mirror for guiding a leader in acting without wrongdoing.

LINE STATEMENTS

Initial Yang ☰☰. Act innocently

If he acts innocently, his move will be auspicious.

If a leader has integrity and sincerity, he will get support not only from the members of the internal organization but also from people in external institutions. Initial Yang in the proper position (a yang line in yang position) indicates that a right act is recommended.

Second Yin ☰☰. To hope to reap without sowing is an absurd desire

If he plows without counting on the harvest and cultivates a waste land without expectation of using it, it will be advantageous in whatever direction he may go.

There is a natural law between plowing and harvesting. A farmer who plows his field should get the appropriate harvest. Similarly, if he cultivates a waste land he expects to be able to use it. This is normal conduct. If on the contrary a farmer does not plow his field but hopes to get a harvest from it, or if he has not cultivated a waste land but hopes to use it, this is against the law of nature. Expectation of gaining something for no effort is an unrealistic desire. When a leader undertakes a project he should not expect to get an immediate return. **Reaping without sowing is an absurd desire. One reaps what one sows.**

Compliance with the law on one's own behalf is in accord with balance and correctness—the qualities of Second Yin. Second Yin in a riding or improper position (a yin line above a yang line), indicating that a desire to gain without effort is impractical.

Third Yin ☳· Unexpected misfortune

An ox that is tied up by someone is carried off by a passer-by.
A passer-by's gain is a villager's loss.

A leader must admit that unexpected misfortune can happen at any time to an organization, even though its policies and operations are proper. He should not without cause blame his subordinate, who may not be responsible. Third Yin in an improper position indicates that an unexpected incident may happen not because of a man's own fault but due to external causes. As long as he knows that he is doing things in the right way, he should persevere in what he is doing without laying the blame at the door of another.

Fourth Yang ☳· Stand firm in an innocent situation

He who is true to himself will be blameless.

If a leader is true (sincere and fair) to himself and trusts his own judgment he will make no mistakes. In this situation, he is advised not to move forward because there is an obstruction (represented by a yang line) ahead as indicated by Fifth Yang which symbolizes strong resistance. On the other hand, a leader in the position of Initial Yang is advised to move forward because Second Yin as a yin line in a yin position indicates that there is no obstruction ahead. Since the senior executive Fourth Yang is close to the top leader Fifth Yang, he must be very careful in his work and act always in the proper way to ward off any danger that may come from the suspicion and distrust of the superior.

Fifth Yang ☳· No action is the best action when there is no wrongdoing

If the causes of his illness are not known, he is advised not to take any medicine.

When a leader faces an unexpected difficulty he should be very cautious in taking any action to solve it, particularly if he believes his present action is correct. He should allow nature to take its course and the difficulty will resolve itself of its own accord.

When a leader launches a new project with full confidence, he should stick to his original principles even if there is an unexpected obstacle. Changing principles rashly will only aggravate the condition. There is no need to take any action in a situation where there is no wrongdoing, because an unreasonable or arbitrary action could change a situation without error to one with error. Unless the leader is absolutely sure about the positive effect of his new action, his present policy should remain as it is. No change is probably the best way to deal with this situation.

Top Yang ䷘ Do not take action in a very favorable situation

Even if he acts without error, he may suffer from his action. Nothing is gained.

Since Top Yang is at the peak of a situation without error, any reckless and excessive move would lead to misfortune. A leader must carefully consider whether he should introduce any new action or new measures in the hope of improvement, for that could turn a rightful situation into a less favorable one.

26

DAXU

The Mountain–Heaven Hexagram

Great Accumulating

IMAGE

Mountain over Heaven or Heaven within Mountain symbolizes the energy of Heaven or the natural resources are that are accumulating within the mountain. The power of heaven is, for the time being, stored within the mountain and will be released for development when the time is ripe. The meaning of this hexagram to an organization is that its leader should constantly plan for the recruitment of competent people, the improvement of the standard of technology, and the preparation of adequate funds for further development. The classic interpretation of this hexagram, however, refers to an accumulation of one's knowledge and virtue. The outer trigram GEN 艮 [Mountain] represents steadiness and the inner trigram QIAN 乾 [Heaven] stands for initiative. If a leader is stable outwardly and creative inwardly, he will be able to meet the fundamental requirements for leadership as suggested by this hexagram.

Heaven symbolizes power and Mountain stands for stopping. A leader should know when to restrain himself from using his power in the wrong way; it is beneficial to accumulate virtue. By the same token, a subordinate should know when to stop his superior from acting unrighteously. This is also a virtuous act. Accumulation of virtue can be found in both superior and subordinate.

HEXAGRAM STATEMENT

Great accumulation in a right way is beneficial. He who has an independent mind does not stay home at leisure, his action is auspicious. It is favorable for him to cross great rivers.

A wise leader should be able to accumulate his resources in terms of knowledge, experience, friends, special abilities, and most of all his virtue. These accumulated resources would mean power to a leader. However, he must know how to use this power in the right way as a misuse of power would result in disaster. **Power is a servant of a wise leader, not the master!**

STRUCTURE

Like the previous hexagram WUWANG 無妄 [No Error] (25), the hexagram DAXU also has a structure with two yin and four yang lines, but the two yin lines are located in the upper trigram instead of the lower trigram. The two yin lines are surrounded by the four yang lines which mean that the evil, as represented by the yin lines or the negative forces of an organization, are under the control of the good (the yang lines) or the positive forces. Under such circumstances, it is favorable for the organization to accumulate its resources.

LINE STATEMENTS

Initial Yang ☶. Stop the advance when there are obstructions ahead

When there is a danger ahead, it is beneficial to stop.

When the leader of an organization realizes that there are obstructions to his advance, as represented by the upper trigram Mountain, he should stop his operations and wait calmly until the appropriate time comes since he is not strong enough (the first line at the bottom of the hexagram) yet to rush ahead. A wise leader knows when he should move and when he should stop, whereas an incapable leader does not.

Second Yang ☶. Stop when the situation is out of balance

The axle falls off the cart.

A disconnection between the body and wheels of the cart symbolizes a breakdown of relationships or a situation which is out of balance. Under such circumstances, a leader can no longer continue his task but should stop. In the meantime, he should prepare to accumulate energy for his later advance. Although the yang line represents a man with strong character, his position is weak (a yin position) and not favorable for moving forward.

Third Yang ☰· Be well prepared and cautious when moving forward

He acts with a strong will and goes forward like a good horse rivaling others.
He should be aware of difficulties ahead. By practicing driving and defensive skills, his advance will be favorable.

Even if a leader is strong and decisive he must be aware of the obstacles (represented by the mountain) ahead that could divert him from his path if he is not alert to them. A yang line in a yang position represents a situation in which a leader could become more energetic but less cautious in his actions.

Fourth Yin ☲· Take precautions against the dangers generated by energetic activities

The horns of a young bull are covered by a board. There will be good fortune.

A young bull signifies a young man's energy and its horns stands for the harm that can be caused by the energy of the young man. The placing of a board across the horns of a young bull is done to prevent injury to other people. Initial Yang represents the horns of a young bull or an energetic young man, whereas Fourth Yin represents the board for covering the horns or the measures to restrain the energy of this young man. By the same token, a leader should pay attention to those young executives who are too energetic and prevent them from doing something harmful to the organization. For example, overmarketing can bring losses to a company.

Fifth Yin ☵· Remove the ultimate trouble

A gelded boar will not hurt people with its tusks. It is auspicious.

When a leader is found in a dangerous situation, he should not try to solve the dangers directly but should use an indirect approach to remove the sting from the situation so that there will be no further trouble. Second Yang is stronger than Initial Yang because of its higher position. However, as a soft-style leader Fifth Yin (symbolized by a yin line) should be able to control Second Yang effectively, as gelding the young boar removes its jungle instincts.

Top Yang On the road to success

He is on a wide and unobstructed road. There will be success.

The leader of an organization can at last use the resources accumulated in the past to achieve his objective; nothing can hold him back from his move. Since Top Yang is at the end of the Hexagram Great Accumulation the leader has brought all resources together under his control and they can be used at last. With these accumulated resources, he is able to take action to achieve his aims successfully.

27

頤
YI

The Mountain–Thunder Hexagram

Nourishing

IMAGE

Mountain over Thunder forms a picture of an open mouth. The two yang lines at the top and the bottom of this hexagram are seen as the jaws of a man. The upper trigram GEN 艮 [Mountain] and the lower trigram ZHEN 震 [Thunder] can be seen as the upper and lower jaw of a man respectively. A man's mouth is where he takes in nourishing food and this hexagram is therefore symbolic of nourishment. Nourishment is considered correct if it is self-nourishment (for one's body or virtue) and nourishment of others (for support). Nourishment by others is acceptable only if there is such a need. A strong person seeking nourishment from a weak person is against the norm and is considered inauspicious.

In an organization, nourishment could mean knowledge and information which are important to the development of the organization. A leader should provide nourishment to the members of his organization, such as the appropriate programs of education and training in order to improve their qualities. Similarly, the leader of a country should have appropriate policies for increasing the living standards of the people.

The hexagram has also an image of "steady movement" as indicated by the characteristics of the upper and lower trigram. The lower trigram Thunder symbolizes movement whereas the upper trigram Mountain stands for steadiness. The hexagram therefore means that the moves made by an organization should be at a steady pace rather as a rash advance.

HEXAGRAM STATEMENT

Nourishing in the right way is auspicious. In observation of the ways of nourishment, he should seek the proper way to nourish himself.

Nourishment has a broad meaning including nourishment of the body, nourishment of others, nourishment by others, nourishment of life, and nourishment of virtue. Regardless of what kind of nourishment it is, the principle is to do it in the right way. A leader should in particular know how to nourish himself by **self-development in respect to virtue and knowledge**.

STRUCTURE

The two yang lines at the top and the bottom indicate a situation in which the four yin lines are completely under their control. The activities of the yin lines are limited by Top Yang and Initial Yang. One should know what food or idea one should use to nourish oneself and others, as well as how to nourish. Nourishing the right things in the right way is beneficial to oneself as it is to a leader of an organization.

LINE STATEMENTS

Initial Yang ☶. Do not ignore your own strength

You ignore your characteristic of a magic tortoise (not eating) but watch me eating with your mouth open. There will be misfortune.

The leader of a company has lost his confidence in the policy that has made the company successful in the past, but admires that of others. His unstable character and irresolution may lead the company in a wrong direction and into danger. He should be content with his own path if he cannot find any negative signs in it. He should appreciate what he has achieved in the past and have stronger self-confidence. If his mind is confused, he will be unfortunate.

The interconnection of Initial Yang with Fourth Yin indicates a situation in which a person in the former position should give his support to the person in the latter position, because a person with a yang character is generally stronger than a person with a yin character. But if the stronger ignores his own strength and seeks support from the weaker his act is not proper and hence he will face an inauspicious situation as indicated in the text. One should not simply envy others' success or fortune but should appreciate what one does have and seek a better way to strengthen oneself. This will restore one's self-confidence and self-reliance and prevent one from falling into self-pity and discontent. Comparing oneself with others can make one unpleasant and restless.

Second Yin ☷. Need self-reliance

He seeks nourishment from those at a lower or higher position; either way contravenes the norm. There will be misfortune in advancing.

Normally, a person in a higher position should provide nourishment to those below him rather than the reverse. If a person in the position of Second Yin seeks nourishment from those at the lower position of Initial Yang, this act is a kind of "reverse nourishment." If he seeks nourishment from Top Yang his act will also be considered "reverse nourishment" because there is no formal interconnection between the two. He tries to get the support from Top Yang through an improper way and so his act is incorrect. Seeking nourishment from others must be done in a right way.

The question is why a person in the position of Second Yin wants to seek nourishment from Initial Yang or Top Yang. It is because of his weakness (a yin line in a yin position), which means he cannot nourish himself. As Second Yin is in the central position of the lower trigram, a person in this situation must possess the quality of persistence and the ability to deal with adversity. Therefore, he should have the will to self-reliance and try to solve problems by himself. Also a person who always seeks nourishment from others may lose his dignity and hence his influence and power. A leader in this position needs more self-confidence and self-reliance in overcoming difficulty. Since there is no interconnection between Second Yin and Fifth Yin, Second Yin seeks a relationship with Initial Yang. This conduct is not normal— The normal practice is to seek nourishment from those above not those below.

Third Yin ☳. Dependence on others damages one's own initiative

He seeks nourishment from those above within a normal relationship. Still there will be misfortune. He cannot be trusted even for ten years, so he will gain nothing.

An executive who relies on the support of those above may lose his spirit of self-reliance and his own initiative. Third Yin is an improper position (a yin line in a yang position). A person in this position is advised to keep to the right path and act properly—self-reliance. The improper position of Third Yin symbolizes an improper motive in seeking nourishment from a wrong target.

Fourth Yin ☷˙ **Mutual support does not hurt the principle of self-reliance**

He who seeks nourishment from those below is not the proper way, but this reverse nourishment can still bring good fortune.
He looks down with intense desire like a tiger glares with full force and concentration. There will be no fault.

An executive in the fourth place of a hexagram represents a position which is close to the leader of an organization in the fifth position. To accomplish his assignment, the executive needs a capable person to assist him, so he seeks the support of Initial Yang as indicated by their interconnection. This is a case in which a person at the upper level of an organization seeks nourishment or support from a person below. His act is not against the principle of self-reliance as stated above for he is weak (a yin line in a yin position) in a certain functional area and the support of Initial Yang can complement him. When the senior executive Fourth Yin has difficulty in his work he seeks the capable person Initial Yang below to help him. This kind of reverse nourishment is auspicious and has no blame. As a result, Fourth Yin is as eager to get such a relationship with Initial Yang as a tiger is when it glares at its prey.

As in the situation Second Yin faces, this is also a "reverse nourishment." Why is the first case is considered unfortunate and the second case is without blame? The main reason for this is that Second Yin above Initial Yang indicates a "riding position" or an unfavorable position and it also lacks an interconnection with Fifth Yin. Under such circumstances, Second Yin needs self-reliance rather than seeking nourishment or support from others. The "reverse nourishment" of Second Yin is therefore considered unfavorable. The "reverse nourishment" of Fourth Yin is, however, favorable due to its interconnection with Initial Yang, through which a yin–yang union is produced. The question of whether a "reverse nourishment" is considered favorable or not is much dependent on the time and place, for the judgment can be different at different time and places as shown by the above two cases.

Fifth Yin ☶ Seek the support of the able

He seeks nourishment of those above. He will be auspicious if he can keep in the right way, but he cannot cross the great river.

Because of his powerful position the leader, Fifth Yin should be able to nourish the members of his organization, but he does not have the necessary abilities to do so because he is weak as indicated by the yin line. He thus seeks the help of the able member Top Yang. He can use a capable person to do difficult things that he himself cannot do. In order to nourish the organization the top leader Fifth Yin relies on the help of the wise and capable man Top Yang.

Top Yang ☶ Bear the responsibility for nourishment

Being the main source of nourishment, he should be cautious and beware of danger. Keeping in this way he will be able to cross the great river.

The person Top Yang who provides his assistance to the leader Fifth Yin becomes the main source of nourishment in the organization. Since he has such a big responsibility, he must be careful in advising the members.

28

大過 DAGUO **The Lake–Wind Hexagram**

Great Exceeding, Preponderance of the Great

IMAGE

The Lake–Wind (or Wood) Hexagram is named DAGUO or Great Exceeding, giving a picture of trees under the lake or water above the trees. This hexagram is the opposite form of the Mountain–Thunder Hexagram YI 頤 [Nourishing] (27) ☶☳, with four yin lines inside and two yang lines outside. The four yang lines are like a beam which is hardy in the middle but soft at the edges. The beam can support a strong weight but the two edges are too weak to support it and might collapse at any moment. The following situations may lead to imbalance:

1. The responsibility assumed by an executive is greater than the authority he has been given. In this situation, his responsibility and authority are out of balance.

2. In a reverse case, the authority delegated to an executive could be more than he actually needs to accomplish his work. In this situation, the authority of the executive exceeds his responsibility.

Both cases stated above indicate a situation in which the relationship between yin and yang is not in balance; the yang element has a predominant position to the yin element. If a leader of an organization is too aggressive in undertaking a project for expansion (yang) beyond the resources (yin) available, he will soon find himself in a difficult position as his great ambition lacks the appropriate resources. As a consequence, his overly strong character could endanger the organization's development and stability.

To avoid a predominance of hardness, it is advisable to adopt a middle way or a centering approach. The leader needs to change his attitude and leadership or management style through canvassing various opinions in order that he may benefit from them. By adding a soft element to his decision-making process, the weakness of a hard leadership can be avoided.

Nevertheless, a predominance of hardness can provide an organization with advantages in a particular situation. When the organization is suffering from inappropriate structure or policies, an overall reform in the whole organization is vital. A strong leader is probably more suitable to this situation for he has the courage to do what he must do.

If a person's yang energy is too strong, his yin energy becomes correspondingly too weak. He will lose his inner equilibrium and independence as yin and yang are not in harmony. When a person's yang energy is in Great Exceeding, he tends to be overconfident, obstinate, and arrogant, making him impulsive, impatient, reckless, and egocentric in his decisions and actions. As a result, people keep distance from him and he stands alone.

HEXAGRAM STATEMENT

The ridgepole bends down under the excess weight. It is beneficial to find a solution that can lead to success.

If a leader is too aggressive he may put most of the resources of his organization into a particular project in which he has strong confidence. As a result, the allocation of the resources of the organization is out of balance and may cause an unstable situation. It is necessary for the leader to take action to solve this problem in order to avoid an even more serious situation later.

STRUCTURE

The lower trigram XUN 巽 [Wind] has the character of gentle penetration whereas the upper trigram DUI 兌 [Lake] has the attribute of joy. The hexagram as a whole means that a gentle penetration is considered the more desirable approach for organizational reform even under a tough leadership, for only through this approach will the members of the organization be joyful. Any forcible measures could demoralize the people in the organization.

There are two yin–yang interconnections in the hexagram, Initial Yin with Fourth Yang and Third Yang with Top Yin. These two yin–yang interactions indicate that harmony can be found even in a situation that is predominated by hardness.

LINE STATEMENTS

Initial Yin ☲. Be cautious in doing things at the beginning

He puts white rushes under the offerings. It is blameless.

The characteristic of rushes is that they are white and thin but can bear heavy loads. To put white rushes under the offerings means respectfulness and carefulness. Since Initial Yin is in the first position of the hexagram, it also means that careful preparations are required in the early stages of a new venture.

Second Yang ☱. Strength is balanced with gentleness

A withered willow produces sprouts. An old man gets a young wife. Nothing is inauspicious.

Second Yang symbolizes an old man (a yang line) whereas Initial Yin stands for a young wife (a yin line in the first position). The marriage of an old man to a young wife is considered auspicious due to the combination of strength and gentleness. If a declining company with old-fashioned management and obsolete technology can merge with another company that has a group of young and energetic people with the most up-to-date technical know-how, it will be good for the company, since a merger of yin and yang brings harmony.

A New Explanation

Since Second Yang is the first yang line among the four yangs in the hexagram it can be seen as "a young man" instead of "an old man" as interpreted in the traditional way stated above. The old statement therefore can be modified as follows:

A flourishing willow produces sprouts. A young man gets a young wife. It is very auspicious.

A merger of two companies with complementary new technology will contribute to the efficiency of both sides.

Third Yang ☲· Be not stubborn and arrogant

The ridgepole sags. It is misfortunate.

Third Yang is located at the upper position of the lower trigram, representing a predominance of the great or hardness. A yang line in a yang position means hardness. An executive who is found in such situation is likely to be stubborn and arrogant as he is not willing to accept the advice of others, insists on going his own way, and blindly plunges ahead. Consequently he will isolate himself. His difficulties or burden will grow and, like a sagging ridgepole, he will collapse in due course.

Fourth Yang ☵· Pay more attention to the above

The ridgepole bulges upward, this means good fortune. Otherwise it is regrettable.

A yang line in a yin position is normally considered improper but it does have an advantage in a situation that requires docility and flexibility as in the case of Fourth Yang. Fourth Yang is near the leadership position, Fifth Yang, and represents a senior executive who has authority delegated by the top leader. On the one hand he is seen to be strong, but he is also soft and docile on the other. So Fourth Yang possesses the essential qualities of an assistant to a top leader who has a strong character and is in a powerful position. A strong top leader with the support of a balanced assistant could be a good match.

He should give advice and support to the top leader in order to keep the organization moving on the right path. When an organization is under a hard structure and management style it would be an advantage to have a person like Fourth Yang in the organization. Spending too much time in supervising those below may not be a good choice. This is why the line statement suggests that Fourth Yang should pay more attention to those above rather than those below.

Fifth Yang ☵· Need a careful evaluation of a merger

The aging willow blooms. The old woman gets a young husband for herself; there is neither misfortune nor praise.

Top yin represents an old woman and Fifth Yang her young husband. The "old" and "young" here are relative terms. Since Fifth Yang has no interconnection with Second Yang he can only seek help from Top Yin for the purpose of obtaining the favorable effect of a yin–yang merge. But the marriage of an old woman with a young man is unlikely to result in a child so the expected effect of this yin–yang merge would be that it is fruitless.

Similarly, the merger of a young company with an old company may not bring advantages to the former since the management style and technology of the latter may not be able to meet the needs of the market despite its experiences and reputation in the past.

Top Yin ☷ **Do not overextend one's capability**

He crosses the river and the water goes over his head. There is danger but no blame.

A yin line in an extreme position indicates a weak and dangerous situation. If a leader goes beyond his capability, he will have trouble. However, he will get through it if he behaves properly and sensibly.

A Comparison of Six Hexagrams with Four Yang and Two Yin Lines

As well as the hexagram DAGUO, there are another five hexagrams with four yang and two yin lines that can also have the same name based on their line structures as shown below:

Daguo 大過 **Dazhuang** 大壯 **Dun** 遯   **Li** 離   **Xun** 巽   **Dui** 兌
[Great Exceeding] [Great Strength] [Retreating] [Brightness] [Penetrating] [Pleasing]

All the six hexagrams stated above have a similar line structure in which the four yang lines are in the predominant position as compared with that of the two yin lines. In the Hexagram Retreating, the positions of the four yang lines are obviously superior to that of the two yin lines. The hexagram DAZHUANG indicates a situation in which the four yang lines are moving upward and will eventually take over the positions of the two yin lines. In the hexagram LI, the two yin lines are encircled by the four yang lines whereas the two yin lines are segregated from each other in its trigrams. Based on the predominant position of the yang lines in the line structure of the six hexagrams they can all in fact be named Predominance of the Great or Great Strength if the focus is place on the line structure of a hexagram.

29

 KAN

The Water Hexagram

Double Pitfall, Danger within

Danger

IMAGE

The hexagram KAN is made up of two KAN trigrams which indicate an image of Water over Water—Double Pitfall. Water means danger or trouble and therefore double water represents double danger or double trouble. The hexagram symbolizes a situation in which a person moves away from one danger but another danger comes to him.

In both upper and lower trigrams, the yang line as the virtuous perseverance is surrounded by two yin lines which represent evil. This gives an image of the virtuous perseverance in a pitfall. The hexagram has two pitfalls, which stand for double danger. One must have perseverance in holding to the principle of centrality or the centering approach as indicated by the two yang lines in the central position of each trigram. Through perseverance in the right way, evil will not triumph over the virtuous.

Although the Hexagram Double Pitfall has a negative meaning—double danger—it also has a positive meaning for it indicates the principles of centrality and integrity when dealing with a dangerous situation. This will make a capable leader prepare against the coming danger in a timely manner. So realizing danger is in fact favorable to an organization rather than unfavorable. Danger can sharpen the sensitivity of a leader, enabling him to take the corresponding action to protect his organization from harm. If danger is perceived by a leader not as an obstruction but an opportunity the adaptability of the organization to the changing conditions will be higher, as will be its effectiveness.

HEXAGRAM STATEMENT

The hexagram KAN signifies double danger, danger within danger.
If his mind is sincerely wholehearted with strong confidence, he will
get through danger and difficulty. Whatever he does is worthwhile.

When a leader is surrounded by difficulties he must remain confident and determined to find the way through. Like water which flows without stopping through mountain and rivers, he must maintain an unshakable confidence in his own understanding of what is right. A strong leader will not avoid the dangers but will confront them with patience, perseverance, and determination, like water flowing downhill.

STRUCTURE

This is a hexagram with four yin and two yang lines. The situation is dominated by the yin factors. The image of water over water illustrates the dangers faced by an organization both internally and externally. The inner (lower) trigram represents the internal danger whereas the outer (upper) trigram represents the external danger.

LINE STATEMENTS

Initial Yin ☵. Do not over-estimate one's ability

From a pit to another pit, he falls into an abyss. It is misfortune.

Initial Yin is at the bottom of the inner trigram symbolizes that a person has just fallen into a pit but he has no interconnection with those above. So he has to solve the problem himself without getting any help from others. The bottom of the lower trigram KAN 坎 [Water] represents an abyss, which means a danger of the dangers.

A leader who is less experienced may think little of the danger he faces. He believes he is able to get out of it without the help of others. But overestimating his ability in dealing with danger may make it even worse. **An ignorance of danger enhances the danger.**

Second Yang ☵. Try to get small gains first

He falls into the deep inside a pit and should strive for small gains.

When a leader realizes that his organization is surrounded by dangers (the yang line is encircled by the two yin lines) he should try to solve the minor problem first and then look for other possibilities to get out of the danger. It is not realistic to solve the problems once and for all. A step-by-step approach appears to be more sensible. Small gains are the basis for larger gains.

Third Yin ䷜· Remain still and wait

He is confronted with pitfalls whether he moves forward or back, he should not act but remain still and wait. Otherwise he will fall into the abyss.

An executive stands at the juncture between the inner and outer trigrams or between two pitfalls. Whatever direction he moves, forward or backward, he will face danger. He is in a dilemma. Either advance or retreat is dangerous. The leader is advised to stay where he is until the conditions change in his favor. Otherwise, he will fall into the abyss.

Fourth Yin ䷜· Sincerity, simplicity, and openness are the basis for a sound relationship

A jug of wine and two bowls of rice contained in a plain vessel are handed in through the window. No misfortune in the end.

This line text suggests that the principle of a sound relationship is based on sincerity and simplicity. Fourth Yin represents a senior executive who is close to the top leader Fifth Yang. He must be careful in handling his relationship with his superior. If he always follows his superior's will without putting forward his own views or any argument, he will appear docile in the eyes of his superior but his colleagues will tend to think he is rather a flatterer. Even an open-minded superior may not like this type of subordinate. The senior executive in this position should give appropriate advice to the superior if there is such a need in order to avoid doing wrong things or moving in the wrong direction. He should develop a relationship of mutual trust with his superior based on sincerity. The text "a plain vessel" means simplicity.

The "window" of a room in the text symbolizes openness and light. Without the window a room is in darkness. The text "through the window" means to let the light in and the "light" here means "an understanding" between the persons. If the senior executive wants to be more persuasive in advising his superior he should keep his communication with the superior sincere, simple, and open.

Fifth Yang ☵ Need strength, perseverance, and balance

The water has not yet filled the pit, it has only reached a level; there will be no blame.

Fifth Yang is in the central position of the outer trigram, indicating that the top leader of an organization is still in the midst of danger. The text "the pit is not filled" means that the top leader should not be conceited with respect to his ability and ambition when dealing with the difficult situation. If he believes he is capable of getting out of danger through his actions, he tends to be obstinate and overoptimistic. Since there is no interconnection between Fifth Yang and Second Yang, no help is expected from the members of the internal organization. He must go on alone. Consequently he will face even more dangers. Under such circumstances, it would be safe not to do great things.

A yang line in a yang and central position gives another suggestion to the top leader: he should persevere in his strength and principle of balance in a time of adversity.

Top Yin ☷ Pay the price for an improper act

He is tied with ropes in a prison surrounded with thorn bushes.
For three years he is unable to be released. It is misfortunate.

This is a dangerous position as indicated by the yin line in the extreme end of the upper trigram. A leader who has misjudged his direction or operation is now to pay the price. A yin line in a yin position indicates a weak leader in a dangerous situation; he has deeply fallen into a pitfall and has little chance of getting out.

30

離
LI

The Fire Hexagram

Brightness, Shining, Clinging

IMAGE

Fire within Fire is the image of this hexagram. The two yin lines cling to the yang lines in each trigram. Fire has no definite form but is given form by the burning object to which it clings. This implies that a person's action is influenced by the person to whom he adheres. To cling to something is a general phenomenon in nature. Sun and moon cling to the sky and trees and grass cling to the earth. Man also clings to someone who is advantageous to him in respect to knowledge, belief, power, and finance. Whether or not he can achieve his goal is much dependent on the object or the person whom he has chosen to cling. If this person is sincere and honest, he could achieve success through this close connection. If not, he could be hurt. Another factor affecting his success is his personal character. If he is tender and gentle like a cow, he will be fortunate.

Fire also symbolizes brightness. The Hexagram Double Fire hence stands for double brightness or constant brightness. To maintain its brightness the fire must cling closely to its source of energy. If a leader wants to prolong his organization's brightness, he must know what its causes are and should strengthen the factors that would affect them.

This Hexagram Brightness can be used to explain **Laozi's** saying: **"He who knows others is learned; He who knows himself is wise."**

A man who knows others can be represented by the outer trigram LI 離 [Fire] and a man who knows himself by the inner trigram Fire. If a man only knows others, he is learned but not necessarily wise. A wise man must know himself. To know oneself is more difficult than to know others. A wise leader is a person who knows his own strengths and weaknesses; he knows when and where he can use his strength and overcome his weakness. A man who has inner clarity as represented by the inner trigram Illumination is in a good situation to cultivate his wisdom.

This hexagram can also be used to illustrate the well-known saying of **Sunzi: "Know the other and know yourself, one hundred battles without danger."** Fire symbolizes brightness, illumination, or knowledge. The outer trigram Fire suggests that a leader should "know the other" and the inner trigram that he should "know yourself":

Hexagram Brightness

Outer trigram: "know the other"
Inner trigram: "know yourself"

To know the other is not easy but it is even more difficult for one to know oneself as Laozi said above.

HEXAGRAM STATEMENT

The hexagram LI signifies clinging and brightness. It is favorable for one to cling to what is right as that can bring him a bright future.
If he cultivates a gentle character in himself like a docile cow, he will have a good outlook.

Sun and moon clings to the sky, plants cling to the earth, and fire also clings to something. A leader should choose the right object to cling to, such as the vision and values of the organization. Clinging to a right object brings fortune but clinging to a wrong object brings misfortune. If a leader has a gentle character like that of a cow, people will accept him for his openness and adaptability.

STRUCTURE

This is a hexagram with two yin and four yang lines in which the two yin lines are encircled by the four yang lines, symbolizing that good is able completely to control the evil this is the condition for bringing brightness. However, the hidden hexagram of the Double Fire Hexagram is the hexagram DAGUO 大過 [Great Exceeding] (28) ☰, which warns a leader to avoid overexpanding his operations merely because of the brightness of the current situation. Similarly the opposite hexagram KAN 坎 [Double Pitfall] (29) also indicates the possible dangers of taking an action that is based merely on optimism.

In the middle position of the two trigrams are two yin lines, indicating there is a need for a soft-based centrality as contrasted to a hard centrality in the hexagram KAN where the two yang lines are in the middle position of the two trigrams. Under the principle of soft centrality, a person is in compliance with the person to whom he clings while maintaining his balance and integrity.

LINE STATEMENTS

Initial Yang ☰. Identify the right direction at the beginning of a development

If he can think carefully and avoid mistakes at the beginning of his move, he will receive no blame.

It is important to a leader to identify the right direction for his organization at the beginning of a new task. Before making a move, he should have made all necessary preparations for the task. A yang line in a yang position indicates a situation in which a leader with strong character and in a strong position tends to make rash decisions in order to advance. However, if he carefully takes all risk factors into consideration before taking any action he should make no mistakes.

Second Yin ☲. Do not take extreme actions

Yellow light is auspicious.

Yellow light refers to the sun at midday; it is also a color that stands for centrality as indicated by Second Yin. The environment of an organization is likely to be favorable. A proper position (a yin line in a yin position) together with centrality is favorable for taking action but the leader is advised not to go to extremes.

Third Yang ☲. Follow the law of nature

If an old person does not sing and beat his pot in the light of the setting sun, he will bewail his old age later. There will be misfortune.

Initial Yang represents the rising sun in the morning, Second Yin the centering sun at noon, and Third Yang the setting sun in the afternoon. The three phases of the "movement" of the sun symbolizes the life of a man. The sun in the afternoon indicates that the golden part of life is already gone and the life is approaching its end. Third Yang is located at the end of the lower trigram Fire which means that the light will vanish quite soon. Similarly, a man's life has an end. It is the law of nature or an eternal pattern. If a man cannot accept this fact but laments in his old age it is sad to have such an attitude toward the law of nature. But if he really understands that everything has an end according to the natural law he will change his attitude toward life and death. If he acts in this way he will have no more fear of death but will appreciate life. He will sing and beat his pot in the light of the setting sun.

When the executives of an organization have not reached their planned target because of unexpected changes in the market, it is not really their fault, but they feel guilty and become frustrated. Their morale is therefore affected. The leader of the organization should encourage them instead of giving punishment. A positive approach is sometimes more effective than a negative approach. Even in a desperate time the leader has the responsibility to maintain enthusiasm among the members in his organization.

Fourth Yang ☲· Troubles made by oneself

His reckless action, like fire, burns all things into ashes.
He is abandoned by others.

Fourth Yang in an improper position (a yang line in a yin position) indicates an executive who is hot-tempered like a flash of lightning and a burning fire. Once he gets a new idea he wants to put it into practice immediately without considering whether it is feasible or not. He will force people to follow him and blame them if their performance cannot meet his standards. People will eventually abandon him. His act burns himself.

Fifth Yin ☵· Think of the time of peril in the time of peace

He cries in floods of tears and bemoans. It is auspicious.

Although Fifth Yang is in both a central and an inappropriate position the advantage of the former compensates for the disadvantage of the latter. As a leader with yin characteristics—softness, broadmindedness, docility, and caution—he makes the necessary preparations for the time of peril in the time of peace. A man who is aware of the need to be concerned and wary should be auspicious.

Top Yang   Keep the good and get rid of the bad

The king trusts him to lead an expedition. He kills the leader of the enemy but spares the followers. There is no mistake.

Top Yang is at the end of the outer trigram Fire, symbolizing strength and understanding. A leader needs strength to get rid of the weaknesses in the organization and to understand the right direction in which to move. A leader should root out his own fundamental weaknesses but should tolerate those who are harmless.

31

The Lake–Mountain Hexagram

Interaction, Conjoining, Sensing

IMAGE

The Lake–Mountain Hexagram indicates a close interaction between the two objects as the lake rests on the mountain and the mountain slopes are nourished by the moisture of the lake. The lake and the mountain are interdependent; the lake needs to rest on the mountain as much as the mountain needs the lake for its moisture. So there is an interactive or interdependent relationship between Lake and Mountain.

The inner trigram GEN 艮 [Mountain] means stillness which can lead one's mind to be innocent, selfless, and free from egocentric pressure—the basis for interaction with others. The result of such a sincere interaction is joyfulness as represented by the outer trigram DUI 兑 [Lake]. Stillness leads to joyfulness and joyfulness strengthens stillness. As a superior–subordinate relationship is like that of the lake and mountain, a wise leader should keep his mind in stillness like a mountain when developing relationships with his colleagues and subordinates in order to obtain a joyful harmony within the organization.

An open-minded leader is needed to achieve effective interaction in an organization. He should be able to set up a mutual benefit system for building and strengthening the coherence of the members within the organization. The Hexagram Interaction gives an example of a mutually beneficial relationship between two parties. Objectivity and sincerity from both parties are the basic condition needed to maintain a good relationship.

HEXAGRAM STATEMENT

The Lake–Mountain Hexagram signifies interaction. A right interaction is favorable like a good marriage with a woman.

Since the interaction between Heaven and Earth or yin and yang can make myriad things grow, a relationship between people that follows this way is favorable. A leader should know how to use this principle to improve human relations. When a leader and his subordinates are sincerely interactive with each other, the organization will benefit.

STRUCTURE

In this hexagram, there are three yin–yang interactions between the upper and the lower trigrams:

1. Initial Yin and Fourth Yang
2. Second Yin and Fifth Yang
3. Third Yang and Top Yin

This is one of the sixty-four hexagrams that have three yin–yang interactions between two trigrams, indicating a high degree of harmony in an organization where two-way communication and mutual trust are well developed. The other three hexagrams that have three yin–yang interactions are HENG 恆 [Perseverance] (32) ☲☴, JIJI 既濟 [Already Accomplished] (63) ☲☵, and WEIJI 未濟 [Not Yet Accomplished] (64) ☲☵. All these four hexagrams with three yin–yang interactions have a particular meaning for a leader.

LINE STATEMENTS

Initial Yin ☲☴. Avoid taking action based on intuition

He acts through the feeling in his big toe.

Initial Yin interacts with Fourth Yang, indicating that the former is enthusiastic to move out of its present place to meet the latter. This implies that one feels the time is favorable for him to move forward as he expects to get support from a powerful person represented by Fourth Yang through their interactive relationship. But he should not do it based on his intuition.

To move, it is necessary for a person to use his foot, not his feeling in the big toe even though he has an interaction with someone who is in a position to give him help. However, movement is not dependent on one's intuition but on one's ability to take action. As Initial Yin is at the bottom of the hexagram, this implies that a person's intuition alone is not sufficient to justify taking action as he may not have the necessary energy or resources to bring success. A leader should not take action simply based on his personal intuition but should stay where he is as the conditions required for such a move may not yet exist, even though the opportunity looks good. For example, the resources required may not be available at present. An action which is merely based on a subtle hunch (like a feeling in the big toe) is risky. Taking action hastily at an early stage can result in danger. However, this is not to say that personal intuition is not important in making decisions; it merely indicates that the necessary conditions for taking an action should also be considered.

Second Yin ☷. Avoid action by impulse

He acts through the feeling in his calves, he will be inauspicious.
If he stays where he is, he will be auspicious.

The calves cannot move themselves but follows the legs. Second Yin is a weak position, as indicated by a yin line in a yin position. An executive in this position should not act impetuously simply because of his good relationship with the top leader Fifth Yin. As Second Yin is in a central position, representing balance and uprightness, the executive in this situation should resist the impulse to rush forward but should stay where he is until the friendly attitude of Fifth Yang is fairly certain. A premature action may be unfortunate.

Third Yang ☶. Do not follow others blindly

He acts through the feeling in his thighs; it is shameful for him to follow others.

The thighs are at the top of the legs. Like the calves in the situation of Second Yin, they cannot move themselves but follow the legs. An executive in the position of Third Yang is characterized by hardness (a yang line in a yang position); he should not make any move because hardness can make him impulsive and obstinate. Blindly following others is like thighs follow calves. If he insists on following others blindly, there will be regret.

Fourth Yang ☷` Keep one's mind sincere and clear in interaction with others

If he can hold his interaction in a just way, he is auspicious and regret disappears.
If he interacts with others out of personal interest, he will be inauspicious and only a few friends will follow him.

If a leader intends to interact with the members of his organization, he should keep his mind sincere and stable without any disturbance including those involving personal interests. Otherwise, only a few of them will follow him and so create a clique under him. Sincerity is a driving power in interaction.

Fifth Yang ☳` Be objective and strong in interaction with others

He interacts with others through his back, he will have no regrets.

The back of the human body is opposite to the heart and is not visible by a man himself. The text suggests the importance of the **principle of objectivity** to a leader when he interacts with others. In interacting with others he must have a strong will and a clear mind as indicated by the character of the yang line and yang position. Fifth Yang is interconnected with Second Yin, indicating that there is a need for a leader to maintain his objectivity and integrity.

Top Yin ☱` Interact with substance

He interacts with others through words.

If a leader only uses words to influence the members of his organization, whatever he says is meaningless. A leader cannot persuade people by just talking. His words can be effective only if they are backed up by something solid, for example, actions.

32

恆 HENG
The Thunder–Wind Hexagram
Persevering, Duration, Constancy

IMAGE

The Thunder–Wind Hexagram indicates a constant relationship between the two objects. When the thunder rolls, the wind also blows; their coming and going are governed by the law of nature. The wind carries the thunder further and the thunder strengthens the wind. The close relationship between these two is long-lasting and gives an image of duration or a perseverance. Thunder represents movement or yang, and wind stands for gentleness or yin. A joint relationship between thunder and wind signifies a merge of yin–yang.

The leader of an organization must be able to distinguish which values are longlasting and which are changeable with time and place. For example, "providing good services to the community" could be a long-term objective of a company and this has a long-term nature. If the organization is on course he should persist. Otherwise, he should change his course. Persistence in incorrectness leads to harm.

HEXAGRAM STATEMENT

Persevering is favorable without blame. Persevering in the right way is advantageous and favorable to go forward.

Persevering means "long lasting." A constant perseverance in the right way is favorable and blameless. But a constant perseverance in the wrong way is harmful and needs to be changed. A leader must know with what and when he should keep constancy and with what and when he should not.

STRUCTURE

This is a hexagram with three yin and three yang lines in which the three yang lines are surrounded by the three yin lines. As compared with the hexagram DAGUO 大過 [Great Exceeding] (28), the hexagram HENG has one yang line less but one yin line more. An increase of yin and a decrease of yang in the hexagram structure have changed the dominant position of the yang over the yin, making the relationship between **yin and yang in balance** and hence creating the basic condition for duration.

The upper trigram ZHEN 震 [Thunder] symbolizes a husband (yang) who works outside the home whereas the lower trigram XUN 巽 [Wind] shows a wife (yin) who works quietly inside the home. The structure indicates the division of labor within a family. This relationship is projected from that between the thunder and the wind. A similar situation is also found in today's business firms where the responsibilities of the various departments or people can be divided into internal and external according to their nature. The difference between internal and external responsibilities can remain unchanged for a certain time but not forever. It cannot last permanently. Nothing in the world remains unchanged as change is the law of nature.

But change can still include constancy. For example, if "providing good services to the community" is the objective of a business firm with a constant nature, as time and place change, the needs of the people will change too. The firm cannot provide the same services to the community as those in the past; they have to be changed and modified to adapt to the new needs. Under such circumstances, the primary objective of the business firm still remains unchanged but the ways of achieving the objective differ from those in the past. Based on the above a general principle can be developed: **"Persevering within change and change within persevering."** This is one of the yin–yang laws: **"Yin within yang and yang within yin."** There are nine yin–yang laws explaining changes in nature or human actions. They will be further elaborated in Part Three of this book.

LINE STATEMENTS

Initial Yin ☷. Be patient in making a long-term commitment

An emphasis on further perseverance will be misfortune.

If an executive is eager to gain long-term business with a potential customer just at the beginning of their interaction he may not be able to reach his objective, because a good relationship between the two should be first established before making any deals. He must be patient in developing a long-term relationship rather than a short one. If he wants too much too soon, he may end up empty-handed. To get immediate success, under most circumstances, is too optimistic; he should work step by step toward his long-term objective. Building up a long-term commitment needs perseverance.

Second Yang ☳. Persevere in centrality

Regret vanishes.

Out of 384 line statements of the *Yijing* there are three commentaries on the situation which indicates merely whether it is "fortunate" or "blameless," or "no regret" without giving any reasons. They are Second Yin of the hexagram DAZHUANG 大壯 [Great Strength] (34) ☰, Initial Yin of the hexagram XIE 解 [Loosening] (40) ☵, and the Second Yang of this hexagram ☳. One of the reasons for this is that the image of the line is self-explanatory so there is no need for further explanations. Since Second Yang is in a central position, the disadvantages of its improper position (a yang line in a yin position) are offset by the advantages of its central position. In the philosophy of the *Yijing*, the principle of centrality, with a few exceptions, has a predominant role in the judgment of whether a situation is fortunate or unfortunate. Also, Second Yang is interconnected with Fifth Yin which is also in the center with balance. Two lines with the characteristic of balance are more than sufficient to make regret disappear.

If an executive who has a strong character like the yang line is constantly able to persevere in centrality, he will have no reason for regret.

Third Yang ☳. Persevere in a stable character

He cannot keep his virtue constantly; he may bring on disgrace for that. If he persists, he will have regrets.

A yang line in a yang position indicates a proper situation but one that is too strong. An executive in this situation is likely to have a strong but also unstable character; so he is likely often to change his mind, making it difficult for the people under him to follow him. If he is unpredictable, people will lose confidence and respect for him. He should be in control of his moods, not his moods in control of him.

Fourth Yang ䷝ Do not persevere in a wrong direction

No creatures and birds are found in the hunting place.

If a leader has chosen a wrong plan or direction for the development of his organization he will not be able to achieve his goal and his efforts will be in vain. He should review his plan in order to decide whether it is realistic or not. If the decision is negative, the plan should be abandoned. A yang line in a yin position gives a warning to a person not to take any action in an improper position; otherwise he will regret it. He should not stay in a place which is not appropriate for the achievement of his plan. To stay in a hunting place where no creatures and birds are found is a waste of time. If he persists in continuing his action, he will not gain anything no matter how much effort he has made. Persevering in a wrong direction is inauspicious. A wise decision is requires between perseverance and change.

Fifth Yin ䷝ Adapt to the conditions of time and place

Persevering in virtue is auspicious for a woman but not for a man.

Fifth Yin represents both the characteristics of flexibility (a yin line) and firmness (a yang position); its position also represents leadership. If a wife is constantly obedient and flexible as she is expected to be, she is auspicious. But this may not be right for a husband, for he is supposed to be active and strong. If he constantly follows others, he will lose his proper character of yang. A leader should have definite views.

As leadership style can be classified to two types: a yin type and a yang type. Both are considered right if used in the right time and place. In the position of Fifth Yin, it is desirable for the leadership to be a yin type rather than a yang type in order to meet the conditions of this specific time. Continued perseverance is one of the essential characteristics of yin.

Top Yin ䷝ Be relaxed and calm

Persevering in activity is misfortune.

Activity is one of the important qualities of a leader but if he constantly acts actively regardless of the changing conditions of time and place he will be inauspicious, for he doesn't know when and where he should stop. Top Yin is at the extreme of the upper trigram Thunder; the position symbolizes a hasty movement which can make the situation unstable. Furthermore Top Yin is in a position of double yin (a yin line in a yin position) at the highest position of persevering, suggesting that he should calm down rather than stirring thing up. It is better for him to remain still instead of moving.

33

 DUN

The Heaven–Mountain Hexagram

Retreat, Withdrawal

IMAGE

Heaven over Mountain indicates a situation in which heaven retreats upward to keep mountain at a distance. In the traditional view, Heaven represents the superior man and Mountain the inferior man. The image of this hexagram indicates that the superior man guards against the inferior man by keeping a distance which is so great that the latter cannot reach the former. For a leader of an organization, it could mean that he decides to withdraw from a strategic move that was planned earlier. The reason is because changes in the environment make any move at this time unfavorable. But this retreat is not to be confused with giving up or running away. Rather it should be considered as a strategic withdrawal as the leader realizes that his chance to win the battle is low. To withdraw from an action is merely to follow the natural cycle of advance and retreat. A wise leader knows when and how he should retreat whereas an unwise leader does not.

HEXAGRAM STATEMENT

It is favorable to retreat and deal with the small matters.

In a time when unfavorable factors (as indicated by the yin lines) are growing and favorable factors (as indicated by the yang lines) are decreasing, a wise leader must know the conditions are not to his favor so he should quickly make a firm decision to retreat from the action that is being undertaken, even though he is still in a favorable position. In such a situation, he is advised to deal only with the small matters.

An executive is involved in a power struggle and is confused on which side he should stand. He does not want to be involved in it and therefore asks the top leader to assign him to a new position in order to keep a distance from the present battle field, even though this position may be less important. When a person is aware of a danger and he is not in a position to deal with it, he should retreat from it as soon as possible.

STRUCTURE

This is a hexagram with two yin and four yang lines. The two yin lines tend to move upwards and push the yang lines into retreat from their present position. In the hexagram the two yin lines of the lower trigram represent the rising negative forces, or evil people, in an organization. Under such circumstances, capable people do not want to associate with the evil people and are likely to leave the organization. Top Yang represents the capable people whereas Initial Yin and Second Yin represent the evil people. The former wants to keep a distance from the latter as far as possible. As a result, good people retreat backward as evil people advance forward. Capable people are unwilling to work with people they despise. The hexagram DUN therefore has two meanings: the first one is a strategic move whereas the second one is a moral concept.

LINE STATEMENTS

Initial Yin ☷. An earlier retreat is advantageous

Retreating at the rear is dangerous. He should not try to move.

As soon as a leader is aware of the danger ahead and realizes that he is not in the position to cope with it, he should withdraw from involvement. A late retreat would be harmful. The first line in the other hexagrams is the "head," but in the hexagram DUN it is seen as its "tail." In a time of retreat the situation is considered dangerous if he stays behind.

Second Yin ☷. Make a good relationship unshakable

He fastens something tightly with yellow ox hide, nothing can unloose it.

This line statement advises that a good relationship between two parties must be unshakable. Second Yin and Fifth Yang have an interconnection which is mutually beneficial to both and hence it should be maintained with steadfast determination. In the text "ox" represents docility, "yellow" the color of the center, and "hide" the hardness. It means that the relationship between the two parties should be based on cooperation, balance, and steadfastness like an ox hide.

Once a person has decided to keep a distance far from his inferiors he should firmly persist in his way and not change, as if he is tied with yellow ox hide and "nothing can unloose it."

Third Yang ☰ · Retreat with determination

He retreats with deep concern, this makes him ill.
He should keep domestic servants and concubines, it will be auspicious.

A leader is concerned with his retreat from a business because it is seriously affected by a change in the economic structure. If he retreats, he will lose his investment and all his efforts in the past years will have been in vain. But if he continues to stay in the business, the outlook is rather bleak. After he weighs the pros and cons of these two alternatives, he decides to retreat from his present business but with much concern; he will no longer be master of the situation. In this case, the advice in the text to him is to retreat in a stately and relaxed way and to restore his energy for starting a new venture when the right time comes.

A person who is in a strong position (a yang line in a yang position) is likely to be tempted to take an action that may first appear to be beneficial to him but which may hurt him later. To protect himself from danger, he should know when and how to control his emotion. This is a retreat from impulsive action.

Fourth Yang ☴ · Retreat without concerns

The superior man retreats calmly and peacefully without looking back while the inferior man cannot make his mind to leave.
It is auspicious for the superior man but not for the inferior man.

The interconnection of Fourth Yang with Initial Yin symbolizes the relationship between the two. A wise leader in the position of Fourth

Yang will, however, give up it without concern if he realizes that such a relationship is incorrect and harmful. Fourth Yang illustrates a situation in which a strong leader (a yang line) who is in a weak position (a yin position) is still able to act in the right way. A wise man can control his emotions and desires while an inferior man cannot because his involvement is with personal interests and motives.

Fifth Yang ☷ Retreat in a timely and properly way

He retreats in a timely and properly way, he is auspicious.

A wise leader knows when and how to retreat. He has strong determination in making decisions on his retreat neither early nor late. He will make the necessary and proper arrangements for his retreat so that the operations of the organization can continue normally even without him. He knows when he should retreat and does it properly. The position of Fifth Yang suggests the principle of centrality for a person when he plans to retreat.

Top Yang ☷ Retreat in a favorable position in a carefree way

He who retreats serenely is auspicious.

Top Yang is located at the end of the upper trigram and has no interconnection with any other line. This suggests two conditions for a person to retreat serenely: First, his position must be favorable for his retreat as Top Yang at the extremity of the outer trigram; second, he must retreat in a carefree way as Top Yang has no resonance with other lines.

34

大 壯
DAZHUANG

The Thunder–Heaven Hexagram

Great Strength, Great Invigorating

IMAGE

This is the Thunder–Heaven Hexagram or Hexagram Great Strength. Thunder signifies action whereas Heaven stands for strength. Thunder over Heaven indicates that the energy of heaven moves into the action of the thunder. There is a close relationship between strength and action. The greater the strength, the more powerful is the action. A union of strength and action gives the image of Great Strength.

A leader who is in the situation of Great Strength has both pros and cons. On the positive side, he could use his favorable position to do things to benefit the organization. On the negative side, he tends to believe that he is a powerful person and can do anything he wants; he may overestimate his ability and ignore the strength of his colleagues or subordinates. He may become an arrogant person and make decisions on his own judgment without listening to others. A person who has power and successful experiences tends to believe that what he is doing is always right.

Great things in the world need not be great in their strength. Greatness not over strength will be able to avoid misfortune. Greatness over strength will be the opposite—misfortune. If a large corporation continuously increases its size through acquisitions and mergers, it could lead to overexpansion and make adverse impact on the organization, such as inefficiency and high debts. Overexpansion leads to an imbalance between yin and yang and hence disharmony.

The hexagram DAZHUANG suggests a balance between the three qualities: great, strength, and right. A leader who can keep a balance in these three is a wise man. **He who least uses his formal power has the real power; he who tries to dominate others by using his formal power is not powerful.**

Hexagram Statement

In a time of great strength, it is favorable to keep to the right way.

In a time of great strength a wise leader should know how to use his power properly. If he has too much self-confidence and becomes obstinate, he may use his power in an incorrect way. A wise leader is the one who has the formal power but uses it least.

Structure

One of the reasons for giving the name Great Strength to this hexagram is because of its structure, in which four yang lines are moving upward from the initial position to the fourth position and the fourth yang line passes beyond the median line of the hexagram, showing thus its Great Strength.

The Hexagram Great Strength is obtained by a change of the fourth line from yin to yang in the Hexagram Harmony as shown by the following:

Harmony   Great Strength

Among the sixty-four hexagrams there are sixteen hexagrams that have four yang and two yin lines. They all can be named Great Strength if the number of yang lines over that of the yin lines is the main criterion for naming a hexagram. If this argument is accepted, the principle of naming can also be applied to other hexagrams with five yang lines and one yin line; in this case, hexagrams similar in their line structure can share their names. This argument here indicates that the hexagram names in the *Yijing* are not objectively determined.

Line Statements

Initial Yang . **Do not act recklessly because of one's own eagerness**

He feels the strength lies in his toes.
If he moves forward, his misfortune is certain.

If a leader is enthusiastic in taking a rash move just at the beginning of an operation, he may make a mistake because the conditions may not be ready yet for him to go ahead. He has overconfidence in his strength and wants to demonstrate his ability, yet he is not well prepared to start such a move. An impetuous person is likely to act impulsively without careful thinking. He will consequently suffer from his reckless action.

A yang line in a yang position symbolizes strength and activity. It is also a part of the lower trigram QIAN 乾 [Heaven] which makes it even stronger. In a situation of Great Strength, a mild action is seen to be more appropriate than a hard one. Since there are three yang lines (Second Yang, Third Yang, and Fourth Yang) ahead, it means that an executive in the position of Initial Yang moving forward will meet difficulties as represented by the hardness of the yang lines.

Second Yin ☷. Keep strength and uprightness

Uprightness brings good fortune.

If a leader is able to keep his strength and uprightness, things will turn out well. The advantages of the central position of Second Yang offset the disadvantages of its improper position.

Both Initial Yang and Second Yang are yang lines. The question is why Initial Yang is seen as "inauspicious" whereas Second Yang is seen as "auspicious." The reason is that Second Yang represents a combination of strength (the yang line) and gentleness (the yin position). By using the principle of centrality, a leader in this position is able to avoid overenthusiasm, exuberant self-confidence, impulsion, and extreme behavior. A wise leader knows to maintain a modest attitude in a time of great strength.

Third Yang ☷. To throw one's weight around may cause one to fall into a dilemma.

The inferior man uses force while the superior man does not.
If one does not remain upright, there will be danger like a ram butts against fence and gets its horns stuck.

The less a leader uses his formal power, the more a truly powerful person he is. **A leader should cultivate his inner strength before he makes a show of his power.** To avoid a situation as when a ram gets its horns caught at a fence, a leader should think twice before he makes any move. In a very strong position as indicated by a yang line in a yang position, a leader is tempted to take offensive actions against others.

Fourth Yang ☳ Keep inner strength in advancement

If he remains persevering and true, regrets disappear.
He approaches an opened fence not to get stuck just as a large cart
with a strong axle is ready for a ride.

A yang line in a yin position as Fourth Yang advises a leader to be mild rather than obstinate. If he changes his attitude and actions, he will be auspicious. The two yin lines (Fifth Yin and Top Yin) are in front of Fourth Yang, indicating that no barriers against advancement exist. The leader should use his inner strength, like a large cart's strong axle, for advancement.

Fifth Yin ☵ Lessen toughness by adding gentleness

He uses a mild method to tame the strong ram. He has no regret.

If a leader acts like a stubborn ram he will have trouble with people both inside and outside the organization. Fifth yin as a yin line in a yang position indicates the possibility of using a moderate (yin) approach to lessen the hard (yang) character or the ram-like nature of a person.

It should be noted that all proper positions (yang line in yang position and yin line in yin position) in this hexagram are judged as unfortunate and improper positions (yang line in yin position and yin line in yang position) as fortunate. For example, Initial Yang and Third Yang are considered unfortunate whereas Second Yin, Fourth Yang, and Fifth Yin are fortunate. These judgments are, however, not in line with the definition of proper or improper positions in normal situations. Both Initial Yang and Third Yang have the nature of toughness but in the situation of Great Strength gentleness is preferable for balancing toughness. Proper positions cannot meet this requirement but improper positions can. This is why a proper position is judged unfortunate whereas an improper position is judged fortunate in this hexagram.

Top Yin ☳ **Stuck in the middle**

The ram butts a fence and gets trapped, it cannot advance or retreat.
He can gain nothing in this situation.
If he understands the difficulties and prepares the appropriate
measures for them, he will be auspicious.

Top Yin is at the end of the hexagram. It cannot go any further but cannot retreat either, resulting in a dilemma. A leader will be found in a similar situation when he is unable to either advance or retreat; whatever action he takes will only make the situation more complicated and worse. However, he should not stand at the crossroads but should actively seek the proper measures to escape from adversity.

35

晉
JIN

The Fire–Earth Hexagram

Advancing, Progressing

IMAGE

This hexagram is the image of Fire rising over Earth. Fire symbolizes the sun and the light. The higher the sun rises, the stronger is the light of the sun and the wider is the area under the sunlight. The rise of the sun symbolizes progress with brightness. The sun is indicated by the upper trigram, representing brightness and clarity as important qualities in a leader of an organization, whereas the earth as represented by the lower trigram means obedience, an important quality in subordinates. The hexagram gives therefore an image that **the subordinates of an organization are willing to follow a bright leader quietly, or people will follow an organization which has a bright future.**

HEXAGRAM STATEMENT

The marquis who contributed to the stability and peace of the country was bestowed gifts of horses by the king and received the award three times within one day.

This is a good time for progress as the capable subordinates make contributions to the organization and the leader admires their performance. This situation is indicated by the image of the hexagram in which the sun rises from the earth and the earth docilely attaches itself to the sun, symbolizing an interdependent relationship between the leader and his subordinates toward a common goal.

STRUCTURE

This is a hexagram with two yang and four yin lines. The two centering positions of the lower and upper trigram are occupied by the two yin lines, Second Yin and Fifth Yin respectively. Fifth position is the ruler (the key line) of the hexagram. A leader in this position is likely to act in a soft style. However, progress is not without difficulty as indicated by the nuclear or hidden Hexagram Obstacles:

Advancing   **Obstacles**

☲   ⟶   ☲

As the hidden hexagram shows there may be danger ahead. It suggests that precautionary measures should be prepared for when possible problems occur.

LINE STATEMENTS

Initial Yin ☷. Keep a steadfast and sincere attitude

He can either advance or retreat as long as he remains steadfast and true, he will be fortunate.
If he has not won the trust of others, he should remain calm and keep a cheerful manner. He will be free from blame.

At the beginning of a move forward an executive tends to advance as he expects assistance from the person with whom he has a good relationship, as indicated by an interconnection with Fourth Yang; but he may face difficulties because this person will not be able to help him for some reasons at present since Fourth Yin is in an improper position. However, this does not mean that he will not get such help later so he should keep a steadfast and sincere attitude. If he thinks he should move forward he can do so but with the expectation of meeting trouble (as indicated by the two yin lines ahead). What he should do now is to keep a steadfast and sincere attitude in either case. Sooner or later he will gain the confidence of others (Initial Yin is in the low position of the hexagram, not a respectable position).

Second Yin ☷. Get help from the experienced

He advances in sorrow. If he remains steadfast and true, he will receive blessing from his grandmother.

Second Yin is located at the bottom of the trigram GEN 艮 [Mountain] (Second Yin, Third Yin, and Fourth Yang) or the foot of a mountain, indicating obstacles ahead. Furthermore, Second Yin has no interaction with Fifth Yin above. This is why the text says "he advances in sorrow." Both Fifth Yin and Second Yin are yin lines; the former is seen as "grandmother" of the latter. In ancient times, the relationship between the grandmother (Fifth Yin) and the grandson's wife (Second Yin) was close, through which the latter could influence the former in order to help the grandson. Today the "grandmother" can be seen as the "experienced people." If a leader meets difficulties in his advance, he should not be depressed. Instead, he should persevere in his task and try to get help from those experienced people (Fifth Yin).

Second Yin as a yin line in a yin position in the middle of the lower trigram suggests for a leader in this position it is advantageous to hold to the principle of centrality during his advance.

Third Yin ☷. Get the support of colleagues

He gets support from his colleagues, regret vanishes.

In order to advance, a leader has to get support from the members of his organization, as indicated by other two yin lines below Third Yin. He can obtain this by emphasizing a common goal and also through good two-way communications. If his colleagues trust him, joint action will overcome the obstacles.

Although Third Yin is in an improper position (a yin line in a yang position) it is at the top of the lower trigram KUN 坤 [Earth], symbolizing high docility. It has an interconnection with Top Yang on one hand and shares the common goal for advance with the two yin lines on the other. An executive in this position must understand how to get support from his colleagues as his first priority in his plan for advancement.

Fourth Yang ☲. Do not be greedy and timid

He advances like a big rat. It is dangerous for him to go on.

A big rat is said to be greedy and timid. In an organization it symbolizes a senior executive who is close to the top leader and hopes to get certain benefits through this relationship. On the other hand, he also worries about resistance from the people (as indicated by the three yin lines below Fourth Yang) because of his misuse of his relationship with the top leader. If an organization contains a person like the big rat his conduct will affect harmony among the members and hence the efficiency of the organization. The rat-like person is not only greedy but is also incapable of performing his duties, as reflected by the improper position of Fourth Yin (a yang line in a yin position). A rat-like person lacks both ability and integrity.

Fifth Yin ☷ Principles for a yin-style leadership

All regrets are gone. He does not worry about gains and losses. It is auspicious to advance.

A person with yin character (tolerance and open-minded) in a top position (the fifth position) has the opportunity to be an effective, influential, and successful leader if he adopts the following three principles:

1. His tolerance and open-mindedness will lead him to employ capable people in their best roles. This is a yin-style leadership where the leader will use the strength of the members of the organization to offset his weaknesses.
2. His open mind will lead him to seek different views when formulating his plans for advancement.
3. He does not care whether the plan will bring him personal gains or losses as long as it is beneficial to the organization as a whole.

As long as a leader is on the right path, he should have confidence in going forward.

Top Yang ☷ Be firm but not impulsive

He advances to the extreme corner. If he can conquer his own land, he will be auspicious. There will be blame even he acts properly.

When a leader realizes that the progress of his present move has reached its upper limit (Top Yang is located at the extreme of the hexagram), he could be tempted to take another aggressive action to maintain his performance regardless of its difficulty and risk. If he can restrain his impulsive emotion, he will make no mistakes. Impulsiveness can be eliminated by self-restraint. But self-restraint may be against one's nature, so there may be regret by acting in this way. If he moves along the middle path, he will not go to extremes, so there is no need to correct his direction and hence there will be no regret.

36

明夷
MINGYI

The Earth–Fire Hexagram

Brightness Dimmed, Hiding
Brightness

IMAGE

The Earth–Fire Hexagram or Brightness Dimmed is the inverse of the previous Fire–Earth Hexagram JIN 晉 [Advancing] (35). The image of the sun over the earth in the Hexagram Advancing is now changed that of the sun under the earth in the Hexagram Brightness Dimmed. When the sun goes down behind the earth, the world is in darkness as brightness is dimmed. Hence, the hexagram is named Brightness Dimmed or Darkening of the Light, indicating that the Light is overshadowed by the Earth.

A leader who is extremely autocratic and incapable will lead his organization into bureaucracy, inefficiency, and corruption. The morale of the people in the organization declines. What actions should people take in this situation? This hexagram suggests some guidelines for people who find themselves in a time of darkness. Let the upper trigram KUN 坤 [Earth] represent the people and the lower trigram LI 離 [Fire] (brightness) the wisdom, then the hexagram has another meaning that indicates that wisdom is rooted in the people or the members of his organization. They know how to protect themselves by using their wisdom in the time of darkness. One of the approaches is to conceal their real intentions. On the other hand, if the leader neglects their wisdom, he will regret it later.

HEXAGRAM STATEMENT

In a time of brightness dimmed, it is beneficial to keep to the right way in order to get through the difficulties.

In adversity or in a dark period, a leader must remain true to his ideals and not lose sight of his goal but try to pursue it quietly. His actions may not be understood and appreciated by the people around him, but he should pay no attention to them and continue to keep a low profile. His optimism, perseverance, and patience will be rewarded when the right time comes.

STRUCTURE

This is a hexagram with four yin and two yang lines. The four yin lines have a dominate position against the two yang lines in the hexagram, reflecting a situation in which **the justice (yang) is overshadowed by the evil (yin).**

LINE STATEMENTS

Initial Yang ☲. An enlightened person will not stand at a dangerous wall

When brightness is dimmed, the superior man runs away swiftly like a wounded bird with dropping wings during flight.
On his escape, he does not eat for three days. His leave is criticized by the master.

Following the meaning of the Chinese saying: "A superior man will not stand at a dangerous wall," an upright man will silently and swiftly leave a corrupt and rotten organization because he believes that this situation will not change as the administration is likely to be under the present leadership for a considerable time. He is sensitive to what troubles or dangers will come later, but his act is not understood by the top leader and colleagues who fail to see this. Similarly an executive should not be involved in an activity which appears to be dishonest or deceptive. The sooner he gets out of it, the safer he is.

During the regime of Zhou Wang 紂王, the last king of the Shang Dynasty (Yin Dynasty: 1600–1045 B.C.), Weizi 微子, the king's brother, fled from Shang to the neighboring state Zhou because of his detestation of King Zhou's tyranny and cruelties. The text refers to this event.

Second Yin ☲☷. Find protection

Brightness is dimmed. He is injured in the left thigh but he can be rescued if he is able to get a strong horse and then there will be good fortune.

Even if an executive is upright and docile as symbolized by the position of Second Yin, he can still be hurt by inferior people in the "time of darkness." He should be able to find a way to protect himself from danger. "A strong horse" as suggested by the text refers to a person in the position of Third Yang. Since Second Yin lacks the ability (a yin line) to move out of the organization, he has to stay where he is and seek the aid of a strong man within the organization, like Third Yang, for safety.

Third Yang ☲☷. Do not make corrections hastily

Brightness is dimmed. He goes hunting in the south. Even if he captures the great chief, he should not restore order hastily.

Even if the leader is able to identify the main cause of corruption within his organization, he should make his adjustments and reforms slowly and carefully, for any change for the better will not happen overnight. Resistance to change from the members of the organization could be so strong that he would meet great difficulties in his reforms unless the corresponding plans for overcoming them are well prepared.

In the *Yijing*, the hexagram KUN 坤 [Earth] (2) represents the south. As the characteristic of the earth is gentleness, the text "hunting in the south" therefore means taking an action for reforms in a gentle way or a gradual approach instead of a hasty one, as things cannot be changed overnight and hasty actions may possibly result in an unstable situation or even chaos.

Fourth Yin ☷☲. Exit quickly from a dark place

He enters the left side of the belly. He reaches the heart of that which dims the brightness. He leaves the courtyard.

Fourth Yin represents a senior official who is close to the leader Fifth Yang. The text "left side of the belly" refers to a place which is close to the main organ of a man's body—the heart. "He enters the left side of the belly" means that this senior official is close to the power center of the organization. "He reaches the heart of that which dims the brightness" indicates that he has gained the heart or confidence of the top leader, a man whose actions bring the organization into darkness. But Fourth Yin has a weak character as indicated by the yin line; he lacks the courage to say "no" to the top leader. Consequently, he will not express his opposition to a decision made by the top leader or the key members of the organization. If he realizes that the organization is deeply corrupted and there is no possibility that matters will improve in the foreseeable future, his best choice is to leave the organization as suggested by the text "he leaves the courtyard."

Fifth Yin ☷ **Conceal true sentiments but hold integrity in the time of darkness**

When uprightness is dimmed, he should act like Prince Jizi who pretended to be insane to protect his dignity. It is good to be upright and true.

Jizi 箕子, who was the uncle of the tyrant King Zhou, could not escape from the court so he concealed his understanding and feigned insanity to protect himself. King Zhou killed another uncle Bi Gan 比干 for remonstrating with him. The fifth line in this hexagram, unlike in the other hexagrams, is not the leadership position but a very senior official to the top leader who is represented by Top Yin here. For some reason this senior official decides not to leave the organization despite the corruption. For example, this could be because of his strong loyalty to the organization. In order not to be involved in the corruption, he should try to find a good excuse to stay away from the decision circle and so keep his inner light bright.

To protect himself he should conceal his true sentiments. The purpose of this is the hope that the top leader as represented by Top Yin here and his followers will eventually be removed. At that time his self-restraint and patience will be rewarded. Even in the darkest time, this senior executive should hold onto his integrity.

Confucius highly praised the three superior men of the Shang Dynasty—Weizi, Jizi, and Bi Gan as mentioned above. He said: **"There were three benevolent men at the end of Yin (Shang) dynasty"** in *The Analects* [*Lunyu* 論語]. Weizi kept a far distance from evil, Jizi persevered with his integrity in the time of darkness, and Bi Gan had the courage to correct evil. Courage, concealment, and retreat are all the essential qualities of a superior (benevolent) man or a bright leader.

Top Yin ☷ Maintain as a bright leader

First he climbs up heaven, brightness is everywhere.
Then he plunges into the earth, darkness comes.

A top leader of an organization must understand the law of nature between brightness and darkness. If he lacks the qualities of a bright leader, he will not be able to hold his position like King Zhou in the Shang dynasty. Top Yin is in a weak position, giving a warning to a top leader who lacks uprightness and integrity.

37

家人
JIAREN **The Wind–Fire Hexagram**
The Family

IMAGE

The Wind–Fire Hexagram illustrates the nature and structure of a family. In the framework of the *Yijing*, wind also represents wood. In ancient China, wood and fire were found in every family, so both together represent a family. Wood over Fire makes the flames which produce smoke; smoke from the chimney of a house symbolizes wind blowing outside. So the image of this hexagram is Fire inside and Wind outside. When there is smoke from a chimney, there is a house or a family.

Fifth Yang and Second Yin symbolize the proper positions of the husband and wife outside and within a family respectively. It means the duty of a man is to work outside whereas that of a woman is to do housework inside.

From another aspect, the hexagram can also indicate the different positions of the members of a family as follows:

——	Top Yang	Grandfather
——	Fifth Yang	Father, chief of the family
– –	Fourth Yin	Wife
——	Third Yang	The elder son
– –	Second Yin	Daughter
——	Initial Yang	The younger son

1. The relationship between father and son or daughter:
   Top Yang and Fifth Yang, Fifth Yang and Third Yang, Fifth Yang and Initial Yang, Fifth Yang and Second Yin

2. The relationship between husband and wife:
   Fifth Yang and Fourth Yin
3. The relationship between brothers and between brothers and sisters:
   Third Yang and Initial Yang, Third Yang and Second Yin, Second
   Yin, and Initial Yang
4. The relationship between grandfather and grandson/granddaughter:
   Top Yang and Third Yang, Second Yin, Initial Yang
5. The relationship between father and daughter-in law:
   Top Yang and Fourth Yin

The hexagram describes three main relationships in a family: father
and son, husband and wife, brother and brother (or brother and sister).
These family relationships can also be extended to those between mother
and son, sister and sister.

Father and mother are strict leaders of a family. Each member of
the family has a role to play. If the father acts as a father, the son as a
son, the husband as a husband, and the wife as a wife, the family is in
order. When the family is in order, according to **Confucius**, all other
social relationships, for example, that between superior and subordinate
or among friends or colleagues, will also be in order. **If one can manage
his own family well, he should be capable of managing other social
organizations just as well, including the government. So the family is
considered the foundation of a society or a country.** This is like fire
that generates energy outwardly. Family values have primarily four
fundamental benefits that can be applied to other social organizations:

- A group spirit
- A mutually supportive relationship
- A harmonious relationship
- A close cooperation in difficult times

HEXAGRAM STATEMENT

The hexagram JIAREN illustrates the **dao** *of a family. It is favorable for
women to act their right role in a family.*

In a family each member has a particular role to play according to the
dao of the family or the proper function in a home. In the family, the
father usually deals more with the outer world whereas wife performs
the inner work. The children prepare themselves for their future by

learning and assisting their parents in domestic work. Following the example of a harmonious family, other organizations should be responsible for making the functions of their members clear so that these people can fulfill their roles effectively.

STRUCTURE

This is a yang-dominated hexagram in which two yin lines are encircled by the yang lines. This signifies that in traditional Chinese society the male plays the major role in a family. The fifth and top lines are yang, representing the positions where the family decisions are made.

All the five lines from the initial to the fifth are in proper positions, that is, a yang line in a yang position and a yin line in a yin position. A right position in a family means each member knows what family orders he or she should follow and what role and duty they have. The yang line at top, however, is in a yin position or an improper position. This line represents the most senior member of the family—a grandfather who has given his authority to his son for managing the family but could reserve the ultimate authority for major decisions and who sits behind the chief of the family, Fifth Yang. This is why the grandfather is assigned an improper position rather than a proper position as the father who has the formal power in the family.

The inverse hexagram of the hexagram JIAREN is the Fire–Lake Hexagram KUI 睽 [Diverging] (38) ☲☱, indicating that there may be conflicts or confrontations among the family members which would hurt their relationships and cooperation, resulting in disharmony within the family. This concept can be applied to other organizations as well.

Wood over Fire indicates a situation in which the wood is burnt by the fire. This warns a family or an organization that harmony can be destroyed by members fighting amongst themselves for their own benefit. The leader must understand that internal harmony is the foundation of stability in a family or an organization.

The hidden hexagram is the Fire–Water Hexagram WEIJI 未濟 [Not Yet Accomplished] (64) ☲☵ in which Fire blazes up and Water flows down, symbolizing that the mission of a family or an organization is not yet completed. All members should thus have the spirit of Not Yet Accomplished. With this mentality, the members of a family or of an organization will cooperate better with each other.

THE SIMILARITY BETWEEN HEXAGRAMS JIAREN AND HEXAGRAM JIJI

From a structural aspect the hexagram JIJI 既濟 [Already Accomplished] (63) can also be used to symbolize a family:

	JIJI
Grandmother	▬ ▬
Father	▬▬▬
Mother	▬ ▬
Son	▬▬▬
Daughter	▬ ▬
Grandson	▬▬▬

The difference between the structure of the two hexagrams JIAREN and JIJI is the nature of the top line. The former has a yang line whereas the latter has a yin line. The top yin line of the hexagram JIJI can be interpreted as the grandmother of a family and the other five lines represent the family members. In this book, the author has repeatedly indicated the fact that the names of hexagrams in the *Yijing* appear to be unfixed because the interpretation of a hexagram structure can be different if approached from a different angle. Different approaches have different interpretations. In fact, each hexagram in the *Yijing* can be renamed according to different perceptions or understanding. If the hexagrams names in the *Yijing* were changed, the hexagram and line statements as well as their interpretations would correspondingly be changed too.

LINE STATEMENTS

Initial Yang ☰. Set the rules clearly to prevent misconduct

He sets up the rules and regulations for the family to follow, regret vanishes.

A family that has rules will make the members understand their roles and duties within the family so that disorder can be avoided. This principle is equally applicable to other organizations in the community. At the beginning of any activity, the role and responsibility of each member in a group or team must be clearly defined. Once misconduct is tolerated and allowed to spread within an organization, it will be difficult to correct this later. Clear rules help maintain order within an organization. The yang line symbolizes that there is a need for something hard, for example, rules.

Second Yin ☲. **Assign responsibility to a person according to his ability**

She follows her husband and does not make decisions herself.
Her proper role in the family is the kitchen. It is auspicious to be
steadfast and true.

The yin characteristic of the second line stands for a person who is not suitable for external work but very capable of assuming internal functions. When assigning a person's responsibility in an organization the principle is to let him have the opportunity to use the best of his ability, just as a wife does kitchen work in the traditional Chinese community.

Third Yang ☳. **Find a balance between discipline and leniency**

The family members complain about the strict rules.
Nevertheless, it is auspicious. When women and children are
frivolous, there will be shame in the end.

Rules are required in all organizations. The question is how strict they should be. Too much discipline will make the organization highly bureaucratic and will cause resentment. Consequently people's initiative may suffer. On the other hand, if discipline is too soft, disorder may arise in the organization. Neither way is correct. The desirable approach is to find a balance between discipline and leniency. If this is not possible the line statement suggests that a strict approach is more preferable to a soft one, because disorder can ruin an organization. Third Yang is in a strong position (a yang line in a yang position), representing the attitude towards discipline.

Fourth Yin ☴. **Provide valuable assistance**

She enriches the family. There is great good fortune.

Fourth Yin represents the character of the wife and her role in a family: docility, domestic service, and assistance to her husband. Her work helps create a harmonious and prosperous family. By the same token, a senior executive who is close to the top leader can provide valuable advice and assistance to the organization even though he is not the top leader.

Fifth Yang ☲ Set a good example for the members

He sets a good example for the members of the family. It is auspicious without worry.

A leader should be able to bring to fruition the way of the *dao* in maintaining his organization. He must be open-minded and true as indicated by the characteristics of Fifth Yang—balance, sincerity, and uprightness. He should give guidance to the members of the organization around him as a father does in the family. If all family members act as they should (father as father, son as son, husband as husband, wife as wife), family relationships will become harmonious and amicable and the foundation of a stable family will be established. Following the same principle, other organizations will also be able to achieve harmony and stability.

Top Yang ☲ Need both sincerity and dignity

He inspires people with sincerity and dignity. The end is auspicious.

There are two important principles for managing organizations: sincerity and dignity. A leader can gain trust and respect from the members of his organization if he is true to himself and has dignified sternness. Sincerity comes from his cultivation and dignity from his sincerity. Top Yang is at the end of hexagram, indicating that sincerity and dignity are considered as the *dao* or the important principles in leading a family or an organization.

38

 KUI

The Fire–Lake Hexagram
Diverging, Opposition

IMAGE

Fire over Lake indicates a situation of opposition based on the nature of the two entities, the fire flames up while water in the lake flows down. These two opposite movements constitute the image of opposition. Between Fire and Water there are differences and similarities. The main difference between the two is in the direction of their movement and the similarity is in their function as fire illuminates the earth and water nourishes the earth. Both benefit people even though they move in different directions.

Knowing the different characteristics of Fire and Water in the nature, the leader of an organization must understand that differences in the views or abilities of the members within his organization are inevitable. To achieve harmony and higher efficiency in the organization, he should not expect to get a uniform view or the same kind of people. Instead, he should seek a shared value from the group members by allowing them to hold their own views. **Similarity within difference or difference within similarity** is an important principle that a leader of any organization should be able to master.

Like yin and yang in a *taiji*, **union and division are the two polar forces within a whole**. When a union reaches its higher level, a division starts to develop and vice versa as indicated by the yin–yang cycle. In the development of an organization, union and division or convergence and divergence can be used as strategies in different times and places. In good times, a division strategy or diversification is often used for catching rising opportunities while in bad times a union or integration strategy appears to be more appropriate as it concentrates the resources and achieves better efficiency.

Division or opposition is not necessarily a disadvantage to an organization, for it is the law of nature. **If there is a union, there must have a division on the opposite side and vice versa**. The division between the heaven and the earth creates myriad things which are in different categories. **The difference in things provides the basis or condition for the union of things. Without difference there is no way to have a union**. Following this concept, a division of the views among the members of an organization is considered normal. What a wise leader should know is how to integrate these different views into a one that will be accepted by the majority of the members. Division or opposition should not be seen as an absolute term since the chance of a reunion between different things is always there.

Hexagram Statement

When there is opposition, it is appropriate to deal with small matters.

When there are diverging viewpoints in a policy among the members of a decision group, the leader should get the group members to agree on a minor point first and postpone the major conflicting issues later, so that he can have more time to convince the key opponents by his sound arguments. Using a gradual approach in a time of opposition is beneficial.

Structure

The Hexagram Diverging with four yang and two yin lines indicates a hexagram that is dominated by the yang; it means that the respective organization is stable. Though there are opposite views or forces, they are, however, under the control. Third Yin in an "improper position" weakens the opposite forces and Fifth Yin as encircled by the two yang lines is also an indication of its weak position. So the positive forces as represented by the four yang lines have the chance to beat the opposite forces back to the road to a reunion.

Line Statements

Initial Yang ☲. Do not create enemies too early

His regret disappears. There is no need for him to chase the runaway horse, it will return on its accord just as he meets someone who is unfriendly but harmless.

If opposition crops up, the leader should not try to alter it immediately, for the situation will possibly return to normal as a runaway horse comes back on its own. A premature response could make the matter worse. When there are people who disagree with the views of the leader, he should not give up on them too early. Otherwise, the gap between them and himself will deepen and an opposed force may be created. Instead, he should try to settle or reduce the differences between the two sides by persuasion and communication in a sincere way. To achieve his goal, the leader should know how to use **the principle of similarity within difference** or **the principle of difference in similarity**.

Initial Yang stands alone as it has no interconnection with Fourth Yang, but it dose share a common value with Fourth Yang (both are yang lines) and this could make the gap between the two disappear. On other hand, Initial Yang symbolizes the early stage of an opposition; it is advantageous to solve this problem now before it escalates.

Second Yang ☱. Use an informal way to unite people

He meets his master in a lane. There is no blame.

An informal approach can be used for an interconnection between a leader and his colleagues or subordinates instead of a formal one, since this is a better way to remove the misunderstanding between the two parties.

Second Yang and Fifth Yin indicate the principle of similarity within differences as both are improper positions (a yang line in a yang position and a yin line in a yin position) but different line characters (a yang and a yin line). Based on this principle, the leader is able to unite the people on their common values even though they have different views on other things.

Third Yin ☲· Seek for help from those with common value

The wagon is dragged backward and the ox halted in front.
The driver's hair is shaved and his nose is cut off. This is not a good start but things will end well.

Third Yin is at an improper position, signifying a person in a difficult situation which is just like a wagon described in the text; it is blocked by Fourth Yang above and seized by Second Yang from below. Third yin is in a yang position that will induce a person to move ahead, but he will not succeed as he is in a dilemma.

The interconnection between Third Yin and Top Yang indicates a complementary relationship. To get out of this situation, the executive should seek the help from a person (Top Yang) who is like-minded, capable, and trustful. Despite the difficulty arising from the opposition, he should not be discouraged as things will turn out well for him if he tries to find the way out.

Fourth Yang ☱ Build up fellowship with one who has similar character

He is alone in opposition, but he meets a capable man; both are sincere to each other. Although there is danger, there will be no harm.

The position of Fourth Yang is between two yin lines, indicating a situation of isolation. When a leader is being isolated by others due to different values or interests, he should find someone of like minds, for example, Initial Yang, and communicate in truth and sincerity. Although Fourth Yang has no interconnection with Initial Yang, both do have a common characteristic—the yang element, for example, great energy. This may become the basis for building up fellowship or comradeship between the two particularly in a time of opposition and isolation.

Fifth Yin ☲ Get assistance from a partner who has a shared value

Regret disappears. His relationship with the clansman is close as he bites a soft meat. What is wrong with going forward?

Fifth Yin has an interconnection with Second Yang which is seen as the clansman of the former as both are in a central position with the characteristics of sincerity, balance, and uprightness. Through this interconnection a union of yin and yang is achievable. When a leader is in a weak (yin) position, he should seek the complement from a strong person (Second Yang) with whom he has a close relationship and a shared value. Through this he will be able to get the needed assistance as easily as "biting a soft meat."

Top Yang ☱ Tensions and suspicions in a time of extreme
opposition

When he is isolated by opposition, he sees his clansman as a pig
covered with mud and carries a wagon full of demons.
First he draws his bow, and then he puts it by as the man is not a
robber but a suitor. Going forward, it is auspicious if rain is
encountered.

When the situation of opposition is at extreme, a leader may become
impulsive and suspicious of the people he is working with and thereby
creating rifts. The leader (Top Yang) and the person who can support
him (Third Yin) are true complements at the extreme situation of
opposition. But the leader may misjudge his partner by taking him as
a "dirty pig" or a "demon." Since he is in the extreme position of
opposition, he is not certain about the changes in the future. Therefore,
his doubts create tensions and suspicions towards his colleagues.
However, his delusion will not last long and he will return to reality in
the end. The leader or Top Yang first doubts Third Yin and turns away;
when this opposition comes to end, Top Yang no longer has doubts and
joins Third Yin. The situation of opposition is harmonized by a union of
yin and yang which is symbolized by rain.

39

JIAN

The Water–Mountain Hexagram

Obstacles, Difficulty, Adversity

IMAGE

Since both Water and Mountain symbolize obstruction, the hexagram of Water over Mountain indicates a situation surrounded by obstacles. Water ahead and mountain behind portray a dilemma. Proceeding will encounter obstacles but to stay behind could risk missing an opportunity for movement. As the mountain also stands for stopping, the hexagram therefore advises that one should not go forward but stay where he is in order to avoid the danger ahead as represented by water. When one is found in a situation of adversity as signified by the outer trigram KAN 坎 [Water] he should not be panicky or frustrated; instead he should keep his mind as stable and peaceful as a mountain while calmly thinking of possible ways out. This is a basic quality required in a wise leader in a time of difficulty.

HEXAGRAM STATEMENT

It is favorable for one to go to the southwest instead of the northeast. It is beneficial to see the great man. If he can keep to the right way, he will be auspicious.

Each of the eight trigrams represents a direction. The direction of the trigram KUN 坤 [Earth] is southwest, which represents softness, and the direction of the trigram ZHEN 震 [Thunder] stands for obstruction. The text "to go to the southeast" rather than "the northeast" therefore means to adopt a safer and easier means of moving forward, avoiding obstacles and dangers. In a time of difficulty, the leader of an organization is advised to choose a safer way and to seek the help of capable people in order to avoid the difficulty.

STRUCTURE

This is a four-yin–two-yang hexagram. The two yangs are surrounded by four yins, indicating the difficulties represented by three trigrams which are the lower trigram GEN 艮 [Mountain] and two trigrams KAN as follows:

1. First KAN (a hidden or nuclear trigram): formed by Second Yin, Third Yang, and Fourth Yin
2. Second KAN: Formed by Fourth Yin, Fifth Yang, and Top Yin
3. GEN: Formed by Initial Yin, Second Yin, and Third Yang

A hexagram which has two trigrams KAN and one trigram GEN indicates a situation of obstacles. The reciprocal hexagram of this hexagram is the Thunder–Water Hexagram XIE 解 [Release] (40) ䷧ , suggesting that an action is required to overcome the obstacles.

LINE STATEMENTS

Initial Yin ䷂. Wait for the right moment to advance

If he goes forward, he will meet obstacles.
If he comes back, he will have praise.

When faced with an obstacle the leader of an organization should consider very carefully whether he should move forward or hold back. Based on the yin character of the first line of this hexagram—caution and passivity—the suggestion is not to move as there is danger ahead represented by the hidden trigram KAN ☵ which is formed by Second Yin, Third Yang and Fourth Yin. Initial Yin is weak (a yin line) and also lacks an interconnection or support from Fourth Yin. Under such circumstances, a wise leader should decide to stay where he is until there is the right time for advancement.

Second Yin ䷂. Dash ahead regardless of one's safety

The minister tries to help the king who is in difficulty but puts himself in a difficult position too. He acts not for his own interest.

When a leader as represented by Fifth Yin is in difficulty, his subordinate Second Yin gives his assistance or support to Fifth Yin even though the subordinate himself is in a weak position (a yin line) and lacks the strength to rescue his superior. He is doing this for the benefit of the whole organization. If all members of the organization follow his example, the obstacles can be overcome. A subordinate who acts in this way will get praise from the leader.

Third Yang ☵· Retreat when the risk in advancing is high

If he goes forward, he will encounter difficulties. So he turns around and comes back.

When a leader believes that he is in a favorable position (a yang line in a yang position and an interconnection with Top Yin), he is tempted to move forward because of his self-confidence or impulsiveness. But when he realizes that he will fall into a pitfall or danger as indicated by the second hidden trigram KAN ☵ (formed by Fourth Yin, Fifth Yang, and Top Yin) and the weakness of his partner (Top Yin), it is wise for him not to advance. Instead he should return to a place where it is more secure. This means that he should stay where he is and seek support from those below as represented by Second Yin and Initial Yin which carry Third Yang in the line structure. Since Third Yang is in the midst of the first trigram KAN ☵ as indicated by the yang line, an executive in this position is advised to preserve his strength for the future.

Fourth Yin ☷· Form alliances for advancement

If he goes forward, he will encounter difficulties. He should come back to form alliances before moving forward.

When a leader realizes there is a danger ahead he should not to go forward but should try to increase his strength by obtaining assistance from those below such as Third Yang, Second Yin, and Initial Yin. Third Yang can offer complementary assistance based on a yin–yang interaction, whereas Initial Yin and Second Yin share the same values as Fourth Yin as all three are yin lines. With a united force the leader will be in a better position for both defensive and offensive purposes with regard to his organization.

Fifth Yang ☵ Integrity brings support

When he is in great difficulty, friends will come to his help.

When a leader who is sincere, balanced, and upright is in difficulties he will get assistance from colleagues and friends because of his integrity. Fifth Yang is in the midst of the Second KAN which represents not only a great obstruction but also represents a man's perseverance. As there is an interconnection between Fifth Yang and Second Yin, it seems that the latter could give his assistance to the former. He is, however, rather weak, as indicated by the nature of the yin line, so the assistance provided by Second Yin would be considered insufficient. Therefore, the leader Fifth Yang should not rely on help from those below, but should actively seeks a possible way out by himself.

Top Yin ☵ Seek help from capable people

If he goes forward, he will encounter difficulties. It is better if he turns back. It is favorable to call on a great man.

Top Yin is at the extreme of the hexagram and the trigram KAN, signifying a situation with great difficulties. A senior executive in this position has to make a choice whether he should go forward or not. According to the advice in the text, he should seek help from the top leader Fifth Yang, who is capable and upright.

40

 解
XIE

The Thunder–Water Hexagram

Loosening, Release, Removal

IMAGE

Thunder represents movement and Water stands for danger. Moving around the outside of danger means getting out of difficulties. The hexagram XIE gives the image of release from danger or difficulties. After the thunder and rain, clouds part and the sky is once clearer, symbolizing the fact that tensions and complications are beginning to ease. Thunder stands for the yang and rain for the yin. A union of yin–yang will restore balance or harmony in nature and obstacles will then fade away naturally. The upper trigram ZHEN 震 [Thunder] means that one should make a move when there are difficulties, so movement or action is the foundation for removing danger.

HEXAGRAM STATEMENT

For a removal of danger it is advantageous to be in the southwest.
In a stable and peaceful situation, nonaction is most appropriate.
But when there is obstruction, a quick removal of it is auspicious.

The southwest is the direction of the trigram KUN 坤 [Earth], which represents softness and docility. When there is obstruction, a leader should remove it in a timely way. He is advised to use a soft approach to remove any difficulty that he faces. Once the obstruction is removed, no further action is needed to maintain harmony in the organization.

STRUCTURE

This is a hexagram with four yins and two yangs. The two yang lines are surrounded by the four yin lines, indicating difficulties that have to be overcome. The hexagram has two trigrams of KAN 坎 [Water] ☵ , the first KAN includes Initial Yin, Second Yang, and Third Yin and the second Kan is a nuclear or hidden one which includes Third Yin, Fourth Yang, and Fifth Yin. The Hexagram Release thereby indicates double dangers.

To overcome difficulties or to obtain deliverance from dangers, it is necessary to take the appropriate action. Between Third Yin and Top Yin there is a trigram ZHEN (Fourth Yang, Fifth Yin, and Top Yin) and a hidden trigram KAN 坎 (Third Yin, Fourth Yang, and Fifth Yin). Thus these two trigrams form the second hexagram XIE within the original hexagram XIE. The two hexagrams are of the same nature as both of them indicate a difficult situation that needs to be dealt with.

LINE STATEMENTS

Initial Yin ☵. Solve the problem right at the beginning

There will be no mistakes.

If a leader can solve his problem right at the beginning, there will be no harm or the harm will be limited. Initial Yin is the first line of the lower trigram Water, indicating that the difficulties have just arisen. It is beneficial to take action and get rid of them at an early stage.

There are two favorable conditions for action as denoted by the line structure. First, as a yin (soft) line in a yang (strong) position, Initial Yin receives the benefit of a yin–yang union. The yang character of the position together with the yin nature of the line provides a balanced way of solving the problem. Second, Initial Yin obtains assistance from Fourth Yang and through this interconnection Initial Yin is thereby able to work with Fourth Yang, and this can provide the strength Initial Yin needs. A problem should be resolved by using a moderate approach at an early stage before it proliferates.

Second Yang ☵. Remove the evil by keeping centrality

He catches three foxes on the hunt and gets a yellow arrow.
Uprightness brings good fortune.

The three foxes refer to the three yin lines except Fifth Yin, symbolizing three cunning or petty men in an organization. Second Yang as a subordinate is given a position of trust by the leader Fifth Yin to remove the three petty men. As a person with uprightness, Second Yang uses a moderate approach (as symbolized by a yellow arrow) to get rid of them. Three foxes also symbolize one's evil thoughts; one can remove them by keeping centrality.

Third Yin ☷· Know the limit of one's own strength

He carries a burden on his back and rides in a carriage; this will attract robbers. Such conduct is shameful.

Third Yin is in an improper position as it rides above Second Yang and carries Fourth Yin on its back. This describes a situation in which a man is doing something which is beyond his capabilities. A leader should know his own limits.

Fourth Yang ☳· Cut off relationships with the petty man

He moves his big toe, friends will come in sincerity.

Fourth Yang represents an honorable senior official and Initial Yin the petty man, as symbolized by the big toe in the text. In order to get friends or capable people, Fourth Yin should cut off his close relationship (interconnection) with the petty man.

Fifth Yin ☵· Influence the inferior man by a right act

If a superior man keeps a distance from the inferior man but gets close to good men, he will be auspicious. His act will influence the act of the inferior man, too.

If a leader who is a noble man only uses people who are also sincere with integrity, inferior people will be positively influenced by his actions and may therefore change their attitude and move in the right direction.

Top Yin ☵· Overcome difficulties by using tough measures

The lord shoots a hawk on a high wall. He hits it with an arrow. An act like this is favorable for every action.

Top Yin symbolizes a hawk or an inferior man who occupies a high position in an organization. The inferior man or Top Yin is in a place above two KANs. First KAN is represented by Initial Yin, Second Yang and Third Yin; second KAN is represented by Third Yin, Fourth Yang, and Fifth Yin. The situation indicates double dangers. The leader should take this opportunity to remove the inferior man in his organization.

41

SUN

The Mountain–Lake Hexagram

Decreasing, Diminishing, Reduction

IMAGE

Mountain over Lake indicates a negative relationship between these two objects. The mountain will become higher if the lake is dredged deeper. A decrease in the lake is therefore an increase in the mountain. Also the moisture in the lake rises upward and nourishes the slopes of the mountain as well as the plants and trees on it. This means a decrease for those below in favor of those above.

The hexagram SUN is formed by exchanging the Third Yang line with the Top Yin Line in the hexagram TAI 泰 [Harmony] (11):

Hexagram Harmony   Hexagram Decreasing

After transformation of these two lines, the third position of the Hexagram Harmony which is originally strong becomes weak in the Hexagram Decreasing. Such a relationship can be found in the situation of a business group where the size of the subsidiary is reduced for the benefit of the parent company or the group as a whole. In the product profile of a company, a shift of resources from a declining sector to a growing sector is another example of an action of decrease. Since the gains from the growing sector are able to offset the losses from the declining sector, the total gains of the company can still be increased; an action of decrease can be seen as "a positive sum game" rather than "a zero-sum game." In this hexagram, the lower trigram, therefore, can represent the declining sector and the upper trigram the growing sector in a company. However, the definition of "decrease" here refers only to a particular unit of an organization, not the whole organization. From the point of view, the whole organization a "decrease" could actually be an "increase." The definition depends on from which angle it is viewed.

There will be a limit to the transfer of resources between the sacrificed unit (the decreased) and the benefiting unit (the increased) of an organization. Any move beyond this would result in total losses rather than total gains: "a negative-sum game." To obtain an appropriate balance in a transfer of resources between the sacrificed and benefiting unit, a leader should be able to master the principle of centrality, under which the initiative of both sacrificed and benefiting units are not damaged.

When a leader uses the decrease method to profit those above at the expense of those below as indicated in the hexagram, the success of the action is dependent on two conditions. First, he must be sincere and trustworthy in order to obtain the support of the sacrificed unit. Second, the time of the action must be appropriate so that the sacrificed unit will not resist it.

The concept of "decrease" and "increase" can be extended to other opposing terms, for example, "gains" and "losses." In a space aspect, what one unit loses become the gains of another unit. If the gains are equal to the losses, it is a "zero-sum game." If the gains overcompensate for the losses, it becomes a "positive-sum game." In a time aspect, losses today could become the gains of tomorrow and vice versa; the gains of today could be the losses of tomorrow.

"Decrease" can also be seen as a method of self-cultivation. One tries to reduce his ego including all self-images, for example, self-centeredness, self-importance, self-esteem, self-assertion, self-defense, self-satisfaction, self-indulgence, self-seeking, and self-will. If a leader is controlled by his ego he tends to be insincere and unreliable. The ego usurps the true self of the leader. To be a selfless leader, he needs to subsume his ego and enable the inner truth to prevail. This is an inner shift of evil to good in order to keep an inner balance in one's self-development.

HEXAGRAM STATEMENT

To decrease with sincerity is very auspicious. To do it perseveringly in the right way is blameless. With this in mind it is beneficial to go anywhere.

The sincere way of decreasing can be expressed by using two sacrificial bowls of rice for offerings.

Within an organization the members should be able to adopt the attitude of decreasing their own interests in order to support the whole if there is such a need; for example, taking a salary cut or a reduction in fringe benefits in a bad time. However, this decrease should be voluntary. A compulsory decrease imposed by the top management will probably have an adverse effect on the interests of the whole organization.

STRUCTURE

All the three lines of the lower trigram are interconnected with their counterparts in the upper trigram, indicating three complementary relationships between the upper and lower positions in an organization. Maintaining harmony is therefore an important condition when taking a decreasing action in an organization.

This hexagram is named Decreasing because the object of the decrease is in the lower trigram. But if the judgment criterion is changed to Increase instead of Decrease, the object of the increased unit is then in the upper trigram rather than in the lower trigram. If this is the case, the Hexagram Decreasing can also be called Increasing and the name of the next hexagram Increasing should correspondingly be changed to Decreasing. The hexagram name is therefore dependent on which trigram the object is located or focused.

LINE STATEMENTS

Initial Yang ☳. Give proper help to the weaker

Once he completes his task, he should go right away, so there will be no blame.
He should carefully consider what appropriate help he can give to others.

Initial Yang is interconnected with Fourth Yin, indicating a situation in which the stronger unit of an organization gives its help to the weaker one. The leader of an organization should carefully consider how much the stronger unit can help the weaker. Overextending the stronger unit's resources to support the weaker unit could harm both, since too much support given to the weaker unit could affect the stronger unit's own initiative and efficiency. The leader should be concerned about whether this action could make the weaker unit dependent on the stronger unit. The support of a stronger unit given to a weaker unit should be on an appropriate scale. It will not do to go too far or alternatively not to go far enough.

To keep harmony in the whole organization, the stronger unit should not complain about what sacrifices it has made to other units of the organization, but should maintain a moderate attitude toward the decrease policy of the organization.

Second Yang ☳. No decreasing is increasing

It is beneficial for him to be steadfast and not to move forward, otherwise there will be misfortune. He can help others better only if he will not decrease himself.

Second Yang is in the center of the lower trigram, suggesting that the executive in this position should maintain the principle of centrality in his leadership. Since Second Yang stands at the beginning of the hidden trigram ZHEN 震 [Thunder] ☳, his moves forward will meet with difficulties as indicated by the Big Mountain ahead as formed by Third Yin, Fourth Yin, Fifth Yin, and Top Yang.

Fifth Yin needs the help of Second Yang as indicated by the interconnection between the two. An executive in the position of Second Yang should examine the situation carefully and consider whether he should give his help to Fifth Yin. If Fifth Yin represents a top leader who is weak and incapable, particularly when he appears to have led the organization in the wrong direction, any help provided by Second Yang under such circumstances would be ineffective but will hurt Second Yang instead. Therefore, it is better for Second Yang to stay where he is. In the meantime, he should try to manage the resources under him in a more efficient way. His action can contribute to the organization as a whole. This is a situation which can be called "no decrease of self but an increase of the whole" or "increasing without decreasing." In some cases, a person must not lose his own strength, in order that he can give help to others. The three foxes refer to the three yin lines except Fifth Yin, symbolizing three cunning or petty men in an organization. Second Yang as a subordinate is given a position of trust by the leader Fifth Yin to remove the three petty men. As a person with uprightness, Second Yang uses a moderate approach (as symbolized by a yellow arrow) to get rid of them. Three foxes also symbolize one's evil thoughts; one can remove them by keeping centrality.

Third Yin ☶· Make the size right

When three people walk together, one will be diminished.
When one person walks alone, he will get a companion.

Jealousy or conflict often arises among three people, so one person has to leave in order to achieve a harmonious relationship. "Two" here symbolizes Heaven and Earth or yin and yang. Like one coin with two sides, yin and yang is "two" within "one," which means *taiji*. "One" represents an entire group (*taiji*) and the "two" represent the two subgroups (yin and yang) within it.

The hexagram SUN is obtained by exchanging the third yang line with the top yin line in the hexagram TAI:

Hexagram TAI: **Hexagram SUN**

In the text "three people walk together" refers to the three yang lines or three yin lines of the hexagram TAI whereas "one will be diminished" indicates the upward movement of the Third Yang or the downward movement of Top Yin. The text "one person walks alone, he will get a companion" refers to the situation of Third Yang or Top Yin. When Third Yang shifts upward from the lower trigram to the top position of the upper trigram, it meets Fifth Yin as its companion in which Top Yang and Fifth Yin form a yin–yang pair in the upper trigram of the hexagram SUN. The same situation is applied to Top Yin when it shifts downward from the upper trigram to the third position of the lower trigram; it meets Second Yang and forms a yin–yang pair.

After the exchange of the positions of Third Yang and Top Yin, Top Yang stands above Fifth Yin and Third Yin above Second Yang resulting in a "one-plus-one" situation or a union of yin and yang, the basis for achieving harmony. In an organization "one" could also stand for the team spirit or the mission of the group. When the members of a group are focused on "one-group–one-spirit," a higher initiative can be expected.

Fourth Yin ☷˙ Correct faults quickly and get support quickly

If he quickly reduces his faults, those at the lower echelon will soon come to give their support to him.

Fourth Yin in a proper position (a yin line in a yin position) indicates the weaknesses of a senior executive. If he knows his weaknesses and corrects them quickly, his act will enhance the trust of the members of the organization in him and hence they will be willing to give him the necessary support.

Fifth Yin ☷˙ Persist in the right principles

People come to help him. He will follow their will and will not change his mind even if ten pairs of valuable tortoise shells are offered to him. It is highly auspicious.

The fifth line is yin and in a central position in the upper trigram, symbolizing a leader who is balanced and broad-minded. He uses the principle of decentralization in his organization. In response people are willing to support him wholeheartedly. It is advantageous for a leader to persist in his right principles. He will not change his mind even if he can get a fortune as in "ten pairs of valuable tortoise shells." The interconnection between Fifth Yin and Second Yang indicates support from the members of an organization to the leader due to his integrity and leadership style.

Top Yang ☷˙ Increase but not decrease others

He does not decrease others but will increase them. There will be no harm.
It is auspicious to stay upright and favorable to go forward. He wins the people's hearts.

Unlike Fourth Yin and Fifth Yin, Top Yang represents a leader who is strong in nature so he does not need a decrease of the people below him, for example, Third Yin, to benefit himself. On the contrary, he can even give help to Third Yin (an interconnection between Top Yang and Third Yin). People will follow a leader if he is selfless.

42

YI

The Wind–Thunder Hexagram

Increasing, Augmenting

IMAGE

The inverse hexagram of SUN 損 [Decreasing] (41) is the hexagram YI, in which Wind is above Thunder. The relationship between wind and thunder are complementary in nature. The fierce and harsh winds come together with the swift and intense thunder. Each enhances or increases the other. This complementary relationship between wind and thunder results in a "win–win situation" or a positive game. A joint movement of Wind and Thunder brings increase. It indicates a good time for moving forward. The Hexagram Increasing is obtained by an exchange between the fourth yang line and the first yin line in the hexagram PI 否 [Obstruction] (12) as follows:

In the Hexagram Obstruction, the fourth line or Fourth Yang moves downward from the upper trigram to the lower trigram, indicating that the benefit from the upper level which is symbolized by the yang line is now transferred to the lower level in order to increase the latter. This is why this hexagram is named Increasing. Judgment on a situation as to whether an action is Decreasing or Increasing should be made from the standpoint of the lower trigram or the lower level of an organization in the perspective of the *Yijing*. If the benefit of the upper level is considered as the basis for judgment as indicated in the previous Hexagram Decreasing, the situation will be the opposite. The concept of decrease and increase are therefore interchangeable, depending from which level the benefit is viewed.

If a leader wants to limit the percentage growth of the salary of his senior executives but increase that of those at the lower echelon, it is a situation of increasing. The purpose of this increasing is to create a sense of cohesion and cooperation within the whole organization. Another example is when a multinational corporation transfers its capital to its subsidiary in order to support a new development plan in that area. It appears that the act of increasing is taken by the multinational corporation to benefit its subsidiary; however, it can also be seen as an act of increasing to benefit the company as a whole.

HEXAGRAM STATEMENT

Through increasing, it is favorable to go forward and cross the great rivers.

If an organization will take action to decrease the benefit of the people at the upper level and increase that of those at the lower level, this is a balanced policy which will harmonize the relationships between these two echelons and contribute to internal stability. Similarly if a person is willing to decrease his fortune in order to increase that of others who are suffering, this will increase his happiness if such an action springs from his sincere heart rather than from a specific motive with a hidden interest. Helping others can therefore be a mutually beneficial action.

STRUCTURE

Like the Hexagram Decreasing, the Hexagram Increasing also has a line structure of three yin and three yang lines. The three lines of the upper trigram are interconnected with their counterparts in the lower trigram, indicating the good relationship between the respective units of those at upper level and those below in an organization. In both hexagrams Increasing and Decreasing, the fifth line corresponds with the second line. The difference between the two patterns of relationship is the leadership style. In the Hexagram Increasing the leadership style is hard as indicated by Fifth Yang whereas in the Hexagram Decreasing it is soft as indicated by Fifth Yin.

LINE STATEMENTS

Initial Yang ☳. Need help from above

It is favorable to do great deeds. There will be great fortune and no harm.

As Initial Yang is the first line of the lower trigram ZHEN 震 [Thunder] it symbolizes the virtues of energy and initiative. An executive in this position may be tempted to undertake a big project even though he is in a lower position. Since he has a good relationship with a senior executive Fourth Yin, who is close to the top leader Fifth Yang, he is able to get the necessary help from above.

Second Yin ☷. Increase through sincerity and balance

People come to increase him. He will not resist them even if he is offered a tortoise worth of ten pairs of shells. He will always be fortunate if he behaves properly.
The king presents him before the Lord of Heaven and he will be auspicious.

Since the Hexagram Increasing is the inverse of the Hexagram Decreasing, Second Yin in the former is therefore equivalent to Fifth Yin in the latter and so is the meaning of the two line statements. The difference between these two statements is the position of the benefactor and the position of the beneficiary. In the Hexagram Decreasing, Second Yang is the benefactor and Fifth Yin the beneficiary whereas in the Hexagram Increasing, Second Yin is the beneficiary and Fifth Yang is the benefactor.

If a leader who is in the position of Second Yin of the Hexagram Increasing follows the principle of centrality that embodies receptivity, tolerance, flexibility, and broad-mindedness, he will draw people to him and benefit from them. Since he is in a weak position (a yin line in a yin position), his relationship with the top leader will be secured if he perseveres in his principles.

Third Yin ☷· Give benefit to those below in times of misery

He gives benefits to those below in times of misery, so he will be free from blame.

He sincerely adopts the principle of centrality and gets permission from his superior before he takes any action to benefit those below.

Third Yin represents weakness (yin) yet it is in a strong (yang) position, indicating an executive who lacks power but has a strong will and the strength to provide every possibility to the people at the lower echelon in times of misery. However, his action needs the approval and blessing of his superior despite using the centrality principle.

Fourth Yin ☷ Act on the principle of centrality

He acts in a moderate way, so the duke trusts him and accepts his advice on the relocation of the capital.

Fourth Yin symbolizes a senior executive who is very close to the top leader Fifth Yang of an organization. If he always acts on the principle of centrality, the top leader will trust him and accept his proposals because he is a man of integrity and credibility. On the other hand, he also gets the capable people (Initial Yang) below to help him as indicated by the interconnection between Fourth Yin and Initial Yang.

Fifth Yang ☵ To give is more fortunate than to receive

If he is sincere and has a kind heart toward others, others will in turn sincerely appreciate him. There is no question about his fortune.

The characteristics of a leader in this position are strength, power, and balance. He will act for what is good for others even at his own expense. Since he is sincere in carrying out actions that benefit the members of his organization, particularly those below him, people will accept his leadership sincerely. Acting in this way he not only strengthens his formal authority but also creates an informal authority that appears to be more influential and powerful in an organization. Anyone who is true to himself and has a kind heart will receive an appropriate return.

Top Yang ☷ Persevere in the action of increase

If he lacks perseverance in the increase of others, no one will come to increase him but will attack him. He will be unfortunate.

Top Yang is at the extreme end of the Hexagram Increasing, indicating a situation that is likely to change. If a leader in this situation persists in his action for increase on behalf of those below, he will be fortunate. Otherwise, there will be misfortune and no one will come to increase him but will attack him.

43

The Lake–Heaven Hexagram

Determination, Decision, Resolution

IMAGE

Lake over Heaven indicates water rising up to the sky; a rainstorm is expected to come down. This is an image a of breakthrough or a resolution as indicated by the hexagram structure in which five yang lines move upward to remove the one yin at the top. When a leader makes a resolution to remove evil as represented by inferior people or unrighteous practices in the organization, his action is indicated by the hexagram. The five yang lines represent decisive action whereas the yin line stands for the object to be eliminated. Top Yin can also represent a man's egoism and the five yangs his determination to remove it.

Another image of this hexagram illustrates a harmonious relationship between the lower and the upper trigrams rather than a hostile one as described above. The lower trigram QIAN 乾 [Heaven] ☰ is a pure yang trigram and the upper trigram DUI 兌 [Lake] ☱ a yin one. The nature of a trigram, whether it is yin or yang, is determined by the least number of the yin or yang lines in that trigram. As the nature of yang is to move upward and that of yin to move downward, an interaction between yin and yang creates harmony. It implies that a harmonious relationship between the upper and the lower trigrams is to be expected. Removal of evil from an organization or from one's mind is favorable in restoring a state of balance and harmony.

HEXAGRAM STATEMENT

The superior man is determined to take action openly against the inferior man in the king's court and sincerely warns people about the existence of danger.
He tells the people in his domain that it is not favorable to attack by resorting to arms.

When a leader wants to remove a senior official who lacks integrity and has hence seriously affected the efficiency of the organization, his action should be taken in an open way so that people understand the reasons why this inferior man should be removed. This is particularly the case if the man is generally perceived by the members of the organization as capable and reputable. It is advisable to use a moderate approach in dealing with this matter.

STRUCTURE

This is a hexagram that is dominated by five yangs which are formed into a group threatening Top Yin. Whether Top Yin can be removed by the five yangs depends on the power and skills of the opposing force on the one hand and the strength of the determination of the group on the other. If Top Yin can get support from Third Yang as indicated by the interconnection between the two, the strength of the group of yangs against Top Yin may be weakened.

LINE STATEMENTS

Initial Yang ☰. Do not be hasty in making the first move

He puts strength in his front toe for advancement, but he is not successful and regrets this.

A yang line in a yang position symbolizes excessive toughness and obstinacy. A leader in this position is tempted to take action hastily without cautious thinking or planning. The danger he is facing comes from his overconfidence and exuberant enthusiasm. This is particularly true for a leader who is young and energetic. If he overestimates his capabilities and ignores the difficulties or dangers ahead, he could be jeopardized.

Second Yang ☱. Be alert against dangers

If he is cautious and alert he does not need to worry even if he is attacked at night.

Second Yang in a central position suggests that a leader should be upright, reasonable, cautious, and modest. If he is fully aware of unforeseen difficulties around him and takes the corresponding measures against them in a timely manner, he will be safe. He needs to be confident but not act rashly.

Third Yang ☱· Hide anger with the inferior man

Anger on the face is inauspicious. He walks alone and encounters rain, and is therefore soaked and annoyed.
People are irritated by his act, but he suffers no harm.

The third yang line is at the top of and in a yin position of the lower trigram, representing a person who is one of the members of the opposing group. However, he has a personal relationship with this inferior man as indicated by the interconnection between Third Yang and Top Yin. During his contact with Top Yin, he should hide his anger with the inferior man whom he wants to remove. The reason for this is to prevent the inferior man from alerting the opposition. But the conduct of Third Yang may not be understood by the members of the opposing group since it is contrary to the principle of solidarity. His conduct is as the text describes: "He walks alone and encounters rain, and is therefore soaked and annoyed." His intention and conduct, however, will eventually be understood by the others when the inferior man is removed.

Fourth Yang ☱· Do not be obstinate but go along with the group

Since he has no skin on his buttocks, he staggers as he walks.
If he can restrain himself as he pulls the sheep along, he will have no regrets. However, he will not accept the advice.

When a senior executive of an organization is active, tough, but obstinate, he tends to do things in his own way regardless of the circumstances and the advice of others. His situation is like a yang line in a weak position; he is therefore not able to lead his group forward. If he reduces his obstinacy and goes along with the group like sheep moving in flocks, he will have no regrets. Since he is in a weak position, he may not want to do so. If he does not correct his attitude, he will suffer from it.

Fifth Yang ☰ Be decisive and balanced

If he is determined, he will get rid of the inferior man like removing weeds from a lawn.
By following the right way, he will be free from any trouble.

As a leader of the opposing group in an organization, his determination to remove the inferior man or the evil must be as firm as that to get rid of the weeds in his garden. As the Fifth Yang line he is advised to maintain centrality and balance, as suits the line's character.

Top Yin ☰ Inferior is replaced by superior

He doesn't need to cry, there will be danger in the end.

Top Yin located at the end of the hexagram symbolizes the inferior man; he is about to wane and will soon be replaced by the forces of the group opposing him. Since this is an inevitable development, there is no one to blame.

ISSUES FOR DISCUSSION

Should Top Yin be considered as a symbol of evil?

In the traditional view, Top Yin of this hexagram represents evil. For example, as the inferior man, he will eventually be removed by a group of upright people as represented by the five yang lines. However, this assumption is dependent on what the definition of Top Yin is. Top Yin can be considered as a leader whose management style is soft or gentle. He adopts a policy of decentralization under which the managers at all levels of the organization obtain adequate authority as required by their responsibilities. His management style follows the doctrine of Laozi: "Gentleness overcomes strength," under which a soft leader is highly efficient in managing all capable people who are active and energetic as represented by the yangs in the hexagram. As a contrast to the traditional view, this hexagram therefore can be interpreted in a rather positive way as stated above. The meaning of determination or resolution should not be restricted only to the traditional interpretation "strength overcomes gentleness." It can also mean the opposite, "gentleness overcomes strength," if the hexagram structure is interpreted as indicated above.

Are the two hexagrams named Determination and Stripping interchangeable?

The hexagram GUAI 夬 [Determination] ☱ is the opposite form of the hexagram PO 剝 [Stripping] ☶. The former has one yin and five yangs whereas the latter is just the opposite with one yang and five yins. The Hexagram Determination describes a situation in which a group of noble people, as represented by the five yang lines, are strongly determined to remove the inferior man represented by Top Yin. But Top Yin can also represent a leader who adopts a soft style of leadership as stated above. In this case, the five yangs then become the supporters or followers of Top Yin. However, they can also become a powerful group in opposition to Top Yin. If this happens, this soft style of leadership can be "stripped" away or replaced by a new hard style of leadership when the time or place or conditions change. In such circumstances, **the name of the hexagram Determination can be changed to Stripping without changing the pattern of the lines**. In a contrary case, **the name of the hexagram Stripping can be changed to Determination** if the organization is well under the control of a strong leader (Top Yang) and the people below (the five yin lines) are obedient to him.

In conclusion, the names Determination and Stripping of these two respective hexagrams are interchangeable depending how the pattern of lines is interpreted. This point has already been discussed in the Hexagram Stripping.

44

姤	**The Heaven–Wind**
GOU	**Hexagram**

Meeting, Encounter

IMAGE

Wind under heaven blows to every corner of the earth and can touch almost everything on the ground, illustrating a meeting. This hexagram has one yin and five yangs, symbolizing a situation in which a woman is chased by five men. The woman tends to be arrogant because of her favorable position and thereby has a strong desire to dominate. According to the classic view, a woman should be gentle and agreeable in order to fulfill the requirements of family life. But if she is a strong, aggressive, and dominant woman, her actions may affect the harmony of the family. A "strong woman" can be seen as a strong business partner in a joint venture. If the business partner is ambitious for power and domination, the harmony of a joint venture will eventually be damaged. On the other hand, a woman meeting five men symbolizes a merge of yin–yang which is considered fortunate and favorable to the development of an organization. From the yin–yang point of view, the situation of Gou is judged to be more on the positive side. What a leader should do in this situation is to keep alert and not let business partners dominate him.

The upper trigram 乾 [Heaven] can symbolize a particular policy of an organization, whereas the lower trigram Xun 巽 [Wind] stands for penetration. The hexagram as a whole can be interpreted as a policy which is implemented by using a soft approach to penetrate into a broad area.

The yin line at the bottom of the hexagram can be considered as the beginning of the rise of yin, or unfavorable factors in an organization. This is a sign of danger as already indicated in the line statement of Initial Yin of the Hexagram Kun 坤 [Earth] (2): **"When frost appears**

under his feet, it is a sign that hard ice is coming." The leader should take precautionary measures against the danger in its early stages. This also means that a person should not allow his evil thoughts to develop further. It would be better to curb his ego and inferiors at the beginning of the dangerous stage.

HEXAGRAM STATEMENT

If a woman is too strong, one should not take her as a wife.

The meaning of the text is already explained and discussed above. Before selecting the right business partner, a leader should consider carefully the impact of this cooperation—whether it is favorable or not.

STRUCTURE

As yin appears at the bottom of the hexagram, the five yangs should be able to restrain it from further movement if they can unite as one group. If not the yin will have a chance to penetrate the territory of the yangs. Since the character of the lower trigram Wind ☴ is penetration, the yangs should not ignore the possibility of an upward movement by the yin since Initial Yin could get support from Fourth Yang (an interconnection between the two). From the structural point of view, one yin at the bottom of the hexagram is not yet harmful to the organization as the strength of the five yangs should still be able to stop or control it if they are united and act as a group.

LINE STATEMENTS

Initial Yang ☰. Stop a destructive thing right at the beginning

If he can control his carriage with a metal brake he will be fortunate as further movement is dangerous.
A lean pig rushes around.

If a destructive thing happens a leader should take action to stop it before it becomes harmful to the organization. As the Chinese proverb says: **"A spark may cause a conflagration."** A leader should not ignore small things which may cause big troubles, like a lean pig growing into a fat one. He should immediately stop any harmful developments that will lead the organization into a difficult position. Similarly a leader should be able to control his emotions or evil ideas and not let them develop further.

Second Yang ☰. Control the inferior things

To wrap a fish in a bag is no fault. To let other people get it is inauspicious.

The character of fish is categorized as yin. Here, it refers to the first yin line, which represents an inferior thing. A leader in the position of Second Yang is strong and balanced so he should be firm and able to restrain the inferior things, for example, improper or unethical practices in his organization. If misconduct is already under control, it will not exert an influence on others.

Third Yang ☰· Keep a distance from the inferior

He has no skin on his buttocks, he staggers as he walks, but he does not make any mistakes even though there is a danger.

A leader with a strong character (a yang line in a yang position) finds himself in a dilemma. He seeks for an interconnection with the people both above and below but he does not succeed. He cannot get support from the people below, represented by Initial Yin, because there is an obstruction indicated by Second Yang standing in between. Neither can he get it from Top Yang, because both have similar characters. He is in a situation as if he had difficulty in sitting and walking. However, he will have no trouble even if he has no association with others as long as he can keep a distance from the inferior people. When there are negative thoughts in the organization, the leader should be able to stop them in a timely manner.

Fourth Yang ☰· Do not lose the relationship with those below

His bag has no fish, he will have misfortune.

When a leader cuts himself off from the people below and stands apart he will lose their confidence or assistance. Here, "fish" refers to the people below as represented by Initial Yin. "No fish" means that a leader loses the trust and support of the people under him. Fourth Yang is in an improper position, symbolizing a leadership that lacks balance and tolerance. As a result, he does not receive support from the people below him, as the text says: "His bag has no fish."

Fifth Yang ☰ Surround the evil and eliminate it when the conditions are ripe

The melon is covered by the willow's leaves; he waits quietly for it to be ripe.

A leader who embodies strength, balance, and uprightness (the properties of Fifth Yang) will be able to surround inferior people as represented by Initial Yin just like the willow wraps a melon in its long leaves. He will be able to remove them easily when the conditions are ripe, just as a melon falls off its stem when it is ripe. Before that he should not show his feelings or intentions.

Top Yang ☰ Do not be ignorant of incorrectness

He encounters the horns. It is regrettable, but there is no blame.

Top Yang is at the end of the hexagram, symbolizing a leader who is arrogant and obstinate. He keeps his distance from the inferior people (Initial Yin) but has not tried to correct their improper conduct. His lofty morals make him ignorant of incorrectness. It is regrettable that he has not tried to prevent the situation from occurring earlier on.

45

CUI

The Lake–Earth Hexagram

Gathering, Collecting Together

IMAGE

A lake on the earth symbolizes a place where water gathers. The lake collects the water which flows over the earth and nourishes myriad things. The hexagram illustrates an image of gathering. The lower trigram KUN 坤 [Earth] ☷ represents the people of an organization following the instructions and policies made by the top leader Fifth Yang and who get assistance from the senior executive Fourth Yang. People gather around the leader as they are influenced by his balance, sincerity, and uprightness. Above all, he offers people a promising vision of the organization and common values. People like him and are willing to follow him joyfully as indicated by the characteristic of the upper trigram DUI 兌 [Lake]—pleasing. This is like a situation in ancient times in which a king went to the ancestral temple to unify the will of the masses. The leader's sincerity in gathering people must be as great as the sacrifice offered at the ceremony. Once people gather together, conflicts amongst them may arise. The leader should deal with these problems carefully and patiently.

HEXAGRAM STATEMENT

The king comes to the ancestral temple for the sacrifice. It is favorable for the great man to come out.
If he can keep in the right way, he will have good prospects.
His sincerity should be as great as the large offerings for the sacrifice at the ceremony.

The purpose of people gathering together at the ancestral temple is to express their sincerity for and solidarity with the group to which they belong. A leader must possess something that attracts members to follow him from their innermost feelings. It can be his admirable personality, say, trustfulness, fairness, balance, and capability, which build up his charisma. The members within his organization know that they can depend on him and will give him full confidence and respect.

STRUCTURE

In this hexagram, four yins gather around the power center as represented by Fifth Yang (leader) and Fourth Yang (senior executive). The two yang lines represent the decision-making center of an organization. All the yin lines, particularly those below, are the units that execute the policies made by the power center. Although the number of yin lines is double that of the yang lines, the latter occupy the strategic positions. Top Yin has a high ranking position but lacks formal power.

The hexagram illustrates the importance of the decision-maker or power center as formed by Fifth Yang and Fourth Yang to the organization. Fifth Yang and Fourth Yang share the characteristics of activity, creativity, and hardness but Fourth Yang has the advantage of a yin–yang union (a yang line in a yin position), making the power center adaptable and flexible. This is complementary to the strong leadership of Fifth Yang (a yang line in a yang position).

LINE STATEMENTS

Initial Yin ☷. Vacillation damages the relationship

If he cannot keep his sincerity to the end, it will ruin his relationship with the man of his heart. But if he can express his sincerity in seeking the assistance of the man, the two will be able to join together happily. Acting in this way he will not have to worry wherever he goes, and there will be no mistakes.

There is an interconnection between Initial Yin and Fourth Yang, indicating the possible relationship between the persons in two positions at different levels. But if the person in the position of Initial Yin also tries to seek a relationship with the top leader Fifth Yang of the power center, his relationship with Fourth Yang will deteriorate. The vacillation of Initial Yin between Fourth Yang and Fifth Yang indicates that he cannot keep his sincerity with the former; this will not only damage the relationship between the two but will also result in conflicts and disharmony within the organization. A man who is vacillating cannot be a good leader.

Second Yin ☷. To be invited in by the leader based on sincerity and trust is auspicious.

If he is invited in by the leader based on trust, this gathering is auspicious.

As an upright man Second Yin would like to work with the top leader Fifth Yang, but he is advised not to take an active part in their interaction. Instead he should be invited in by the leader. The main reason for this is that a wise and capable leader must be in the position to know or identify the right person with whom he really wants to work. A capable man with dignity will only want to work under a leader who will respect him.

Third Yin ☶. Seek association with one who is in the decision-making circle

He sighs for not being able to associate with the right person.
The situation is not particularly favorable, yet going forward is blameless even though there is a little regret.

Both Initial Yin and Second Yin are interconnected with Fourth Yang and Fifth Yang respectively, but Third Yin does not have association with Top Yin. It is not always possible to get together with the desirable person as nothing is perfect in the world. Instead an executive in this position should associate with a person in the decision-making circle like Fourth Yang, even though he is not the ideal. Since Fourth Yang is close to the top leader of the organization, and has an important role to play in the decision-making circle, a relationship with him is considered useful and favorable.

Fourth Yang ☳. Need great fortune

He needs great fortune in order not to be blamed.

A senior executive in this position has both advantages and disadvantages. His closeness to the top leader is advantageous to him in getting both formal and informal power in making decisions within the organization. However, if he tries to flatter the top leader, his colleagues or followers will despise him and that could jeopardize his position. There are three yins under Fifth Yang, symbolizing the hidden dangers that this position faces. Since Fourth Yang is an improper position (a yang line in a yin position) it indicates that the person in this position could act in the wrong way. This is why the text says that there is need for "great fortune" for one who is in this position.

Fifth Yang ☵ Need the virtues of leadership

He is in the proper position for gathering people together if he has the virtues of leadership. He always needs to be correct and stable in his actions to avoid any regrets, otherwise people will not trust him.

When a person is in this honored position, his actions should be in accordance with it, that is, he should cultivate the virtues or the qualities of leadership. A leader should not rely on his formal position to win respect from the members of his organization; rather he has to earn the trust of the members through his virtues such as uprightness, sincerity, and centrality. A leader who knows how to inspire others will be able to gain their confidence.

Top Yin ☷ Examine oneself

He sighs and weeps, but there will be no blame.

A senior man in an organization, like Top Yin, seeks to gather to him the people below but no one will want to associate with him (no interconnection between Top Yin and Third Yin), so he sighs and weeps from frustration. He needs to examine his past actions and make the corresponding corrections.

46

升
SHENG

The Earth–Wind Hexagram

Rising, Ascending, Progress Upward

IMAGE

The upper trigram of the Hexagram Rising is represented by Earth and the lower trigram by Wood. Trees grow in the earth and become taller as they mature, so the image of this hexagram is a rising or upward progression. The energy is moving upward and outward. Like trees that grow gradually and patiently, an enlightened person should follow this pattern in order to accumulate knowledge or to build virtue. In this manner, an efficient organization can also move forward gradually. The hexagram SHENG emphasizes a "soft rising" instead of an "aggressive rising" when adapting to the conditions of a particular time and place. Different approaches should be used in different times and places. Soft progress means steady growth, an approach particularly adaptable to a time of natural growth, whereas an aggressive progress can be harmful in this situation.

HEXAGRAM STATEMENT

The prospects for rising are extremely good. It is the favorable time to see the great man. There is no need to worry about going to the south for it will bring good fortune.

Even if the time is favorable for moving forward, an organization still needs different types of capable people in different functional areas in order to build up a strong basis for its advancement. The term "great man" refers to a great leader who will use those capable people for his advancement.

STRUCTURE

This hexagram has four yins and two yangs. The two yangs are surrounded by the four yins. It is a yin-dominated hexagram. The lower trigram XUN 巽 [Wind] symbolizes penetration and the upper trigram KUN 坤 [Earth] stands for docility. Therefore, the hexagram as a whole means "a steady penetration" or "a steady rising." Fifth Yin represents the leader of an organization who adopts a soft style of leadership whereas Second Yang represents the capable action-leader. The interconnection between Fifth Yin and Second Yang would bring increase the positive effect of a yin–yang union.

LINE STATEMENTS

Initial Yin ☷. Follow an experienced senior

If he rises up through trust, he should have great good fortune.

A person in a low position of an organization, like Initial Yin, who wants to rise through the organization needs a strong person from above to give him a hand. Since there is no interconnection between Initial Yin and Fourth Yin the most suitable person is Second Yang, for he is strong, sincere, and balanced. Therefore, Initial Yin should follow the direction of Second Yang by being trustful and faithful. He will rise together with his superior—Second Yang.

Second Yang ☷. Rising with sincerity

If he is sincere, he can present simple offerings at the sacrifice ceremony. Acting in this way, he will be free from blame.

The position of Second Yang symbolizes an executive who obtains power from the top leader Fifth Yin who is a gentle and sincere person. A combination of a strong subordinate with a gentle leader results in a yin–yang union, providing a favorable condition for rising. Since Second Yang is sincere too, he does not need to use any outward adornment in his interaction with the top leader but he acts in a simple way. Through acting with sincerity and loyalty he will receive the appropriate reward.

Third Yang ☷· Rising with courage and caution

His courage rises as if he walked up into an empty city.

Third Yang is in a proper position (a yang line in a yang position). An executive in this situation may be tempted to move forward, for he anticipates no obstacles ahead. But he may be overconfident in his calculations and fall into the trap of obstinacy. The upper trigram Earth symbolizes emptiness. When an executive intends to move forward solely based on his optimistic outlook, he needs to check out the real worth of such an action before forging on. Courage alone will not guarantee success unless it is accompanied by cautiousness.

Fourth Yin ☷· Rising with obedience

The king uses him as a helper at an offering to the ancestors on Mount Qi. It is fortunate.

Mount Qi 祁山 was the site of the ancestral temple of the royal family in the Zhou dynasty. The king as represented in the text by Fifth Yang lets his senior official Fourth Yin take part in the ceremonial sacrifices. In modern terms, the senior official is invited by the top leader to participate in the center of power, signifying a bright future for him. One of the main reasons for his promotion is due to his docility, modesty, and faithfulness as represented by the characters of the yin line. Obedience of the subordinate can win the trust of the leader.

Fifth Yin ☷· Rising up by steps

If he remains steadfast, he is auspicious. It is favorable for him to rise by step by step.

In a time of rising a leader should use the capable person below (Second Yang) properly by giving him adequate authority to meet his responsibilities. With the assistance of a capable subordinate the leader can move upward steadily. A movement made patiently and steadily, like climbing stairs, is likely to achieve the goal of an organization. The three yins of the upper trigram Earth indicates that the leader Fifth Yin has successfully formed a close-knit group that would contribute to harmony at the upper management level, which forms a solid foundation for a steady rising.

Top Yin ☷ Rising with persistence and energy

*He rises in the dark. It is beneficial to him to keep persisting
unceasingly.*

Yin at the top of the hexagram means that rising has reached its limit.
When the future is uncertain as if one was in the dark a leader should be
cautious and avoid any impulsive action.

A COMPARISON OF SHENG ䷭ [RISING] WITH SHI ䷆ [LEADING TROOPS]

In the hexagram SHI 師 [Leading Troops] (7), Second Yang represents
the commander of an army while the other five yins stand for the troops
or people under him. Similarly in the hexagram SHENG 升 [Rising] (46),
Second Yang can also be considered as the commander of an army as in
the case of the hexagram SHI. Third Yang can be considered his chief
military adviser. The comparison of these two hexagrams illustrates the
important fact that the hexagram names in the *Yijing* are interchangeable,
depending on how the hexagram structure is interpreted.

47

困
KUN

The Lake–Water Hexagram

Adversity, Confinement, Exhaustion

IMAGE

The Hexagram Adversity combines Lake and Water in the upper and lower trigrams respectively. The water should be in the lake but in the hexagram it is below the lake, indicating that the water is leaking out and the lake is drying up. As a result, the lake may eventually have no water. This is the image of the Hexagram Adversity.

In a time of adversity, the leader must stay on the path of centrality with his strength as advised by the hexagram; the two yang lines in both second and fifth positions indicate the principles in dealing with this situation. The two yang lines located in the central position imply a double strength with centrality. These are the essential qualities a leader requires in a time of adversity.

In a time of exhaustion a leader needs to have perseverance, patience, inner balance, and self-confidence while preparing the necessary action to combat difficulties. He should be able to unite all available forces (the three yang lines) in order to find a way out.

The hexagram advises a leader to keep to his will even though he is in a difficult position. As **Confucius** said: **"An army can be deprived of its commanding officer, yet a man cannot be deprived of his will."** When a leader realizes that he is in a dangerous situation as symbolized by the inner trigram KAN 坎 [Danger], he should keep calm and joyful outwardly, as is the character of the outer trigram DUI 兌 [Pleasing].

HEXAGRAM STATEMENT

Adversity can lead him to a successful future if he acts in the right way as a great man. But in adversity, no one believes him.

Adversity can be seen as a training ground for a future leader. In adversity a man needs to persevere in his belief and to have the courage to combat difficulties enthusiastically. He must be a man of integrity so that people will trust him and be willing to give him corresponding help if needed. Acting in this way he has a good chance of escaping adversity, and of becoming a person who is able to deal with all kinds of difficulties in the future. Adversity is the source of success.

STRUCTURE

All three yang lines are surrounded by three yin lines, indicating a situation in which the yangs are overshadowed by the yins. Second Yang is trapped between two yins in the lower trigram KAN ☵, which means difficulty or danger. Both Fifth Yang and Fourth Yang are also encircled by Third Yin and Top Yin indicating a bigger KAN ☵ or a big danger. Although both yangs and yins are equal in number, the positions of the yangs are seen as less favorable since the yangs are oppressed by the yins.

LINE STATEMENTS

Initial Yin ☷. Keep inner balance and remain true in adversity

He sits exhausted under a bare tree. He walks into a dark valley. For three years he is not seen.

Initial Yin at the bottom of the hexagram and the beginning of the trigram KAN gives an image of a man sitting under a bare tree, which cannot provide shade. Since it is also at the beginning of danger (the lower part of the trigram KAN) it symbolizes a person going into a dark valley. He is a weak person as indicated by the yin line and so he lacks the ability to extricate himself from difficulty. He is in adversity.

Initial Yin can get support from Fourth Yang through their interconnection, but Fourth Yang is not in a proper position (a yang line in a yin position) and is therefore not strong enough to help Initial Yang.

Furthermore, the way between Initial Yin and Fourth Yang is blocked by Second Yang which symbolizes obstruction, so Initial Yin cannot find a means of getting through. Under such circumstances, it is essential that a leader who is in adversity should keep his inner balance and remain true to the right path. A rash move forward could result in danger. Hence, he should wait with patience and optimism. The way out will show itself at the right time.

Second Yang ☵. Persevere in one's principles

He is in adversity even though he has enough wine and food and has just received the crimson garment (a symbol of high position). It is favorable to offer a simple sacrifice.
Moving forward brings misfortune. If no move is made, there will be no mistakes.

An executive Second Yang is at the center of danger as indicated by the central position of the yang line in the lower trigram KAN. In this position he should not worry about gains and losses, but should keep belief in the direction and the principles he has chosen. His hardness and strength give him confidence to overcome the difficulties encountered. He should maintain a high level of sincerity and should trust in himself, as if he offered a simple sacrifice as suggested by the text. In a time of adversity, a rash move to overcome a difficulty can lead to misfortune.

Third Yin ☷· Do not make a move in a situation when there are obstructions from the front and the rear

He is blocked by rocks in front and is surrounded by brambles behind. When he returns home, he does not see his wife. There will be misfortune.

If Third Yin moves upwards there are two yangs ahead of it (Fourth Yang and Fifth Yang) and it is not strong enough to overcome them. On the other hand if it moves downward, Second Yang blocks its way back. Similarly an executive in this position will find himself in a dilemma. He will meet obstructions to his forward or backward moves. Under such circumstances, he decides to seek help from someone close to him (here it refers to another yin line, the Top Yin). But there is no interconnection between these two so he should wait until there is a way out.

Fourth Yang ☵ **Do not seek assistance in haste**

He comes down slowly and has difficulty managing the golden carriage.
There is regret, but all will be well in the end.

In a time of adversity, it is reasonable for a senior executive to find someone above or below who can give him assistance. Fourth Yang and Initial Yin are true complementaries. Fourth Yang wants Initial Yin as his partner, but his way downward is blocked by Second Yang symbolized by a golden carriage in the hexagram (Initial Yin can be seen as the subordinate of Second Yang). It would be advantageous to Fourth Yang to improve his relationship with Second Yang in order to get assistance from Initial Yin.

Fifth Yang ☵ **Seek a way out with an unhurried manner**

He is restless and restricted in his high position. He can remove himself from adversity with sincerity and in an unhurried manner, as if he is offering a sacrifice.

A leader in adversity may become restless and restricted but he should remain calm and actively seek the way out in an unhurried manner. On the other hand, he should maintain sincerity and high spirits as if he were offering a sacrifice.

In a time of adversity, a leader needs all kinds of capable people to help the organization out of its difficulties. Although there is no interconnection between Fifth Yang and Second Yang because of their similar character, the top leader Fifth Yang should seek any possible cooperation with the latter. If he can unite all the capable people below him, as symbolized by the three yangs, into one force to combat the yins it should help him to find a way out. However, these actions should be undertaken in an unhurried manner—little by little. To escape adversity the leader should tread the path of centrality (a yang line in a central position). If he can maintain his sincerity as if he was offering a sacrifice, he will turn things to his favor. When Second Yang becomes his partner he will be in a better position to escape adversity.

Both the top leader Fifth Yang and the action leader Second Yang are surrounded by yins, which symbolize danger. Fifth Yang and Fourth Yang are in a Big KAN ☵ formed by Third Yin, Fourth Yang, Fifth Yang, and Top Yin.

Top Yin ☷ **Take action at the extreme of adversity**

He is exhausted in creeping vines on unsteady ground. He understands that he will have regrets if he moves forward, but he will have even more regrets if he doesn't. It is auspicious for him to proceed.

Top Yin is at the extreme of the Hexagram Adversity. This is a situation which will change the negative to the positive based on the law of reversion or the law of cyclical change. It is therefore favorable for a leader to take action to break free from whatever has been holding him back.

48

JING 井 The Water–Wind (Wood) Hexagram

The Well

IMAGE

The shape of the hexagram JING is like a well. The upper trigram KAN 坎 [Water] represents the water of a well while the lower trigram XUN 巽 [Wood] symbolizes a wooden bucket that is lowered into a well to bring up water for people to drink. This hexagram describes a situation in which people use a bucket to fetch water from a well. If they can successfully draw the water up they will achieve their purpose. However, it would be inauspicious if the bucket overturned before the water could be drawn from the well.

The well represents the **virtue of nourishment** since it supplies an endless source of water to people but does not ask for anything in return. This symbolizes a situation in which a man offers his services to the community without expecting any return. It illustrates the virtue of the well. An enlightened leader should have the qualities of a well when serving the organization he works for, particularly in public institutions. However, he may not be able to provide his services if he acts incorrectly, as when using a cracked bucket to fetch water from a well. This means that even with a high standard of integrity, an enlightened leader will not be able to reach his goal successfully if he is careless in performing his duties. He must think things through carefully.

Among all sixty-four hexagrams only two of them use the name of substantial things, the well of the hexagram JING and the cauldron of the hexagram DING 鼎 [Renewing] (50). Both are related to how people live. Water can be drawn from a well. Food can be boiled in a cauldron as it were in ancient China.

HEXAGRAM STATEMENT

A village can be moved to another place but the well cannot.
The water in the well does not shrink or grow despite people coming
and going to fetch water from the well. The bucket breaks when it is
almost drawn out of the well, there will be misfortune.

The hexagram statement implies that a person's position can be
changed as a village can be moved, but his principles as represented
by the unmoved well cannot be changed. The two yang lines—Fifth
Yang and Second Yang—symbolize the strong will of a person in
maintaining his principles. People draw water from the well but
the well is neither exhausted nor does it overflow. There is no gain or
loss in the well, which indicates the constant nature of the well or
of people's perseverance in their right principles. Since all people can
draw water from the well, the well is unselfish and has a universal
nature. A leader of any organization should have these two qualities of
the well.

STRUCTURE

The hexagram JING ☵ is the reciprocal of the hexagram KUN 困
[Adversity] (47) ☷ . In both hexagrams three yangs are surrounded
by three yins. The difference between these two hexagrams is the position
of their third and fourth line. Through an exchange of the position
between Forth Yang and Third Yin of the Hexagram Adversity, Adversity
then becomes The Well:

Adversity   **The Well**

The upper trigram KAN of the hexagram The Well indicates
danger whereas the Big KAN ☵ , constructed by Initial Yin, Second Yang,
Third Yang, and Fourth Yin, symbolizes an even bigger danger.
Something that originally had a useful function like that of a well can
be lost if an improper method is used, as the case of using a cracked
bucket to fetch water as indicated in this hexagram. A promising action
can fail before success simply because the obstructions in its execution
are ignored.

LINE STATEMENTS

Initial Yin ☵. **Need self-development and self-preservation**

The well is muddy; no one drinks the water from it. There are no birds around this deserted well.

Initial Yin is at the bottom of the hexagram. It is compared to the muddy bottom of a well. If a company can no longer provide the right products or services to the market, it will be abandoned by the buyers. Similarly, a government will be abandoned by the people if it cannot provide them with efficient administration and services to meet their needs. Any organization which neglects self-development or self-preservation will face the danger of elimination.

Second Yang ☵. **A capable person should use his abilities in a more efficient way**

The well is like a broken and leaking jug; water from it is just enough for pouring small fishes.

In the text "water" symbolizes the ability of an executive and "water leaking from a broken jug" means that the ability of the executive cannot be used in an effective way. This is like the situation faced by a capable executive in the position of Second Yang. He may originally give his support to the top leader Fifth Yang in order to benefit the whole organization, but there is no interconnection between the two. As a result, his abilities can only be used at a lower level. When a capable executive uses his abilities in a less efficient way, he is wasting his energy on unworthy pursuits like water leaking from a broken jug. An executive in this position should let the senior leader know that he has the ability to assume more important responsibilities.

Third Yang ☵. **Do not let the resources go unused**

The well is cleaned, but no one drinks from it. This creates pain in his heart.
If the ruler is brilliant, all would share the blessings.

Third Yang is in a right position, indicating a situation in which the well water is pure and drinkable but no one drinks from it. This symbolizes that the capable people in an organization have not yet been used by the top management. If the top leader is brilliant, he should put these capable people in the right positions to increase efficiency so that the whole organization will benefit from this reshuffle. When the abilities of people are not being put to good use, it is a great loss to an organization. Once their values are recognized, the whole organization will benefit.

Fourth Yin ☷ Need a reform

He repairs the wall of the well, there is no fault.

To repair the wall of the well means to improve oneself by self-development or self-cultivation. Fourth Yin represents a weak position (a yin line in a yin position), lacking the strength to help others. An executive in this position is advised to improve his knowledge and ability for the benefit of the organization as a whole. Like a person's self-development, an organization can improve its effectiveness and efficiency by launching a reform. To reform an organization rather than to liquidate it is just like repairing the wall of well instead of digging a new well. The hexagram JING advises that in some occasions a reform is preferable to a revolution.

Fifth Yang ☵ Keep leadership qualities as pure and cool as spring water

The water in the well is clear and cool, it is good for drinking.

The qualities of a leader in Fifth Yang should be as clean and cool as spring water. He is seen as a source of strength and wisdom which others can draw on. The purity and coolness of the spring water symbolize a positive strength that is balanced and upright, as represented by Fifth Yang (a yang line in a yang position).

Top Yin ☷ Provide unselfish services

He draws up water and leaves the well uncovered. His sincerity is auspicious.

Top Yin at the end of the hexagram means that people are finally able to drink the water from the well. After drawing the water he leaves the well uncovered, indicating that he does not want to use the well exclusively but will also let others use the well. His unselfishness will make people trust him.

49

 革
GE

The Lake–Fire Hexagram

Reform, Revolution, Revolutionary Change

IMAGE

Lake above Fire indicates an **incompatible relationship** between the water and the fire as the former goes down and the latter goes up. Water can extinguish fire and fire can also evaporate water. The incompatible nature of the water and the fire would result in conflicts between the two and lead to **reformation** or **revolutionary change**.

A radical change means getting rid of the old and building the new. But people are likely to resist it in defending their own interests. A leader should have the ability to persuade them to believe that such a change is advantageous not only to the organization but also to them. Before a radical change occurs, people may not believe in it unless they are convinced that such a change is really necessary. The measures for change must be appropriate to the conditions.

The right timing is another factor that will affect the success of a revolutionary change. If the change is too early, people will resist it due to their feelings of insecurity. But if the change comes too late its impact will be less effective and the resistance is likely to be even greater.

If a leader wants to make a revolutionary change without encountering strong resistance he will need the support of the members of his organization, and whether this is provided is much dependent on whether people trust him or not. Again **the leader's sincerity and creditability affect the trust of people in him**. If the leader's motive is to benefit the whole organization rather than himself, his unselfish act will enable him to win the support of the members of his organization.

Snakes and birds change their skins and feathers periodically. So an organization needs to discard its old structures and practices and adopt new ones, so does a man need to remove his weaknesses in order to rebuild strengths.

An effective revolution should be neither excessive nor ineffective, for an excessive change will make people confused and frustrated whereas an ineffective one results in a waste of resources and energy. Both ways are inefficient. To lead a revolutionary change is a difficult task but is possible if the leader can make the objective of the revolution clear to people and utilize the proper measures.

HEXAGRAM STATEMENT

Recognizing this and keeping in the right way, the prospects for reform are bright and regrets will disappear.

Since people in an organization generally have a suspicion of any revolutionary change and dislike it, a leader should therefore not make the change hastily but should convince them through effective communication. **Gaining the understanding and trust of people** is an important condition for the success of a revolutionary change.

STRUCTURE

This is a yang-dominated hexagram in which the two yins are under the control of the four yangs. This indicates that a revolutionary change needs strength and activity, as represented by the characteristics of the four yangs. The inner trigram LI 離 [Fire] and the outer trigram DUI 兌 [Joy] symbolize enthusiasm and optimism respectively. Both are the qualities needed in a leader who leads a revolutionary change.

LINE STATEMENTS

Initial Yang ☲. Secure his own position before a move

He uses the yellow ox hide to bind himself tight.

Initial Yang is at the bottom of the hexagram, signifying the beginning of a revolutionary change. The leader is tempted to make a hasty move forward as influenced by his active (yang) character. However, the conditions for such a move may not exist at present; any rash action could bring danger in the future. It is not the right time to take action now but it is the right time for preparations for a move to the next stage. There is no interconnection between Initial Yang and Fourth Yang. This means that no assistance from other units of the organization can be expected. To take action in this position is obviously not one taken at the right time.

A leader should stay where he is, as if he is wrapped tightly in yellow ox hide. Yellow signifies the Golden Mean or centrality and the ox hide is a symbol of docility. A leader at the beginning of a revolutionary change should be cautious, should not act on impulse, and should not move forward until the time is ripe.

Second Yin ☷. Take action at the right time

He makes a revolutionary change at the right time when the conditions for moving forward are favorable without having mistakes.

Second Yin has a favorable time and position for carrying out the revolutionary changes because it has centrality, flexibility, and a relationship (interconnection) with Fifth Yang. Centrality and flexibility will enable the executive to win the confidence of people. A relationship with Fifth Yang means that the necessary support of the top leader is obtainable. Based on these, it is the right time for the executive to introduce changes step by step.

Third Yang ☳. Examine the plans repeatedly in order to integrate the views of others

If he takes a rash action he will meet misfortune; but if he does not then there is danger too. He should repeatedly discuss his plans and actions with people until they are convinced.

Since Third Yang is at the top of the lower trigram, an executive in this position is tempted to act hastily. He could rush into trying to change things. As a consequence he would suffer misfortune. The proper way for him is to prepare his revolutionary plans very carefully so that the members of the organization will have strong confidence in him. To be effective, he should discuss his reform plans with people many times until they are convinced.

Fourth Yang Implement reforms backed up by the trust of people

His regret vanishes as people believe in the revolutionary change and give their trust and support to him. The change brings good fortune.

Fourth Yang is at the lower position of the upper trigram, signifying that the revolutionary change is on the way to success as backed by people's trust. A leader in this situation should show that he is a person of strong character, as indicated by the yang line.

Fifth Yang Obtain the trust of people through capability and uprightness

The great man changes like a tiger's skin pattern, bright and clear. People believe in him even without divination.

Like the dragon, a tiger is also a symbol of a great man. Fifth Yang represents a great leader with the characteristics of strength, sincerity, balance, and uprightness. His actions are clear like the stripes of a tiger. People trust him and will gladly follow his lead.

Top Yin Consolidate the position in order to attract people

The superior man changes like the skin pattern of a leopard, bright and splendid.
The inferior man changes only his countenance.
Further reform will meet troubles. To keep in the right way will bring good fortune.

Top Yin is at the end of the hexagram, symbolizing that the reform is complete. Senior people in the organization adapt themselves to the conditions of the new environment like a leopard changing its spots. The inferior people change their attitude and behavior to show their obedience to the new leader. After a revolutionary reform, the leader should not push matters further as the organization now needs stability.

50

 DING

The Fire–Wind (Wood) Hexagram

The Cauldron, Renewing

IMAGE

Fire above Wood means the rise of flame from wood in the Hexagram Cauldron. A cauldron is a bronze vessel which was used by the king in ancient China to prepare food as offerings to Lord of Heaven or ancestors; it can also be used as a cooking pot in a banquet for eminent people. In a family the cauldron was used to serve food to a guest. The function of a cauldron is to change things through cooking; the nature and shape of the raw is transformed from hard to soft. To an organization a cauldron symbolizes an action that introduces new vision, new structure, new personnel, and new strategies aimed at improving the efficiency of the organization.

As indicated in the hexagram JING 井 [The Well] (48), a well has the meaning of giving nourishment to the people of the community. A cauldron also has the meaning of nourishing the capable people in an organization.

The lower trigram Wood under the upper trigram LI 離 [Fire] illustrates the relationship between input and output (cause and effect): output can only be obtained if there is input. The absence of input produces no output. If an organization lacks any plans or fails to action to develop and train its personnel, there could be obstruction to its future expansion.

The hexagrams JING and DING are the only two among the sixty-four hexagrams that use the name of the concrete subjects. In the Hexagram Cauldron, Initial Yin symbolizes the legs, Second Yang, Third Yang, and Fourth Yang represent the belly, Fifth Yin represents the handle and Top Yang the carrying rod. The six lines represent the image of a cauldron.

HEXAGRAM STATEMENT

The cauldron signifies a good beginning and great fortune.

The cauldron signifies a new stage of an organization where old obstructions to development are removed and new visions, new values, and new ways of doing things are introduced. The members of the organization feel as if they were reborn so they are now enthusiastic to do their best in their jobs. After a time of radical change, the time to create a new order begins. As long as the actions are proper, the reforms will have good prospects.

STRUCTURE

Since the hexagram DING ☶ is the reciprocal of the hexagram GE 革 [Reforming] ☱ (49) it is also a yang-dominated hexagram even though the positions of the lines of these two hexagrams are different. The two yins are segregated by the four yangs. However, the power position of Fifth Yin does not represent a weak leader but one who is willing to delegate his authority to his subordinates so that they may implement their responsibility. Before and during a revolutionary change, the leader should be a person with energy and hardness as represented by Fifth Yang in the hexagram GE. But once the revolutionary change is complete the old things should go out and the new come in. Correspondingly there is **a need to change the leadership style** in order to better adapt to the new environment. The leader should know how to assign the right people to the right positions. Based on this principle, a **decentralized type of leadership** appears to be desirable. The leadership should be **soft and tolerant**. Fifth Yin of this hexagram represents therefore the need for a new style of leadership in the new organization.

LINE STATEMENTS

Initial Yin ☴. Get rid of the old

When a cauldron is overturned on its base it is beneficial to take out the dregs inside.
When one takes a concubine, there is no blame as long as she gives birth to a son.

Initial Yin at the bottom of the hexagram symbolizes the legs of a cauldron. Its interconnection with Fourth Yang above is an upward movement, symbolizing that the legs are on top—an image of overturning. The old food is thrown out and fresh one put in. In the same way, an organization should get rid of any inefficient systems, structures, and practices before setting out new plans.

The text considers that to take a concubine is bad but to get a son is good, so on the whole there is no blame. The text points out that a new action can have both positive and negative effects. If a leader wants his new plans to be effective, he has to get rid of his old values and practices as he cannot have both at the same time. He should clear his mind of obsolete and preconceived ideas before introducing new plans.

Second Yang ☲. Keep a distance from an inferior man

The cauldron is replete here. The opponent is beset with affliction.
If he can keep his principles, the opponent cannot harm him.

Initial Yin represents the inferior man who shows obedience to his superior Second Yang. If the relationship between the two becomes closer, the inferior man will be able to influence Second Yang in a harmful way. So it is beneficial for Second Yang to keep the inferior man at a distance.

Third Yang ☴. Do not ignore capable people

When the handles of the cauldron are changed, the cauldron cannot be lifted.
Delicious food is not eaten.
Once it rains, regret vanishes. There is a good future in the end.

The function of the handles or "ears" of a cauldron is to provide assistance to a move. The handles here refer to Fifth Yin, representing the ruler of the hexagram or the leader of an organization. If the handles are changed, the cauldron cannot be moved, indicating that the leader will have difficulties in taking action. Since there is no interconnection between Third Yang and Fifth Yin, this means that the leader has no relationship with his subordinate who is in the third position. The subordinate Third Yang is a capable and energetic person but he is not recognized as such and used by the leader Fifth Yin, as in "delicious food is not eaten."

Nonetheless, the leader will recognize his capability in due course and put him in the right position. This act is like a union of yin–yang through which rain can be produced.

Fourth Yang ☲ˑ Do not put an incompetent person in a responsible position

The legs of the cauldron are broken. The food for the duke spills out in a mess. His clothes are spoiled. There will be misfortune.

Fourth Yang represents a high official in an organization who is close to the leader Fifth Yin. He chooses Initial Yin as his assistant as indicated by the interconnection between the two. But Initial Yin is weak and incompetent (a yin line in the lowest position of the hexagram); his capabilities are inadequate to assume the responsibility required by the position as he has neither the strength nor the experience. The organization suffers from a wrong assignment given by Fourth Yang. This situation is bad like food spilt out from an upside down cauldron.

Fifth Yin ☲ˑ Keep a central balance in facilitating a new development.

The cauldron has yellow handles and a metal carrying rod. It is favorable to persevere.

The cauldron is carried by a rod slipped through the handles. A cauldron can only benefit people if it can be carried and moved to their place. To do this both handles and a carrying rod are needed. The leader of an organization is like the yellow handles of a cauldron which represent the virtue of central balance (the yellow color is considered the color of soil or centrality in traditional Chinese culture). Although his leadership style tends to be on the soft side (a yin line) he obtains complementary support from a person who is strong, capable, and balanced as represented by Second Yang. A cooperative relationship between Fifth Yin and Second Yang indicates a desirable combination of yin and yang. While Fifth Yin represents the handles of a cauldron, Second Yang is the carrying rod. A leader who has a well-balanced attitude is favorable to the new development of an organization.

Top Yang ☰ **A combination of hardness and softness**

The cauldron has a jade carrying rod. It is very auspicious and beneficial to all around.

The top position of the hexagram DING, like the hexagram JING, symbolizes good fortune. At this stage, food is well cooked and ready to be taken out for eating—the function of the cauldron is fulfilled.

Jade has the characteristics of hardness and gentleness; a jade rod symbolizes therefore a combination of yin and yang. This advises the leader to use measures in this stage which are firm (yang) and yet to use them in a flexible (yin) manner. A well-balanced situation brings harmony and good fortune.

51

ZHEN

The Thunder Hexagram
Shake, Shock, Quake

IMAGE

Both upper and lower trigrams in the hexagram ZHEN represent Thunder and this Double Thunder gives an image of enormous shock. The yang line of the two trigrams stands for the power of movement whereas the two yin lines above it illustrate an image of shake-up from a movement of power. A thunder movement startles people; they are frightened and may lose self-control. The hexagram therefore symbolizes a situation in which a leader faces shock. If he remains calm, steadfast, and maintains self-control, he will be able to find a way out without being affected by the danger.

Thunder means danger. It is an alarm to the leader of an organization about safety. With a calm manner he should immediately prepare all necessary measures for the emergency. Fear comes from danger, but fear can also lead to safety and good fortune if the corresponding action against the danger are prepared in a timely way. A leader must have the qualities of calmness and steadfastness which are particularly meaningful in a dangerous situation.

HEXAGRAM STATEMENT

When thunder comes, the superior man shivers and shakes, but his fear can lead to success. At this time he talks and laughs as usual. The thunder startles for a hundred miles, yet he remains calm and does not drop the sacrificial ladle and the fragrant wine.

When there is a danger, a cultivated leader keeps calm and outwardly alert even though inwardly he is shocked. However, the shock can be considered positive if he takes the necessary precautions and looks ahead with concern. Danger also means challenge. If he is prepared to rise to the challenge, the shock will have a positive effect on his actions. In a time of panic, a leader should have strong self-confidence and maintain an optimistic attitude. This hexagram gives a leader an important principle: **one who has fear now will not have fear later and one who doesn't have fear now will have it later**.

STRUCTURE

This is a hexagram with four yins and two yangs. Two yins above one yang in each of the trigrams signify the domination of the yins over the yangs: a dangerous situation. The hidden hexagram of the Hexagram Thunder is the Water–Mountain Hexagram JIAN 蹇 [Obstacles] (39) ☵☶, indicating that difficulties will arise from a shock. The opposite hexagram GEN 艮 [Mountain] (52) ☶☶ gives the leader advice on how he should react to the danger he faces. The image of the Hexagram Mountain is stillness and stopping, suggesting that the leader should maintain his position as steady as the mountain despite having emergency measures in place to deal with the dangers that surround him.

LINE STATEMENTS

Initial Yang ☳. Be calm and steadfast in a panic

When thunder comes he is fearful but he keeps calm and alert, then he talks with laughter. It is auspicious.

When the leader of an organization is shocked by a sudden danger he should remain calm and steadfast so that the organization can operate peacefully and smoothly as if it were not affected by the shock. In the meantime he will find a solution. He must have strong confidence that the tension will ease in due course and everything will be restored to balance. **A situation looks bad on the surface but it can be good in disguise**.

A leader should have "fear" or caution in a panic even though it is a minor problem. Equally, he should keep calm when it is a serious problem.

Second Yin ☳. **Do not worry about an inevitable loss as it can be regained later**

When thunder comes, he is in danger and may lose his treasures.
He should climb up the high mountain without going after them,
for he will regain them in seven days.

Second Yin rides on Initial Yang which is the origin of a powerful movement. The position of Second Yin is therefore unstable and dangerous. If a leader finds his organization in a similar situation, for example, suffering from financial losses, he should take measures to avoid further losses. But he should not take any rash and speculative action to obtain income in the hope of compensating for the losses. A hasty move could make the situation even worse.

If the danger from a shake-up is believed to be only of a temporary nature and that normality will be restored later, the leader should not react too early, since after the shock the organization will be able to regain what it has lost.

Third Yin ☳. **Do not panic in a shock but stay calm**

Thunder makes him agitated and disturbed. If he strives forward, he will not be hurt.

Third Yin is in an improper position (a yin line in a yang position), indicating a situation in which a leader is agitated and disturbed by shock. If his sense of danger is induced by shock, he will tend to be cautious and will leave what is wrong and take what is right; then he will stay free of danger. A shock can make a leader change his mind and possibly change to a new way. If he acts in this way, he will not have trouble. Since Third Yin carries (below) Fourth Yang, its movement forward is considered right.

Fourth Yang ☳. **Stuck in the mud**

When thunder strikes, he falls in the mire.

When a leader does not react to danger his insensitivity can lead him to be less alert and incapable of adapting to an incident. Consequently, he will fall in the mud. Fourth Yang between two yins (Fifth Yin and Third Yin) forms a hidden trigram KAN 坎 [Water] which represents a dangerous situation. The position of Fourth Yang is not balanced and not correct (a yang line in a yin position), indicating its weaknesses.

Fifth Yin ☷ Keep strength under a threat

Thunder goes and comes. He will not lose his right of presiding over the sacrifice at the ancestral temple.

When a leader is surrounded by dangers, he must not lose centered balance or the principle of centrality. This will enable him to control himself and give him the strength to resist threats. To keep balanced is like keeping the right to preside over the sacrifice at the ancestral temple. A leader should not lose his strength even under threat.

Top Yin ☷ Need self-control

Thunder makes him shaken and restless, He is anxious to look around. If he acts this way, there will be trouble.
If he takes precautions he will not have misfortune. The short-sighted people, however, may speak against him.

In a dangerous situation a leader, fearful and anxious though, should be able to control himself by staying calm and steadfast. If he does not take any moves forward, the organization will be safe. If the leader's views and acts are different from those of other people, they may dislike him, but the leader should do what he believes is right.

52

The Mountain Hexagram
艮 GEN · Stillness, Stopping, Restraint

IMAGE

This Double Mountain Hexagram has Mountain as both the upper and lower trigrams. Mountain stands for stillness or stopping in contrast to a movement as represented by the Thunder Hexagram. A leader of an organization should know when he should move and when he should stop. He should not move when the time or the place is not favorable, even if his action is well planned. Vice versa, he should take action when the conditions are favorable even if action has not been planned. This hexagram illustrates an important principle: **advancing and stopping at the right time and place.**

In some cases, a leader wants to undertake an ambitious project not for the organization's benefit but rather for his personal interest and goal. His personal desire leads him in a direction that could be neither at a right time nor at a right place. Therefore, a leader should not let his personal ego dominate his mind. **If he is able to remain calm and to restrain his inner desire at the right time and place, he will make no mistakes.**

Mountains are linked one to the other. But each Mountain has its own position, implying that a person should not move out of his position but should keep still so that his inner desire will not affect others. Confucius had a similar view that a superior man should not become involved in affairs that are not his responsibility. He said: **"Do not interfere in others' business if you are not in their position."**

Hexagram Statement

The hexagram Gen *signifies stillness. He keeps his back still, but he cannot see it himself. It is like two persons walking back to back in the same courtyard, but they do not see each other. There will be no blame.*

Man is moved by desires, or desires induce a man's act. If a man has no desires, he will not move but will stand in stillness like a mountain. But desires can be classified into two categories: "positive desires" and "negative desires," or "superior desires" and "inferior desires." "Superior desires" refers to those which will lead a man to act in the right way by following the principles of sincerity, balance, and uprightness whereas the "inferior desires" are those with selfish purposes and evil intentions. Stable emotion can be included in the first category and unstable or impulsive emotion in the second. Moves led by "superior desires' should be encouraged but not those led by "inferior desires."

Man should be able to control his "inferior desires" so as to act in the right way. He should know when to move by "superior desires" and when to stop through his "inferior desires." Advancing and stopping at the right time/place is the key principle suggested by this hexagram. The text "he keeps his back still" means he stops his "inferior desires" at the right time or place. As the back of a man is unseen by himself unless mirror is used, so stopping at what is unseen means there are no "inferior desires" to disturb his mind. The text "he walks in the courtyard but he can not see it himself" implies that he forgets his own wishes or he is selfless because he has no "inferior desires."

Structure

This is a hexagram with two yangs and four yins, indicating a situation which is dominated by the two yangs. Both are at the top of each trigram and have a favorable position for controlling the two yins below. Fifth Yin (a top leadership position) and Fourth Yin (an action-leader position) are encircled by Top Yang and Third Yang as in the big trigram Li 離 [Fire], symbolizing a situation of weakness inside and strength outside:

Big Fire

Top Yang	———
Fifth Yin	— —
Fourth Yin	— —
Third Yang	———

Although Fifth Yin is in a leadership position with formal power, it is weak due to its yin character and the absence of complementary support from the people below as represented by Second Yin and Fourth Yin. Third Yang, however, is surrounded by four yins, indicating a big trigram KAN which signifies Big Danger faced by a person:

Big Danger

Fifth Yin	— —
Fourth Yin	— —
Third Yang	———
Second Yin	— —
Initial Yin	— —

If a leader does not know when he should move and when he should stop, he will face Big Danger.

LINE STATEMENTS

Initial Yin ☶. **Restraint at the beginning**

It is favorable for him always to keep steadfast at the beginning like he keeps his toes still. There will be no blame.

Initial Yin has six weaknesses: a yin line, an improper position, a noncentral position, a low position, a position under a yin line, and no interconnection with the fourth line. A person in this position should therefore restrain his impulsive action to move forward and so prevent falling into danger. He should stay where he is. If he can constantly control his emotion, he will always benefit.

Second Yin ☶. **Do not follow others in a wrong direction. Be true to yourself**

He should keep his calf still. If he is unable to correct the person above but follows him, he will not be happy.

Second Yin represents the calf and Third Yin the thigh. When the thigh moves, the calf follows. If the thigh symbolizes the superior of an organization and the calf the subordinate, the superior is the one who makes the decision whether to move or stop and the subordinate is just the follower. Even though a subordinate is as upright and sincere as Second Yin in a central position, he has to follow his superior's action even if it is incorrect. Consequently, he is not happy. If he is true to himself, he should advise his superior to stop the incorrect action. If the superior insists on moving forward according to his original plan, how should the subordinate behave? Should he resign from his position? Or just follow his superior?

Third Yang ☶· Do not restrain at a wrong time and a wrong place

He restrains at the waist and splits his back flesh, the danger worries him.

The waist is at the midsection of the human body; stopping or restraint at this position causes a split of the back into two parts, the upper and the lower. This situation is illustrated by Third Yang which symbolizes the waist of the upper and lower trigrams. For a leader, a split of the members of the organization into two or more groups would mean conflicts and contradictions. If he ignores this situation and leaves it as it is, the dangers will escalate and will damage the organization in due course.

In other lower trigrams, a person in the position of Third Yang is often advised not to take any action but to stay where he is as obstinacy or overconfidence would lead to danger. But in a situation of conflict a nonaction is considered incorrect. An action which can reduce or remove the conflict between the groups is required and desirable in order that cooperation and harmony within the organization can be restored. Restraint at the wrong time and in the wrong place is harmful.

Fourth Yin ☷· Know when and where one should have self-restraint

He keeps his body still. There will be no mistakes.

A senior executive Fourth Yin in a weak position (a yin line in a yin position) follows the top leader Fifth Yin. He can only restrain himself without influencing others (no interconnection with Initial Yin). If he knows when and where he should have self-restraint he will be unaffected by the dangers around him.

Fifth Yin ⚍ Be cautious in speaking

He keeps his mouth shut and speaks only at the proper time. There will be no regrets.

A leader must know when and how he should speak so as to avoid making mistakes through his words. He should choose his words carefully. Once spoken they cannot be taken back. He should not exaggerate but speak frankly and with substance, being brief and precise. Whenever he speaks he should sound convincing. Fifth Yin is a weak and improper position (a yin line in a yang position). A leader in this situation must be careful not only in his actions but also in his speech.

Top Yang ⚍ Control emotions and desires with honesty when at the top

He keeps still with honesty. There will be good fortune.

Top Yang is at the end of the hexagram, symbolizing that one should keep still with honesty to the end. A leader must be able to restrain his emotions and desires when he is at the top. If he acts honestly in this way, he will be auspicious. It is noticeable that the hexagrams that have the upper trigram GEN 艮 [Mountain] all have favorable commentaries on the top lines, such as in the hexagrams MENG 蒙 [Enlightenment] (4), GU 蠱 [Decay] (18), BI 賁 [Adornment] (22), PO 剝 [Stripping] (23), DAXU 大畜 [Great Accumulating] (26), YI 頤 [Nourishment] (27), and SUN 損 [Decrease] (41). All top positions of these eight hexagrams are considered favorable due to restraint at the right time and place. The reason for this is that the characteristics of Mountain are, like those of Earth, tolerance, caution, and patience. With these qualities a leader will be in a safe position, even though he is at the turning point of a cyclical change.

53

JIAN

The Wind (Wood)– Mountain Hexagram

Gradual Progress

IMAGE

The outer trigram Wind or Wood stands for tree which is above the inner trigram Mountain, symbolizing that a tree on a mountain grows gradually. The inner trigram Mountain means restraint as elaborated in the previous hexagram; the tree as represented by the outer trigram grows with an orderly pace. This principle of gradual progress can be applied to human organizations too. For example, a change in the basic structure of the organization. A hasty change of the structure will result in resistance and hence disharmony. A gradual progress under certain circumstances is less risky than a hasty change. A gradual progress, however, does not mean being conservative but does mean being cautious. When the internal conditions do not suit a rapid change and the external conditions are not clear, gradual progress appears to be a better choice.

According to the hexagram statement, an orderly progress is considered the necessary principle for a woman's marriage in ancient China. If a marriage did not follow this principle, it would be unfortunate. Like marriage, a lasting relationship between people or between business partners does not develop overnight but develops gradually with the increase of their mutual trust. Events must be allowed to develop gradually. As Confucius said: **"Do not make haste, do not covet small gains. If one makes haste, one cannot reach one's goal."**

The principle of gradual progress is meaningful to a person in cultivating character. Like the slow growth of a tree, it is not realistic to expect a person to change his character within a short time since the pace of development is slow.

A leader who is strong and active should in particular not be too eager for success if he sees only immediate advantages. Under some circumstances he needs patience and perseverance to reach his goal. A Chinese saying advises one to **"to plant one's feet on solid ground"** or to do a job honestly and with dedication. For the cultivation of one's character, Laozi said: **"To overcome the difficult should begin with the easy; to accomplish what is big should begin with the small. The difficult things in the world must originate in the easy; the big things in the world must take root in the small."** For a capable leader the principle of gradual progress should always be kept in mind.

HEXAGRAM STATEMENT

The marriage of a woman that proceeds in a gradual way is auspicious. It is favorable to keep to the right way.

The traditional marriage of a woman in ancient China was a rather long process because of the belief that a good and lasting marriage cannot be developed overnight. The text advises that certain matters should be done slowly with great thought and care. However, gradual progress is considered appropriate only if it can bring benefit at a particular time; otherwise it might not be correct.

STRUCTURE

This is a hexagram with three yin and three yang lines. Fifth Yang signifies that a leader in this position is active and creative with the support of the docile Second Yin. All three yins are under the control of the three yangs, indicating that the gradual progress is still yang in nature and is active and energetic.

The nuclear or hidden hexagram is WEIJI 未濟 [Not Yet Accomplished] (64) ☲☵, indicating that the development has not ended and there is a need for ongoing progress and creativity. In an unsettled time, a gradual approach is considered to be safer. The nuclear hexagram WEIJI implies that the benefits provided by gradual progress are unlimited.

The four lines including Second Yin, third Yang, Fourth Yin, and Fifth Yang are all in the proper positions. In particular, Fifth Yang holds a central balance that can represent the right direction of a move.

LINE STATEMENTS

Initial Yin ☶. Progress according to one's strength and conditions

The wild goose gradually advances to the shore. A young man thinks it should not stop there and should go further. But the goose is right and makes no mistakes.

Initial Yin is at the bottom of the hexagram, indicating its weak position (a yin line) in the early stage of development in a project. Under such circumstances, a leader realizes that he could meet with difficulties if he moves recklessly as the conditions for taking a big step are not yet established and he also lacks complementary support from above (Fourth Yin). A wise leader who has a long-term vision will be patient; it is better for him to stay where he is. But his action is not understood by those who are uncultivated and short-sighted.

Second Yin ☵. On the right track

The wild goose progresses onto the rock at the shore and here it eats and drinks happily. There will be good fortune.

Second Yin in a position of centrality and correctness together with its complementary relationship with Fifth Yang makes the situation stable, secure, and favorable. A leader in this position feels relaxed and optimistic and will share this harmonious delight with his colleagues.

Third Yang ☳. Secure the present position rather than moving forward

The wild goose progresses onto the high plain. This is like a husband who goes out but does not return or a wife who is pregnant but cannot give birth.
There will be misfortune. It is advantageous to defend against brigands.

A leader in the position of Third Yang tends to be obstinate as indicated by a yang line in a yang position at the top of the lower trigram as he always believes his own judgment and choice. He seldom considers other people's views and prefers a rash advance to a gradual one, so he falls into danger. This is a situation like the text says "a husband who goes out but does not return or a wife who is pregnant but cannot give birth." However, his tough character is seen "advantageous to defend against brigands."

Fourth Yin ☶. Manage a difficult position

The wild goose flies onto a tree. If it can find a big flat branch, it will have no trouble.

Since a goose has webbed feet, it has difficulty in gripping a tree branch and so needs to find a big flat branch to rest on. This means that the position of Fourth Yin is proper. On the other hand, it rides on Third Yang that wants to move up, putting pressure on Fourth Yin and thereby creating an unstable situation. Fourth Yin carries Fifth Yang and may get the necessary support from above (Fifth Yang), so its position can be secured just like a goose perching on a flat tree branch. An executive should be able to get the support of his superior in order to secure his position when he faces pressure from the people below him.

Fifth Yang ☵. Keep strength and flexibility

The wild goose progresses to the hills. A wife does not become pregnant for three years. In the end, she conceives as nothing can prevent this. It is auspicious.

A leader who can keep his strength and correctness will be able to achieve his goal. For example, the high stage of a gradual development as represented by the position of Fifth Yang. He needs the complementary assistance of capable people below (Second Yin). There are hindrances between Fifth Yang and Second Yin as represented by the fourth yin line and the third yang line, like the text says "a wife does not become pregnant for three years." But the difficulties will eventually be resolved as long as he can maintain his principles.

Top Yang ☶. One's attainment can serve as a model for inspiring others

The wild goose progresses into the sky. Its feathers can be used as ornaments for a ceremony.

When a leader has accomplished something great, his attainment can be seen as a standard for the inspiration of others. Top Yin symbolizes the virtue or integrity of a superior man, which is seen by the ordinary people as a high model for emulation.

54

The Thunder–Lake Hexagram

The Marrying Maiden, Irregular Progress

IMAGE

The upper trigram Thunder represents an older man whereas the lower trigram Lake a young woman. Thunder also represents movement and Lake represents joy. The hexagram GUIMEI portrays a young woman pleased to go along with an older man. A marriage based on the likes of the young woman was considered abnormal in ancient China. A young woman's marriage which proceeded in an orderly manner was seen as the correct practice. The marriage would be considered unfortunate if a young woman took an active part in it. This sort of marriage for a young woman is the opposite to the conventional type of gradual progress as illustrated by the previous hexagram JIAN 漸 [Gradual Progress] (53). In fact GUIMEI is the opposite hexagram of JIAN:

JIAN   GUIMEI

The upper trigram Thunder symbolizes action. An action which is based on an individual's own likes or optimistic outlook as represented by the lower trigram Lake or Pleasing would face risks. This kind of merger is also applicable to a business partnership that is primarily based on the people's likes or dislikes rather than on the objective factors.

HEXAGRAM STATEMENT

The marriage of the young woman is unfortunate and there is nothing to be gained.

Any action that is decided by a leader alone based on his personal likes or dislikes will involve a certain risk if there is no any objective study made before it. However, the action can also be considered positive if the leader's judgment is correct. Generally an action-decision should follow a regular process, but a nonordinary approach can also be used to react quickly and catch an opportunity. This hexagram emphasizes action that is based on an ordinary approach. However, nonordinary approaches should not be excluded from a decision-making for they can be creative and effective.

STRUCTURE

This hexagram has three yins and three yangs. Four of them are not in the proper positions: Second Yang, Third Yin, Fourth Yang, and Fifth Yin. Improper position means that an improper act or improper behavior that would lead to misfortune, like the marriage of young woman that does not follow the gradual or ordinary way as illustrated by this hexagram.

LINE STATEMENTS

Initial Yang ☳. Do the best despite limited resources

The young woman is married as a junior wife. If she acts as a lame person who can still walk, there will be good fortune.

A junior wife has a lower status in the family than that of the first wife. But if she is upright, capable, modest, and able to prove her worth to others, she acts in the same way as a lame person who can manage to get along.

An executive in a low position with limited authority, like a second wife or a lame person who can walk, will still be able to make contributions to the organization if he can offer his services to the benefit of the whole group by using his limited resources. An executive can do his best even though he plays a subordinate role in an organization, like a concubine in a family.

Since there is no interconnection between Initial Yang and Fourth Yang, Initial Yang lacks support from above. An executive in this position has to rely on his own strength when he takes action. The situation is like a person who walks with a limp.

Second Yang ☳. Keep uprightness and perseverance

A concubine is like a person who can see only with one eye. It is favorable to be steadfast like a person who loses his freedom but remains upright and firm.

Second Yang indicates a situation in which a concubine can still offer her services to the family despite her limited authority, as a one-eyed man can see. Second Yang represents a capable and upright woman and Fifth Yin stands for a weak and not upright husband. Through an interconnection between the two, Second Yang can help Fifth Yin to manage a family by providing her services even though she has limited resources at hand. Second Yang is obviously in a better position to assist the upper management than Initial Yang does. Based on the text, an executive with limited authority and resources can still make contributions to the organization if he does not lose his loyalty and uprightness.

Third Yin ☳. Do not aim too high

A young woman wants to get married as a first wife like her elder sister, but she is married as a concubine in the end.

Third Yin is in an improper position symbolizing a woman who seeks marriage based on her own wish that is, however, beyond reality. If an executive wants to attain his objective through an irregular process, he may not reach it.

Fourth Yang ☳. Postpone an action until the time is ripe

A young woman spins out the time to her marriage, for she has expectations and there is a time for her.

Fourth Yang represents a young woman of high status who does not want to marry a man who cannot meet her expectations. She prefers to postpone her wedding until she gets the right person. Her situation is indicated by the absence of interconnection or complement with Initial Yang. Similarly a leader does not want to undertake an operation now because of his belief that the time and space are not favorable; he has every right to postpone his plans until the time is ripe.

Fifth Yin ☷ **Act in a proper way**

The emperor Di Yi gave his young sister in marriage as the concubine of the Lord of Zhou. The dress of the princess was not as fine as that of the second wife of the Lord. She behaved like an almost full moon and therefore enjoyed good fortune.

Fifth Yin symbolizes the noble status of the royal princess whereas Second Yang the Lord of Zhou. The relationship between Fifth Yin and Second Yang indicates a situation in which the former has a higher political status than that of the latter. The text "the dress of the princess was not as fine as that of the second wife" is a praise of the princess for her simplicity and modesty, even though she has a noble status. It means that she does not need to decorate herself outwardly to please others. The dress of the first wife of the emperor is not as fine as that of the second wife.

The text advices the leader of an organization that he should act properly according to his position and avoid competing with others to show how strong and powerful he is. As moon represents yin, the full moon symbolizes the full growth of yin as indicated by Top Yin and "an almost full moon" is therefore represented by Fifth Yin. Since the position of Fifth Yin is lower than that of Top Yin, its situation is just like "an almost full moon." The text advises a leader not to act in an extreme way, for example, by seeking maximum benefit. If he follows this principle, he will be auspicious.

Top Yin ☷ **A person's ability must meet the requirements of his position**

A woman carrying an empty basket and a man slaughters a sheep with no blood. There is nothing to be gained.

At the sacrificial ceremony held by the lords for their ancestors in ancient China, the husband played the major role in presenting the offerings and was accompanied by his wife. His function was to slaughter a sheep and the wife's was to carry a basket with the offerings. The text "a woman carries an empty basket" implies that the wife does not perform her function in the sacrifice ceremony and her husband too as he slaughters a sheep with no blood. In a modern organization, this means that an executive and his subordinates are not capable of carrying out their duties, like the husband and his wife with the offerings.

Top Yin is in a proper position (a yin line in a yin position), but it is weak in nature and lacks interconnection with Third Yin. This indicates a situation in which a man's ability cannot meet the requirements of his position, or the situation of a man who does have the ability to fulfill his duties as required by his position but does not have the chance to fulfill his part because of the restrictions of the present system or policy. The statement of this hexagram, like some others, can be interpreted in both positive and negative ways dependant on different times and places.

55

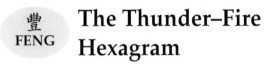 **The Thunder–Fire Hexagram**

FENG

Abundance, Prosperity, Fullness

IMAGE

Thunder signifies movement whereas Fire stands for light. Thunder above Fire symbolizes action with clarity. The precondition for taking action includes clarity, a good understanding of the rationale for it, and an estimation of the difficulties that will be encountered in the move. The relationship between clarity and action is interdependent. With clarity one can perceive matters better and with action one is able to move toward the goal. Clarity can reduce the risks of an action and provide the basis of the road to success or abundance. **Action with clarity brings fortune.**

Abundance represents a situation that is like the sun at midday. In this situation, the leader of an organization should understand the law of nature. At noon the sun begins to set and the full noon begins to wane. His major task is therefore to prolong the stage of abundance within the cycle and to adapt to the situation when the cycle goes downward.

HEXAGRAM STATEMENT

Abundance can be achieved under the governance of a king. There is nothing to worry about if it can last like the sun at high noon.

The king in the text can be interpreted as a wise and capable leader of an organization. He understands well the law of nature in which downward movement will begin once the peak of abundance or prosperity is reached. To maintain long-lasting prosperity, like the sun at high noon, is desirable. But this is difficult or unrealistic because of the law of nature or the cyclical change in the universe. What the leader of an organization can do is to try to use every possible measure within his capability and resources to prolong the peak of the cycle. There are six principles that can be useful for maintaining or prolonging the good time of an organization as stated in the following six line statements.

STRUCTURE

According to the structure of the six lines, three yin lines are located in good positions including the two central lines: Second Yin and Fifth Yin. As both Initial Yang and Fourth Yang are below Second Yin and Fifth Yin respectively, this indicates that a soft management appears to be more appropriate and adaptable in a time of abundance.

In the Hexagram Abundance ䷶ and the Hexagram Biting Through ䷔, the positions of the upper and lower trigrams are interchanged. In the Hexagram Abundance, Fire is considered as the "independent variable" whereas Thunder acts as the "dependent variable." Action is based on clarity. With clarity success or abundance is achievable through action. In the Hexagram Biting Through, the positions of these two "variables" are reversed: Thunder acts as the "independent variable" and Fire as the "dependent variable." Action that represents law can lead people to act in the right way.

LINE STATEMENTS

Initial Yang ䷶. Strengthen the position by having a partner with common characteristics

He gets his partner as they have common characteristics.
The cooperation between the two will be valuable to go on without any blame.

Both Initial Yang and Fourth Yang are in the beginning of the lower and upper trigrams respectively, sharing the common characteristics of firmness and strength as both have the nature of the yang line. But there is no interconnection between the two lines. Without a yin–yang union, how can they cooperate with each other? To maintain prosperity, it is necessary for an executive to get support from someone who shares common values even though the person cannot provide complementary assistance. His strength, however, can still be advantageous to the organization. The principle of complementarity or a yin–yang union will not be used here, but rather the principle of similarity so long as it is adaptable to the present conditions.

Second Yin ☲· Be sincere and faithful

When abundance is in the shade, the North Star is seen at midday. Going forward he gets mistrust and suspicion. It is auspicious if he is sincere and faithful.

Second Yin in the central position of the lower trigram Fire or Lightening symbolizes an executive who is sensible. The North Star that is at the center of the stars symbolizes the leading position of Fifth Yin. The North Star can only be seen in the night. If it is seen at midday, it means that the light is lost as if at night. This implies that Fifth Yin is an ignorant and unfair leader and does not trust Second Yin because of Fifth Yin's suspicious nature. Under such circumstances, it is difficult for the organization to maintain its abundance because of the internal disharmony. If the executive Second Yin can keep his sincerity, he may earn the trust of the leader Fifth Yin, through which the organization will be able to maintain its good position.

Third Yang ☳· Persevere and be strong when unable to do anything

Abundance is screened, so that even the tiny stars can be seen at midday. He can do nothing as if his right arm were broken.

The darkness that Third Yang faces is even greater than that which Second Yin does, for the tiny stars can be seen at noon. It means that the sun is in eclipse which brings darkness at midday, symbolizing that abundance is screened. Although Third Yang has interconnection with Top Six, the latter is weak and cannot give Third Yang sufficient support needed to reach the objective. Therefore, Third Yang is like a man without a right arm. An executive in this position, although he is willing to do something positive for the organization, is unable to do it due to the absence of support from his superior who is weak and incompetent. In such a situation, he should be patient, persevere, and keep strong as shown by the characteristics of a yang line.

Third Yang is in a strong position (a yang line in a yang position), implying that the executive may be tempted to take forward action. If he acts in this way, his efforts will be in vain as the conditions for doing things in this stage are unfavorable.

Fourth Yang ☳ Seek cooperation with a capable peer

When abundance is screened, the North Star is seen at midday.
He meets a peer and will have good fortune.

The first part of the statement is same as that of Second Yang. In both situations the leader Fifth Yin is weak and incapable and the whole organization is operating as if in darkness. Fourth Yang is considered the master of action as it is the first position of the upper trigram ZHEN 震 [Thunder]. To make action more effective, the senior executive in this position should obtain the assistance of a capable person from a lower echelon as represented by Initial Yang. As Initial Yang is at the beginning of the lower trigram LI 離 [Fire], the executive in this position is considered enlightened and capable. Fourth Yang should seek cooperation with him to overcome the darkness.

Fifth Yin ☴ Get the assistance of different capable people

He who can attract excellent people will have joy and reputation.
It is auspicious.

Fifth Yin represents a top leader who is weak but open-minded and tolerant; he is willing to use the capable people in his organization and to delegate as much authority as is needed. Although he appears to be soft, the people as represented by Initial Yang, Third Yang, and Fourth Yang are all strong and active. By acting in this way, he is able to strengthen his leadership position through the joint efforts of all the capable people in the organization.

His relationship with Second Yin is not complementary as both are yins. But Second Yin does have the qualities of balance and uprightness that can help the leader Fifth Yin in a significant way. With the assistance of capable people under him, Fifth Yin will be able to have joy and reputation.

Top Yin ䷶ Do not be isolated at the top

He makes his house huge and magnificent but encloses himself inside. Peeking through the gate, no one can be seen there. He does not see anyone for three years. There will be misfortune.

When a leader reaches a top position he could become a person who is conceited or complacent. Acting in this way, he will meet danger. A leader in a time of abundance should be modest and particularly should not be arrogant toward those who have supported him. If he wants to keep his success and riches to himself, he will become isolated.

56

The Fire–Mountain Hexagram

The Wanderer, Traveling

IMAGE

Mountain is stationary as represented by the inner trigram GEN 艮 [Mountain], signifying a person's hometown dwelling which cannot move. Fire is free to move on elsewhere as represented by the outer trigram LI 離 [Fire], symbolizing the movement of a person traveling outside his hometown. The hexagram LÜ, where Fire is above Mountain, is therefore called The Wanderer or Traveling.

A person's life is like traveling as he will face different circumstances at different times and in different places. There are good times and bad times as well as good places and bad places. As a wanderer he should be careful and alert so as to not fall into any pit. He should also be flexible and adaptable to changing conditions. During his travel through life, he must have a strong will to keep to his objectives or his aim while acting in the right way, that is, sensibly and honestly.

The world today is globalized. Business executives are required to make trips to different parts of the world and they can be assigned to different foreign countries for a certain period of time. Due to differences in cultures, an international business executive needs higher adaptability and flexibility to cope with the conditions of the local environment.

The outer trigram LI implies that one who travels or works outside his hometown should have a quiet and understanding heart in order to realize what is happening around him and to understand the need for him to follow local practices and rules.

A person who works outside his hometown faces an unfamiliar place where there are uncertainties and difficulties. To him the situation is like the hexagram Pɪ 否 [Obstruction] (12) ☰☷. Many obstacles stand in the way of further progress as symbolized by the three yin lines. To adapt to the new environment an executive who is assigned to an unfamiliar place or a foreign country needs to be correct, modest, flexible and balanced. The hexagram Lü or The Wanderer is obtained by exchanging Third Yin of the lower trigram Kun with Fifth Yang of the upper trigram Qɪᴀɴ in the original hexagram Pɪ:

The Fifth Yin of the hexagram Lü suggests the required qualities an international business executive should possess (sincerity, adaptability, flexibility, and balance) when he is a stranger in a foreign country. By acting in this way, he will win the cooperation of and a welcome from the local people.

HEXAGRAM STATEMENT

The prospects of progress are moderate. If the traveler behaves properly, there will be good fortune.

Like a wanderer, an international business executive is exposed to uncertainties and dangers when he is on the road as the environment of the host country is different from that of his home country. As he is in a vulnerable position, he should be flexible and should adapt to the local conditions, and in particular pay respect to the local laws. By acting in this way, he will make sure progress with the least danger.

STRUCTURE

This is a hexagram with an equal number of yin and yang lines. Two yins however occupy the two important positions, the fifth and the second. Both carry the hard lines or the yangs, indicating that a soft style of leadership or management should be adopted when operating outside one's hometown.

The upper trigram Fire is a yin trigram (one yin line only) whereas the lower trigram Mountain is a yang trigram (one yang line only), implying that a person should have clarity like fire outside and perseverance like a mountain internally when in a strange land.

LINE STATEMENTS

Initial Yin ☶. Do not engage in trivial matters but focus on major things

If he is engaged in trivial matters during his travels, he is inviting trouble.

An executive who uses his energy and time on engaging in trivial matters will most likely ignore the major points or the key issues facing him. He could be a person who lacks great insight or vision. A short-sighted executive is interested only in actions that can bring profits in the short run but will lose the opportunity to make large gains in the long run. However, his competitor may move in a direction that he has ignored. As a result, the organization will face pressure in the future. This is the situation in which one obtains a small gain but loses a large one.

Second Yin ☷. Require basic qualities

During his travels he has a place to live, sufficient money to spend and a dependable attendant at his service.

An executive who is correct, flexible, and balanced as suggested by Second Yin will be able to win the trust of the local people and the needed capital and manpower.

Third Yang ☶. Do not be obstinate but flexible and adaptable

The inn where the traveler stays at is burnt down and he loses his faithful attendant. Even if he acts properly there is danger.

Third Yang as a yang line in a yang position at the top of the lower trigram symbolizes hardness. If an executive in this position is obstinate or exceedingly adamant in taking a reckless action without considering the unfavorable conditions around him and the advice of his colleagues, he will lose the faith of the people under him. People will lose faith in him and leave the organization. The situation is as if a traveler's inn was burned down. Should hardness be reduced, Third Yang can be replaced by Third Yin to obtain the hexagram JIN 晉 [Advancing] (35) ☷. It suggests that a soft steady progress under a soft (yin) style of leadership should be adopted instead of a rash advance under a hard (yang) style of leadership.

Fourth Yang ⚎ Capabilities are restrained by mismatched team members

He finds shelter in his travel and has the axe for defense. But his heart is not at ease.

The executive Fourth Yang, who is under a soft leadership of Fifth Yin has a good plan and connections for penetrating the local market of a foreign country, like a traveler who gets an axe for defense. But he is not happy due to the indecision of his superior Fifth Yin and the incapability of his subordinate Initial Yin. Under such circumstances, he cannot give full play to his abilities and do what he really wants to do. In consequence, he is not able to achieve his initial objective.

Different times and places require different superiors and subordinates to be matched accordingly. There is no standard pattern. If Fifth Yin is replaced by Fifth Yang, the present hexagram LÜ ⚌ will be changed to the hexagram DUN 遯 [Retreating] (33) ⚌, a strong leadership in the organization. Whether a strong leadership is preferable to a soft one depends very much on the conditions in the respective foreign country. The top leader of at the headquarters needs to consider carefully before making a decision for change.

Fifth Yin ⚏ Do not emphasize gains and losses when establishing contacts

He shoots a pheasant but loses his arrow. He obtains fame and entitlement in the end.

The leader of an organization in a foreign country should be balanced, flexible, and correct as indicated by the yin line in the fifth position. This style is more adaptable to the local conditions. The gains from this are like getting a pheasant and the losses comparatively low, like losing just "an arrow." As a whole, the gains outweigh the losses. The executive should be able to cultivate the right contacts with influential people in a foreign country so that he can establish himself in the new situation.

Top Yang ☶ᐧ **Do not be adamant and too self-confident in a high position**

The bird's nest burns up. The wanderer laughs at first and then later cries for the loss of the ox in the field. It is unfortunate.

The yang line at the top of the hexagram signifies a bird's nest that is built in too high a position. When a person is in a high position he easily becomes adamant and overly self-confident. Consequently he believes that whatever decision he makes is always right and rarely accepts other people's views. He will gradually lose the support of his superiors, colleagues, and subordinates. Few people are willing to associate with him. This is a situation where, as the text says, "the bird's nest burns up." He may laugh at first when he is in a high position but then he cries later when he realizes that no one will work with him. The situation is just like "the loss of the ox in the field."

57

The Wind Hexagram

XUN

Penetration, Compliance, Obedience

IMAGE

This is a Double Wind Hexagram. Since winds can blow through myriad things, this hexagram means penetration. A Double Wind Hexagram indicates that action needs double penetration and should be led by people with strong character like Fifth Yang and Second Yang. In the structure of each trigram two yang lines are above the yin line, indicating that a yin or soft approach appears to be desirable for the purpose of penetrating into an organizational structure which is dominated by the yang force.

It is important for the leader of an organization to understand the views and needs of its members. He can acquire such information by quiet observation, through opening channels for suggestions, opinion polling, group discussions, personal discussions, and forums. The responses of the members of the organization should be used as the reference point or basis for formulating an action policy. This is a gentle approach to communication with the members of an organization in order to investigate problems encountered and formulate corresponding policies. To avoid internal conflict and confrontation, it is beneficial to use a soft approach instead of a hard one. With a soft approach a leader will be in an advantageous position to achieve a harmonious state.

HEXAGRAM STATEMENT

The prospect of a gentle influence is moderate. It is beneficial to go forward and for the great man to come out.

Using a gentle approach in an organization with a hard structure is useful, but it can achieve only moderate success. As long as the hard style of leadership or management remains unchanged in an organization, the effect of gentle influence could be limited unless there are fundamental changes in the organizational structure.

STRUCTURE

From a structural aspect the hexagram XUN symbolizes a hard type of organization since the yin lines in both the lower and upper trigrams are below two yang lines. This organization is obviously dominated by executives with yang characteristics. Their subordinates Initial Yin and Fourth Yin show their obedience to their superiors, Second Yang and Fifth Yang, respectively. A question arises whether the subordinates who are obedient to the superiors are advantageous to the organization as a whole or not. The hard style leaders may appreciate their obedient character, but they may not be favorable to the organization as the leaders can be misled into deciding and acting on their own. **Absolute obedience creates absolute autocracy.**

LINE STATEMENTS

Initial Yin ☴. **Do not be indecisive**

He cannot decide whether he should move forward or backward.
It is favorable for him to be decisive like a warrior.

A leader should be decisive. If his mind is full of doubts and fears he tends to be hesitant and indecisive. This will lead to a situation of irresolution. The yin line in a low position of the lower trigram symbolizes an executive who is too weak and soft to make a decision. One of the reasons for his weakness in making a decision could be that he does not have any support from above as there is no interconnection between Initial Yin and Fourth Yin.

Second Yang ☴· **Find out the causes of the problems thoroughly and remove them meticulously**

He finds out the causes of the problems thoroughly and resolves them
by using extremely careful measures, as the witch exorcises the evil

spirit hidden under the bed. He will have good fortune and make no mistakes.

When problems are found in an organization the leader should thoroughly investigate the real causes for them rather than the surface ones. Once the causes of the problems are identified, the leader can resolve these problems by using appropriate methods together with professional assistance and suggestions, just as people in ancient times employed a witch to exorcize the evil spirits under the bed.

The evil can be interpreted as one's ego. One should search for this hidden enemy in one's mind and remove it, like a witch exorcizing evil.

Third Yang ☴· Be self-confident and stable in emotion

He changes his mind frequently, he will have regrets.

If an executive lacks self-confidence and his emotions are not stable he tends to change his mind frequently. This will lead his subordinates into difficulties as they want to know which of his decisions is right. If they blindly follow his orders, the action could in fact be wrong. But if they express their differing views frankly, the superior may not accept them. This, they think, could damage their relationship with their superior. In either case the efficiency of the organization is negatively affected.

Fourth Yin ☴· Be docile in a proper position

There are no regrets. He catches three kinds of game in hunting.

Fourth Yin represents a senior executive who is in an unfavorable position between two yang lines—Fifth Yang and Third Yang—but he is in a proper position (a yin line in a yin position) and obedient to the superior Fifth Yang. By taking advantage of his closeness to the top leader and his own managerial skills, the senior executive in this position should be able to develop a good relationship with all people above and below him like "he catches three kinds of game in hunting."

Fifth Yang ☴· Ponder over a situation

It is good to be steadfast and true. Regret vanishes and nothing is unfavorable.

There is no beginning but an end. It bodes well to be careful before a change and reflective after it.

If a leader can act in the right way as indicated by the central balance of Fifth Yang, he will be auspicious without regrets. When making a change, the leader needs to consider the situation. Before making a change, he must think carefully about the possible impact of it and re-examine the situation and the possible effects. The term "no beginning" means a lack of careful thinking before a change, and "an end" refers to the necessary revisions after a change.

Top Yang Do not be excessively docile

He is excessively obedient as if he were under the bed. He loses possessions and axe. His persistence in obedience is harmful.

Top Yang is at the extreme of the Hexagram Penetrating, indicating a man who is excessively obedient in this position. If an executive is too obedient or docile, he may lose the creativity and strength to do new things, which the original nature of a yang line should have. An axe is a cutting tool which symbolizes a man's strength or determination. If a person loses his axe as indicated in the text, it means that he loses his strength and determination. An executive who lacks these two qualities will not be able to lead his organization in change as required by the new conditions.

58

| 兌 |
| DUI |

The Lake Hexagram
Interlinking, Pleasing, Joyous
Interaction

IMAGE

This is a Double Lake Hexagram. When two lakes are joined water flows between them, so neither will dry up. This linked relationship between two lakes symbolizes a companionship between two persons who can learn from each other or a partnership between two corporations for the purpose of mutual support. Through companionship or a friendly partnership, the two parties involved can both benefit and hence both of them are happy.

If the upper trigram represents the upper management of an organization and the lower trigram the people at the lower echelon, mutual support and a harmonious relationship between the two will lead both groups to happiness. This can be the motivating force for the whole organization. If the members of an organization are joyful, they are pleased to associate with the organization. However, the way of pleasing people must be correct; if not, there will be regret.

HEXAGRAM STATEMENT

The hexagram signifies pleasing. If he can keep in the right way, he will achieve success.

If a leader can please others, others will please him too. A joyful relationship between them will lead to harmonious cooperation both internally and externally through which the success of the organization can be ensured.

STRUCTURE

The two yang lines Fifth Yang and Second Yang represent sincerity, balance, and strength, whereas the two yin lines Top Yin and Third Yin represent gentleness, docility, and flexibility. Therefore, yang stands for hardness and yin for softness. In both upper and lower trigrams one yin is above and two yangs are below, symbolizing softness outside and hardness inside. In fact, hardness and softness are interdependent; a leader with outward gentleness (yin) without inward firmness (yang) has an unbalanced character. Conversely, a leader with outward firmness without inward gentleness results in an unbalanced character too. The Hexagram Double Lake symbolizes a man who is soft outwardly but hard inwardly, the ideal type of a superior from the classic perspective. A leader of this type tends to be friendly, warm, and helpful to others while keeping the principles of sincerity and balance.

Like the hexagram Xun 巽 [Obedience] (57) ☴, Dui is also a four-yangs-dominated hexagram. The difference between the two is the positions of the two yins. Xun is the reciprocal hexagram of Dui—the two yins are at the bottom of each trigram in Xun as compared with that of Dui where they are at the top of the two trigrams. Dui has a structure of outward softness and inward hardness whereas Xun has a structure of outward hardness and inward softness.

LINE STATEMENTS

Initial Yang ☱. Be amiable to people

As he is amiable to people, he is auspicious.

Initial Yang at the bottom of the hexagram symbolizes a person who is friendly and amiable. He is not an ambitious person as he is content with his life as it is. He is open-minded and willing to accept other people's views, so people make good relationships with him without having doubts. A man who has the above personality will rarely come under the suspicion of others.

Second Yang ☱. Be sincere to others

He gets joy through sincerity to others. Acting in this way he will have no regrets.

If a leader treats people with sincerity and fairness by following the characteristics of Second Yang, he is in the right way to please people. Although Second Yang is not in a proper position (a yang line in a yin position), its weakness is compensated for by the strength of the principle of centrality.

Third Yin ☱· Do not please others in an improper way

If he pleases others to seek harmony, he will have misfortune.

If a leader intends to achieve harmony with others through improper ways or at the expense of his integrity, he is inviting trouble and will have regrets. The improper position of Third Yin (a yin line in a yang position) symbolizes the improper measures used.

Fourth Yang ☴· Keep close to good and away from evil

He weighs in which direction the joy lies, so his mind is not in peace. If he can ward off harm, he will have pleasure.

Fourth Yang is between Fifth Yang and Third Yin. The former represents a leader who is upright whereas the latter represents an inferior man who knows how to please others. Both can give Fourth Yang pleasure even though they are not the same. An executive in this position must make a decision as to which he should associate with. Since yang stands for good and yin represents bad, he will have true pleasure if he can keep distance from what is wrong (Third Yin) and close to what is right (Fifth Yang).

Fifth Yang ☱· Be wary of flatterers

He who trusts an inferior man will encounter danger.

It will be harmful to a leader if he trusts flatterers as they may be hiding their intentions and take advantage of him. It is beneficial for a leader to identify which of the people who surround him are truly sincere. In the text, the flatterers or inferior people are represented by Top Yin.

Top Yin ☱· Beware of the seductive act of an inferior man

He seduces others to be joyful.

One should not seduce others to reach one's own objective. If a person acts this way, the relationship between the parties is unstable and can easily be broken. Both Top Yin and Third Yin try to seduce each other as indicated by the interconnection between them. Since their positions are different, the effect of their seductive act are different too. Third Yin is in a yang position which is open in nature whereas Top Yin is in a yin position with a hidden nature. Consequently, people are able to identify the seductive actions of Third Yin but find it more difficult to recognize those of Top Yin. This is why the line statement of Third Yang is considered unfortunate and the one of Top Yin as neutral.

59

 ## The Wind–Water Hexagram

Dispersing, Scattering, Disintegration

IMAGE

When the wind blows across the surface of a lake, it causes waves. This is the image of Wind over Lake. To a leader of an organization, wind symbolizes the events that are around him and the waves in the lake stand for the problems or troubles that are caused by these events. Within an organization the values and views of the members can be different. If they cannot be integrated into one that will be accepted by the different members, people will disperse into several groups either in an overt or a covert way.

For a leader, a difference of views among the members in his organization is almost unavoidable. His task is to unite the people by building up coherence, for example, through the values or the culture of his organization. Since coherence and dispersion are opposed, higher coherence means lower dispersion and vice versa.

HEXAGRAM STATEMENT

Dispersal can be resolved if the king would summon the people at the ancestral temple for a united purpose.
Acting in the right way, it is favorable to cross great rivers.

As the text indicates, the king who offers sacrifices at the ancestral temple is trying to reunite the hearts of the people by emphasizing the contributions or values of their ancestors. Offering sacrifices at the ancestral temple in ancient China can be seen as a way for a king to build up the group spirit or coherence of his people. Similarly a leader in modern times can also use this means to build up group values and team spirit as soon as dispersion in the organization is identified. However, the measures for building the group spirit must be right.

A leader must understand that there is an opposing relationship between dispersion and gathering. When he faces a situation of dispersal, he should not only think of using forcible measures to stop it but also of the ways to strengthen the spirit of gathering or coherence in the organization.

STRUCTURE

This hexagram is dominated by hardness as the two central positions are occupied by the yang lines: Fifth Yang, Second Yang, and Top Yang. Fifth Yang and Second Yang encircle Fourth Yin and Third Yin, resulting in a situation of Big Fire ☲. Under such a hard organization people tend to be dissatisfied, disagreeable, and disappointed, either overtly or covertly. As a consequence, members of the organization diverge and disperse.

LINE STATEMENTS

Initial Yin ☶. Reconcile conflicts at an early stage and use all the help one can get

If he can get a strong horse, he will have good fortune.

When dispersal starts to develop in an organization the leader should seek the help from a capable person as symbolized by a strong horse, or Second Yang in the text. A horse can also symbolize the fact that a quick action is required to solve the conflict. When dispersion starts the leader should not allow it to develop further but should act promptly in order to reduce the differences among the members and between the members and the organization.

Second Yang ☶. Rely on a support

In a time of dispersion, he runs to support. His regret vanishes.

In a time of dispersal or disintegration, an executive in the position of Second Yang should get a support. Since he has no interconnection with

Fifth Yang he cannot get support from above but he can from Initial Yin below. The relationship between Second Yang and Initial Yin is complementary, as Second Yang is seen by Initial Yin as "a strong horse" and Second Yang considers Initial Yin a support. To take effective action to resolve conflicts in a time of dispersion, a leader needs complementary support.

Third Yin ☵· Dissolve one's ego

He who disregards his own desires has no regret.

If a leader can put away all his personal and selfish concerns and be concerned about other people's problems, he will have no reason for regret. Third Yin is in an improper position (a yin line in a yang position) symbolizing a man who has personal desires. The relationship (interconnection) between Third Yin and Top Yang indicates that he is willing to dissolve his ego and support others.

Fourth Yin ☵· Dissolve the clique

He breaks up his clique and then gathers a large group, there will be good fortune. Ordinary people would not consider doing this.

As the senior executive of an organization he should dissolve his own clique and gather together people in general, looking out for the interest of the whole organization. An executive who can give up his own interests for the benefit of the organization as a whole will get support. The senior executive Fourth Yin will follow the top leader Fifth Yang, who represents the interests of the organization, while keeping a distance from Third Yin which symbolizes his ego.

Fifth Yang ☵· Inspire others to remedy an unhealthy situation

In a time of dispersion, the king makes his orders reach everywhere in the country as a sick man sweating in a fever. There is nothing wrong in this.

To remedy dispersal, a leader can make imperative directives to all members of his organization in order to inspire them to go along with him, as if sweating to cool a fever. A leader who has the characteristics of sincerity, balance, and uprightness as represented by Fifth Yang will be in a good position to restore healthy order in his organization.

Top Yang ䷿ Prepare safety measures and contingency plans

In a time of dispersion, he keeps far away from harm for not causing bloodshed, so there is no fault.

When there is a danger in the time of dispersal the leader must be able to protect the interests of the organization as a whole. Top Yang is at the end of the hexagram, symbolizing an extreme situation of dispersal and Third Yin is at the top of the lower trigram KAN 坎 [Water], representing a high danger. Since the distance between Top Yang and Third Yin is far, a leader in this position will not be hurt by the danger if he can prepare timely safety measures and contingency plans.

60

節
JIE

The Water–Lake
Hexagram

Regulating, Restraint, Limitation

IMAGE

Water over Lake implies that the water needs to be regulated, for too much water causes flooding and too little causes drought. The Water–Lake Hexagram advises a controlled way of life. Conduct should be centered and balanced, neither excessive nor demeaning, neither extravagant nor restricted. If a person is balanced, he will be joyful and not suffer pain. As long as the restraint does not create pain, a disciplined life is acceptable.

A leader of an organization should keep his actions in balance through control. For example, in the following areas:

- In an economic recession, a lay-off should not be excessive so that the long-term effectiveness of the organization is not adversely affected. A balance between corporate responsibility and social responsibility is desirable.
- In a time of economic expansion, development should not be concentrated in one single sector even though this has a "promising prospect." Diverse or balanced growth is most appropriate.
- Expenditure should not exceed income if the deficit cannot be turned around in the near future.

A leader should not be overambitious and demanding from others more than they are capable of. He restrains from pushing beyond the limit for he knows when and where he should stop. He knows when he should control his temper and emotions in order not to go too far, so that the principle of centrality will not be violated. There is another reason for centrality, as too excessive a restraint leads to rigidity but inadequate restraint can also lead to dispersal. An appropriate restraint is the one that meets the conditions of a particular time and place.

An ambitious leader wants to do great things to reach his high aims but he may ignore the resources available. If he insists on moving forward regardless of the limitations he may exhaust himself and face danger. One reason for the failure of a strong man is often his inability to restrain himself. As Laozi said: **"He who conquers others is forceful; he who conquers himself is powerful."**

HEXAGRAM STATEMENT

Regulation can be successful if it is not over done.

Regulation is required in any organization but it should be kept in balance. Overrestriction is disadvantageous to development and hence cannot be lasting. Between overall restraint and total freedom there is always a middle way to consider.

STRUCTURE

Like the previous Hexagram Dispersing, Regulation is also a hexagram with three yins and three yangs. The difference between the two is the positions in the respective hexagrams. The Hexagram Dispersion can be transformed into the Hexagram Regulation by exchanging its Top Yang with Initial Yin as shown below:

Dispersing   Regulating

Regulation is the inversed Hexagram of Dispersing. Once there is dispersal in an organization, it is necessary for the leader to use the appropriate measures in a timely way to restrain this in order to restore stability, harmony, and efficiency within the organization.

LINE STATEMENTS

Initial Yang ☵. Maintain self-control

He does not go out of the house to the courtyard. There will be no mistakes.

The leader of an organization should be able to restrain his action and not move forward if there are obstructions ahead. Initial Yang represents the present position whereas Second Yang the obstruction. When difficulties are anticipated the leader should control his emotions even if he has a strong desire to take action in order to attain his personal objective. If the time is not favorable at present, it is advantageous to wait for an opportunity in future. Initial Yang in a proper position (a yang line in a yang position) indicates that waiting at the present place is the correct decision. Knowing what will succeed and what will be thwarted is wisdom.

Second Yang ☵. Move forward when the time is favorable

He does not go out of the gate of his courtyard, there will be misfortune.

In front of Second Yang is Third Yin, which signifies weakness or least obstruction. At this time and position, the leader Second Yang should move forward and not let the opportunity slip by. If he holds back he will fail to seize the opportunity and will have regrets. He should take action when the time and place are advantageous to do so.

The text of Initial Yang and Second Yang are similar. Why is the commentary in the former considered "no mistakes" whereas in the latter is "misfortune"? It is because of the time/place factor. In the first case, Second Yang, which represents obstruction, is in front of Initial Yang; the right action therefore is to stay at one's present position instead of moving forward. But in the second case, the situation facing Second Yang is different as the obstruction ahead is rather weak, which is illustrated by the third yin line. Under such circumstances, a leader in the position of Second Yang should move forward. Otherwise he will miss the opportunity.

Third Yin ☷· Lack of self-control is regrettable

If he does not know how to restrain himself, he will lament it.
But if he can change his mind, he will be free from blame.

If a leader does not know how to exercise self-control, he has no one to blame but himself.

Third yin is an improper position (a yin line in a yang position) which signifies incorrectness and unbalance, leading to a situation lacking restraint. But if the leader in this position knows his weakness and is willing to change it, his regrets will disappear.

Fourth Yin ☷ Restrain oneself naturally

He restrains himself in a natural manner, he will succeed.

Fourth Yin is in a proper position (a yin line in a yin position) and it carries (below) Fifth Yang, indicating its obedience or support to the ruler (Fifth Yang). But it is not necessary for a senior executive to act passively through getting orders or instructions from the leader in order to control certain activities of the organization. Instead, he can act in a spontaneous and natural way to adapt to different conditions. He should be able to do the best he can within the limits of the resources available. Restraint in a natural manner is most appropriate.

Fifth Yang ☵ Restraint in balance

A balanced restraint is auspicious and gets wide praise.

Fifth Yang is in a proper position, indicating its characters of strength, balance, and correctness. With these qualities the leader of an organization can exercise his restraint appropriately, neither excessively nor inadequately. A balanced restraint is pleasing to and appreciated by the members of an organization.

Top Yang ☵ Avoid excessive restraint

Persistence in excessive restraint is inauspicious. If it can be eliminated in a timely way, regret will disappear.

If a leader is exercises excessive restraint and does not adapt to new conditions, he will have regrets as too much restriction can lead to resistance or even rebellion. Excessive restraint is not advisable and should not be exercised unless there is such a need in a special situation for a short time.

61

中孚 ZHONGFU The Wind–Lake Hexagram

Inner Truth, Sincerity, Truthfulness

IMAGE

Wind over Lake symbolizes the wind blowing moisture from the lake in all directions, like spreading sincerity to every corner. The upper trigram is also associated with wood or a wooden boat. Wood over Lake portrays a picture of a boat floating on a lake. A boat is empty inside and strong outside. The four yang lines represent the outside of a boat and the two yin lines the inside. The emptiness inside and firmness outside are the characteristics of a boat, symbolizing sincerity. If a leader is sincere inside, he is like an empty boat. If he is sincere outside, he is like a strong wooden boat as both emptiness (tolerance) and firmness (strength) are the basic qualities of sincerity. When a leader is sincere, he is able to overcome the difficulties as if taking a boat to cross a great river safely through a number of obstructions. Sincerity comes from the inner heart of a person and not the surface.

HEXAGRAM STATEMENT

Sincerity can even affect pigs and fishes. It is advantageous to cross great rivers and keep the correct path.

A person with a sincere heart can touch and motivate others even if they are as dumb as pigs and fishes. People will follow a person with sincerity and cooperate with him. To preserve sincerity, a person needs to be steadfast and correct.

STRUCTURE

The two yin lines are in the center of the hexagram, symbolizing emptiness. The larger the emptiness, the larger is its capacity to take in different things or views and the greater the truthfulness. The two yin lines surrounded by four yang lines indicate an organization which is under a hard type structure since Third Yin is not an obstruction to Second Yang, and Fourth Yin follows Fifth Yang. Although there is no interconnection between Fifth Yang and Second Yang, the two do have a common objective or interest that enables them to cooperate in controlling the activities in the organization.

The Hexagrams Sincerity and the Hexagram Great Exceeding (28) both have four yang and two yin lines. The difference between the two hexagrams is the location of the four yang lines:

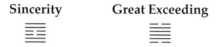

Sincerity   **Great Exceeding**

In both hexagrams the yang lines are in the majority. The question is whether the Hexagram Sincerity can also be named Great Exceeding if "Great" is defined as sincerity and firmness.

LINE STATEMENTS

Initial Yang ☳. Sincerity is from the inner heart

If he is satisfied with his position, he will be auspicious.
If his will is unsteady, he will be uneasy.

When a person is contented with his position he will have a peaceful mind and internal stability, from which springs a sincere attitude toward other people. If his will is unsteady he will be uneasy. His actions should be based on the inner truth.

A leader must keep his sincerity unchanged and show it to a person whom he meets the first time. As the sincerity of a person stems from his inner world, it cannot be obtained from the outer world. So it would be wrong for a person as Initial Yang in the inner trigram to seek sincerity through the relationship with Fourth Yin in the outer trigram. Normally an interconnection of a yang line with a yin line is considered favorable, but not in the situation in the Hexagram Sincerity which emphasizes sincerity from a person's inner heart, not from the surface.

Second Yang ☱. Sincerity enables a relationship to be deep and lasting

The crane calls in the shade, its chick answers back.
I have good wine and will share it with you.

Second Yang is in the center of the lower trigram, representing sincerity at the center. A leader who is sincere will influence the members of his organization. People will respond to him as the young cranes (represented by Initial Yang) respond to the older crane (Second Yang). "The crane calls in the shade" refers to the situation in which Second Yang is below the two yin lines (Third Yin and Fourth Yin), or at the foot of a mountain ☶.

Sincerity is the basis of the link between people. If a leader is truly sincere, people will be sincere in return. If he is insincere, people will avoid him. "Good wine" here means sincerity that can be shared with others. The call and response of the cranes symbolizes that sincerity should come from the inner heart spontaneously, not be deliberately manufactured. Relationships between the people made on the basis of sincerity will be deep and lasting.

Third Yin ☳. Be more self-confident and self-reliant

He follows the act of his mate on beating drums, resting, weeping, and sighing.

Top Yang is the partner of Third Yin through their interconnection. Due to its improper position, Third Yin tends to be indecisive. If a leader lacks self-confidence, he tends to be emotional and will be affected by his moods. He is likely to follow what his partner is doing. Without self-confidence his sincerity could be unstable and would come to rely on his partner's acts. It is beneficial for a leader to be more independent and self-reliant.

Fourth Yin ☵ Choose a right and capable partner

The moon is almost full. The horse abandons its mate.
There is no blame.

Fourth Yin is in a proper position. Its closeness to Fifth Yang—the position of power—is like the moon being almost full. On the other hand, Fourth

Yin and Initial Yang are complementary or partners; the relationship between the two is like a horse and its mate. Fourth Yin has to choose between the top leader Fifth Yang and the partner Initial Yang as to which of them is his real partner as a person in this position cannot be truthful to both sides. If Fourth Yin decides to be true to the top leader rather than to his partner below, the situation is like "a horse abandoning its mate." Fourth Yin chooses Fifth Yang as the object of truthfulness as indicated by the obedient relationship between Fourth Yin and Fifth Yang, in which the former follows the later.

Fifth Yang ☲ Sincerity links others in a close union

He unites others closely with sincerity. There is no blame.

Fifth Yang is a leadership position. As a leader, his sincerity and integrity will attract people to follow him in a close and firm relationship. Sincerity has the power to unify people.

Top Yang ☲ The reputation is not supported by fact

The crow of a cock rises up to the sky. It is inauspicious to persist.

The crow of a cock rises up to the sky but the cock itself is on the ground. The sound flies, but the substance does not follow it. If a leader seeks fame through exaggerating his contributions or achievements without factual support then his sincerity is doubtful. The line text also gives a warning to a leader who should recognize his own limited strength and not step beyond his ability.

A yang line in a yang position at the extreme of the upper trigram should give advice to a person as to when and where he should stop rather than moving forward. Any further movement will remove him from the center of sincerity as symbolized by Fifth Yang.

62

小 過
XIAOGUO
The Thunder–Mountain Hexagram

Small Exceeding

IMAGE

Thunder stands for action and Mountain symbolizes stillness or restraint. Thunder over Mountain means action with restraint. An action that exceeds the norm (the mean) should be limited only to a small range. To increase adaptability to the changing conditions, a small excess over the norm is allowed and considered favorable. If the Mean or centrality is the criterion for a corrective action, a small flexibility around it is desirable. In reality, the application of the principle of centrality should be a range aspect rather than a point. However, great excess in any matter is not favorable. The concept of small excess is therefore associated with humility. A man who is modest will most likely not overextend himself.

HEXAGRAM STATEMENT

Small exceeding is favorable by keeping to the right way. This is appropriate for small matters, but not for great matters.
If the flying bird goes up, it would lose its voice. But if it goes down, there would be great fortune.

The shape of the Hexagram Small Exceeding is like a flying bird. The two yang lines in the center of the hexagram symbolize the back of a bird whereas the two yin lines are the wings on either side. If the bird flies upward, its cry becomes inaudible; if it flies downward, its cry is audible. A flying bird should not go up but go down because it cannot find a place to stop in the sky, but it can find somewhere on the ground to rest. Here, "goes up" means great excess and "goes down" small excess. **A man who fails to recognize the limits of his own strength is like a bird flying upwards**. The leader of an organization should not be a flying bird that aims too high.

STRUCTURE

The meaning of the Hexagram Small Exceeding is the opposite of that of the hexagram DAGUO 大過 [Great Exceeding] (28) as stated earlier, although their lines are not opposite in structure:

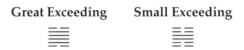

In both structures, firmness is on the inside of the hexagram and softness on the outside. The difference between the two is the degree of excess: great in the former but small in the latter. In respect to structure the Hexagram Small Exceeding is the opposite to that of the hexagram ZHONGFU 中孚 [Sincerity] (61):

Sincerity   Small Exceeding

The structure of the Hexagram Small Exceeding is soft outside and firm inside whereas the structure of the Hexagram Sincerity is firm outside and soft inside. Hence the meanings of the two hexagrams are different. From a conventional perspective, a superior man should possess the qualities of the Hexagram Small Exceeding, soft outside but firm inside.

LINE STATEMENTS

Initial Yin ☶. Stand on solid ground

A flying bird is misfortune.

Initial Yin is at the lowest position of the hexagram and has an interconnection with Fourth Yang. An executive who is not strong (a yin line) yet ambitious to move forward believes he would get the assistance from above (Fourth Yang). It is possible that he will fail in his mission because of his incompetence and the assistance from above may not be as adequate as expected. An executive with high aims but without the capabilities and resources to back up him will fail in his action like the fate of a flying bird going upward.

Second Yin ☷· Small exceeding and small inadequacy is appropriate

He passes by his grandfather to meet his grandmother. The minister does not go to see the king, but the king comes to meet him. There is no blame.

Second Yin represents the daughter-in-law of a family in ancient China whereas Fourth Yang stands for the grandfather and Fifth Yin the grandmother. The daughter-in-law has a closer relationship with the grandmother than with the grandfather, as indicated by the similar character of the two respective yin lines: Second Yin and Fifth Yin. This behavior of the daughter-in-law, Second Yin, in the traditional Chinese family is considered normal due to the closer relationship between the two. As the grandfather is represented by great and the grandmother by small, bypassing the grandfather to meet the grandmother is therefore considered a case of small exceeding, and thus appropriate behavior.

In an organization, a subordinate normally has defined duties under the supervision of his immediate superior, but he can be assigned to a special task by the top leader for a certain period of time although he is officially still affiliated to his original department. During this time, he has a direct relationship with the top leader, bypassing his direct superior. The connection between the two deviates from the normal practice but is justified in a special case. This is a situation of Small Exceeding. However, this practice is not considered right for longer periods since it can damage the unitary chain of command. What the top leader should do is either relocate the subordinate Second Yang or get another person to assume responsibility for the special task. Small Exceeding is temporary in nature. Other examples of small exceeding are as follows:

- Increasing the expenditure for promotion over the planned budget
- Giving special allowances to the staff in an emergency
- Hiring temporary staff

Small Inadequacy is the reverse case of Small Exceeding. For example, the executive Second Yang is normally not in the position to reach the top leader Fifth Yin even though he has useful suggestions or different views on the practices of the organization. The top leader however can take an active part to approach him. This is a case of small inadequacy. Other examples are a temporary cut of expenditures for promotion under the planned budget, or a temporary cut in the number of staff.

The concepts of Small Exceeding and Small Inadequacy indicate the importance of the principle of centrality.

Third Yang ☳· Do not be overconfident of your own strength and be careless of danger

He should be careful not to go too far, for someone may come up and attack him from behind. If he does not act in this way, he will be inauspicious.

Third Yang in a hard position (a yang line in a yang position) signifies excessive strength. An executive in this position may insist on his own standpoint and rarely take other people's advice. If he can avoid being overconfident and be very cautious, he will be auspicious.

Fourth Yang ☳· Be cautious in seeking a relationship with an inferior man

He is firm but also flexible, and does not seek relations with the inferior man.
There is danger ahead, he should not move forward but keep alert.

Although Fourth Yang is in a yin or improper position, the hardness of the yang line can be balanced and harmonized by the softness of the yin position. An executive in this position should therefore know how to control his emotions and not make impulsive decisions. In a time when yin is predominant, as indicated by the line structure with four yins and two yangs, yin will be very unlikely to follow yang or the inferior to be obedient to the superior man. Under such circumstances, it is favorable for the superior man to keep a distance from the inferior man as a safeguard against his harmful influence. Fourth Yang symbolizes the superior man and Initial Yin the inferior man. This is the reason why the text advises Fourth Yang not to have a relationship with Initial Yin even though there is an interconnection between the two.

Fifth Yin ☵ Flog a dead horse

The duke who attempts to shoot the bird in the cave does so in vain, as when dense clouds gather over the western suburbs but it does not rain.

A weak leader (a yin line) in a noble position (a yang position) cannot do much for his organization—just as when "dense clouds gather over the western suburbs but it does not rain" or "the duke who attempts to shoot the bird in the cave does so in vain." A good idea may not always be practicable because the conditions for taking the corresponding action are not there. He can seek help from those below to support him in his plan for advance but their capabilities are not adequate to meet the requirements. This situation is reflected by the absence of an interconnection between Fifth Yin and Second Yin, or a complementary relationship between the two.

Top Yin ☷ Do not overrate one's own abilities

He passes the target by too far like a bird flies too far away and will eventually be caught in the hunter's net. There is misfortune and a sign of disaster.

As Top Yin is at the extreme of excess a leader in this position should look downward and seek an interconnection with those below as represented by Third Yang in order to get the benefit of a yin–yang union. But if he insists on his way and goes farther and farther away from where he should stop, he will suffer from his action. The situation is just like a bird which flies too far away and eventually will be caught in the net. If a leader cannot curb his arrogance, he will lose the trust of people who respect him and he will become totally isolated.

63

| 既 濟 | **The Water–Fire Hexagram** |
| JIJI | Already Accomplished, Settled |

IMAGE

The Wate–Fire Hexagram signifies a mission has already been accomplished. Both water and fire are the two basic elements for cooking. Water above Fire is in the right position for these two to perform their functions. If their positions are reversed, Fire above Water, it is no longer possible to cook and so the mission cannot be accomplished. Of the sixty-four hexagrams JIJI is the only one in which the six lines are all in their proper positions, indicating that all the basic elements for performing a mission must be assigned their right positions so that they can function effectively to reach the objective.

Fire rises and warms the water whereas water drops down and cools the fire. However, there are some worries. If the fire is too strong, the water will dry up; if the fire is too weak, the soup may not be hot enough. Only when both water and fire are in an appropriate relationship can a tasty soup be cooked. Therefore, the relationship between water and fire needs the right balance.

Water symbolizes danger or trouble and Fire stands for illumination, clarity, or understanding. If a leader has a good understanding of the nature of the project, he is undertaking and the nature of the troubles that he is facing this will help him plan his action and accomplish his task.

The question is whether the state of Already Accomplished is favorable to future development, because a success may lead to a failure. If the leader of an organization is too proud of his achievement, he may lose the initiative. His success can be seen as just the beginning of his later failure. When a development reaches its extreme, a reverse movement can be expected. Cyclical change is one of the important concepts of the *Yijing* and also emphasized by Laozi: **"The** *dao* **is cyclical"**. *Dao* is interpreted as the law of nature which can be used to interpret a cyclical movement between success and failure. When either of them reaches its extreme, a reverse movement will start.

HEXAGRAM STATEMENT

It is successfully accomplished even in the small matters.
It is favorable to keep to the right way.
Although good fortune prevails in the beginning, things may end in misfortune.

When a person has achieved a success, he must not become complacent. If he does so and he loses his initiative and energy, the situation will become unfavorable. This is a warning to a successful leader who reaches a peak. He needs to be steadfast in keeping to the right way and creating new foundations for a new start. **A leader must be as cautious in the end of an action as at the beginning.**

STRUCTURE

The reason why the small matters are also considered auspicious in the hexagram statement can be explained by the relationships between a yin line and a yang line. Yin represents the small and yang the great. Both Second Yin and Fourth Yin carry (or are below) Third Yang and Fifth Yang respectively, indicating favorable relationships between the small and the great. In addition, the three yin–yang interconnections as represented by Initial Yang and Fourth Yin, Second Yin and Fifth Yang, Third Yang and Top Yin, are all to the favor of the small as the three yins are backed up by the three yangs.

In the hexagram JIJI, the nuclear or hidden hexagram is WEIJI 未濟 [Not Yet Accomplished] (64):

	WEIJI
Top Yang	———
Fifth Yin	— —
Fourth Yang	———
Third Yin	— —
Second Yang	———
Initial Yin	— —

The hidden hexagram WEIJI indicates that **the stage of Already Accomplished is not the final stage of a development as a whole but can be seen as the beginning of a new development**. According to the *Yijing*, a development is infinite. The stage of Already Accomplished refers merely to the "end situation" of one of many stages during this infinite development.

The hexagram JIJI is derived from the hexagram TAI 泰 [Harmony] (11) by exchanging its Second Yang with Fifth Yin:

Harmony   **Already Accomplished**

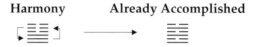

Based on the commentaries on the lines, the situation as indicated by the three lines of the lower trigram Accomplished (Initial Yang, Second Yin, and Third Yang) appears to be more favorable than that of the three of the upper trigram (Fourth Yin, Fifth Yang, and Top Yin). This is because the first part of the hexagram TAI is seen to be more favorable than that of the second part. The reason is that in the first part of the hexagram JIJI people are more energetic, cautious, and better prepared for possible future perils while enjoying peace. But in the second part of this hexagram, people may become complacent about their achievements and show less initiative and caution. This is why the hexagram statement for JIJI warns that a fortune can be turned into misfortune if a person is not able to persevere in his will and principles.

LINE STATEMENTS

Initial Yang ☳. **Hold back from forward movement at early stage**

He puts the brakes on the wheel of his carriage like a fox wets its tail in crossing a river. He is blameless.

If a driver wants to stop his forward movement he brakes the wheels of his carriage. If a fox wants to hold back when crossing a river, it wets its tail. If a leader does not want to push ahead too quickly after a success is achieved, he should pull back and put on the brakes at an early stage. **By being careful in the beginning, there will be no mistakes in the end**.

Initial Yang is at the bottom of the hexagram, indicating that it has a strong drive to move forward (a yang line in a yang position) but lacks adequate strength to do so (being in a low position). If a leader in this position intends to move forward, he will face dangers ahead as indicated by the hidden trigram Water (Second Yin, Third Yang, and Fourth Yin). Although Initial Yang has a possible interconnection with Fourth Yin this is blocked by Third Yang, so help cannot be obtained from above. Due to these obstructions, one should not go forward.

Second Yin ䷾. Be calm and patient and wait for the right time to come

The woman loses the curtain of her carriage, but she should not look for it as she will be able to get it back in seven days.

The line statement describes a situation in ancient times when a woman drove out in her carriage and needed a curtain to veil her from the people outside. It symbolizes the fact that a man with the qualities of balance and uprightness (the characteristics of Second Yin) is not realized by the superior (Fifth Yang). The situation of Second Yin is like the text says: "The woman loses the curtain of her carriage." If he can maintain his principles and act in the right way as in the past, **what he has lost today will be gained back tomorrow**, as stated in the text. His qualities will eventually be recognized by the top leader.

Third Yang ䷾. Do not employ inferior people after a success

The King Wu Ding of Yin dynasty attacked the country Guifang and conquered it in three years of hard battles. Inferior people must not be employed.

Third Yang is in a proper but strong position, representing great strength. A leader in this position, particularly in a time of Already Accomplished, is tempted to take an aggressive action like King Wu Ding 武丁 of the Yin dynasty attacking the neighboring country Guifang 鬼方. However, there is a great need for resources for such an ambitious task. A leader is advised to consider two important factors before undertaking a large operation. First, he must realize the fact that a large operation needs not only a lot of resources but also considerable time. Second, after the task has been accomplished those people who are not capable and reliable should not be employed.

Fourth Yin ☵ **Take precautions against predictable dangers**

He prepares the rags to stop leaks in his boat. He is careful all day.

In this situation, a leader must take precautions against predictable dangers as if he had the rags ready to stop the leaks in his boat when sailing. He should be able to sense danger ahead and take the appropriate precautions to prevent this from happening. Fourth Yin is located at the beginning of the upper trigram KAN 坎 [Water], indicating there is surrounding danger.

Fifth Yang ☲ **Sincere respect can be expressed by presenting a simple thing rather than an expensive one**

The neighbor in the east slaughters an ox at the sacrifice, but this is not as good as the simple offerings with sincerity made by the neighbor in the east. The latter will enjoy great blessings.

A pompous sacrifice may not be effective as a small one made with sincerity. A leader should not use great things to impress others, but should do things simply and with sincerity. In some cases, a simple presentation with sincerity counts for more than a grand but insincere one. Fifth Yang symbolizes a leader in a successful position in which he should restrain himself from being boastful.

Top Yin ☷ **Be careful at the end of a venture**

He gets his head wet like a fox when crossing a river. He is in danger.

The yin line at the top position of the hexagram symbolizes that a person is in a dangerous position. If a leader is carelessly complacent at the end of a venture, he will think he can relax and enjoy his success. But things could slide and he will lose all he has gained, like a little fox gets its head wet in the water as it nears the river bank at the other side. He suffers defeat on the verge of success.

64

WEIJI

The Fire–Water Hexagram

Not Yet Accomplished, Unsettled

IMAGE

WEIJI or Not Yet Accomplished is the inverse hexagram of JIJI 既濟 [Already Accomplished] (63). Fire over Water symbolizes a situation in which work has not yet been accomplished. Fire rises upward and water flows downward, indicating that the two forces yin (water) and yang (fire) are moving away from each other. This disintegration of yin and yang signifies a work not yet accomplished. It is favorable for a leader always to keep in mind that he has not yet completed his task so that he will continue to maintain his enthusiasm and initiative in moving forward.

The hexagram QIAN 乾 [Heaven] (1) is the start of the sixty-four hexagrams and the hexagram JIJI is the final stage of a development. As the movement of Heaven is a never-ending process, so the ending of the sixty-three hexagrams as indicated by the hexagram JIJI is in fact **the beginning of another new development** as represented by the hexagram WEIJI. A leader who has the attitude of Not Yet Accomplished will make himself strong and untiring as Heaven. Therefore, the hexagram WEIJI has the spirit of the Hexagram Heaven.

HEXAGRAM STATEMENT

Not Yet Accomplished is favorable.
The young fox gets its tail wet when crossing the river. Nothing is gained.

To achieve success the leader of an organization must be as alert and careful as an old fox which erects its tail to prevent it from getting wet when crossing a river. "To erect its tail" here means "to remain cautious." The text takes the view that a wet tail is a hindrance for a fox crossing the river. A young fox is, however, careless, so its tail gets wet and consequently it fails to reach its goal. The text warns people that they may fail within reach of success if they are careless, just like the young fox. With courage alone but without deliberation and caution, a leader will have difficulty in achieving success. On the other hand, a leader may miss an opportunity to take on a project with good prospects if he is too cautious. A capable leader should have both qualities—the courage of the young fox and the caution of the old fox. A combination of yin and yang is the basis for success.

STRUCTURE

All six lines in this hexagram are in the improper positions, implying difficulties are encountered in accomplishing a task. However three yin–yang interactions (Initial Yin and Fourth Yang, Second Yang and Fifth Yin, Third Yin, and Top Yang) provide favorable conditions for overcoming the difficulties since close cooperation between the members of an organization is essential for the accomplishment of a task.

The hexagram WEIJI is derived from the hexagram PI 否 [Obstruction] (12) by exchanging its Second Yin with Fifth Yang:

PI   WEIJI

The three lines of the lower trigram of WEIJI (Initial Yin, Second Yang, and Third Yin) indicate the situation in the first part of the development, which is considered less favorable as obstructions increase. In the second part of the development as indicated by the upper trigram, the three line statements (Fourth Yang, Fifth Yin, and Top Yang) become more favorable because the members of the organization are able to maintain their initiative and sincerity in accomplishing their task.

LINE STATEMENTS

Initial Yin ☵. Know one's own limit

The young fox gets its tail wet when it crosses the river. It is a shame.

Initial Yin is in a weak position (a yin line in a low position) at the beginning of the lower trigram KAN 坎 [Water] and will face danger if it moves forward without caution. Although Initial Yin is interconnected with Fourth Yang, Fourth Yang is not balanced correctly and thus may not be able to help Initial Yin. When an executive is tasked he should assess whether he has the abilities, resources, and authority to accomplish that task. If he does not, he will not be able to finish it.

Second Yang ☵. Do not be rash but exercise self-control

He puts the brakes on the wheels of his carriage. This will bring good fortune.

Second Yang represents an executive who practices the principle of centrality. He has a complementary relationship with the top leader Fifth Yang but he prefers to proceed slowly and carefully because of his unfavorable position. Second Yang is located at the center of the lower trigram Water, which symbolizes danger. An executive in this situation must keep remain his firm and keep his strength and balance in order to safeguard himself. When the right time comes, the top leader who has a soft character will use him. So he must be patient and in the meantime prepare to strengthen himself for his future move.

Third Yin ☵· Overcome adversity by strengthening oneself

He has not crossed the river, further advancement will be inauspicious. It will be disadvantageous for him to cross the great river unless he can get help.

Third Yin is in an improper position (a yin line in a yang position); it is incapable of accomplishing a task due to its weakness and lack of balance. However, Third Yin can get help from Top Yang in crossing the danger which is indicated by the hidden trigram Water (Third Yin, Fourth Yang, and Fifth Yin). When an executive is in a weak and unfavorable position to handle a situation which is beyond his own strength, he should get help from someone who is capable like Top Yang.

Fourth Yin ☵· Be steadfast when taking a venture

It is fortunate to be steadfast. All regrets will pass away.

He should actively take an action as the King Wu Ding conquered the country Guifang through three years of battles. He will be rewarded for his efforts.

A senior executive in the position of Fourth Yang is close to the top leader Fifth Yin. He should therefore use his advantages and strengths to undertake an ambitious project through which he will get the appropriate reward in due course. The yang line implies that he needs strong determination and courage in carrying out his duties.

Fifth Yin ☲ Draw people in through integrity

His uprightness brings him fortune and no regret. He has won people's trust because of his integrity.

The upper trigram LI 離 [Fire] symbolizes brightness and Fifth Yin in the center represents a brilliant leader with correctness and integrity. With these qualities the leader is able to attract followers. For example, a capable person like Second Yang is willing to assist him, as indicated by the interconnection between the two.

Top Yang ☲ Avoid overindulgence

He celebrates what he has achieved so far with confidence by drinking wine. It is blameless.
However, if he is overindulgent in drinking and gets drunk, his confidence will be misplaced.

If a leader is fully confident in his ability to accomplish his task in the near future without taking any precautionary measures he may suffer from it, since overoptimism can lead to failure. When a leader indulges in the belief that success is in sight, he must still maintain a sense of danger in order to guard against any unexpected events. The text can also be applied to a case in which a leader is fully confident in delegating his authority to his subordinate to carry out his duties to accomplish a task which appears to be without problems. The reason he acts in such a way is because he believes that having contributed so many efforts in the past it is now the right time for him to relax. But the subordinate is incapable of performing his functions and makes a misjudgment, so that the task is not yet accomplished. Delegation of authority is an effective principle of leadership but the person to whom the authority is delegated must be a capable man. A wrong delegation of authority can adversely affect the efficiency of the organization. A leader must be constantly on alert even though success is close at hand.

Top Yang is at the end of the hexagram, indicating a situation in which success is near. However, it is in an improper position (a yang line in a yin position) which can induce a person, because of his exuberance, to do something that he should not to do.

PART THREE

A Leadership Model from the *Book of Change*

A Leadership Model from the *Book of Change*

❧ ❧ ❧

The Graphic Model

Having explained the sixty-four hexagrams of the *Yijing* [the *Book of Change*] it is useful to build up a leadership model based on the nature of the hexagrams and the meaning of the statements. A conceptual model provides a framework for the qualities of leadership and the guidelines for proper action in an organization. A graphic model is shown below:

A Leadership Model from the *Book of Change*

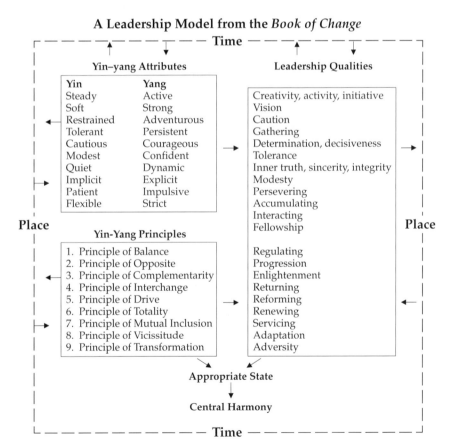

A Leader's Yin–Yang Attributes

A leader's attributes can be classified into two categories: yin and yang. A leader with yang attributes is seen as active, strong, adventurous, persistent, courageous, confident, dynamic, explicit, impulsive, and strict, whereas a leader with yin attributes tends to be steady, soft, restrained, tolerant, cautious, modest, quiet, implicit, patient, and flexible. In the real world, there is probably no pure yang- or yin-type of leader as is the case of the hexagrams in the *Yijing*, where the pure yang hexagram Qian 乾 [Heaven] (1) and the pure yin hexagram Kun 坤 [Earth] (2) are the "parent" or origin of the other sixty-two hexagrams which are yin–yang mixed. In reality, the character of a leader is most likely a mixture of yin–yang—He can be seen as more yang than yin or more yin than yang. A yang-type leader can have yin characteristics and a yin-type leader can also have yang characteristics. The attributes of a leader can also be influenced by time/place as they can change in order to meet different conditions. In time/place I a leader can be seen as a yang type more than a yin type and in time/place II he can be considered a yin type more than a yang type. So when speaking about a yang- or yin-type leader, this refers to his main characteristics which are explicitly identified. The attributes of the two elements yin and yang which can be found in a person are listed on the left side of the upper part of the leadership model figure.

Nature–Human Union

The nine yin–yang principles or the natural laws are listed on the left side of the lower part of leadership model figure, indicating that the natural forces are applicable equally to the human world. The natural laws as represented by the yin–yang principles are transferable to the human world and bring people's attitudes, outlook, and behavior into harmony with them. The concept of nature–human union is the essence of the *Yijing*'s philosophy and is also the cornerstone of Daoism and Confucianism.

Nine Yin–Yang Principles: Nine Forces of Nature

The relationship between yin and yang can be summarized in nine laws:

1. Principle of balance
2. Principle of opposites
3. Principle of complementarity
4. Principle of interdependence
5. Principle of totality
6. Principle of drive
7. Principle of mutual inclusion
8. Principle of transformation
9. Principle of vicissitude

The nine yin-yang principles are illustrated in the following diagram:

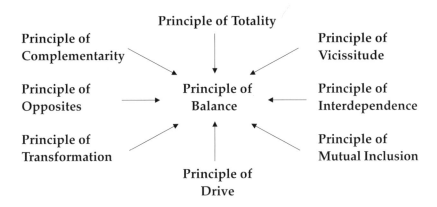

A successful leader must first be able to master these nine yin–yang principles because they can effectively guide him to move to a right direction or to avoid misfortune. These nine yin–yang principles are in fact the nine forces of nature which, according to the philosophy of the *Yijing*, cannot be changed by the people but must be adapted to. A leader needs to have a good understanding of these nine forces and adapt to them well in order effectively to lead using the *Yijing* model.

The Principle of Balance

The principle of balance is a key concept in the leadership model given by the *Yijing*. The reason why the second and fifth line of a hexagram are in most cases considered favorable or fortunate is because of their central position, which represents the concept of centrality or the Mean or the moderate way. In the *taiji* diagram yin and yang are represented by the black and white fishes respectively. The equal size of these two fish indicates the importance of a balance between yin and yang in the development of all things.

However, the relationship between yin and yang may not be always in balance during a development, as reflected by the relationship between the black fish and the white fish (the white fish's head is in opposite to the black fish's tail and vice versa). But the ultimate target of a yin or yang movement is to achieve a balanced state between the two, even though it is a temporal one.

The principle of balance suggests a leader should not act in an extreme manner. By following this principle, a leader will correspondingly pay high attention to ethical standards such as integrity, fairness, and openness.

The Principle of Opposites

Everything has an opposite. Yin is the opposite of yang and vice versa. In any organization the leader has to face different views of the members. Different views are not necessarily harmful or negative. The result much depends on how the leader handles them. A capable leader may consider opposite views useful to himself or to the organization as a whole because from them he will be able to identify and recognize what he has overlooked or neglected in his plans. If he can accept and absorb the meaningful and useful views of other members, and integrate them with his original plan, this will bring about a synergy which favors the development of his organization.

A leader should have the capability to turn inferiors into superiors, or a negative state into a positive one. It would be unwise for a leader to turn down the opposite views of the members of his organization during discussion. With the principle of balance in mind, a wise leader should be willing to incorporate constructive ideas into his action plans.

The Principle of Complementarity

The opposite nature of yin to yang should not be seen as unfavorable but rather in a favorable light. What one element lacks can be complementary to another. A complementary union of yin and yang produces a positive effect.

An interconnection between a yang line in a lower trigram and a yin line in the same position of an upper trigram (Initial Yang and Fourth

Yin, Second Yang and Fifth Yin, or Third Yang and Top Yin) are generally considered favorable. The rationale for this is based on the complementary effect of a yin–yang union, for it provides harmony in the whole organization. The interlocked relationship between the white fish and the black fish in the *taiji* diagram also presents the same image. A complementary union of yin and yang provides a favorable basis on which to practice the principle of drive.

The Principle of Interdependence

If everything has an opposite, it should also have a dependent. As the *taiji* diagram indicates the relationship between yin (black fish) and yang (white fish) should not be looked at only as opposites, they should also be seen as interdependents as neither of the two can exist alone. The existence of yin is the precondition for the existence of yang and vice versa. Without yin there will be no yang and the reverse is also true. The relationship between yin and yang is therefore dual in nature, as illustrated in the *taiji* diagram. The sixty-two hexagrams, except QIAN (1) and KUN (2), are formed by yin and yang lines, indicating clearly the interdependent relationship between these two elements or forces. However, an interdependent relationship does not show whether it is positive or negative. The principle of complementarity indicates both the complementary effect and the synergic effect of the yin–yang interdependent relationship, whereas the principle of opposites shows the restraining effect of the yin–yang interdependency.

The Principle of Drive

A yang alone cannot grow things, nor can a single yin. The drive for growth comes from a yin–yang union. As indicated in the *taiji* diagram, yin and yang cannot be separated from each other—The two must be considered as one. But to better understand the attributes of the two, they are treated separately in the hexagram system of the *Yijing*.

The attributes of the yang force correspond to creativity, activity, and strength whereas yin is seen as receptive, tolerant, and soft. Elements which are complementary in nature can produce new things. Except in the parental hexagrams QIAN (1) and KUN (2), all other sixty-two hexagrams are constructed by both yin and yang lines. Yin and yang provide the forces needed for growth. A good match between these two forces will produce a greater drive for change.

The Principle of Totality

Taiji comprises both the yin and yang forces, but neither of the two can form a *taiji*. *Taiji* is a concept of totality; yin or yang is only a part of the whole. Yin and yang are the two sides of a whole like the two sides of a coin. A leader must first think of the whole organization because without a whole there will be no individual. However, an overemphasis on the benefits of the whole unit could hurt the initiative of an individual subunit. A wise leader should keep an appropriate balance between the benefits of the whole unit and those of the individual. The principle of balance provides the basis for solving this conflict.

In the sixty-four hexagrams, each individual hexagram is only a part of the whole hexagram system. Although each hexagram can be transformed into another hexagram by changing its line(s), the changing hexagram still remains within the whole system of the sixty-four hexagrams. This is the principle of totality.

The Principle of Mutual Inclusion

In the real world, there is no situation which is completely yin or yang. In a yin-dominated situation, a yang element will be found and a yin element is also identifiable in a yang-dominated situation. Yin within yang and yang within yin form the principle of mutual inclusion. In the *taiji* diagram the white fish has a black eye and the black fish a white eye, indicating the principle of mutual inclusion.

The main difference between the principle of complementarity and the principle of mutual inclusion is that in the former the two forces of yin and yang are approximately equal in size and power whereas in the latter, one has apparently a dominant position as compared with the other.

The principle of mutual inclusion points out the fact that neither a yin or a yang situation can last long because the opposite force (yin or yang) will eventually gain strength until finally it becomes the dominating factor in a new or reverse situation. The principle of vicissitude therefore follows the principle of mutual inclusion.

The Principle of Vicissitude

The inverse relationship between yin and yang is another characteristic of these two elements. When yin rises yang falls and vice versa, as indicated by the following hexagrams:

QIAN 乾 **GOU** 姤 **DUN** 遯 **PI** 否 **GUAN** 觀 **PO** 剝
[Heaven] [Meeting] [Retreating] [Obstruction] [Observing] [Stripping]
(1) (44) (33) (12) (20) (23)

≡≡ ≣≡ ≣≣ ≣≣ ☷≣ ☷☷

KUN 坤 **FU** 復 **LIN** 臨 **TAI** 泰 **DAZHUANG** 大壯 **GUAI** 夬
[Earth] [Returning] [Approaching] [Harmony] [Great Strength] [Determination]
(2) (24) (19) (11) (34) (43)

☷☷ ☷≣ ☷≡ ☷≡ ☰≡ ☰≡

In the above twelve hexagrams, an inverse relationship between yin and yang is clearly indicated. Both yin and yang move in the opposite direction. An increase of yin reflects a decrease of yang and vice versa. This inverse relationship between yin and yang is also found in the *taiji* diagram as indicated by the changing relationship between the white fish and the black fish; the tail of the black fish is opposite the head of the white fish and the head of the black fish is opposite the tail of the white fish. The changes in the relationships between yin and yang are reflected by these two interlocked fish. The principle of vicissitude between yin and yang is another illustration of the concept of cyclical change. A leader who can master this principle will be able to improve the ability of his organization to adapt to changing conditions both external and internal.

The Principle of Transformation

In a hexagram a yang line can be changed to a yin line or a yin line can be changed to a yang line. Through such a change in a line, the original of the primary hexagram will transformed into another hexagram. For example, a change of the yang line to a yin line in the fourth position of the hexagram TONGREN 同仁 [Fellowship] (13) ≣≡ will transform the primary hexagram into the hexagram JIAREN 家人 [The Family] (37) ≣≡ .

In any time or place, the position of yin and yang can be interchanged under the principle of transformation. The color of the two fish in the *taiji* diagram is interchangeable too, since the white fish can be transformed into the black fish and vice versa. The principle of transformation indicates that flexibility and adaptability can be obtained through an interchange between yin and yang.

LEADERSHIP QUALITIES

The leadership qualities listed on the right side of the leadership model figure influenced by yin–yang attributes and yin–yang principles. The hexagrams of the *Yijing* have not only provided the nine yin–yang principles or thinking methodologies to leaders, but they also suggest the qualities expected from them. All the sixty-four hexagrams and 384 line statements (or 386 statements if the two rules of "using yang" or "using yin" are included) give advice on how to approach "fortune" and how to avert "misfortune." Some essential guidelines regarding leadership qualities are summarized as follows (the numbers in brackets are those of the hexagrams related to the leadership qualities mentioned):

- Creativity, activity, initiative, and vision (1, 64)
- Vision (64)
- Gathering, gathering together (45)
- Tolerance, generosity, and receptivity (2)
- Sincerity, integrity, and fairness (61)
- Perseverance (32)
- Interaction, communication (31)
- Caution (2, 10, 53)
- Fellowship and team spirit (8, 13, 37)
- Modesty (15)
- Determination (43)
- Restraint (52, 60)
- Progression (1, 10, 35, 46, 64)
- Returning (24)
- Reforming (18, 49)
- Renewing (50)
- Accumulating (26)
- Servicing (48)
- Enlightenment (4)
- Steadfastness (39, 47)
- Hiding (36)
- Adornment (22)
- Empowerment (7, 11, 19)
- Discipline (7)
- Adaptation (17, 56)
- Adversity (12, 23, 29, 39, 40, 47, 59)

These leadership qualities are directly or indirectly indicated by the sixty-four hexagrams and the hexagram statements as well as by the 384 or 386 line statements. Twenty-six qualities are selected here to illustrate their relationship with leadership.

Force, **Creativity**, and **activity** are generally seen as the characteristics of the first hexagram QIAN (1). The last hexagram WEIJI 未濟 [Not Yet Accomplished] (64) also has the same spirit of QIAN (1): a leader should be strong and untiring. These two qualities are explicitly indicated in QIAN (1) but implicitly expressed in WEIJI.

The hexagram WEIJI advises that a leader should have **vision** in his activities, just as a compass assists a captain at sea. A wise leader needs vision and courage to create. Vision gives him direction. Without it he would not know where he is, which way he is going, and where he is going to land.

A leader who is merely **creative** and active may face risks unless he is also cautious. A proper balance between **initiative** and **caution** is meaningful. The hexagrams KUN (2), LÜ 履 [Treading] (10), and JIAN 漸 [Gradual Progress] (53) give useful suggestions.

Nourishment, **tolerance**, **generosity**, and **receptivity** are the characteristics of the hexagram KUN (2) that will enable a leader to become a person with whom people would like to associate and follow. A leader with the qualities of earth is most likely to have also a modest attitude toward people.

A leader with a modest attitude does not think of himself as being superior to others. He is open-minded in accepting different opinions and suggestions raised by his colleagues and subordinates. However, modesty does not mean servility. A modest leader does not undervalue himself as he knows when he should reveal his intelligence and ability at an appropriate level. **Modesty** is a virtue that is particularly emphasized by the hexagram QIAN 謙 [Modesty] (15).

The hexagram ZHONGFU 中孚 [Inner Truth] (61) particularly emphasizes **sincerity**, including honesty, trustfulness, and fairness. If a leader is sincere, he must have these three qualities too. Likewise the hexagram WUWANG 無妄 [Innocence] (25) indicates that perfect truthfulness can bring one fortune and success.

How to make people join together for a common objective and companionship or **fellowship** in a group is one of the essential responsibilities of a good leader and the respective principles are indicated in the three hexagrams Bɪ 比 [Joining Together] (8), Tᴏɴɢʀᴇɴ 同人 [Fellowship] (13), and Sᴜɪ 隨 [Following] (17).

A good leader must be able to gather people with different capabilities around him to resolve conflicts and balance the interests among them for the benefit of the whole organization. A successful gathering of people will gain high spirits and efficiency. The hexagram Cᴜɪ 萃 [Gathering] (45) suggests the guidelines for **gathering** people together. An efficient leader needs strong determination in taking action. He should not be easy going but should have the strength to make quick decisions. The hexagram Kᴜᴀɪ 夬 [Determination] (43) suggests guidelines for dealing with this situation.

Interaction or **interconnection** between the people in an organization is meaningful and useful in building harmonious relationships, team spirit, and coherence. The hexagram Xɪᴀɴ 咸 [Interacting] (31) provides guidelines for this.

Perseverance is essential to the success of a leader. He should not expect to achieve success within a short period of time. When facing difficulties he should have patience, confidence, and determination in his plan and not give up easily. However, he should know what and when he should keep persevering and when he should not. The hexagram Hᴇɴɢ 恆 [Persevering] (32) suggests guidelines.

In different times and spaces, different principles for progression should be adopted by an organization. A wrong approach will lead to a wrong direction and thus misfortune. There are five hexagrams which suggest guidelines for **progression**: Qɪᴀɴ (1), Lü (10), Sʜᴇɴɢ 升 [Rising] (46), Jɪᴀɴ (53), and Wᴇɪᴊɪ (64).

In order to continue development a leader should have ongoing plans for the recruitment of high calibre individuals, the improvement of technological standards, and preparations of adequate funds for future actions. The hexagram Dᴀxᴜ 大畜 [Great Accumulating] (26) indicates that an **accumulation** of capable people or resources is beneficial in meeting future needs.

A leader's contribution to his organization cannot be evaluated merely by using the criterion of the current returns he has made. It should also be evaluated on the basis of the services provided by the organization to the community, the country, and the world. The virtue of **service** is indicated by the hexagram Jɪɴɢ 井 [The Well] (48), in which the well nourishes people but is never exhausted.

The hexagram SUI (17) indicates the importance of following or **adaptation**. A leader should keep his mind open and alert to changes in both the external environment and internal conditions. Adaptation to changes in time and space is one of the essential qualities of leadership.

A leader should also have the capacity of an **educator** in his organization by using his wisdom to influence the people below him. If he is willing to share his experience with others, the members of the organization will be able to gain a good number of cultivated people through him. The hexagram MENG 蒙 [Enlightenment] (4) indicates this function of a leader.

In time of **adversity**, a capable leader must remain steadfast, inwardly firm with principles, and outwardly soft with calmness. The hexagrams KAN 坎 [Double Pitfall] (29), JIAN 蹇 [Obstacles] (39), XIE 解 [Loosening] (40), KUN 困 [Adversity] (47), and HUAN 渙 [Dispersing] (59) suggest guidelines for overcoming difficulties in adversity.

A leader should constantly examine his policy and actions to see whether or not they are on the right path. If there is a significant deviation from that path, he should make the corresponding corrections in a timely manner so that the direction of movement can return to the right path. The hexagram FU 復 [Returning] (24) suggests this move. It also advises a leader to **retreat** from ego and overambition.

As time and space change, no organization can survive without change in its structure and policy in a dynamic and competitive world. The two hexagrams GE 革 [Revolution] (49) and GU 蠱 [Decaying] (18) indicate the importance of reforming, whereas the hexagram DING 鼎 [Renewing] (50) emphasizes creative efforts which will bring great benefits to an organization.

A leader should be able to control his temper, emotions, and desires to avoid going too far and violating the principle of centrality. He should know when and where he should move and stop. The hexagram JIE 節 [Regulating] (60) indicates the importance of self-control and restraint to a man who wants to behave correctly.

RELATIONSHIPS BETWEEN YIN–YANG PRINCIPLES AND LEADERSHIP QUALITIES

The relationship between yin–yang attributes and yin–yang principles are not necessarily correlated. Yin–yang attributes have a certain influence on a leader's attitude and behavior, but whether he is an efficient leader of an organization depends much on how well he can master the nine yin–yang principles. A proper use of the yin–yang principles will improve the qualities of a leader. If the nine yin–yang principles are seen as a necessary condition for effective leadership, then proper time and place should suffice. Since it is rather difficult in the human world to master the yin–yang principles perfectly in meeting changes in time and place, the model of perfect leadership serves primarily as a guideline for good leadership.

With changes in time and space (or place) the nine yin–yang principles also change in order to adapt to the changing conditions. But the qualities of leadership remain unchanged since they are considered an eternal truth. A capable leader should be sensitive to changing time and space (as reflected by the six lines) and should follow them, or should adopt the proper yin–yang principles to meet the new conditions. As a result of adapting yin–yang principles to the environment, the leader will be able to retain his qualities during the changes. However, a misuse of yin–yang principles will have an adverse effect on his leadership qualities. A person's ability to master the nine yin–yang principles and leadership qualities is not necessarily inherent, but is cultivable.

APPROPRIATE STATES AND CENTRAL HARMONY

The concepts of centrality and harmony can be divided into four combinations:

- Central harmony
- Central disharmony
- Noncentral harmony
- Noncentral disharmony

In the case of a **central harmony**, if a leader can apply the nine yin–yang principles and maintain his qualities appropriately, he will have the chance of reaching the most desirable state which is called a central harmony. A central harmony is defined as a state in which a yin–yang union is achieved by using the principle of centrality or a centering approach.

A centering approach emphasizes neither too much nor too little. It is an approach of "just right." A central harmony is considered the most desirable or the best situation in which the two forces yin and yang interact and are in balance.

In a hexagram the second and the fifth line are in the central position of the lower and upper trigram respectively. An interaction between a second yin line and a fifth yang line, or between a second yang line and a fifth yin line, can be seen as a state of central harmony. A central harmony is therefore a state that comprises the concept of the Mean and the concept of harmony. This is why the states of most of the lines with central harmony in a hexagram (Fifth Yang, Fifth Yin, Second Yang, and Second Yin) are commented on as "good fortune."

A **central disharmony** is a state in which the centering approach is used but there is no interaction between yin and yang. For example, there is no interaction between Second Yang and Fifth Yang or between Second Yin and Fifth Yin. This situation can still be considered "favorable" even though not "most favorable."

A **noncentral harmony** indicates a situation in which a noncentering approach is used to achieve a harmony, such as the interaction between Initial Yang and Fourth Yin, Third Yang and Top Yin, Initial Yin and Fourth Yang, Third Yin and Top Yang. Whether the situation is "favorable" or "not favorable" depends on the circumstances.

A **noncentral disharmony** is a state in which the approach used is neither central nor harmonious. For example, Initial Yang and Fourth Yang, Initial Yin and Fourth Yin, Third Yang and Top Yang, Third Yin and Top Yin are not in centering positions and have no yin–yang interconnections.

In a comparison of the above four situations, a central harmony appears to be most desirable.

TIME AND SPACE

The Relationship between Time/Space and Yin–Yang Characteristics

As a person, a leader's character should not remain static but should change as time/space changes. In time/space I he behaves strongly and actively, and in time/space II he becomes soft and steady. His yin–yang characteristics should not be seen as unstable but as adaptable to the conditions of different times/spaces. If a leader does not react to the changing conditions in a timely manner, he will suffer from his insensibility.

As time/space changes, a leader should be able to master how to apply the nine yin–yang principles appropriately. The applications of these yin–yang principles are dependent on the time and space. The principle of balance should be seen as the benchmark of a good leadership. The principle of centrality is another expression of a balanced situation—any deviation from it can only be considered a short-run phenomenon. Through an adjustment of the relationships between yin and yang and through the nine laws (principles) of nature, a balanced situation can be restored. In the long run, yin and yang always tend to move towards a balance between each other.

In different times and spaces, the effectiveness of the nine principles can differ depending on whether a leader is able to master them or not. However, no matter how wise a leader is, he cannot always grasp the right timing or the right space. Consequently he will face uncertainties or misfortune.

The Relationship between Time/ Space and Leadership Qualities

A leader's qualities are determined by three factors as indicated in the leadership model figure:

1.	The adaptability of his yin–yang characteristics
2.	The mastery of the nine yin–yang principles
3.	The time/space factor

If a person has adaptable yin–yang attributes and a good mastery of the nine yin–yang principles, this will contribute favorably towards the build-up of his leadership qualities. These two factors are, however, explicit in nature; the implicit factor is time/space which also influences these factors. If a leader is sensitive to changes in time/space, he will correspondingly change his character and adopt the correct yin–yang principle in order to meet the changing conditions. As a result, he will be able to maintain his leadership qualities in an appropriate state and hence a state of central harmony. For example, good foresight, proper activity, timely regulation, adaptable reformation, and so forth.

Necessary and Sufficient Conditions

An effective leadership model derived from the *Yijing* needs two conditions: the necessary condition and the sufficient condition. An adaptable yin–yang character and a skilful mastery of the nine yin–yang principles can be seen as the necessary condition. However, a complete mastery of changes in time and space is almost impossible. Consequently, any change in the outward or inward conditions will involve uncertainties, risks, or misfortune. So a *Yijing* leadership model cannot guarantee a leader's success, but it does provide him with the guidelines to follow in order to act in the right way.

INTEGRITY AND CAPABILITY

Leadership qualities represent a person's capability and integrity; the relationship between the two is not positively related. A person who is highly capable may lack integrity and a person who has a high level of integrity may not be capable. A question is therefore raised about which of the two is most important in the leader of an organization. An ideal leader appears to be a person who is well balanced between integrity and capability. The capability of an ideal leader is determined by whether he is able to master the nine yin–yang principles on the one hand and to create new things, bond people together, and persevere in adversity on the other.

MORALITY AND ETHICS

The *Yijing*-type leader is a cultivated person who has particularly high standard of morality since he knows what is and what is not rightful conduct. According to the philosophy of the *Yijing*, the morality of a leader is considered more important than his capability. A very capable man without a sense of morals may become egocentric as he may use his intelligence in an unrighteous way in order to achieve his personal desires and wants at the expense of the organization. There are many unethical examples in the business sector as illustrated below:

In **marketing**
- Exaggerated or deceptive advertising or sales promotion
- Obtaining business through bribes
- Taking advantage of the consumer's ignorance of the regulations concerning product or service guarantees or insurance compensation
- Setting barriers to competitors in the distribution channel
- Using less or inferior material than that agreed upon
- Ignoring the high standard of product safety for consumers
- Using impulsive or high pressure selling

In **purchasing**
- Receiving bribes to make a deal

- Buying products/services from a company in which one has a personal interest

In **accounting**
- Making a false account by indicating fictitious profit
- Boosting profit by overstating expenditure
- Classifying an item of expenditure as ìinvestmentî
- Hiding profits or losses by manipulating items in accounts

In **finance and investment**
- Inside trading in the equity market
- Acquiring a company in which one has a personal interest at a high price
- Selling company assets to another company in which one has a personal interest at low price
- Ignoring the stakeholders' (consumers, employees, and share-holders) benefit in a business takeover
- Buying back the company's stocks from the acquirers at a higher premium than the market price in order to protect the senior leaders' power status in the organization
- Making a leveraged buy out

Others
- Using the employees' retirement fund in an improper way
- Not taking action about environmental pollution caused by the company's operations
- Receiving an extremely high salary and unreasonable fringe benefits
- Improper collusion in business

Although there are government laws and regulations against unethical practices, people can always find loopholes and use corresponding measures to bypass them. This corresponds to the Chinese saying: **As virtue rises one foot, vice rises ten**. This means that the force of evil is always able to beat the force of law. No matter how effective the laws are they cope only with the symptoms of the evil not its roots. So to improve a leader's business ethics, it is necessary to establish or raise his inner morality first. Only when he attains his original nature of innocence, purity, and goodness will he act as a cultivated person or a "superior man" as opposed to an uncultivated or an "inferior man." In the *Yijing*, a "superior man" is seen as the true self who in his original nature follows the natural laws or *dao*, whereas an "inferior man" is a false self whose nature deviates from *dao*.

Business ethics can be substantially improved only when people act in the right way as a "superior man" as illustrated in the *Yijing*. An individual's morality is the foundation of a well-developed community ethic.

THE EQ PERSON

In an organization people can be classified into two types according to whether they have high intelligence in a specific area or the ability to control their emotion to adapt to different conditions. The first type of person can be called IQ (*intelligence quotient*) person and the second type EQ (*emotion quotient*) person. An IQ person has very good knowledge in his specialized area and is capable of accomplishing his work efficiently. When he has a new idea, he will focus his energy on it. He emphasizes rationality, precision, and direct approach. As a result, he tends to be self-centered and pays no regard to other people's opinions and feelings. Therefore, he may be seen as cold and detached.

In contrast to an IQ person, an EQ person knows when he should control or restrain his emotions in order to avoid hurting others. He is able to interact with others in an appropriate way. He tolerates other people's views and merges his own ideas with them. He has the ability to integrate the individual interest with the group interest. He knows when he should move and when he should stop. He is adaptable to changing conditions. He is seen as warm, fair, and reasonable.

Which of the above two types of person is more suitable to be the leader of an organization? Based on the *Yijing*'s leadership model, an EQ person appears to be more appropriate than an IQ person. While an IQ person fits well into activities related to research and development, an EQ person possesses the important qualities of the *Yijing*-type leader. The hexagrams and the line statements of the sixty-four hexagrams in Part Two of this book have indicated the desirable qualities of an EQ person.

PART FOUR

Divination

Three Coins Method

๛ ๛ ๛

The *Yijing* can be used as a tool to broaden a leader's spectrum of thinking when making decisions. Suppose he is facing a situation in which he is considering whether or not his company should enter a new market niche. Before undertaking market research to get the required information, he can seek advice from the *Yijing*. Here divination can help him get some insight on problems that he is not yet aware of. For example, he may obtain the hexagram JIAN 蹇 [Obstacles] (39) through divination. A leader who is initially very optimistic will now start to think about the future obstacles he will face and the appropriate measures to overcome them. From the six line statements of the hexagram JIAN, useful advice can be derived.

There are many methods of divination. The oldest and the most traditional method is using yarrow stalks. Since this method takes about half an hour to complete, it may not be appropriate for executives who have little time. A simple method is to use three coins.

The Value of the Two Sides of a Coin

A value is given to both sides of a coin: 2 for the head and 3 for the tail:

> Head (yin) = 2
> Tail (yang) = 3

The head of a coin is considered as yin and the tail as yang. The reason for this is based on the way farmers worked in the field in the ancient times. Their back was against the sun while their front in the shade. Also in traditional Chinese medicine, the back of a person is seen as yang. Some diviners, however, use the opposite concept whereby the head is considered as yang with a value of 3 whereas the tail is considered as yin with a value of 2. But these two methods make no difference in obtaining a hexagram.

Total Value of a Coin

Three coins are simultaneously thrown together on a table. There are four combinations of the total value of the three coins:

1. Tail + Tail + Tail or TTT: $3 + 3 + 3 = 9$
2. Tail + Tail + Head or TTH: $3 + 3 + 2 = 8$
3. Head + Head + Tail or HHT: $2 + 2 + 3 = 7$
4. Head + Head + Head or HHH: $2 + 2 + 2 = 6$

An odd number represents a yang line and an even number a yin line. Each of the four values above represents four types of line:

9 = a **changing** yang line (old yang)
8 = a yang line (young yin)
7 = a yin line (young yang)
6 = a **changing** yin line (old yin)

A changing yang line is a yang line which is obtained from the total value of 9. Since 9 represents the extreme of the yang in the primary hexagram divined, it must change to the yin or a yin line in the changing hexagram. For the same reason, if the total value is 6, the extreme of the yin, the original yin line divined in the primary hexagram must change to a yang line in the changing hexagram:

Primary Hexagram	Changing Hexagram
9 ⚊	→ 6 ⚋
6 ⚋	→ 9 ⚊

If the total value is 8 or 7, there is no need to change the line as it is not an extreme value of the yin or the yang.

Primary Hexagram	Changing Hexagram
7 ⚊	→ 7 ⚊
8 ⚋	→ 8 ⚋

According to the binomial distribution of statistics, the chance of obtaining each of the four numbers after throwing three coins is stated as follows:

Numbers	Chance
9	1/8
8	3/8
7	3/8
6	1/8

The chance of obtaining 8 or 7 is 3/8 whereas that of obtaining 9 or 6 is 1/8.

Drawing a Hexagram

The three coins are thrown six times in order to obtain the six lines of a hexagram. The first throw is for the first line, the second throw the second line, and so forth. The first line is placed at the bottom of a hexagram and the rest of the lines are placed accordingly. Following this step a hexagram is obtained as follows:

	Combination of Coins Thrown	Total Value of Coins Thrown	Hexagram Yɪ 益 [Increasing] (42)
Top Line	HHT	7	————
Fifth line	HHT	7	———— Wind
Fourth line	TTH	8	— —
Third line	TTH	8	— —
Second line	TTH	8	— — Thunder
First line	HHT	7	————

Based on the total value of the coins thrown the hexagram Yɪ 益 [Increasing] (42) is obtained. Since all six lines are either 7 (yang) or 8 (yin), there are no changing lines in the hexagram and no changing hexagram is derived.

Primary and Changing Hexagram

If there are one or more changing lines, based on the total value of 6 or 9, in the primary hexagram, the original line(s) must correspondingly change to the opposite line(s) as explained above. Suppose the second and fifth lines are both changing lines. The original hexagram Yɪ must be changed to a derived hexagram or a changing hexagram Sᴜɴ 損 [Decrease] (41) as shown below:

Primary Hexagram Yɪ 益 [Increasing] (42)	Changing Hexagram Sᴜɴ 損 [Decrease] (41)

Wind   ▬ •   ⟶   ▬ ▬ • Mountain

Thunder   ▬ ▬ •   ⟶   ▬ • Lake

There are two changing lines in the primary hexagram Yɪ: Second Yin (obtained from the total value of 6) and Fifth Yang (obtained from the total value of 9). These two lines must be changed to their opposite lines, that is, Second Yang and Fifth Yin respectively. Through the changes in lines the Changing Hexagram Sᴜɴ is obtained.

Iɴᴛᴇʀᴘʀᴇᴛᴀᴛɪᴏɴ ᴏꜰ ᴀ Pʀᴇᴅɪᴄᴛɪᴠᴇ Hᴇxᴀɢʀᴀᴍ

If there is no changing lines in a primary hexagram, the diviner can interpret that respective hexagram, for example, by using the following bases:

1. The hexagram name
2. The image of the hexagram; that is, the relationship between its upper and lower trigrams
3. The hexagram statement
4. The line structure
5. The linear statement
6. The derived hexagrams such as opposite hexagram, inverse hexagram, nuclear hexagram, and interchange hexagram

The different ways to interpret a hexagram have been demonstrated in Part Two of this book. The sixty-four hexagrams provide, with their guidelines, a path to follow in order to act in the right way. Through divination a leader will develop a broader mind and generate new ideas.

The interpretation of a predictive hexagram may also follow traditional rules as suggested by Zhu Xi 朱熹, a philosopher in the Song dynasty (ᴀ.ᴅ. 960–1279), as stated below:

Primary Hexagram	Statement(s) used for Interpretation
1. No changing line	The hexagram statement of the primary hexagram
2. One changing line	The statement of this line

3. Two changing lines   Both line statements, primarily the one above
4. Three changing lines   The hexagram statement of the primary hexagram
5. Four changing lines   The statements of the two nonchanging lines of the changing hexagram, primarily the one below
6. Five changing lines   The statement of the nonchanging line of the changing hexagram
7. Six changing lines   For Hexagram QIAN 乾 [Heaven] (1)
The text of "Using Yang"
For Hexagram KUN 坤 [Earth] (2):
The text of "Using Yin"

The above "rules" are given as suggestions. The diviner can make changes according to his rationale and judgment.

Examples

The CEO of ABC Company is planning to expand his company next year. He has formulated the corresponding strategies, but he would like to know if there are any viewpoints he may have ignored. So he uses the *Yijing* to make a divination in order to broaden his point of view. His question is **"What points should I think about for the expansion of my company next year?"**

In the case of no changing line

First example: **Hexagram TUNGREN 同人**
[Fellowship] (13)

The hexagram statement:

Fellowship can be established in the wilderness.
The prospects are bright.
It is favorable to cross great rivers. If the superior man behaves in the right way, he will reap rewards.

    The CEO is advised to build up his team to expand on a basis that is as broad as it is in a wilderness. The background of the team members should be kept diversified rather than in a specified field. He should use people who are capable and have integrity regardless whether they are from the same town, same clan, or same school. Only with this broad-minded attitude will he be able to overcome the difficulties of expansion.

Second example:

Hexagram JIAN 蹇
[Obstacles] (39)

The hexagram statement:

It is favorable for one to go to the southwest instead of the northeast. It is beneficial to see great man. If he can keep to the right way, he will be auspicious.

As the southwest stands for softness and the northeast for obstruction, the CEO is advised to adopt a market niche which is easier to enter or to penetrate in a business sector which has less entry barriers. He should not enter a sector where there are strong competitors if he lacks adequate strength to combat them.

In the case of one changing line

If the divined hexagram is SHI 師 [Leading Troops] (7) which has one changing line, Second Yang, the primary hexagram Leading Troops will transform to a changing hexagram KUN 坤 [Tolerance] (2) as follows:

Primary Hexagram   **Changing Hexagram**

SHI 師 **[Leading Troops] (7)**   KUN 坤 **[Tolerance] (2)**

The statement for the changing line Second Yang in the primary hexagram is:

He steers a balanced and middle course in the army. He is fortunate without any blame. The king will honor him three times.

The statement of Second Yang suggests that the CEO should select the right person as the action-leader for the expansion who should be sincere, balanced, and able to master the principle of centrality.

According to the structure of this hexagram, the top leader should delegate adequate authority to this action-leader in order that he can effectively fulfil his responsibilities.

Using traditional rules, these interpretations are restricted to the primary hexagram. However, the suggestions provided by the changing hexagram can also be used as a basis for the future scenario. In the above example, the changing hexagram KUN 坤 [Tolerance] (2) suggests that an action-leader should have the qualities of the earth—to be broad-minded, tolerant, and willing to listen to other people's advice.

In the case of two changing lines

Primary Hexagram	Changing Hexagram
KUAI 夬 [Determination] (43)	XIAN 咸 [Interacting] (31)

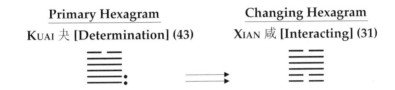

The statement of the first changing line Initial Yang in the primary hexagram:

He puts strength in his front toe for advancement, but he is not successful and regrets this.

The statement of the second changing line Second Yang in the primary hexagram:

If he is cautious and keeps alert, he doesn't need to worry even if he is attacked at night.

According to the traditional rules, the changing line in the above (Second Yang) should be used as the basis for interpretation. The CEO should constantly keep alert and have a sense of the danger around him. He should prepare the necessary measures against unexpected events. But he can also get useful advice from the statement of Initial Yang; he should not be overly confident or too exuberant and enthusiastic.

The changing hexagram XIAN advises the CEO to strengthen his relationships with colleagues and subordinates through better communication, in order to get their useful support.

In the case of three changing lines in the primary hexagram

Primary Hexagram	Changing Hexagram
JIAN 漸 [Gradual Progress] (53)	YI 頤 [Nourishing] (27)

Since there are three changing lines (Initial Yin, Third Yang, and Fifth Yang) in the primary hexagram JIAN 漸 [Gradual Progress] (53), the interpretation is based on the meaning of the hexagram as a whole. The hexagram suggests a step-by-step advancement. Whether this is good advice or not depends on the situation, time, and place faced by the company. If the situation is uncertain or resources are not adequate for a big move, gradual progress appears to be a better way. On the other hand, if the company is in a favorable environment and its resources are adequate for such a big move, the CEO of the company must make a decision on what strategy he should adopt: a gradual progress or a big move. Divination cannot give the diviner a firm answer since the result can differ from one person to another according to their background and character.

The changing hexagram YI 頤 [Nourishing] (27) advises the CEO to provide opportunities for his members to improve their abilities, for example, through training and developments for a future move. It can also mean that the CEO needs to develop his own virtue and knowledge.

In the case of four changing lines in the primary hexagram

Primary Hexagram	Changing Hexagram
KUAI 夬 [Determination] (43)	QIAN 謙 [Modesty] (15)

The primary hexagram KUAI 夬 [Determination] (43) has four changing lines and two non-changing lines—Top Yin and Third Yang. According to the traditional rules given above, Top Yin and Third Yang of the changing hexagram QIAN 謙 [Modesty] (15) become the basis for interpretation, with emphasis on the one below. The statement for the Third Yang is:

He is diligent yet modest. By keeping this way he will enjoy good fortune.

Even if the company has achieved a great success, the CEO is advised to maintain a modest attitude, particularly with members who have contributed a lot of effort to the development. Also the CEO must not be complacent over his achieved success but must continue to maintain a high spirit to strive for an even better success.

However, the CEO can also learn from the statement for Top Yin about how to treat people. The statement is:

When his explicit modesty becomes a fault, it is beneficial to mobilize the army to overrun his own state.

When the CEO interacts with the members of his organization in a "too humble" way, people may be skeptical of his sincerity. In this case, he needs strength as symbolized by "the army" to restrain his "over-docility." He should restrain his modesty appropriately.

In the case of five changing lines in the primary hexagram

Primary Hexagram		Changing Hexagram
Cui 萃 [Gathering] (45)		Tai 泰 [Harmony] (11)

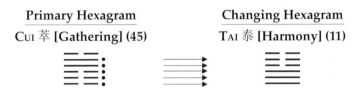

Since Top Yin is the only nonchanging line of the primary hexagram Cui 萃 [Gathering] (45), the statement for Top Yin of the changing hexagram Tai 泰 [Harmony] (11) becomes the basis for an interpretation. The statement for Top Yang is:

As the wall of the castle collapses into the moat, it is not possible to mobilize a military action. The orders can only be carried out by people around him. Even if he keeps to the right way, he will not be able to change the direction.

The CEO must be able to realize what situation the company is facing. When the peak of a business cycle is reached he should follow the trend, not go against it, that is, he should stop his expansion and make preparations for a downturn. If he acts in this way, his company will be in safe.

In the case of six changing yang lines in the primary hexagram

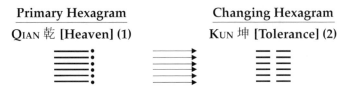

Primary Hexagram		Changing Hexagram
QIAN 乾 [Heaven] (1)		KUN 坤 [Tolerance] (2)

If all the six yang lines obtained in the primary hexagram QIAN 乾 [Heaven] (or Force) (1) are based on the number 9, they must be transformed into six yin lines which form the changing hexagram KUN 坤 [Tolerance] (2). The interpretation of the hexagram QIAN is based on the statement of "Using Yang":

A group of dragons has no head. It is auspicious.

The six dragons signify the strength of the Heaven whereas "no head" refers to the characteristic of Earth. This is a situation in which yang merges with yin and it will bring harmony. The CEO should keep a good balance between the forces yin and yang during the expansion of his company. "No head" also means that there is no domination of a situation; it symbolizes a leader with an open mind.

If all six yang lines are divined based on the number 7 (young yang), there is no need to change the lines. Since the hexagram is QIAN (1), the basis of the interpretation is the hexagram statement, or the meaning of the hexagram as a whole.

In the case of six changing yin lines

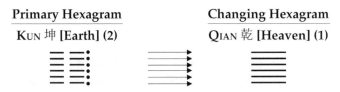

Primary Hexagram		Changing Hexagram
KUN 坤 [Earth] (2)		QIAN 乾 [Heaven] (1)

If all the six yin lines are divined from the number 6 in the primary hexagram, they must be transformed to six yang lines in the changing hexagram which forms QIAN (1) (Force). The interpretation of the primary hexagram Earth is based on the statement of "Using Yin." This statement is:

It is always beneficial to keep a docile way.

The CEO should keep the characteristics of Earth, that is, docility, tolerance, and caution, even if he will be moving into a very favorable situation for expansion like a pure yang hexagram QIAN (1). Based on the principle of mutual inclusion of yin and yang, yin is within yang, and vice versa. In reality there is no pure yang or pure yin situation.

If all six yin lines are divined from the number 8 there is no need for changes. The interpretation of the hexagram KUN 坤 [Earth] (2) is based on the hexagram statement or the hexagram structure:

A minor change in the rules for interpretation.

Since divination is used in this book as a thinking tool, it is not necessary to follow the traditional rules exactly in the interpretation of the hexagrams. A minor change in the rules is recommended to adapt to different times and places.

Yarrow Stalk Method

✍ ✍ ✍

The Yarrow Stalk Method is the oldest method of divination. As the name indicates, yarrow stalks are used in the process of divination. The Yarrow Stalk Method was introduced in the *Xici zhuan* 繫辭傳 [the Great Commentary on the Appended Phrases], but this method of divination was not clearly explained. The method was perfected by Zhu Xi, a philosopher in the Song dynasty. The method presented in the following is based on his interpretation with some modifications.

FORTY-NINE STALKS

The diviner prepares fifty stalks and places them on a table. One stalk must be set aside and will not be used in the divination. This stalk is considered as the *taiji*, the beginning of the development of things, and a divination is one of these. Forty-nine stalks are used for divining the six lines of a hexagram. Three mutations are required to get one line of a hexagram, so eighteen mutations yield six lines or one hexagram.

First Mutation

1. The forty-nine stalks are randomly divided into two bunches which are roughly similar in size and are placed on the right and the left. The two bunches symbolize Heaven (Yang) and Earth (Yin). Suppose that the number of stalks in the right bunch is 26 and that in the left bunch is 23.
2. One stalk is taken out of the right bunch to symbolize Man, so the total number of stalks in the right bunch is now 25 (26 −1 = 25).
   The right bunch is divided into groups of four (as a symbol of four states, for example, four seasons); the last group has one stalk and this is put aside. The number of stalks in the last group is obtained by dividing 25 by 4 (25/4); the residual represents the number of

stalks in the last group. In this case, the last group has one remaining stalk. In general, the total number of remaining stalks in the last group will range from one to four stalks. If the last group has no remaining stalks because the total number of stalks is divisible by 4, say, 24, the numeral 4 is used to represent the number of remaining stalks in the last group. For example, if the number of stalks in the bunch is 24 instead of 25, there will be no residual stalks in the last group, so the numeral 4 is used to represent the number of remaining stalks and they are put aside.

In the above example, the total number of stalks remaining in the right bunch is now 24 (26 – 1 – 1 = 24).

3. The left bunch is also divided into groups of fours; the last group has three stalks (23/4, the residual is 3) and these are put aside. The total number of remaining stalks in the left bunch is now 20 (23 – 3 = 20).

    The total number of the stalks put aside: 1 + 1 + 3 = 5.

4. The stalks in both the right and left bunches are put together. The total number of remaining stalks is 44 (24 + 20 = 44), which can also be obtained by reducing the total number of stalks put aside (5) from the number 49 after the first mutation: 49 – 5 = 44.

Second Mutation

1. The newly combined bunch is randomly divided again into two, a right and a left bunch. Assume that the number of stalks in the right bunch is 21 and that in the left 23.

2. One stalk is taken out of the right bunch and put aside. The total number of stalks in the right bunch is now 20 (21 – 1 = 20).

    The right bunch is divided into groups of four, that is, 20 stalks are divided by 4. Since there is no residual, 4 is used as the total number of the remaining stalks in the last group and these are put aside. The total number of remaining stalks in the right bunch is now 16 (20 – 4 = 16).

3. The left bunch is divided into groups of four. The last group has three stalks (23/4, the residual is 3) and they are put aside. The total number of remaining stalks in the left bunch is now 20 (23 – 3 = 20). The total number of stalks put aside is: 1+ 4 + 3 = 8.

4. The stalks in the right and left bunches are put together. The total number of remaining stalks is now 36 (16+ 20 = 36 or 44 – 8 = 36).

Third Mutation

1. The newly combined bunch is randomly divided into two, a right and a left bunch. Assume that the number of stalks in the right bunch is 19 and that in the left 17.
2. One stalk is taken out of the right bunch and put aside. The total number of stalks in the right bunch is now 18 (19 – 1= 18).
   The right bunch is divided into groups of four; the last group has two stalks (18/4, the residual is 2) and these are put aside. The total number of remaining stalks in the right bunch is now 16 (18 – 2 = 16).
3. The left bunch is divided into groups of fours the last group has one stalk (17/4, the residual is 1) and it is put aside. The total number of remaining stalks in the left bunch is now 16 (17 – 1 = 16).
   The total number of stalks put aside is 4 (1 + 2 + 1 = 4).
4. The total number of remaining stalks after the third mutation is 32 (16 + 16 = 32). Alternatively, the total number of stalks used in the divination (49) minus the total number of stalks put aside in three mutations (5 + 8 + 4 = 17) is 32 (49 – 17 = 32).

After three rounds of casting, the total number of remaining stalks is 32. Dividing 32 by 4 gives 8, which represents the nature of the divined line. There are four numbers that can be obtained after the three mutations: 36, 32, 28, or 24. These four numbers are used as the basis to determine what the type of the divined line is. Dividing each of these four numbers by four (or group of fours), four significant numbers 6, 7, 8, and 9 are obtained and these are used as the basis for conversion of the numbers into the respective lines:

36/4 = 9	Old Yang	the changing yang line
32/4 = 8	Young Yin	the unchanged yin line
28/4 = 7	Young Yang	the unchanged yang line
24/6 = 6	Old Yin	the changing yin line

Based on the above conversion table, these four numbers are transformed into the respective four lines. In the above example, the total number of remaining stalks after three mutations is 32. When this is divided by four, the number 8 is then the number obtained which represents Young Yin or the first yin line of the divined hexagram.

Alternatively the total number of stalks put aside during the three mutations can be used as the basis for deriving the line sought after:

Stalks put aside in first mutation: $1 + 1 + 3 = 5$
Stalks put aside in second mutation: $1 + 4 + 3 = 8$
Stalks put aside in third mutation: $1 + 2 + 1 = 4$
   Total stalks put aside: $5 + 8 + 4 = 17$
   $(49 – 17)/4 = 32/4 = 8$, the same result as given above.

Summary of the Three Mutations for the First Line

Start	**50 stalks**
I. Take one stalk out of **total** stalks:	$50 – 1 = 49$
Divide the total stalks randomly into two bunches.	23 26
Take out of one stalk out of the **right** bunch and one stalk of the last group after dividing 25 by 4:	$26 – 1 – 1 = 24$
Take three stalks out of the **left** bunch after dividing 23 by 4:	$23 – 3 = 20$
II. Combine the stalks of the **two** bunches:	$20 + 24 = 44$
Divide the total stalks randomly into two bunches:	23 21
Take out one stalk out of the **right** bunch and four stalks after dividing 20 by 4:	$21 – 1 – 4 = 16$
Take three stalks out of the **left** bunch after dividing 23 by 4:	$23 – 3 = 20$
III. Combine the stalks of the **two** bunches:	$20 + 16 = 36$
Divide total stalks randomly into two bunches:	17 19
Take out 1 stalk of the **right** bunch and 2 stalks after dividing 18 by 4:	$19 – 1 – 2 = 16$
Take out 1 stalk of the **left** bunch after dividing 17 by 4:	$17 – 1 = 16$
Combine the stalks of the two bunches:	$16 + 16 = 32$
Alternatively, total number of stalks used minus total number of stalks put aside after three mutations:	$49 – (5 + 8 + 4) = 32$

By dividing 32 by 4 the number 8 is obtained,
representing an unchanged yin line (young yin): $32/4 = 8$

   Following the same procedure the other five lines of the divined hexagram are obtainable.

A Further Example

First mutation

1. Take one stalk out of 50 stalks: $\qquad$ 50 − 1 = 49
2. Divide 49 stalks randomly into two bunches: $\quad$ 23 $\quad$ 26
3. Take one stalk out of the right bunch: $\qquad$ 26 − 1 =25
4. Divide the stalks of each bunch by 4 and put the residual aside. The remaining stalks in each bunch are:

   25 − 1 = 24

   23 − 3 = 20
5. Combine the stalks of the two bunches: $\qquad$ 20 + 24 = 44
6. Total stalks put aside: $\qquad$ 1 + 3 + 1= 5

Second mutation

1. Divide the 44 stalks randomly into two bunches: $\qquad$ 23 $\quad$ 21
2. Take one stalk out of the right bunch $\qquad$ 21 − 1 = 20
3. Divide the stalks of each bunch by 4 and put the residual aside. The remaining stalks of each bunch are:

   23 − 3 = 20

   20 − 4 = 16
4. Combine the stalks of the two bunches: $\qquad$ 20 + 16 = **36**
5. Total stalks put aside: $\qquad$ 1 + 3 + 4 = **8**

Third mutation

1. Divide the 36 stalks randomly into two bunches: $\qquad$ 20 $\quad$ 16
2. Take one stalk out of the right bunch: $\qquad$ 16 − 1 = 15
3. Divide the stalks of each bunch by four and put the residual aside. The remaining stalks of each bunch are:

   15 − 3 = 12

   20 − 4 = 16
4. Combine the stalks of the two bunches $\qquad$ 16 +12 = **28**
5. Total stalks put aside: $\qquad$ 5 + 8 + 8 = **21**

The first line of the divined hexagram can be obtained by using either of the following two methods:

1. Dividing the total number of remaining stalks after three mutations by four:

   28/4 = 7
2. Dividing the difference between the total number of the stalks used

in the casting and the total number of stalks put aside after three mutations by four:

$$(49 - 21) / 4 = 7$$

The first line of the divined hexagram is an unchanged young line (young yang) as represented by the number 7.

Hypothetical Results of Another Fifteen Mutations in the First Example

First, second, and third mutation for the first line:
 $32/4 = 8$ Young Yin, the yin line
Fourth, fifth, and sixth mutation for the second line:
 $36/4 = 9$ Old Yang, the changing yang line
Seventh, eighth, and ninth mutation for the third line:
 $24/4 = 6$ Old Yin, the changing yin line
Tenth, eleventh, and twelfth mutation for the fourth line:
 $28/4 = 7$ Young Yang, the yang line
Thirteen, fourteen, and fifth mutation for the fifth line:
 $32/4 = 8$ Young Yin, the yin line
Sixteenth, seventeenth, and eighteenth mutation for the sixth line:
 $36/4 = 9$ Old Yang, the changing yang line

Based on the six numbers obtained from the eighteen mutations, a hexagram is divined as follows:

Primary Hexagram	Changing Hexagram
WEIJI 未濟	**X**IAOGUO 小過
[Not Yet Accomplished] (64)	**[Small Exceeding] (62)**

Top Yang (9)	—— •	——→	— —
Fifth Yin (8)	— —		— —
Fourth Yang (7)	——		——
Third Yin (6)	— — •	——→	——
Second Yang (9)	—— •	——→	— —
Initial Yin (8)	— —		— —

Two Numbers Method

A more simple method for divination is the two numbers method. To obtain a hexagram, two numbers are required:

1. The number of the upper trigram
2. The number of the lower trigram

Each of the eight trigrams has a particular number assigned to it by the philosopher Shao Yung 邵雍 in the first century of the Song Dynasty, as stated below:

QIAN 乾 [Heaven]	☰	1
DUI 兌 [Lake]	☱	2
LI 離 [Fire]	☲	3
ZHEN 震 [Thunder]	☳	4
XUN 巽 [Wind]	☴	5
KAN 坎 [Water]	☵	6
GEN 艮 [Mountain]	☶	7
KUN 坤 [Earth]	☷	8

The first number obtained will decide the upper trigram and the second number the lower trigram. For example, if the first number is 1, then the trigram QIAN 乾 [Heaven] will be used as the upper trigram. Similarly if the second number is 7, the trigram GEN 艮 [Mountain] will be the lower trigram. The whole then forms the Heaven–Mountain Hexagram DUN 遯 [Retreating] (33):

Hexagram DUN 遯
[Retreating] (33)

Heaven (1)

Mountain (7)

The time of making a divination is not considered, nor is the changing line. The interpretation of the divined hexagram is based on

1. the hexagram statement
2. the image of the hexagram
3. the structure of the hexagram
4. the imagination of the diviner

How do we get the two numbers for the upper and lower trigrams of a hexagram? There are different methods of obtaining these two key numbers for a divination, as stated later.

Three Numbers Method

In using the Three Numbers Method, both the **time** factor and the **changing line** are considered. To obtain a hexagram, three numbers are required:

1. the number of the upper trigram
2. the number of the lower trigram
3. the number of the time of making the divination

In the Three Numbers Method, the time of making a divination as the third number is included in the formula. The reason for this is that any change in things is related to the change in time. For the sake of simplicity, the formula used here will not include the year, month, and day of making a divination, but only the time at which hour the divination is made. As there are twenty-four hours in a day, a number can be assigned to represent each hour of a day.

In the traditional Chinese calendar, the twenty-four hours of a day are combined into twelve time units with two hours each starting at 11:00 p.m. to 1:00 a.m., so there are a total of twelve numbers representing the twelve time units of a day. Each time unit (two hours) has a specific name in Chinese. In order not to confuse readers of this book, the twelve Chinese names for the twelve time units of a day will not be used here. Suppose that the time of a divination is at 11:30 p.m. The number that represents this time unit (11:00 p.m. to 1:00 a.m.) is 1. If the divination starts at 3:30 p.m. the number that represents this time unit (3:00 p.m. to 5:00 p.m.) is 9. The time conversion is stated below:

Time	Number of Time Unit
11:00 p.m. – 1:00 a.m.	1
1:00 a.m. – 3:00 a.m.	2
3:00 a.m. – 5:00 a.m.	3
5:00 a.m. – 7:00 a.m.	4
7:00 a.m. – 9:00 a.m.	5

9:00 a.m. – 11:00 a.m.	6
11:00 a.m. – 1:00 p.m.	7
1:00 p.m. – 3:00 p.m.	8
3:00 p.m. – 5:00 p.m.	9
5:00 p.m. – 7:00 p.m.	10
7:00 p.m. – 9:00 p.m.	11
9:00 p.m. – 11:00 p.m.	12

Assuming that the time of a divination is 4:15 p.m., the number of this time unit is therefore 9. The time factor of a divination as represented by this number 9 must be added to the two numbers of the upper trigram Heaven (1) and the lower trigram Mountain (7) together. The sum of these three numbers $(1 + 7 + 9)$ is divided by 6 (there are six lines in a hexagram), so the number for the representation of the changing line is obtained:

$$(1 + 7 + 9)/6 = 17/6 = 2\,^5/_6.$$

The 5 is used to represent the number of the changing line which is Fifth Yang of the predictive Hexagram Dun 遯 [Retreating]:

Hexagram Dun 遯
[Retreating] (33)

Upper Trigram Heaven (1)　　　　☰·　　The changing line
Lower Trigram Mountain (7)

If the sum of the three numbers is divisible by 6, for example, $(5 + 4 + 9)/\mathbf{6} = 3$, there is no residual, so 6 is used to represent the number of the changing line of the respective hexagram, the top line:

Hexagram Dun

Upper Trigram Heaven (1)　　　　☰·　　The changing line
Lower Trigram Mountain (7)

If the number of a divined trigram is larger than 8, say, 32, it must be divided by 8. The reason for this is that there are in total eight trigrams. Since the number 32 is divisible by 8, the denominator 8 is treated as the number of the trigram Kun 坤 [Earth] ☷. If a number is indivisible by 8, for example 35, the residual 3 $(35/8 = 4\,^3/_8)$ represents the number of the trigram Li 離 [Fire] ☲.

How to Get the Two Key Numbers

The fundamentals of The Three Numbers method has been introduced above. To use these two and three numbers methods the key numbers are the two that represent the upper and the lower trigrams, as the number of a respective time unit is already given and the number of the changing line is in fact a number that is derived from the three numbers.

How do we get the two key numbers for the upper and lower trigrams in a divination? There are many methods of getting these two key numbers. Any method can be used as long as it is objective. It is like a sampling in marketing research—the respondents should be selected on a random basis so that the results are objective rather than biased. The methods stated below are suggestions; readers of this book can develop their own methods as long as these are objective.

The Peanut Method

The diviner randomly takes some peanuts from a plate twice and counts how many peanuts are taken each time. If the number of the peanuts on the first draw is 8, the upper trigram, according the numbers assigned to the eight hexagrams as shown above, is Kun 坤 [Earth]. Following the same rule, four peanuts represent the trigram Zhen 震 [Thunder]. If the number of peanuts taken is more than eight, say 20, they must be divided by 8 because there are eight trigrams. If the number is divisible by 8, such as 24, then 8 is the number of the predictive hexagram which is the trigram Kun [Earth]. If the number is 33, which is indivisible by 8, the residual 1 is used as the number of the upper trigram which is Qian 乾 [Heaven] in this case. The number of peanuts taken in the second draw will indicate what the lower trigram should be. For example, the number 6 represents the trigram Kan 坎 [Water]. If the number is 19, the residual of 19/8 is 3 which is the number of the trigram Li 離 [Fire].

The third number represents the time of a divination. It can be obtained from the time conversion table given above. Where three numbers are obtained, the changing line of the predictive hexagram is determined as elaborated in the above examples.

The word "peanut" as used in this method is adopted arbitrarily. The object can be anything that will serve the same purpose as the peanuts, for example, other nuts, rice grains, matches, toothpicks, or candies.

The Dice Method

There are two kinds of the Dice Method. The first kind uses three ordinary dice as the medium to get a predictive hexagram, whereas the second kind needs three specially made dice to serve this purpose.

The Ordinary Dice Method

The diviner uses three ordinary dice to generate a hexagram. The total number of each throw of three dice ranges from 3 to 18. If the total number obtained from the first throw is between 1 and 8, the upper trigram is determined. If the total number is larger than 8, say, 16, it must be divided by 8. Since 16 is divisible by 8, then 8 is used as the number of the upper trigram; in this case it is the trigram KUN [Earth]. If the total number given by the throw of the three dice is indivisible by 8, say, 11, 13, 15, or 17, the residual is used to represent the number of the trigram sought. The total number obtained from the second throw of the three dice will determine the lower trigram. The changing line can be obtained by using the method indicated above.

The Special-Made Dice Method

For the purpose of divination, three dice are specially made in a way that each of them has only two numbers: 2 and 3. The total number of the three dice ranges from 6 to 9. With these four numbers, the six lines of a hexagram are determined as 9 (old yang) represents a changing yang line, 8 (young yin) a yin line, 7 (young yang) a yang line and 6 (old yin) a changing yin line. The diviner needs to make six throws of the three dice to obtain a predictive hexagram. By using this Special-Made Dice Method, there is no need to calculate the number of the changing line as in the ordinary dice method. If the diviner does want a changing line, he or she can use a simple method of determining which of the six lines should be changed. For example, the line number can be obtained by throwing one ordinary dice which has six numbers from 1 to 6.

The Card Method

Method One

In using cards to make a divination, the red colour represents the yang line for its brightness and the black colour the yin line for its darkness. Fifty-two cards are used for a divination from which the diviner arbitrarily picks three cards, since each trigram has three lines. The three cards are placed in vertical order. If all three cards in the first draw are all red (heart/diamond), they are treated as three yang lines, which form the upper trigram QIAN [Heaven] ☰. If all three cards are black, they represent three yin lines or the upper trigram KUN [Earth] ☷. In the case of one black card above and two red cards below, the upper trigram is DUI 兌 [Lake] ☱. In a reverse order, one red card above and two black cards below, this forms the trigram GEN 艮 [Mountain] ☶. A red card at the top and the bottom with a black card in between indicates the trigram LI [Fire] ☲. In reverse, a black card at the top and the bottom with a red card in between makes the trigram KAN [Water] ☵. Using the same method, the lower trigram can be obtained. The methods of getting the changing line are indicated above. The changing line is determined by drawing one from six cards which have the numbers from one to six.

Method Two

There is another method of using fifty-two cards for divination. Since each card has a number from one to thirteen, any card which is arbitrarily drawn from the fifty-two is thereby considered the number of the respective trigram. If the number is larger than 8, say, 12 or 13, it must be divided by 8 in order to get a trigram. If the number is divisible by 8, then 8 represents the respective number of the trigram Earth. If it is indivisible by 8 then the residual will be used as the number of the trigram that is sought. The time element can be taken into consideration in determining the changing line: the sum of the number of the upper trigram, lower trigram, and converted time unit is divided by 6 in order to get the number of the changing line. This method has already been explained above.

Method Three

This method is an extension of the Three Coins Method. Four cards with the number *three* and another four cards with the number *two* are used, so there are all together eight cards. The diviner draws simultaneously three cards out of the eight, the total added number of these three cards will range from 6 to 9, including 7 and 8. If the total number from the three cards is 9, it is an old yang or a changing yang line. Following the same rule, the number 6 represents a changing yin line (old yin), 7 a yang line (young yang), and 8 a yin line (young yin). From each draw the type of a line can be determined, so six lines of a hexagram are obtained through six draws. To determine the changing line a number can arbitrarily be drawn from six cards with the numbers ranged from one to six. The number obtained will determine where the change should be.

Method Four

The diviner can arbitrarily pick **six** cards out of the fifty-two and place them in a **vertical order** like the six lines of a hexagram. An odd-numbered card will be treated as a yang line and an even-numbered one a yin line. The methods of getting the changing line are indicated above.

Method Five

As in Method Two, red cards (heart and diamond) represent the yang line and black cards (spades and club) the yin line. The diviner can draw six cards separately; the color of each card determines the type of line. The first card represents the first line, the second card the second line and so on. The changing line can be obtained by using the methods indicated above.

The Letters Method

The number of letters in a word or words can be used to obtain a hexagram and the changing line. The word or words can be arbitrarily chosen from a book or a newspaper. It may also be the name of a person or the brand name of a product.

One Word Method

The diviner arbitrarily selects a brand name from a newspaper, for example, *Grandluxe*, as the basis for obtaining the three numbers as required in his divination which is made at 3:30 p.m. Since the total number of the letters of this brand name is 9, it is necessary to divide this number into two parts in order to get two numbers to represent the upper and lower trigram of a hexagram. The lower part should have the larger number and the upper part the smaller number. By using this rule, the lower trigram has a number of 5 and the upper trigram a number of 4. The number of the converted time unit is 9. The hexagram Heng 恆 [Persevering] is divined as follows:

Hexagram HENG 恆
Persevering (32)

Thunder (4)    The changing line

Wind (5)

The changing line Top Yin is obtained from the following formula: $(4 + 5 + 9)/6$. Since the numerator 18 is divisible, the denominator 6 is then used as the number of the changing line which is Top Yin.

Two Words Method

The diviner can randomly select two words as the basis for deriving the hexagram sought. The number of letters in the first word represents the number of the upper trigram and the number of letters of the second word that of the lower trigram. For example, suppose the two words selected are judgment and power. The first word has eight letters and the second word five letters. According to the order number of the eight trigrams given above, the no. 8 trigram KUN 坤 [Earth] (46) is the upper trigram and the no. 5 trigram XUN 巽 [Wind] the lower trigram of the hexagram SHENG 升 [Rising] (46):

Hexagram SHENG 升
[Rising] (46)

Earth (8)   

Wind (5)   The changing line

Assuming that the divination is made at 10:30 a.m., the number 6 represents the converted time unit from the conversion table stated above. Then the changing line of the Hexagram Rising is determined: $(8 + 5 + 6)/6 = 3\,^1/_6$. The first line is the changing line.

Suppose a person's name is David Lee. The letters of his first name David has five letters whereas there are three in his surname Lee. The number of the letters of the first name represents the number of the upper trigram and the number of the letters of the surname stands for the lower trigram. Based on the two numbers 5 (upper trigram) and 3 (lower trigram), the hexagram JIAREN 家人 [The Family] (37) is obtained:

Hexagram JIAREN 家人
The Family (37)

Wind (5)   The changing line

Fire (3)

Assuming the time of this divination is 4:15 p.m., then the number of the respective time unit is 9. The changing line is determined by using the formula given above: $(5 + 3 + 9)/6 = 17/6 = 2\,{}^5/_6$. The residual is 5. Fifth Yang is the changing line.

Summary of the General Steps of the Two/Three Numbers Method

Step 1: *The first number represents the upper trigram*

Assuming that the first number is 6, the upper trigram KAN [Water] of a hexagram is determined. If the number is larger than 8, say, 64, it must be divided by 8 as there are eight trigrams. Since the number 64 is divisible by 8, then 8 represents the number of the upper trigram or the trigram KUN [Earth].

If the derived number is 75 which is indivisible by 8, its residual 3 $(75/8 = 9\,{}^3/_8)$ then represents the number of the upper trigram or the trigram LI [Fire]. If the number is 28, its residual 4 stands for the number of the upper trigram which is ZHEN 震 [Thunder].

Step 2: *The second number represents the lower trigram*

The lower trigram of a hexagram can be obtained by using the same method as indicated above.

Step 3: *The third number represents the converted time unit*

If the time element is to be considered in a divination, the number for the respective time unit (each two hours a day) can be obtained from the converted time table given above. For example, if the time of a divination is at 1:30 p.m., the number which represents this time unit is 8.

Step 4: *The changing line*

Assume that the three numbers of the upper trigram, lower trigram and converted time unit are 6, 8, and 8 respectively, then the number that represents the changing line can be determined by dividing the sum 22 by 6. Since the residual is 4, the fourth line of the hexagram is the changing line. If there is no residual, 6 will be the number of the changing line. In this case, the top line of the respective hexagram will be the changing line.

Five Elements Method

❦ ❦ ❦

The Five Elements (or *Wuxing* 五行) Method was originally developed by Shao Yung during the Song dynasty. It is known in China as Plum Blossom Numerology. Unlike other traditional methods such as the Three Coins Method and the Yarrow Stalks Method, this method does not use the hexagram statement or line statement, or the image of the hexagram or the structure of the hexagram, as the basis for prediction but uses the relationships between the five elements. As a refresher, the two relationships between the five elements are restated below:

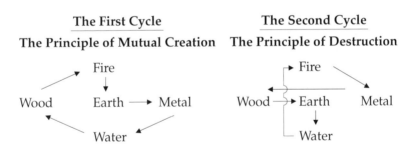

The First Cycle	The Second Cycle
The Principle of Mutual Creation	The Principle of Destruction

The principle of mutual creation indicates a relationship of production or support between the five elements, and the principle of destruction points out the relationship of control or restraint between them. An element which receives support from one other element is considered in a favorable situation but at the same time it can also be destroyed by another element. These two cycles are the basis of the five element method for divination. Since divination by this method is entirely based on the relationships between the five elements, it is therefore necessary to understand the attributes of the eight trigrams which are shared with that of the five elements as stated in the following table:

Eight Trigrams		Five Elements
Qian 乾 [Heaven]	☰	Metal
Dui 兌 [Lake]	☱	Metal
Li 離 [Fire]	☲	Fire
Zhen 震 [Thunder]	☳	Wood
Xun 巽 [Wind]	☴	Wood
Kan 坎 [Water]	☵	Water
Gen 艮 [Mountain]	☶	Earth
Kun 坤 [Earth]	☷	Earth

Based on the framework of the five elements, the attributes of the eight trigrams are reduced to five which are used differently from the ways they are used in the orthodox methods illustrated earlier. In the Five Elements Method, the interpretation of a predictive hexagram is entirely based on the relationships between these five elements and whether they are considered favorable or not. The steps in obtaining a predictive hexagram are similar to those above, but the interpretation focuses on the relationships between the trigrams of the predictive hexagram rather than the hexagram or line statements, or the image of the hexagram or the structure of the hexagram. To do this, the trigrams need to have different names and definitions.

SUBJECT TRIGRAM AND ACTION TRIGRAM

A **subject trigram** is defined as the subject of a divination. For example, the person who is looking for advice from a divination. In a predictive hexagram there are two trigrams. The subject trigram is the one which does not have a changing line. The reason for this is that the person who seeks advice is basically in a static state and so a subject trigram is by nature a static trigram. An **action trigram** has a changing line to represent its movement for a specific purpose. An action trigram is therefore moving in nature and the changing line can also be called the moving line. A subject trigram is a static trigram and an action trigram is a moving trigram. The relationship between a subject and an action trigram of a hexagram is stated as follows: (suppose the changing line is the second line)

**Hexagram Tai 泰
[Harmony] (11)**

Subject trigram (Earth)
Action trigram (Metal)   The changing line

The Relationship between Subject and Action Trigrams

In the hexagram TAI 泰 [Harmony] (11), the upper trigram is the subject trigram with the attribute of Earth whereas the lower trigram is the action trigram and has the changing line. According to the relationships between the five elements, the subject trigram is Earth and the action trigram Metal.

The Productive Relationship

Case 1: The subject trigram produces the action trigram

A productive relationship is one in which an element supports or "produces" another element, for example, Earth "produces" Metal. In the above hexagram TAI, it means that the subject trigram Earth has a productive effect on the action trigram Metal. Which of the two trigrams is the beneficiary of this productive relationship? Is it the subject trigram or the action trigram? At first sight, the subject trigram appears to be the beneficiary of this action. But this may not be the case, for the subject (an organization or a person) has to use its resources to support the action, through which it may exhaust its resources and hence the situation will be **unfavorable**. According to the Five Element Theory, the subject trigram will therefore be disadvantaged in a productive relationship. However, the subject can also benefit from supporting the action if the action can generate returns later, but this point has not been taken into consideration in the traditional view.

Case 2: The action trigram produces the subject trigram

In the reverse case, if the subject trigram gets support from the action trigram or the action trigram produces the subject trigram as shown by the following hexagram, the situation is then considered favorable for the subject trigram or the subject of the divination:

Hexagram Mingyi 明夷
[Brightness Dimmed] (36)

Subject trigram (Earth)

Action trigram (Fire)   The changing line

Since this is a case of "Fire producing Earth," it means that the action trigram will support or reinforce the subject trigram, or the subject of the divination will benefit from the planned action. This situation is considered **favorable**.

If the changing line is in the upper trigram of the predictive hexagram, the lower trigram then becomes the subject trigram and correspondingly the upper trigram is the action trigram. The place of the changing line determines which of the two trigrams should be the action trigram or the subject trigram:

Hexagram Mingyi (36)

Action trigram (Earth)   The changing line

Subject trigram (Fire)

In the above case, the situation of the subject trigram (or the subject of the divination) is not favorable because it produces the action trigram and can exhaust its resources. The subject trigram (or the subject of the divination) will be the loser whereas the action trigram (or the action) is the beneficiary of the productive relationship between the two.

The Destructive Relationship

Following the second principle of the Five Elements Theory, it is necessary to identify what is a destructive relationship between the subject and the action trigram.

Case 1: The subject trigram destroys the action trigram

Hexagram Guan 觀
[Observing] (20)

Subject trigram (Wood)

Action trigram (Earth)   The changing line

In the hexagram Guan 觀 [Observing] (11), the attributes of the subject trigram and the action trigram are Wood and Earth respectively.

Since Wood (tree) can destroy Earth, the subject trigram (or the subject of the divination) will be able to destroy the action trigram or to control the action that will be taken. It appears favorable to the subject trigram or the subject of the divination. However, the subject will exhaust its resources in supporting and controlling the action, so in this aspect it is not favourable. On the whole, the effect of "a subject trigram destroying an action trigram" is considered **mixed**.

Case 2: The action trigram destroys the subject trigram

In a reverse case, if the subject trigram is Earth and the action trigram Wood, then the relationship between the two is unfavorable to the subject trigram as wood will destroy earth.

Hexagram SHENG 升
[Rising] (46)

Subject trigram (Earth)

Action trigram (Wood)   The changing line

The action trigram or the action will injure the subject trigram or the subject of the divination. The situation is **not favorable**.

The Harmonious Relationship

If both subject and action trigrams have the same attribute, say Earth, the situation is considered favorable. The reason for this is that both have same values and interests and hence there is a relationship of mutual support between the two.

Hexagram KUN 坤
[Earth] (2)

Subject trigram (Earth)

Action trigram (Earth)   The changing line

In this situation, the subject trigram or the subject of the divination is considered **favorable**.

The Relationship between Subject and Nuclear Trigrams

After the primary hexagram (the subject and action trigram), for example, the Hexagram Harmony, is divined two nuclear trigrams can be derived from it.

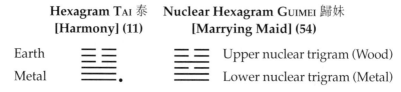

Hexagram Tᴀɪ 泰   **Nuclear Hexagram** Gᴜɪᴍᴇɪ 歸妹
[Harmony] (11)   **[Marrying Maid] (54)**

Earth   Upper nuclear trigram (Wood)

Metal   Lower nuclear trigram (Metal)

The nuclear trigrams symbolize the situation at an **intermediate stage** of action. The relationship between the subject and these two nuclear trigrams will suggest whether or not the situation is favorable. The principles used to compare the two are the same as those given above. In the above hexagram Gᴜɪᴍᴇɪ, the attribute of the subject trigram is Earth and the attribute of the upper nuclear trigram is Wood. It is a situation of "Wood destroying Earth" and hence it is not favorable to the subject trigram. The relationship between the subject trigram and the lower nuclear trigram is unfavorable too as it is a case of "Earth producing Metal"—the subject will exhaust its resources to support the action in the intermediate stage of a development. On the whole, the situation at the intermediate stage of the planned action appears to be not favorable due to these two unfavorable relationships with the subject trigram. If the relationship between the subject trigram and the two nuclear trigrams is that one is favorable and other one unfavorable, the situation at an intermediate stage of the action is considered to be **mixed**.

The Relationship between Subject and Changing Trigrams

The final situation of an action can be predicted by the relationship between the subject and the changing trigram of the hexagram divined.

Primary Hexagram	**Nuclear Hexagram**	**Changing Hexagram**
Harmony	**Marrying Maid**	**Rising**
S.T. (Earth)	U.N.T. (Wood).	Earth
A.T. (Metal).	L.N.T. (Metal)	Wood.

S.T.: Subject trigram   A.T.: Action trigram
U.N.T.: Upper nuclear trigram   L.N.T.: Lower nuclear trigram
•: Changing line

The changing hexagram Sʜᴇɴɢ 升 [Rising] (46) is derived from the primary hexagram Tᴀɪ based on a transformation of the first yang line of TAI into the first yin line of SHENG, since the position of the changing line in the changing hexagram is the same as that in the primary hexagram. The attribute of the subject trigram of the primary hexagram is Earth and that of the changing hexagram is Wood. According to the principle of destruction in the Five Elements Theory, the changing trigram destroys the subject trigram. The final situation of the subject trigram or the subject of the divination is therefore **not favorable**.

By using the Five Elements Method, the situations in three stages of development in a situation can be predicted:

1. The early stage of an event
2. The intermediate stage of an event
3. The final stage of an event

Summary of the Relationships between the Trigrams according to the Principles of the Five Elements Theory

1. Subject trigram produces action trigram: **Not favorable** to the former
2. Subject trigram destroys action trigram: **Mixed**
3. Action trigram produces subject trigram: **Favorable** to the latter
4. Action trigram destroys subject trigram: **Not favorable** to the latter
5. Subject trigram harmonizes with action trigram: **Favorable** to the former
6. Subject trigram produces upper or lower nuclear trigram: **Not favorable** to the former
7. Subject trigram destroys upper or lower nuclear trigram: **Mixed**
8. U.N.T or L.N.T. produces subject trigram: **Favorable** to the latter
9. U.N.T. or L.N.T. destroys subject trigram: **Not favorable** to the latter
10. Subject trigram harmonizes with U.N.T. or L.N.T.: **Favorable** to the former
11. Subject trigram produces changing trigram: **Not favorable** to the former
12. Subject trigram destroys changing trigram: **Mixed**
13. Changing trigram produces subject trigram: **Favorable** to the latter
14. Changing trigram destroys subject trigram: **Not favorable** to the latter
15. Subject trigram harmonizes with changing trigram: **Favorable** to the former

Based on the fifteen predictions from the Five Elements Method, the chance of a diviner obtaining a "favorable" situation is equivalent to that of obtaining a "not favorable" situation. The chance of obtaining a "mixed" situation, however, is lower.

ADVANTAGES AND DISADVANTAGES OF THE FIVE ELEMENTS METHOD

A prediction based on the Five Elements Method can indicate whether or not the situation in each of the three stages of an event is favorable. By using this method there is no need to use the statements of a hexagram as the basis for the interpretation. Rather the interpretation of a predictive hexagram can be entirely based on the four relationships: productive, destructive, harmonious, and changing. The main advantage of this method is that it avoids subjective interpretation of the text or the image or the structure of a hexagram, as presented in this book earlier, and keeps the prediction objective. However, the advantages of this method may also be disadvantages because the diviner will lose the possibility of having a broader spectrum in which to develop his thinking ability or imagination, which it is possible to have through using the orthodox way.

IMPACT OF THE POSITION OF THE CHANGING LINE ON A PREDICTION

One important factor that will affect the three situations from a divination is the position of the changing line of the action trigram. The situations brought about by the changing line being in the first line position are different from those brought about by it being in the second line or third position and so on. The following six examples will illustrate this important fact:

Example 1: Changing line in the *first position* of a hexagram (in action trigram)

Primary Hexagram	Nuclear Hexagram	Changing Hexagram
Harmony	Marrying Maid	Rising

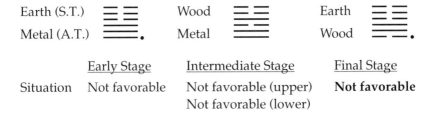

	Early Stage	Intermediate Stage	Final Stage
Situation	Not favorable	Not favorable (upper) Not favorable (lower)	**Not favorable**

Comment:

Think about what difficulties may arise in all three stages of development.

Example 2: Changing line in the *second position* of a hexagram (in action trigram)

Primary Hexagram	Nuclear Hexagram	Changing Hexagram
Harmony	**Marrying Maid**	**Brightness Dimmed**

Earth (S.T.) ⚏   Wood ⚏   Earth ⚏
Metal (A.T.) ⚌•   Metal ⚍   Fire ⚍•

	Early Stage	Intermediate Stage	Final Stage
Situation	Not favorable	Not favorable (upper) Not favorable (lower)	**Favorable**

Comment:

Think about what difficulties may arise in the early and intermediate stage of a development, and what measures will enhance the favorable situation of the final stage.

Example 3: Changing line in the *third position* of a hexagram (in action trigram)

Primary Hexagram	Nuclear Hexagram	Changing Hexagram
Harmony	**Marrying Maid**	**Approaching**

Earth (S.T.) ⚏   Wood ⚏   Earth ⚏
Metal (A.T.) ⚌•   Metal ⚍   Metal ⚌•

	Early Stage	Intermediate Stage	Final Stage
Situation	Not favorable	Not favorable (upper) Not favorable (lower)	**Not favorable**

Comment:

Think about what difficulties may arise in all three stages and the measures for solving them.

Example 4: Changing line in the *fourth position* of a hexagram (in action trigram)

Primary Hexagram	Nuclear Hexagram	Changing Hexagram
Harmony	Marrying Maid	Great Strength
Earth (A.T.)	Wood	Wood
Metal (S.T.)	Metal	Metal

	Early Stage	Intermediate Stage	Final Stage
Situation	**Favorable**	Mixed (upper) **Favorable** (lower)	Mixed

Comment:

Think about what measures can be used for enhancing the favorable situation in the early intermediate stage, and measures for solving the difficulties that may arise in the intermediate and final stages.

Example 5: Changing line in the *fifth position* of a hexagram (in action trigram)

Primary Hexagram	Nuclear Hexagram	Changing Hexagram
Harmony	Marrying Maid	Waiting
Earth (A.T.)	Wood	Water
Metal (S.T.)	Metal	Metal

	Early Stage	Intermediate Stage	Final Stage
Situation	**Favorable**	Mixed (upper) **Favorable** (lower)	Not favorable

Comment:

Think about what measures can be used for enhancing the favorable situation in the early or intermediate stage, and measures for solving the difficulties that may arise in the intermediate and final stages.

Example 6: Changing line in the *sixth position* of a hexagram (in action trigram)

Primary Hexagram	Nuclear Hexagram	Changing Hexagram
Harmony	Marrying Maid	Great Accumulating
Earth (A.T.) ☰☰•	Wood ☰☰	Earth ☰☰•
Metal (S.T.) ☰	Metal ☰	Metal ☰

	Early Stage	Intermediate Stage	Final Stage
Situation	**Favorable**	Mixed (upper) **Favorable** (lower)	**Favorable**

Comment:

This is the best situation among the six given since the situations in both the early and final stages are considered favorable even though the situation in the intermediate stage is mixed. Based on this prediction, the diviner is advised to prepare measures to enhance the favorable situations in all three stages and measures for solving the difficulties that may arise in the intermediate stage.

The above six examples have illustrated the importance of the **place** in divining whether a situation is favorable or not.

COMPLEMENTARY RELATIONSHIP BETWEEN THE FIVE ELEMENTS METHOD AND OTHER METHODS

The main difference between the Five Elements Method and the other methods illustrated above is the focus of the interpretation of a hexagram. The Five Elements Method focuses on the relationships between the five elements, whereas other methods focus on the yin-yang relationships in the structure of a hexagram and the respective statement(s). Since the main purpose of using a divination in this book is to broaden a person's thinking power, there is no reason why the Five Elements Method cannot be used together with other methods despite their different basis for divination. The following example will indicate how two different kinds of methods can be used in a complementary way.

A company leader wants to expand his business and he would like to know what the *Yijing*'s advice is. He uses the Three Coins Method for divination and gets the Lake–Water Hexagram KUN 困 [Adversity] as stated below:

Hexagram Adversity

Lake	⚌⚌	
Water	⚏⚍.	The Changing Line

First, he looks at the name of the hexagram. It is rather discouraging as the hexagram name implies that he may fall into adversity or into a situation of exhaustion or impasse (see the explanations of this hexagram).

Second, the image of the hexagram shows Water under Lake, indicating that the water will leak out and the lake dry up. The situation appears to be not favorable.

Third, he reads the text for the first line which is divined as the changing line. The text says: **"He sits exhausted under a bare tree. He walks into a dark valley. For three years he is not seen."**

According to the line text the leader should not move forward rashly for he will meet danger ahead. What he should do is to wait with patience and optimism until the right time.

The leader does not stop happily with the advice of the *Yijing* based on the Three Coins Method because he has properly prepared his expansion plans with great confidence. So he analyzes the above hexagram by using the Five Elements Method as follows:

Primary Hexagram	**Nuclear Hexagram**	**Changing Hexagram**
Adversity (47)	**The Family (37)**	**Interlinking (58)**
Metal (S.T.) ⚌	Wood ⚌	Metal ⚏
Water (A.T.) ⚍.	Fire ⚌	Metal ⚍.

Initial Yin is the changing line.

	Early Stage	Intermediate Stage	Final Stage
Situation	Not favorable	Mixed (upper) Not favorable (lower)	**Favorable**

Comment:

The early and intermediate stages appear to be not favorable, but the final stage will be favorable.

According to prediction by the Five Elements Method, the operation that the leader has planned is not favorable in the early stage and even in the intermediate stage, but the situation will eventually become fine and favorable. Faced with such a situation, the leader has to make a decision as to whether he should go ahead or to wait. A decision has much to do with the personality of the person concerned.

If he is an indecisive person, he is likely to follow the advice as suggested by the three coins method. But if he is a man with strong self-confidence and an active character, like the one presented in this example, he is more likely to be influenced by the prediction of the Five Elements Method about the situation in the final stage of his development plans. The favorable prediction will strengthen his belief and hence his confidence to move forward. However, he will also prepare measures to solve the difficulties that he might meet in the early and intermediate stages of the development, rather than be optimistic that the possible obstruction could be ignored. The two predictions divined from the three coins method and the five elements method will, however, warn him.

Although the *Yijing* is traditionally seen as a book of divination, the author tends to believe it is rather a book for guiding people in how to behave in the right manner in their daily life. The statements given by the *Yijing* are based on the important assumption that **the future outcome is likely to be determined by today's conduct**. However, there is no absolute relationship between the input of today and the output of tomorrow—merely a possible relationship. Situations as judged by the statements of the *Yijing* can be seen as hypothetical in nature rather than as inevitable, and depend on how a person behaves. If one behaves in proper way, one would be fortunate, but otherwise unfortunate. If a divination is interpreted in this way, it will be meaningful.

In the *Yijing* there are sixty-four hexagram statements and three hundred and eighty-four line statements. All of them can be used as guidelines for people in order to behave as a "superior man." The fundamental spirit of the *Yijing* is to advise people to behave as a well-cultivated man so as to increase the possibility of attaining fortune. A divination using the *Yijing* serves therefore as a guideline or a principle rather than a fact. Based on this, a divination can be considered as another way of preparing a person to be a "superior man" in ordinary life or a wise leader in an organization.

CONCLUSION

Since divination is the original function of the *Yijing* it should not be excluded or ignored when studying the wisdom of the *Yijing*. In ancient China, divination was explicitly placed on the yang side in order to guide people to act in a right way, whereas the philosophy rooted in it was implicitly on the yin side. However, people gradually shift their focus in favor of the latter. While intellectuals have more interest in its philosophy, ordinary people look for guidance in their life through divination in the hope of obtaining "fortune" and avoiding "misfortune." Indeed there is no conflict between these two purposes as long as a divination is used in a proper way rather than superstitiously. As at the beginning of this book, the author advises readers or the executives of all organizations to use divination as a tool to broaden the spectrum of thinking when facing problems.

Bibliography

ℝ ℝ ℝ

Works in Chinese

Jin Jingfang 金景芳 and Lü Shaogang 呂紹綱. Zhouyi *quanjie* 周易全解 [*Commentary on the* Zhouyi]. Changchun: Jilin Daxue chubanshe, 1989.

Zhou Shan 周山. *Jiedu* Zhouyi 解讀周易 [*Interpreting the* Zhouyi]. Shanghai: Shanghai shudian chubanshe, 2002.

Gao Heng 高亨. Zhouyi Dazhuan *jinzhu* 周易大傳今注 [*Contemporary Annotations to the* Zhouyi *and the* Great Commentary]. Jinan: Qi Lu shushe, 1979.

Huang Shouqi 黃壽祺, and Zhang Shanwen 張善文. Zhouyi *yizhu* 周易譯註 [*Annotations to the* Zhouyi]. Shanghai: Shanghai guji chubanshe, 1989.

Liu Dajun 劉大鈞. Zhouyi *gailun* 周易概論 [*Fundamentals of the* Zhouyi]. Chengdu: Bashu shushe, 1988.

Mun Kin Chok 閔建蜀. Yijing *de lingdao zhihui* 易經的領導智慧 [*Leadership Wisdom from the* Yijing]. Hong Kong: The Chinese University Press, 2000.

Nan Huaijin 南懷瑾, and Xu Qinting 徐芹庭. Zhouyi *jinzhu jinyi* 周易今注今譯 [*Contemporary Annotations to and Commentary on the* Zhouyi]. Taipei: Taiwan Commercial Press, 1974.

Zhong Taide 鍾泰德. Yijing *tongyi* 易經通譯 [*General Commentary on the* Yijing]. Taipei: Cheng Chung Book Company, 1999.

Zhu Bokun 朱伯崑. Yixue *jichu jiaocheng* 易學基礎教程 [*Fundamentals of the* Yijing *Studies*]. Beijing: Jiuzhou tushu chubanshe, 2000.

———. Yixue *zhexue shi* 易學哲學史 [*History of the* Yijing *Studies and Philosophy*]. 4 vols. Beijing: Huaxia chubanshe, 1995.

Works in English

Anthony, Carol K. *A Guide to the* I Ching. 3rd ed. Stow, MA: Anthony Publishing Company, 1988.

Cleary, Thomas. I Ching: *The Tao of Organization*. Kuala Lumpur: Eastern Dragon Books, 1991.

Chan Chiu Ming. Books of Changes: *An Interpretation for the Modern Age*. Singapore: AsiaPac Books, 1977.

Dening, Sarah. *The Everyday* I Ching: *Ancient Wisdom for Success Today*. London: Simon & Schuster, 1995.

Fu Huisheng. *The Zhou Book of Change*. Shangdong: Shandong youyi chubanshe, 2000.

Karcher, Stephen. *Total* I Ching: *Myths for Change*. London: Time Warner Books, 2003.

Lynn, Richard John, trans. *The Classic of Changes—A New Translation of the* I Ching *as Interpreted by Wang Bi*. New York: Columbia University Press, 1994.

Moran, Elizabeth, and Joseph Yu. *The Complete Idiot's Guide to the* I Ching. Indianapolis, IN: Alpha Books, 2001.

Markert, Christopher. I Ching: *An Ancient Wisdom for Decision-Making*. Trumbull, CT: Weatherhill, 1998.

Wilhelm, Richard, trans. *The I Ching or Book of Changes*. Rendered into English by Cary F. Baynes. London: Arkana Penguin Books, 1989.

Wu Wei. I Ching *Life: Living It*. Los Angles: Power Press, 1995.